Behind Office Doors
Perspectives on Use and Users in the History of Office Buildings

BEHIND OFFICE DOORS

PERSPECTIVES ON USE AND USERS IN THE HISTORY OF OFFICE BUILDINGS

Edited by Jens van de Maele

LEUVEN UNIVERSITY PRESS

Published with the support of the Research Foundation – Flanders (FWO) and the Luxembourg National Research Fund (FNR), grant reference C21/SC/16326815. For the purpose of open access, and in fulfilment of the obligations arising from the grant agreement, the editor has applied a Creative Commons Attribution 4.0 International (CC BY 4.0) license.

Published with the support of the KU Leuven Fund for Fair Open Access and the Open Book Collective. For details on the supporting institutions participating in the Open Book Collective, see www.lup.be/obc.

Published in 2026 by Leuven University Press / Presses Universitaires de Louvain / Universitaire Pers Leuven. Minderbroedersstraat 4, B-3000 Leuven (Belgium).
Selection and editorial matter © 2026, Jens van de Maele
Individual chapters © 2026, the respective authors

All TDM (Text and Data Mining) rights are reserved.

This book is published under a Creative Commons by Attribution 4.0 International licence.

Attribution should include the following information: Jens van de Maele (ed.), *Behind Office Doors: Perspectives on Use and Users in the History of Office Buildings*. Leuven: Leuven University Press, 2026. (CC BY 4.0)

All images are expressly excluded from the CC BY 4.0 license covering the rest of this publication. Permission for reuse should be sought from the copyright holders.

ISBN 978 94 6270 499 2 (Paperback)
eISBN 978 94 6166 710 6 (ePDF)
eISBN 978 94 6166 711 3 (ePUB)
https://doi.org/10.11116/9789461667113
D/2026/1869/1
NUR: 648

Typesetting: Crius Group
Cover design: Daniel Benneworth-Gray
Cover illustration: Siska Vastesaeger. Belgian artist Siska Vastesaeger creates miniature worlds that subtly balance recognition and alienation. Her work invites viewers to look closely: by shrinking the world, it expands; by zooming in, more becomes visible. In the miniature office depicted on the cover, Vastesaeger questions the (in)visible hands of the worker, manager and designer, as well as the relationships between their respective agencies.

Table of Contents

Acknowledgements   7

Introduction. Retracing Use and Users in the History and Historiography of the 20th-Century Office Building   9
Jens van de Maele

Part 1. Categories and representations of office users   71

Chapter 1. What's the Use? The Users and Usability of the Filing Cabinet   73
Craig Robertson

Chapter 2. The Office in Popular Culture, or the "Plight of the Clerk"   93
Nicola Bishop

Part 2. The impact of normativity and standardisation on the office as an "environment"   119

Chapter 3. Too Cold? Gendered Conflicts over Mechanical Cooling in Early Post-war Japanese Office Spaces   121
Tatsuya Mitsuda

Chapter 4. Thresholds of Comfort: Managing Light, Sound and Focus in the Post-War Office Environment   145
Joeri Bruyninckx

Chapter 5. Surviving the Office: Workplace Design, Activism and the Health of Women Workers in 20th-Century Britain   171
Amy Thomas

Chapter 6. Measuring, Evaluating and Configuring: The German
Debate about Safe and Healthy Screen Work 199
Bernd Holtwick

Part 3. Office uses conceptualised by and for the managerial elite 221

Chapter 7. A "Facility Based on Change" (for the Worse):
Leveraging Labour Process Theory to Understand the Evolution of
Herman Miller's Action Office 223
Petra Seitz

Chapter 8. The European Commission's Office Spaces in the 1950s
and 1960s: Constructing a Materialised Imaginary 249
Marco Ninno

Part 4. Visual essays 273

Chapter 9. "Mimic Men" in the Office Spaces of a "Nervous State":
The Materiality of Bureaucracy in Late Colonial Congo 275
Johan Lagae and Jens van de Maele

Chapter 10. Between Hierarchy, Efficiency and Pragmatism:
Picturing Portuguese Government Offices in Historic Buildings
during the Estado Novo Dictatorship 315
Ana Mehnert Pascoal

Chapter 11. Office Life in Chandigarh 327
Ruth Baumeister (text), Shaun Fynn (photography)

Epilogue 347
Martin Kohlrausch and Andreas Fickers

Contributors 353

Index 357

Acknowledgements

This book originates from a workshop held at the Robert Schuman House in Luxembourg on 20–21 November 2023, following a call for papers issued in early 2023. Most participants developed their presentations into chapters for this volume, while several other contributors were invited independently by the editor. The workshop was part of the BUREU research project (2022–2026) at the Centre for Contemporary and Digital History (University of Luxembourg) and the research group History of Modernity and Society 1800–2000 (KU Leuven). Funded by the National Research Fund Luxembourg (FNR) and the Research Foundation – Flanders (FWO), the BUREU project examined the history of office buildings housing the administrations of the European Union in Brussels and Luxembourg. Interdisciplinary in approach, it focused on the managerial factors shaping interior spaces, integrating perspectives from architectural history, management history and European Union studies.

Financial support from the FWO, the FNR and the KU Leuven Fund for Fair Open Access enabled the production of this volume and its dissemination to as broad an audience as possible. Sarah Cooper (University of Luxembourg) provided invaluable linguistic proofreading, while Anna Derwael (KU Leuven) assisted with the technical editing. The editor thanks the contributors to this volume, the external peer reviewers and the staff at Leuven University Press. Special thanks go to Siska Vastesaeger for providing the cover artwork.

Note on translations. Unless indicated otherwise, all translations in this volume were made by the respective authors.

Note on digital bibliographical references. The URLs of all online resources were last accessed in December 2024.

Introduction
Retracing Use and Users in the History and Historiography of the 20th-Century Office Building

Jens van de Maele

A BANAL WORLD

In the afterword to a 1984 anthology of German-language fiction on "people in offices", the literature scholar Hannes Schwenger reflected on the office as a research object. "It cannot take long", he noted, "before the first office museum will open its doors – probably before the turn of the millennium". Schwenger drew a parallel with 19th-century factories, which by the mid-1980s were gradually becoming museum-worthy because of the ongoing deindustrialisation in Western countries. "Over the course of the 20th century", he continued, "large offices have appeared alongside factories as the 'other side' of the modern world of work, and in them, too, one can discover a piece of cultural history worth documenting".[1] Schwenger turned out to be right: in 1987, Scryption, a museum dedicated to the material history of written communication and office work, opened its doors in the Dutch city of Tilburg. The initiative was followed in 2000 by the establishment of a Museum of Historical Office Technology in the German town of Naunhof. Ironically, neither museum was destined to last. In 2011, a national round of cultural budget cuts led to the closure of Scryption. Without government subsidies, the fate of the museum's collection of "old iron" – as one civil servant described the assortment of typewriters and other office equipment – was sealed.[2] Although part of the collection was saved thanks to the efforts of volunteers, valuable objects did "get lost" around the time of the closure, including rare fountain pens and a typewriter that once belonged to the renowned Dutch novelist Willem Frederik Hermans.[3] The small Saxonian municipality of Naunhof maintained its office museum until 2024, when it decided it could no longer finance an institution for which "the regional population has shown a lack of interest". Following the death of its founder in 2011 and "years of decline", closure became the inevitable outcome.[4]

Sure enough, throughout the world, one can find office-related artefacts in museums addressing topics such as design, labour, skyscrapers and computing.[5] Various large institutions – including the Centre Pompidou and MoMA – have moreover hosted exhibitions on the history of office work.[6] Yet a dedicated (non-virtual) "office museum" may be an overly ambitious leap, as demonstrated by the Tilburg and Naunhof cases, as well as by other unsuccessful attempts to establish lasting initiatives.[7] The limited musealisation of the office, along with the limited heritagisation of office architecture and artefacts, can be explained by the absence of a "compensation effect".[8] Unlike industrial labour, which has largely receded from Western society and thus attained a certain significance for museum collections, administrative work continues to be a persistent and integral aspect of our daily lives. As stated by the architect and labour psychologist Élisabeth Pélegrin-Genel: "The office is a banal world that everyone thinks they know", since "almost everyone experiences it at some point".[9] By the late 20th century, she added, "even the last remaining holdouts, such as farmers, shopkeepers and craftsmen, have no longer been able to avoid spending ever more time in offices".[10] The "banality" of office work and its material culture has two overlapping dimensions, both of which played a role in the demise of the museums in Tilburg and Naunhof: one quantitative and neutral (the office is still everywhere), another qualitative and subjective (the office is unspectacular).

Popular opinion thus seems to be that the omnipresent and "dusty" world of the office, just like bureaucracy itself, warrants *some* critical attention and historical reflection – but certainly not too much.[11] This sentiment is echoed in the visual arts, where administrative work has not been a prominent theme.[12] Until the 1980s, for instance, photographic representations of the office were, as Andreia Alves de Oliveira noted, "marginal or often nonexistent in relation to the documentation of manual labour".[13] Unsurprisingly, recent examples of artistic photography on office life have tended to dwell on its "unbearable ennui" and absurdity.[14] In literature, numerous authors *did* depict the office: unlike factory labourers, many office workers have not only engaged in writing as part of their daily routines, but often also had the time to pursue creative work in their spare moments. Yet while the importance of novels as a primary source for understanding the past dimensions of office work is undeniable, the "office

Fig. 0.1. Interrogation room in the Hohenschönhausen prison complex, Berlin, 2012. Photo by Wikimedia Commons contributor Anagoria / CC BY 3.0.

novel" genre – as historian Sabine Biebl observed – is typically devoid of "heroes" and "events", often focusing instead on aspects external to the office environment itself, such as the protagonist's mental ponderings and interpersonal relationships.[15]

To explore the office of the past, one might nevertheless look to museums of a completely unexpected kind, such as the Hohenschönhausen prison in Berlin. Now a memorial (*Gedenkstätte*), this former Stasi complex features a cell block built around 1960, which also contains a floor with dozens of interrogation rooms, many of which have remained largely unchanged since the fall of the German Democratic Republic. As one journalist observed years after the prison's closure, any of these rooms resembles a "seemingly normal office, with a large wooden desk, an old fashioned green telephone, two comfortable upholstered chairs at one end of the room and one small, meek wooden chair at the other" – the latter evidently intended for those under interrogation.[16] Some tour guides have even been known to point out that "the frilly curtains give the [rooms] a fairly pleasant atmosphere".[17] In these generic-looking spaces, which – aside from the barred windows – could easily be mistaken for the private offices of mid-level administrators in a corporate firm or public administration from the 1960s, the often invoked banality of the office takes on an unsettling quality (Fig. 0.1.). At Hohenschönhausen, the familiar aesthetics of administrative work and its technological culture were mobilised to normalise the violence exerted by the Stasi officers. Rather than being settings for physical torture, the interrogation rooms served a key role in a process of psychological coercion, with interrogation becoming part of a seemingly reasonable and rational process of administrative efficiency.[18] By making the rooms look like ordinary offices, the Stasi effectively reinforced the notion that oppression could be bureaucratised and symbolically embedded within the fabric of everyday life. As such, Hohenschönhausen not only illustrates the societal ubiquity of the office; it also serves as an example – albeit an extreme one – of the deep entanglement of bureaucracy and state power. Meanwhile, in the postwar "capitalist" West, bureaucracy and its material culture – including countless office blocks in the "International Style" – became strongly intertwined with *corporate* power, as has been demonstrated by Reinhold Martin's architectural analysis (2003) of the so-called "organisational complex". This complex complemented the "military-industrial complex", another bureaucratic phenomenon par excellence.[19] Seen from these perspectives, the office is far from "dusty".

A MESSY WORLD

This edited volume aligns with the recent research trend of challenging the long-standing popular perception of the office, particularly its materialities, as a subjectively banal topic.[20] Its focus is not on musealisation or heritagisation, although these themes certainly warrant enquiry at some point in the future.[21] Instead, the volume explores the 20th-century history of office buildings through an exploration of *users* and *use*. Even if one agrees with the common opinion – which also appears to have long characterised historical scholarship, as we will see below – that the office is unspectacular "dry matter", its analysis can reveal important insights about the way in which material and mental infrastructures underpin contemporary societies.[22] There are indeed numerous "boring things", as sociologist Susan Leigh Star provocatively called them, that maintain social stability, naturalise (in)equalities and create standards for conduct. Apart from infrastructures, such "things" include routines, classifications and operating procedures – all of which come together in the architectural and social space that is the modern office.[23] The broad questions this volume thus seeks to address are as follows: How were use and users conceptualised by office planning professionals such as interior designers and architects? How was knowledge about user needs (mis)construed and operationalised? What kind of user categories can be retraced in sources produced by office design experts? How did office technology and management create path dependencies that were both material and mental? How were negative aspects of such path dependencies challenged by users? And what methodological or heuristic challenges emerge when one seeks to analyse histories of everyday use? Focusing on what happened "behind office doors", the volume's case studies thus scrutinise history through various thematic lenses, including (interior) architecture, workplace sociology, management, representations in popular media, and science and technology.[24] Rather than expanding the "jungle of small specialities in different disciplines" that have tackled the office over the past four decades, this volume aims to enhance communication between academic domains, thereby contributing to the development of a more integral perspective that could be termed "historical office studies".[25] After all, like every manifestation of architecture, the office can be considered a "composite phenomenon" and an "assemblage of interlocking disciplines, techniques and strategies", whose history cannot be adequately understood without transdisciplinarity.[26]

The societal importance of office spaces – along with the "office cultures" which have developed in them – cannot be overstated, and that fact was already recognised by some philosophers at an early stage. In the notes for his unfinished *Arcades Project* (1927-1940), Walter Benjamin wrote that around 1900 "the office emerged as the true centre of lived space".[27] This change was rooted in the 19th-century emergence of the bourgeoisie, which pursued its business interests in a public realm separate from the private sphere of domesticity. Dedicated administrative workspaces (first in separate rooms within townhouses, later in dedicated buildings) became the terrain where the bourgeoisie and its white-collar workforce effectively "lived" the majority of their lives. In 1935, another German philosopher, Martin Heidegger, emphasised the role of government bureaucracies in the advancement of office spaces. He did this by posing a rhetorical question: "Wherein lies the essence of the state: in the fact that the police arrest a suspect, or in the fact that many typewriters clatter in the ministries and take dictations from state secretaries and ministerial councillors?"[28] The growing societal importance of bureaucratic environments, as observed by Benjamin and Heidegger, coincided with significant shifts in managerial practices. In 1936, the French philosopher Georges Friedmann argued that Taylorism, with its emphasis on efficiency and standardised management, had shaped Western society more profoundly than "any other moral system proposed by philosophers in the last five decades".[29] The importance of commerce, governance and management continued to grow after the Second World War, resulting in a situation by the late 20th century where a significant portion of the workforce in Western societies was employed in the service sector – the majority in office roles. As such, the British architect and leading authority on office planning Francis Duffy could aptly conclude in 1981 that "never have offices been so central to society", and that "we would do well to take their design seriously".[30]

Paradoxically, the factual significance of the office as a "spatial system" – which interrelates with the office as a "social structure" – is not as well-reflected in historiography as one would expect.[31] The claim that the office has long been a "taboo subject" (Pélegrin-Genel) is undoubtedly hyperbolic, but the historians Gianenrico Bernasconi and Stefan Nellen were right when they observed in their edited volume *Das Büro: Zur Rationalisierung des Interieurs* (2019) that the economic history of the service sector and the social and cultural history of white-collar workers have largely offered analyses of the office without considering its material and architectural dimensions.[32] Yet, even the topic of administrative management – which can be considered the "software" that interacts with the architectural "hardware" of the office – has remained underexplored in historical enquiry.[33] In another recent volume (2019), literature scholars James Dorson and Jasper Verlinden argued that "in the humanities, [management] is often reduced to a Taylorist caricature; [it is also] tangled in a web of signifiers in which most of us are implicated, rather than a well-defined discourse we can define ourselves against".[34] The office's apparent banality resurfaces here – but the personal familiarity many scholars have with it can obscure its historical complexity. Journalist Gideon Haigh has remarked on this familiarity as follows:

> Historians and sociologists gravitate [...] to extremes, directing their scholarship at governing elites and disadvantaged minorities, in a way that the Marxist historian Arno Mayer once observed bordered on the suspicious: "Could it be that social scientists are hesitant to expose the aspirations, life-style, and worldview of the social class in which so many of them originate and from which they seek to escape?"[35]

At first glance, the 20th-century office building may indeed seem like a relatively "simple" environment with "very few [design] variables" (as Duffy argued in 1974), characterised by seemingly static, time-honoured concepts such as open-plan layouts and a managerial preoccupation with efficiency.[36] However, as we will see further on, there is no doubt that this continuity was underpinned by a permanent managerial *flexibility*, which allowed for gradual and piecemeal "fixing" of problems and of wrongful expectations.[37] According to Dorson and Verlinden, "the task of analyzing the culture of management diachronically is complicated by the way it changes in response to critique in order to legitimize itself to workers and society". This "necessity for constant adaptation", they added, "makes [management] inherently messy".[38] Clearly, the "messiness" of management is also the messiness of the office.

MAKING SENSE OF MESSINESS (1): THE CANONICAL FOCUS

Over the past four decades, historical scholarship on the office (understood here as a spatial system interacting with a social structure) has attempted to make sense of this "messiness" using several hermeneutical strategies. This section and the next discuss some of these strategies, thus providing an essayistic (and by no means exhaustive) evaluation of the historiography of the office building, along with insights into its lacunae and limitations. The first major strategy has relied on an architectural canon, in which a number of high-profile office buildings and innovations are listed chronologically and commented upon. Typical inclusions in this canon are Frank Lloyd Wright's Larkin Building (Buffalo, New York, 1906-1950) and Johnson Wax Building (Racine, Wisconsin, 1939), Ludwig Mies van der Rohe's Seagram Building (New York City, 1958), the Quickborner Team's *Bürolandschaft* concept (West Germany, c. 1960), Herman Miller's Action Office furniture series (United States, from 1964 onward), and Herman Hertzberger's Centraal Beheer Building (Apeldoorn, the Netherlands, 1972). This architectural canon usually also doubles as a canon of milestones in management, which can be linked to specific buildings: the advent of the modern "Taylorist" office (Larkin), the partial "humanisation" of Taylorism through the emergence of the "human relations" school (Johnson Wax), the shift toward increasing flexibility reflecting capitalist expansion (Seagram), the growing emphasis on interpersonal communication (*Bürolandschaft*), the development of "ergonomic" expertise (Action Office), and finally the rise of flat hierarchies and "personalisation cultures" as part and parcel of the postmodern condition (Centraal Beheer). Even though the introduction of the computer – first as mainframes (1950s) and later as PCs (1970s and 1980s) – represents an important managerial and technological innovation by gradually integrating various office technologies into one, this evolution is typically not associated with any canonical office building.[39] The same is true for older technological innovations, such as the punched card and addressing machines of the interwar period.[40]

As is the case with any canon, this approach veils as much as it elucidates. Consider, for instance, the Larkin Building. Its originality is beyond question, owing to its innovations in management (such as strict task division and a focus on the swift flow of documents) and environmental control (including sealed windows and air-conditioning), both of which would be adopted by numerous other companies.[41] Yet the Larkin Building was also highly idiosyncratic. As historian Christine Schnaithmann argued, Wright and his client sought to socially legitimise the then novel office typology by presenting it as more than just a space for economic activity; it also had to embody and promote higher ideals. Consequently, the Larkin Building was imbued with a sense of "sacrality", evident in the edifying inscriptions on the interior walls of the central atrium and the celestial daylight streaming in from above.[42] This sacrality, combined with a rhetoric that framed the Larkin workforce as one big "family", can be seen as part of a managerial strategy to counter the effects of the rigid task separation within the Larkin mail order company, which created significant potential for dissatisfaction and deviation among hundreds of atomised workers.[43] In a rare discussion of these workers' perceptions, architectural historian Zeynep Çelik Alexander noted that this strategy was certainly not always successful: "A minor mutiny almost broke out in 1914 [...] when one clerk asked for permission to replace his 'very uncomfortable' Wright-designed chair with another; the clerk's request was denied, and the chair remained in place".[44]

The combination of Wright's highly personal artistic language with a fusion of "the mundane with the profound" makes the Larkin Building an intriguing *Gesamtkunstwerk*, even though its very distinctiveness evidently limited its applicability as a template for widespread adoption.[45] The vast majority of 20th-century office buildings did not resort to the legitimation strategies Wright incorporated, which makes the Larkin Building – at least from this perspective – an anomaly rather than a representative standard. (The 1950 demolition further underscores how the building's unique design was believed to hinder its adaptability in an evolving architectural and managerial landscape.) Similar observations concerning exceptionality can be made about the Centraal Beheer Building, which Pélegrin-Genel has aptly described as a "cult place". The "social spaces" and office rooms – both collective and private – of this insurance company headquarters were intentionally designed to enable a certain ludicity and avoid hierarchical connotations, thus aligning with some of the ideals of the late 1960s countercultural movement. Although it was "visited by the entire world", the Centraal Beheer Building can – once again – not be considered representative of common office practices. In the medium term, this "exceptional outlier" (as architectural historian Amy Thomas refers to it in her contribution to this volume) did not even set a precedent for its own client, who added a number of conventional buildings to its office campus in later decades.[46] At some point, as architect Hertzberger recently remembered, the original building's occupants, too, began to re-embrace ostentatious signs of hierarchy, reportedly without any directive from management: "They started wearing suits again, the ties returned..."[47] (Ironically, the spectre of demolition long hung over the Centraal Beheer Building as well; only after fifteen years of disuse has a redevelopment process recently been initiated.)

Office complexes like Larkin, Seagram and Centraal Beheer have always attracted historians of architecture – not only because of their originality and aesthetic refinement, but also because they embodied the high-minded ideals of their designers and clients. In the case of Seagram, this enduring attention additionally resulted from the fact that the building was a skyscraper: an architectural typology that has long been the focus of a relatively rich secondary literature (in contrast to low- and medium-rise office buildings, as Nikolaus Pevsner noted in his 1976 classic *A History of Building Types*).[48] However, most office buildings were not designed by "messianic" figures like Wright or Mies van der Rohe.[49] Instead, they were the outcome of unspectacular and little-publicised bureaucratic processes, with their collective authorship shared among various little-known designers and specialists.[50] Immediately after the Second World War, the American critic Henry-Russell Hitchcock famously described the outcome of this erosion of personal authorship as the "architecture of bureaucracy", which he opposed to the "architecture of genius". For Hitchcock, the latter applied to just a small number of functional categories – such as religious buildings and townhouses, where the individual artistic expression of great architects was believed to remain crucial.[51] While Hitchcock did not look down on "architecture of bureaucracy" (he indeed considered it as important as "architecture of genius"), the postwar shift towards ever increasing specialisation in ever larger teams did affect the social status of office designers and the objects they created. In a discussion of 1960s Britain, the architect Patrick Hannay (1992) for instance recalled that even among professionals in the building trade, the job of office interior consultant was "hardly [considered] a respectable calling", with interior designers often being "unknown or despised", and office interiors deemed by many "unworthy of serious intellectual consideration".[52] Francis Duffy (1992) added that the profession of "management" held much more prestige in those postwar decades, and that "any crumbs of management consultancy which could be fed to architects were bound to be gratefully received".[53] Amy Thomas noted that the social status of office design professionals further suffered due to "their close relationship with [real estate] developers". As such, they "were criticized by the architectural establishment for the very characteristics that made them attractive to their clients: an economical approach; an affinity for using planning loopholes; and, above all, a working method that privileged cost calculations over other ambitions".[54] In all these accounts, the figure of the architectural expert as a powerful "genius" is notably absent.[55]

Occasionally, designers working for large architectural firms did acquire personal fame – and hence canonical acknowledgment – for their designs, the best-known example being Gordon Bunshaft from the company Skidmore, Owings and Merrill (SOM), who co-designed the Lever House in New York City (1952), among many other office projects. In a recent monograph, Nicholas Adams credited Bunshaft with "providing an identity for SOM that was an alternative to Hitchcock's binary of genius and bureaucracy".[56] While there is no doubt that the corporate modernism of architectural firms like SOM depended on numerous highly talented individuals – smaller and larger "geniuses within the bureaucracy", so to speak – the postwar period inevitably saw the proliferation of myriad "banal" office buildings that had no chance of entering the canon.[57] On the rare occasion when the designers and clients behind such buildings *did* aspire to create an architecture that stood for more than mere businesslike efficiency and profit maximisation, those aspirations were not necessarily recognised as such by the public (including architectural critics). This is illustrated by architectural historian Erik Sigge's account of a large government office complex in Stockholm. Completed in 1972, the so-called Garnisonen complex was "typical of the buildings of its time in its streamlined production and monotonous expression", boasting an almost 350m-long façade and 70,000m² of office space (Fig. 0.2.).[58] However, in the eyes of a leading architect within the design company (who reflected on

Fig. 0.2. Garnisonen office complex, Stockholm, 2014. Photo by Wikimedia Commons contributor Holger Ellgaard / CC BY-SA 4.0.

the commission decades later), the complex had explicitly been conceived as an ambitious "expression of democratic welfare":

> Naively, I had considered government officers the servants of the people. A large building filled with civil servants meant that Sweden was prosperous enough to serve many. Instead, in the public consciousness, the long façade turned out to illustrate that the bureaucracy had risen over our heads.[59]

In the age of mechanical reproducibility, the office typology thus took part in what in Benjamin's philosophy of art has been described as the "disappearance of the aura".[60] When "architects of bureaucracy" did try to emulate examples of "architecture of genius" such as the Seagram Building, the aura immediately vanished, often prompting analysts to condemn the copies as "dismal".[61] The non-auratic character of the vast majority of office buildings has seen its ultimate embodiment in what the Dutch architect Rem Koolhaas dubbed the "Typical Plan". Koolhaas understood this concept as "zero-degree architecture, [...] stripped of all traces of uniqueness and specificity [and] [...] as empty as possible: a floor, a core, a perimeter and a minimum of columns". While Koolhaas saw the "Typical Plan" as a uniquely American phenomenon of the postwar period, it is clear that the tendency of "erasing specificity" has marked business districts throughout the world, leading to parts of cities becoming "an accumulation of [...] deliberately empty containers, programmatical voids and undefined sites to a degree never before experienced in the history of mankind".[62] Such developments – often associated with the destruction of residential urban fabric – did little to improve the image of the "banal" office building among scholars and members of the broader public alike.[63] Even after they became occupied and loaded with "function", society remained wary of these "containers", as has been suggested by cultural scientist Hartmut Böhme:

> An office was and is a formally defined space with an internal structure that regulates information processing and input/output relationships. Therefore, from the outside, an office is perceived as a black box. This is the deeper reason for the widespread mistrust – sometimes silent, sometimes vocal – toward what actually happens "in there".[64]

MAKING SENSE OF MESSINESS (2): THE FOCUS ON SURVEILLANCE

Böhme's observation brings us to a second hermeneutical strategy scholars have often deployed to make sense of the "messiness" of the office, which is directly related to what happens "in there". When discussing the actual functioning of office buildings, two themes have been mobilised significantly more than others: surveillance and gender. This section will focus on the first – although both themes overlap considerably, with surveillance often reinforcing power relations along lines of gender (and class). The concept of surveillance, usually understood as visual and/or auditory control of superiors over subordinates, has become strongly associated with the historical interpretations and social theories of Michel Foucault. His *Surveiller et punir* (1975) in particular has provided an important analytical tool for interpretations of office life, by presenting Jeremy Bentham's panopticon as a metaphor for pervasive surveillance in modern societies. Under conditions of "panopticism", Foucault argued, power is maintained by making individuals feel they are constantly being watched, leading them to regulate their own behaviour.[65] It is telling, in this respect, that one of the first historical accounts of office cultures, *The*

Enormous File: A Social History of the Office by the British author Alan Delgado (1979), did not delve much into control strategies, having appeared just a few years after the publication of the English version of Foucault's book (1977). Rightly stating that his popularising study dealt with "more or less unexplored [historiographical] territory", Delgado discussed the long-term development of office spaces, devoting ample attention to the 19th-century precedents of the modern open office.[66] Up until the early 20th century, he argued, "the idea was to get as many people into as large an area as possible without much thought as to whether the conditions under which they worked contributed to efficiency". The advent of scientific management changed this; from this point on, office managers and architects avoided "crowded" arrangements, the aim being to "correctly [channel] the flow of work", make it "simple to communicate" and establish "easy supervision".[67] As such, for Delgado, surveillance was just one of multiple – and desirable – elements that buttressed the proliferation of the Taylorised open office, while pre-1918 designs were not interpreted as "spaces of control" at all.

Published around the same time, Francis Duffy's short but excellent historical article on "office buildings and organisational change" (1980) remains valuable today for its main argument that "technology and organisation" (or, in other words, office "hardware" and office "software") must be considered in unison. With this conceptualisation of the office as a "socio-technical system",[68] Duffy prefigured similar methodological frameworks later proposed by architect Hans-Joachim Fritz (1982), social psychologist Gustave-Nicolas Fischer (1984), managerial expert Christopher Baldry (1997), architectural historians Chrysanthe Broikos and Donald Albrecht (2000), and historians Michelle Murphy (2006) and Delphine Gardey (2008).[69] However, like Delgado, Duffy did not position surveillance as a major category of analysis. Rather than explaining the advent of the open-plan office as solely driven by "supervision" requirements, he tentatively argued that this design may also have been inspired by the need for efficient ventilation.[70] A few years later, in 1982, Foucault's ideas on disciplinary power did trickle down into Fritz's groundbreaking 1982 monograph on the history of office buildings. Essentially unknown outside of the German-speaking world, the aptly titled *Menschen in Büroarbeitsräumen* (People in Office Workspaces) is probably the first in-depth academic treatment of the topic (Fig. 0.3.).[71] While both Delgado's and Fritz's books adopt a multi-century perspective – an approach largely avoided in present-day academic history, with Fritz even beginning his

Fig. 0.3. Front cover of Hans-Joachim Fritz's 1982 monograph.

narrative in the Middle Ages – the latter work is distinguished by its theoretical ambitions.[72] Arguing that the arranging of office interiors equals "the arranging of the people occupying those spaces", Fritz sought to unravel "the social contexts that play out behind the façades, [by questioning] [...] people's cohabitations and collaborations for the purpose of work".[73]

Central to Fritz's enquiry was the application of Norbert Elias' sociological theory of the "civilising process" (1939), which describes the long-term, intergenerational evolution towards increasing self-regulation, greater control over impulses and the establishment of complex social norms. Fritz linked Elias' macro-historical perspective on the internalisation of behavioural norms to Foucault's more recent focus on the micro-techniques of surveillance and discipline within institutions.[74] According to Fritz, the large office spaces that first emerged in the late 19th century and were further developed after the First World War under Taylorist principles could only function with workers who had duly internalised notions of discipline and shame.[75] Alluding to Max Weber's theories on the 19th-century bureaucratisation process – which was likewise aimed at a "rationalisation" of both mind and body – Fritz described these successful conditions of disciplined office work as a "bureaucratic domestication".[76] This domestication relied strongly on visual surveillance, whose disciplinary force led to increased self-surveillance. Open-plan offices thus served as a Foucauldian *dispositif* that enabled both types of surveillance:

> Unclear spatial zones, obstructed sightlines caused by work materials, [...] hidden niches and concealed areas of the workroom, as well as all forms of disorganised gatherings of people [...] where the human body itself could become a means of shielding, and all undirected diversity of movement, had to give way to [...] spatial-social homogenisation. [...] The increasingly complete visibility of the now ever more segmented work processes corresponded to the permanent visibility of all workers and their spatial-social actions. Only a comprehensive overview of the space and people in the workroom ensured the efficiency of surveillance. As the field of vision expanded step by step, more and more people could be subjected to the controlling gaze of surveillance specialists. Various methods of visual control, as they can be found throughout architectural history in the spatial organisation of different building types, up to the principles of the panopticon developed in prison construction, were now applied to the expansive, single-room solutions of office workspaces.[77]

Fritz's 1982 study was an early application of the concept of panopticism to the study of everyday usage patterns in 20th-century offices, anticipating a wave of similar approaches that gained traction in later scholarship. Many of the subsequent authors who gave surveillance an important role in their historical explorations did so by referring to Foucault and/or Bentham's panopticon.[78] Such references usually pertained to the architectural dimension (viewing panopticism as a phenomenon with crucial spatial ramifications), even though some scholars also used the term in a broader sense, for instance by conceptualising the managerial surveillance of work performed on computers as constitutive of the late-20th-century "information panopticon".[79] Exploring surveillance and self-surveillance has helped illuminate some of the paradoxes related to office users and use. According to historian Dirk van Laak, all types of infrastructure are designed not only to enable but also to regulate and constrain movement.[80] Yet in open-plan offices, where most of the "order" is imposed through the furniture arrangement, the open design – promoted for its inherent flexibility – can still unintentionally allow for a wide range of unscripted movement. From a managerial point of view, this potential for disruption had to be curtailed through (self-)surveillance, which functioned as a mental infrastructure complementing the physical one.[81] Furthermore, while the results of industrial labour are typically visible and easily measurable for supervisors, office work indeed operates more like a black box – also for those *within* the office.[82] Since outcomes are not as directly observable, managers generally shifted their focus to monitoring their workers' presence and seating.[83] A compelling analysis of this phenomenon has been offered by sociologist Rainer Paris:

> [...] [Panoptic] disciplinary power essentially offers two possibilities: either it imposes visibility on people and controls them through actual or presumed constant observation (this is the principle of the factory hall and also of the open-plan office), or it ensures their presence at the desired locations through complete surveillance of the in-between spaces (as in modern prisons). This latter variant, in a weakened form, also applies to the office: the empty corridor signals that everyone is working [...]. From the perspective of smooth organisational operation, office corridors are therefore ideally deserted spaces. The everyday certainty of authority and the completion of work is guided by the maxim "if no one is to be seen, everything is in order".[84]

Much like the canonical approach, however, use of the panoptic metaphor runs the risk of clarifying and obscuring in equal measure. To illustrate this, let us consider a few more paradoxes, this time with regard to historiographical analyses of offices. Firstly, as literature researcher Graham Thompson has observed – and as historian Nicola Bishop (who also contributes to the present volume) later re-emphasised – it is "somewhat surprising" that the office "remained outside the orbit of Foucault's attention in his studies of surveillance [...], especially against the clear facts that the office and its various functions are tied so closely into capitalist development".[85] Foucault saw this development precisely as the driving force behind "disciplinary power", which could be operated "in the most diverse political regimes, apparatuses or institutions".[86] That the French philosopher never analysed offices, is, according to Bishop, yet another indication of "the ways [...] the office is underplayed as a significant part of modern society".[87] While one might argue that the late-19th-century rise of the office typology fell outside Foucault's temporal focus, it is worth noting that the philosopher did (briefly) examine 18th- and 19th-century factories (*ateliers, usines*), whose institutional and architectural forms he regarded as analogous to those of the quintessential typology of surveillance: "Is it any wonder that the prison resembles factories, schools, barracks, hospitals, all of which resemble prisons?"[88] Given the similarities between industrial labour and low-ranking office work (a parallel I will revisit later), it is unsurprising that subsequent authors have applied Foucauldian theory to the office. Ideally, however, such applications must consider continuities and discontinuities in relation to typologies such as the prison and the hospital. This is certainly not always the case. One does not have to be hypercritical of Foucault's legacy – like political philosopher Perry Anderson, for example, who mentioned "the banalization of power in Foucault's overstretching of the concept" – to ascertain that panopticism has become "overused" in the humanities, often serving as a catch-all term for any generic situation where some kind of surveillance is operational.[89]

Architectural historian André Patrão has argued that Foucault's analysis of Bentham's panopticon owes its popularity to the fact that it "reduced a long thorough work into a few clear straightforward pages, written in a captivating style merging eye-opening philosophical insights with powerful imagery, by a highly popular contemporary philosopher addressing current and pressing social issues".[90] This brings us to another paradox: while Foucault never wrote about administrative workspaces, Bentham actually *did*. This fact has gone virtually unacknowledged in the historiography of the office, precisely because Bentham's ideas are rarely examined beyond Foucault's interpretation.[91] The English utilitarian philosopher discussed office spaces in his monumental (but unfinished) treatise *Constitutional Code* (1822-1832), which he intended as a globally applicable blueprint – a "constitution" – for rational governance, aimed at maximising transparency, accountability and efficiency in public administration. A firm believer in the idea that architecture could shape behaviour (a principle nowadays known as architectural determinism), Bentham was convinced that good governance depended on specially designed ministerial office buildings, enabling the aforementioned qualities.[92] Like in all his architectural proposals, he placed enormous importance on surveillance, reflecting a methodological distrust of people – whether prisoners, politicians or civil servants. However, in contrast to his earlier writings on panopticons for prisons, schools, hospitals and factories, *Constitutional Code* did not suggest that the occupants of government office buildings (i.e. ministers and civil servants) had to be subjected to the permanent, monocentric visual gaze of an unseen supervisor. Instead, Bentham proposed that ministers have personal offices, from where they could converse at any moment with their colleagues through so-called "conversation tubes".[93] Meanwhile, any member of the public would be allowed to follow each minister's conversations and actions from adjacent observation spaces, as if they were seated "in the boxes of a theatre". Only in exceptional cases, when informants had to be protected against eavesdroppers, did Bentham suggest allowing the use of private meeting rooms.[94] All users of government office buildings – including visiting citizens – were thus to play a role in a regime of mutual surveillance, with the public observing state officials as well as the other way around.

Consequently, the inventor of the panopticon was not only one of the first theorists on office architecture (with historian Cyprian Blamires even arguing that Bentham "should […] be seen as a progenitor of the open plan office").[95] He also understood well that different social institutions – as well as their corresponding architectural typologies – should rely on different *regimes* of surveillance and management: despite certain similarities with regard to (self-)surveillance, the power dynamics in offices are inherently different from those in prisons.[96] This is why the unmediated application of the panoptic metaphor to the office runs the risk of introducing semantic noise, as has already been observed by a few authors. Rainer Paris emphasised that "bureaucracies are certainly not total institutions and offices are no cells", while Graham Thompson focused on the fact that "workplaces are not prisons, […] and the relationships between employers and employees are not equivalent to those of guards and inmates".[97] Management historians Alan McKinlay and Robbie Guerriero Wilson moreover noted that "the striking, dystopian image of Bentham's Panopticon […] has distracted many from Foucault's insistence on agency and resistance".[98] Even though there is no doubt that offices can be like "hell" and in certain contexts even approximate "a Dickensian sweat shop", they can also – and this in firm contrast to the prison – be an attractive and even glamorous environment.[99] The American office layout consultant John Pile emphasised this diversity of potential experiences in a 1978 handbook:

> Office workers have complex views of their jobs and the places where they work, which are not always easy to discover and explain. The job may be a challenge, a pleasure, or a burden. The office may be a purgatory, a social center, a second home, or some combination of any or all of these things.[100]

Office work, though often characterised by rigidity, structured routines and hierarchical control, also, as social scientist Martin Albrow noted, provided a sense of stability, job security and comforting predictability.[101] This duality is especially evident when considering the gendered history of the office. From the early days of clerical work, women have faced systemic inequalities, with gender functioning as a crucial "signifier of power and difference".[102] Yet, as Francisca de Haan observed in the context of the Netherlands during the pre-war period, office work also offered women opportunities for collegiality, personal development, job satisfaction and financial independence – qualities that helped shape the image of the "modern woman".[103] Michelle Murphy's analysis of American office workers up to the 1960s further underscores this complexity, highlighting how white working-class women were drawn to office work not only for its safety and cleanliness but also for its aura of middle-class respectability. With its codes of dress and decorum, the office became a desirable alternative to factory labour even as women subtly pushed the boundaries of organisational norms through fashion and self-expression.[104] The scholarly association with the panoptic prison has indeed tended to overshadow the fact that office workers – obviously including men as well – generally possess more agency to resist control, deviate from norms and respond to their supervisors. "Complicity or even mere implication in power relations," McKinlay and Guerriero Wilson argue, "necessarily entails latent conflict, from open, perhaps knowing, collaboration, to tacit opposition and open resistance".[105] Conversely, as Foucault stated in one of his studies on the history of sexuality, "power is tolerable only on condition that it masks a substantial part of itself; its success is proportional to its ability to hide its own mechanisms". Manifestations of power that are "entirely cynical", the French philosopher added, have a limited chance of establishing themselves durably.[106]

Most importantly, with regard to questions on the history of use and users, the panoptic regime of surveillance as proposed by Bentham for prisons does not capture the various "codes of visibility" typically present in office spaces, where surveillance was often not unidirectional but *polycentric* – something which Bentham himself already recognised, as is shown above.[107] In the open-plan office, higher-ranking observers were also subject to scrutiny from their subordinates, while within a group of surveilled workers, individuals could observe not only their supervisors but also one another through "sideways glances".[108] In line with the aforementioned notion of workers' resistance, polycentric surveillance could also "turn the hierarchy on its head", as historian Julie Berebitsky argued: "The (male) supervisor kept an eye on the workers, but a (female) worker could also catch the supervisor's eye in a sexual sense, disrupting the efficient, impersonal ideal and complicating the balance of power." In return, "this surveillance could work in the opposite way, too, giving men free rein to gaze on women against their will, while also allowing the men to waste time" – a practice that went against the managerial impulse of efficiency.[109] Obviously, not all components of the office were uniformly "gaze-able": some spaces and workers were more surveilled than others.[110] Combined, however, the complex patterns and relations of visibility in the office – which could reflect, enforce or distort horizontal as well as vertical hierarchies – were clearly more representative of everyday realities of modern surveillance than those prescribed for the Benthamite panoptic prison. These patterns also included "auditory visibility", to use an oxymoron that has been coined, in a different context, by art historian Anna Vemer Andrzejewski.[111] The open-plan office created a dynamic of acoustic proliferation, where silence often functioned as both a shared expectation and a tool of restraint. Even in managerial and architectural settings that actively promoted verbal exchange (such as the *Bürolandschaft*, discussed later), workers who spoke felt constrained by the awareness that their noise disrupted others, while simultaneously relying on their peers' silence to maintain focus.[112] Technologies such as the telephone – and Bentham's much earlier hypothetical "conversation tubes" – further demonstrate how sound could serve as a medium of surveillance.

Therefore, if one catch-all term must be used to describe surveillance patterns in offices, the *omniopticon* might be a better candidate. Proposed by historian Patrick Joyce, "omnioptic" surveillance is not about "the few seeing the many" but about "the many seeing the many". Joyce conceived this notion to describe liberal principles of urban life emerging in the 19th century, when "the city became a place where one watched and was watched; in the public park, in the municipal museum, in the public squares of the city, people were led to present themselves in ways that would be 'publicly' acceptable, and in presenting themselves to others, these others, in a reciprocal 'calculated administration of shame', presented themselves in turn to them".[113] The principle of omniopticity not only aligns better with the mutual surveillance dimension typically present in office buildings; it also reflects the managerial ideas prescribed by the early-20th-century French mining engineer Henri Fayol. A pioneering theorist of administrative work, Fayol's ideas are often overlooked in the historiography of the office building, overshadowed as they are by the more prominent Taylorism (which was originally conceived for *industrial* labour). Highly influential in French-speaking countries from the interwar period onward – a time that also saw the advent of managerial thought more broadly – Fayol's ideas were, according to management historians John C. Wood and Michael C. Wood, integrated into Anglo-Saxon managerial theories after the Second World War.[114] One of the key "Fayolist" principles is the "good example" set by the administrative *chef*, who was expected to maintain a high degree of visibility to subordinates. This visibility was not merely a top-down form of control ("the few seeing the many"); rather, it was designed to foster a reciprocal dynamic in which leaders, under constant observation, were compelled to embody the standards they imposed on others.[115]

In her 1992 study on the history of gender segregation across various architectural typologies, Daphne Spain drew attention to a set of management handbooks by American specialists Harry Levinson and Eugene Emerson Jennings – published between 1968 and 1981 – that align with concerns about managerial visibility also found in Fayol's work. These rarely cited examples of "grey literature" emphasised the need for workplace leaders to "shine and show them" ("them" referring to lower-ranking employees), along with the concept of "visiposure": a blend of "visibility" and "exposure" that described the requirement "to see and be seen by the right people" as a means of accelerating career progression.[116] Whether such ideas emerged through direct transmission from Fayol's work or represent a case of parallel development remains to be fully explored in a transnational framework. Hans-Joachim Fritz, too, in his 1982 monograph, examined dynamics that resonate with Fayolist principles. He did not reference the French theorist, whose possible influence in Germany has likewise received little scholarly attention.[117] Yet his discussion, drawing on the work of Elias and Foucault, highlighted how, from the normative perspective of senior managers and office layout consultants, "the simultaneous presence of supervisor and supervised in a shared workspace guaranteed their mutual disciplining".[118]

BRINGING IN USE AND USERS

Notwithstanding inherent disadvantages, the focus on canonical architecture and panoptic surveillance, together with the focus on gender, has proven crucial to our current understanding of the office building and its workers as historical objects. *Behind Office Doors* seeks to add to this understanding by proposing a double shift in perspective. First, this book moves away from a creator-centred analysis by deconstructing canonical approaches (as seen in Petra Seitz's chapter on the Herman Miller company, and in Ruth Baumeister and Shaun Fynn's contribution on Le Corbusier's Chandigarh project), while also examining lesser-known, non-canonical architectural cases (as the other authors do). Instead of exploring the ideas and ideals of "starchitects" and their "enlightened" clients, we attempt to shed light on the interactions among actors within complex, "messy" frameworks during various moments in a building's lifecycle – from intellectual conception to everyday use. Second, by disassociating the office from the overtones emanating from Bentham's panoptic prison and a reductionist reading of Foucault's "carceral archipelago", this volume seeks to re-emphasise the importance of analysing the everyday interplay between office workers and the managerial and technological norms imposed upon them.

Aspects of this double shift have already informed earlier scholarship. Besides Fritz's monograph, important work on non-canonical "everydayness" has for instance been authored by Adrian Forty (whose 1986 monograph on British interior and furniture design I will to return later), Delphine Gardey (who focused on clerical labour and administrative workspaces in pre-war France), and Michelle Murphy (whose study on Sick Building Syndrome bridged a wide gap between architectural history, environmental history and gender studies). Another example is the recent anthology *Back to the Office*, which did not abandon the notion of the canon but rather sought to expand it by retracing diachronic evolutions in the usage of fifty buildings with either international fame or merely regional renown.[119] Also highly inspiring for our purposes is design historian Jennifer Kaufmann-Buhler's equally recent call for "a more inclusive understanding of the office that gives greater weight to the experiences, intentions, and meanings constructed by workers rather than focusing exclusively on the intentions of designers or the organizations that employ them".[120] In her monograph on the open-plan design in the post-war United States, Kaufmann-Buhler argued that "the real life of the open plan office is in its use over time: the array of mismatched office chairs, dingy systems furniture components, tangled power cords and communication cables under the desk, workstation drawers filled with papers and office supplies, partitions with personal items pinned to their surfaces, and an ever-growing collection of aging computers and other technologies".[121] In an article on the "misuse" of office equipment by workers, she additionally highlighted the strategies office workers have deployed to circumvent the managerial ethos of efficiency and to "reassert their own individuality and autonomy within the organizational system" – for instance through subversive use of photocopiers, telephones and computer software.[122]

A focus on the user perspective, as architectural historian Kenny Cupers has shown in a general discussion of modern architecture, allows for an exploration of "a [...] universe of everyday experience that remains outside of the designer's direct control". Much of "architecture's meaning" is indeed not made "on the drafting board" but "in the complex lifeworld of how it is inhabited, consumed, used, lived or neglected".[123] This lifeworld is "peculiarly under-explored", not only in historiography but also – with regard to the office typology – under-analysed by furniture designers, interior consultants and managers themselves.[124] Of course, important aspects of future use are inherently unknowable, while any act of designing by definition assumes an unequal exchange, as design critic Thomas Hine argued:

> In a sense, design is the enemy of culture. Culture evolves; design is imposed. Culture is tacit; design is explicit. Culture values stability; design is radical. Culture is a complex transaction among large numbers of people; designers may consult with workers but, in the end, design is dictatorial. Culture generates deep and arcane knowledge; design wipes out wisdom and forces everyone to start over.[125]

However, the under exploration of the office lifeworld also resulted from the professional habitus of design, planning and real estate professionals, which often inhibited them from thoroughly enquiring into users' experiences. Kaufmann-Buhler demonstrated this in a discussion of office furniture designers of the 1970s and 1980s, who typically only engaged in "worker participation [...] as a [strategic] [...] means of ensuring that the workers felt heard even if their ideas or comments were not reflected in the final design at all".[126] Speaking from his own experience as an office layout consultant, Francis Duffy (1992) pointed out that "the architect's brief, too often, represents client requirements – not user requirements – and then only at one point in time". Furthermore, Duffy argued, "there is no financial motivation at all for architects to interest themselves in the use of buildings through time".[127] The effect of mercantile impulses has also been highlighted in a historical essay by the engineer Federico Maria Butera, who used post-war office towers as an example to illustrate the disdain architects and engineers often had for the user. Tower interiors, Butera argued, inevitably become either too cold or too hot, while their glazed façades create glare. These problems were usually addressed by installing air conditioning and blinds or tinted glass, which, in turn, tended to create an unpleasant environment that had to be artificially illuminated. Real estate developers – who could expand their marketable surface areas by getting rid of interior courtyards as means of natural illumination – and industrial actors specialising in electricity, lighting, ventilation and glazing obviously benefitted from this, to the extent that they could be characterised as "hidden persuaders" who "manipulated the architectural culture".[128]

Yet, what Butera saw as manipulation was perhaps not so much an anomaly but rather the very essence of the architectural *and* managerial cultures of the office. Indeed, starting with the rise of scientific management in the 1910s and 1920s, the office increasingly became the domain of experts who, to varying degrees, vied for epistemological influence and commercial success.[129] In historiography, the association of Taylorist principles and experts with office work has often – and undoubtedly for good reason – been regarded as an important foundation for phenomena such as the "industrialisation", "mechanisation", "degradation", "alienation" and "proletarisation" of lower-ranking (and often female) clerical labour throughout the 20th century.[130] In the field of science and technology studies (STS), too, Onno de Wit et al. have demonstrated that suppliers of technologies like punched card machines and computers reinforced principles of scientific management by embedding managerial control into office workflows.[131] If we consider Taylor's managerial ideology to be the "original sin", it becomes clear that countless other categories of professionals – architects, interior planners, furniture designers, appliance manufacturers, indoor environment engineers, plant care providers, landscapers, and so on – have succeeded in making a living by *mediating* the problematic effects of Taylorism in office buildings.[132] In so doing, they also tended to "lock in" and perpetuate Taylorism's core features, including the focus on hierarchy, surveillance, depersonalisation and continuous efficiency improvement.[133] Even though "no one today takes Taylorism seriously", Duffy wrote in 1997, "the kinds of office interiors [and] buildings […] that Taylor indirectly created are still being replicated" – despite the advancement of "far more sophisticated and humane ideas and practices in management thinking" since the mid-20th century.[134] Empirical investigations of the history of use and users can reveal how these dynamics of mediation evolved through time and space, thus contributing to our understanding of the reception and practical implementation of managerial ideas (rather than presenting management as a "caricature" of all things dismal, as Dorson and Verlinden urged researchers not to do).[135] Such investigations can also reveal how management, architecture and technology developed their own internal logics and rationalities, intertwining in ways that could lead to unforeseen consequences – with, as in all sociotechnical systems, "winners and losers" along the way.[136]

One of the most prominent examples of mediation is offered by the *Bürolandschaft* model that emerged around 1960.[137] Promising a radical break from the rigidities of Taylorist planning, its German inventors proposed a "cybernetic" paradigm of workplace organisation, aimed at dissolving hierarchies and actively encouraging communication between all workers.[138] Consequently, the paradigm represents an almost ideal-typical example of omniopticism, with open spatial arrangements intended to foster both interpersonal interaction and a more democratic information flow. Another component of the cybernetic paradigm was the notion of actively seeking users' feedback during processes of design and adaptation, which, as John Pile noted in his 1978 handbook, necessitated involving employees "at all hierarchical levels" in planning.[139] Architectural historian Andreas Rumpfhuber argued that this marked "an emancipatory moment in the history of workplace architecture", with "dissenting opinions" becoming appreciated for the first time as "knowledge feedback within the organization".[140] However, in historiography, the Quickborner Team's claims to innovation have also been subject to deconstruction. Joseph L. Clarke pointed out that office landscape designs generally gave workers "much less access to daylight and fresh air" than previous models, without resolving any of the problems related to the open office, especially noisiness and a lack of privacy.[141] Iñaki Ábalos and Juan Herreros saw the *Bürolandschaft* as little more than an "enlightened reexamination of Taylorism", while Kaufmann-Buhler regarded the model as part of "a repeated recycling of the same ideals, the same solutions, and even the same failures over and over again".[142] Old wine in new bottles: this was also the evaluation of architect Peter Blake in a 1974 essay highlighting the gap between everyday reality and the pretensions of the modernist movement. Commenting on the office landscape when it was still fairly new, Blake ironically argued that "few of the architects ever move into one of their own ephemeral creations, since they know what is best for them: places with solid walls, solid doors, and real windows that let in real air and real light". As such, these "creations" were "for somebody else, preferably someone who is deaf to noise, blind to views and equipped with his or her own portable supply of air".[143]

The argument on the relative lack of originality can also be reversed. Many of the "enlightened" ideas propagated by the Quickborner Team had already been proposed in the interwar period by various theorists of office design and management, although most were not widely implemented during the heyday of classic Taylorism. Such ideas include the focus on swift communication between employees (promoted by Henri Fayol in the 1910s), the removal of physical barriers between employees at different hierarchical levels (advocated by, among others, Fayol and the American office planning theorist William Henry Leffingwell in the 1920s), and an emphasis on "feelings of belonging" (promoted by the American "human relations" school in the 1930s).[144] The historiographical questions, then, are why a technical and managerial update like the *Bürolandschaft* came to be perceived as radically new, and what qualities it *did* offer that made it so influential.[145] It is doubtful that the theoretical principle of seeking all users' feedback both during and after the planning stage (as praised by Pile in 1978) was a major factor in the *Bürolandschaft*'s appeal among clients. The Quickborner Team itself, for that matter, was acutely aware of the ease with which this principle could be ignored in practice.[146] According to Rumpfhuber, many organisations indeed loosely adopted office landscape elements without incorporating the Quickborner Team's cybernetic "ideological base" – most importantly the requirement to "incorporate dissenting opinions".[147]

A more plausible explanation for the model's popularity was already suggested in 1986 by architectural historian Adrian Forty, who, in a seminal monograph on interior design, argued that the office landscape owed its popularity to its capacity to symbolically reconcile competing demands. In the post-war context of full employment and increasing worker mobility – with the West German *Wirtschaftswunder* and its corollaries in many other countries in full swing – employers faced growing pressure to attract and retain clerical staff. The office landscape offered a cost-efficient means of enhancing the workspace's appeal: it broke with the industrial appearance of Taylorism by projecting egalitarianism and middle-class respectability, while still preserving top-down managerial dominance.[148] The model thus helped managers "calm anxieties" about the status of office work and deflect the appearance of hierarchical control at a time when democratic and participatory ideals were gaining ground.[149] From this perspective, the office landscape aligns well with the logic of "consociational democracy", a concept from political history used to describe the ideological climate in various Western European countries during the first three post-war decades.¹⁵⁰ In this period, political stability and economic growth were achieved by containing ideological conflict through elite-driven frameworks of consensus and controlled inclusion. Both consociational democracy and the *Bürolandschaft* emerged as mediation devices in response to pressures for democratisation; their approach did not involve dismantling hierarchies, but subtly reconfiguring them. While these systems did introduce tangible, if limited, shifts toward broader participation, they also served to create an *appearance* of democratisation: authority was redistributed just enough to preserve institutional continuity, allowing existing power structures to adapt without fundamentally transforming. Ironically, even the managerial imperative to attract and retain personnel (as observed by Forty) was not entirely new. In 1930, the German cultural critic Siegfried Kracauer already noted in his landmark article series *Die Angestellten* (translated as *The Salaried Masses: Duty and Distraction in Weimar Germany*) that many companies had begun implementing "neo-paternalist ideologies of community" through initiatives such as sports clubs and "Sunday excursions with wives and children" – measures intended to improve "the well-being of their staff" and thereby reduce turnover.¹⁵¹ Across the Atlantic, the "human relations" school, which emerged around the same time, was part of a similar trend.

An elitist and indeed "neo-paternalist" logic was not only embedded in the theoretical underpinnings of the *Bürolandschaft*, but also in its visual language. Rather than inviting genuine input, the Quickborner Team's staggeringly intricate floor plans and communication diagrams could also function as instruments for reinforcing expert authority. They rendered the planning process opaque, lending it the air of a "technique [with] the character of an arcane mystery, from which [workers and uninitiated managers] were excluded and yet to which they were subject".¹⁵² In his 1978 handbook, Pile for instance described the visually chaotic design language of the Quickborner Team as "shocking" to clients and planning professionals of the early 1960s (Fig. 0.4.).¹⁵³ The shock may well have been part of the *Bürolandschaft*'s power. Clarke (2023) observed that the new design language made a strong artistic statement, with "workstations [appearing] to be strewn helter-skelter, flouting the building's structural grid, as though the office had been ransacked by burglars".¹⁵⁴ The layouts symbolised rebellion against the conformist ennui of repetitive desk rows, and in doing so, probably contributed further to the model's popularity. The apparent disorder conveyed a sense of radical innovation, aligning with what historian Peter Gay described as modernism's "lure of heresy"

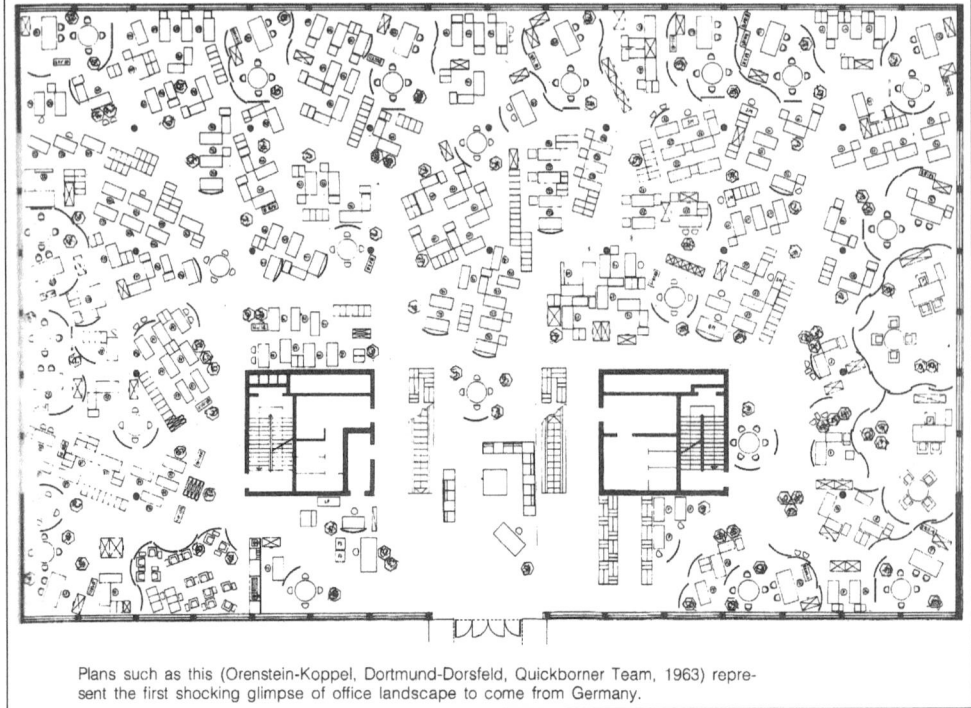

Plans such as this (Orenstein-Koppel, Dortmund-Dorsfeld, Quickborner Team, 1963) represent the first shocking glimpse of office landscape to come from Germany.

Fig. 0.4. A 1963 office layout plan by the Quickborner Team, commented on by John Pile in his 1978 handbook *Open Office Planning*.

– a drive to assert the unprecedented.[155] At the same time, the aura of mystique most likely energised a new inner circle of planning experts who saw themselves as initiates in a specialised knowledge system, reinforcing the model's authority even more. As Clarke argued, the office landscape aligned with an "ascendant managerialism", with layouts not being "the result of employees' positioning their own desks to improve communication from their standpoint", but rather "the result of a rational design process undertaken by specialists".[156] Much like Frederick Winslow Taylor and Henri Fayol in the 1910s and 1920s, the Quickborner Team and later advocates of the office landscape thus excelled at a key aspect of expertise: authoritatively *selling* their ideas – boosted, as journalist Lance Knobel (1987) noted, by their "unequalled [...] polemical ability".[157]

In this volume, contributions such as Joeri Bruyninckx's on light and noise management, Petra Seitz's on the Herman Miller company, and Craig Robertson's on the filing cabinet offer fresh insights into the performative aspects of expertise. These case studies demonstrate that companies pushed for "solutions" by framing established practices as insufficiently "efficient", thus creating a seemingly natural demand for their knowledge and products.[158] In this context, a striking parallel emerges between the trajectory of the *Bürolandschaft* and Herman Miller's Action Office furniture series, whose intended "emancipatory" characteristics were gradually lost through the replication of formal features. Obviously, in the "contested terrain" of the 20th-century office, mediation processes did not originate solely from the impulses of expertise and commerce; they also arose in response to bottom-up pressures driven by various categories of employees. High-ranking personnel for instance resisted the equalising force exerted by the open-plan layout (as shown in Marco Ninno's contribution on the offices of the European Commission in the 1960s), while non-executive workers protested against techno-managerial innovations that threatened their health and, in extreme cases, even their lives (as Amy Thomas' article on workplace activism in Britain and Tatsuya Mitsuda's study on air conditioning in Japan demonstrate).[159] Governments played a role in this process as well, as they imposed another layer of mediation through the enactment of workplace regulations (as shown by Bernd Holtwick's contribution on "screen work" legislation in Germany).

In the wake of Michelle Murphy's groundbreaking study on Sick Building Syndrome in offices, a significant field of enquiry remains vacant for historians to investigate workers' feedback and resistance, most clearly exemplified in this volume by Thomas' contribution (which also brings in a focus on trade union activities). Foucauldian interpretations regarding the "microphysics" of managerial dominance – and the potential for the corresponding microphysics of workers' resistance – will surely continue to provide an essential framework for this, complemented with insights from STS and theorists of "everyday life" such as Henri Lefebvre and Michel de Certeau.[160] Still, alternative approaches invite further exploration. A valuable perspective can for instance be found in the field of (de)industrialisation history, where scholars investigating the post-war West have used the notion of moral economy to refer to the "norms and sentiments regarding the responsibilities and rights of individuals and institutions with respect to others".[161] These mediating principles informally limited how far industrial corporations could exploit their labour force and generate environmental pollution, ensuring a balance between corporate interests and the well-being of workers and their communities. In this context, the French historian Gérard Noiriel has spoken about the existence of a "secret factory" (*usine secrète*): a realm of everyday life beyond official regulations and representations, where workers partook in workplace *flânerie*, casual drinking, petty theft and *bricolage* (i.e. on-the-job tool and material use for personal projects).¹⁶² Tolerated by workplace supervisors to varying degrees, these activities effectively created an omnioptic system of mutual complicity between the observers and observed, fostering personal bonds among them, softening the harsh realities of labour, and generating a sense of autonomy and agency among workers.

There is no doubt that similar types of social contract shaped life in administrative workspaces as well, thus helping to stabilise architectural, managerial and technological regimes.¹⁶³ Like the regimes themselves, these social contracts must have been in constant need of maintenance – sometimes being successfully "repaired", while at other times being the subject of "regrettable substitution", whenever a problem was addressed by introducing a novelty that eventually proved to be just as harmful (or even worse).¹⁶⁴ Of course, one can also point to maintenance in quite a literal sense, performed by workers such as cleaners, technicians and doorkeepers, whose activities are "part of the background and invisible by virtue of routine (and social status)".¹⁶⁵ In this regard, historians might find inspiration in the recent essayistic work *The Office of Good Intentions: Human(s) Work* (2023) by architectural critics Florian Idenburg and LeeAnn Suen. This visually rich book examines present-day life in historical office buildings, shedding light on aspects overlooked in historiography, by drawing on lesser-used source materials (including advertisements) and raising thought-provoking questions, such as the role of window cleaners and the place of breastfeeding employees (or rather the absence of it).¹⁶⁶ The "secret office", we might conclude, calls to be opened for investigation.

*
* *

OVERVIEW OF THE CONTRIBUTIONS

As demonstrated by the preceding historiographical exploration, *Behind Office Doors* aims to develop a new awareness of empirical case studies on places beyond the Anglo-Saxon realm, as well as of secondary literature in languages other than English. Indeed, the articles deal not only with the "usual suspects" – the United States and the United Kingdom – but also with Germany, Japan, Portugal, India, the Belgian Congo and the workspaces of the transnational European Commission. (Evidently, one could argue that this selection is still not quite generous enough, given the near-universality of the office.) By primarily focusing on the post-war decades, this volume moreover aims to complement the chronological scope of previous key studies, such as Delphine Gardey's monographs and the edited volume *Das Büro*, both of which focus on the interwar period and the *fin de siècle*. On a related note: embedding analyses of the office within a broad chronological context will undoubtedly remain one of the most effective ways to offer nuanced interpretations of important recent developments, such as the widespread rise of remote working from 2020 onwards. Although generally viewed as a radical shift, the technological foundation for this change was laid as early as the 1980s with the emergence of the personal computer.[167] Likewise, the advent of the home office is not quite the revolutionary novelty it is often portrayed as, but rather a partial return to the 19th-century paradigm of domesticity, which Walter Benjamin noted had begun to transform around 1900.

Unlike the other contributions, which are grounded in specific case studies, the first two chapters take a broader view, offering interpretive frameworks for thinking about how office users have been categorised and represented. By problematising the notion of the "user" in relation to a single new technology – the filing cabinet in the early 20th-century United States – **Craig Robertson**'s essay urges reflection on the varied categories of users in the office and the sources available for investigating them. In line with Gardey's call to "situate [oneself] at the level of understanding as experienced by [...] the actors themselves", Robertson demonstrates that filing cabinet users were not a homogeneous group.[168] Instead, "in defining one group of users, sources defined other groups of [...] users in a hierarchical relationship of use based on the intersection of class and gender". These groups – characterised by Robertson as including "expert users", "valuable users" and "enthusiastic users" – held different degrees of status and visibility. While expert users and manufacturers played a role in defining ideal practices, the design of filing cabinets relied heavily on assumptions about gendered and class-based labour, particularly targeting women for repetitive, manual tasks. The chapter highlights the epistemological challenge posed by the top-down nature of design, which often renders the experiences of the most common users, such as low-ranking female clerks, invisible. Robertson, however, succeeds in tracing how filing cabinets materialised Taylorist ideologies of efficiency and control while also exploring how such technologies inscribed power relations and stratified labour. The filing cabinet, he argues, simultaneously embodied and reinforced hierarchical relationships in the office, shaping users into categories of status and skill, while excluding many from practices of innovation and influence.

Focusing on 20th-century Britain, **Nicola Bishop** examines the representation of the office in popular culture. Although "office novels" have received significant attention in historical scholarship, Bishop explores them alongside less-studied media like television and film, providing perspectives on how the office is portrayed across various formats.[169] She finds evidence of a persistent trope that views it as a "negative cultural space", with "longstanding prejudices against office work, bureaucracy, administration and the people who engage with it professionally [remaining] deeply entrenched". In contrast to Robertson's fine-grained user categorisations, Bishop argues that popular opinion commonly homogenises all experiences of the office into the category "singularly boring": "Without question, assumptions are drawn from the four-word phrase 'work in an office' about the nature of the architectural space [...], the activities the users within are occupied with and, by extension, the type of person that they are." As such, Bishop suggests that the long-term stability of Taylorist principles is mirrored by the popular association of these principles with the character of office workers: "Office types are much more likely to be used as a shorthand that implies rigidity, pedantry, method and a lack of humanity than those who work in the factory environments for which rationalisation was originally intended." Of course, the degree to which this perception reflects reality, is another question. Bishop offers some insight into this issue by stating that "users of the office space [have been] particularly vocal in exploring their own status and in offering critical and creative responses to their experiences". One typical criticism can for instance be found in numerous novels that describe the unhealthy nature of administrative work, with clerks often falling victim to the rapid spread of diseases in crowded rooms. These representations were also strongly linked to gender, with the majority of office novels written by men and featuring male protagonists, whose masculine identity was often at odds with the enervating environment the office was perceived to be.

In the next part, four chapters further explore workplace health and well-being and how these were often compromised in pursuit of efficiency. **Tatsuya Mitsuda**'s analysis of air-conditioning in Japan during the first post-war decades contributes to the expanding literature on the history of climate control technologies. While much of this research has focused on the West (particularly the United States), where such technologies were a driving force behind the evolution of socio-technical regimes, Mitsuda's work shows that in Japan, too, climate control was far from "a neutral piece of technology".[170] The introduction of mechanical cooling in the subtropical Japanese climate "served as a techno-economic tool for extracting the maximum amount of labour from both humans and machines", while it also "helped reinforce office hierarchies and discipline female bodies". Driven by a desire for predictability, the architecture and business communities called on physicians to determine norms for the "optimum climatic conditions that offices should achieve". Such "objective" norms inevitably created winners and losers, as rooms often became too cold for women who, in line with recent trends in female emancipation, "dressed lightly". The solution to one problem – hot and humid summers – was thus subsumed into a new one, with female workers being told "to wear trousers, jumpers and cardigans to keep warm". Like Craig Robertson, who notes that clothes were "a site of struggle over control and individuality in the office", Mitsuda observes a tendency to standardise not only the physical environment but also the physical appearance of workers, thus reinforcing gendered expectations and limiting personal autonomy.[171] In this context, he operationalises the notion of the social contract, arguing that such a contract was severely lacking. Despite the fact that female office workers "knew in their bodies" that the temperature was abnormal (to paraphrase a recent study from the field of repair studies on the "cold office problem"), and despite numerous complaints attesting to this embodied knowledge, they usually had to endure an uncomfortable indoor climate.[172] Senior managers indeed believed that their norms, and the promise of efficiency embedded in them, far outweighed the "subjective" experience of individual, low-ranking users.

Notions of comfort and a top-down interpretation of efficiency by historical actors are also central to the next contribution on "light, sound and focus" in British and American offices. This chapter by **Joeri Bruyninckx** retraces the emergence of the concept of the workplace "environment" during the mid-1960s. The concept was a typical update of older ideas: Bruyninckx for instance mentions the influence of the "human relations" management school, though one could also point to precedents such as the quantitative standardisation of building design championed by the German architect Ernst Neufert from the mid-1930s onwards, the attention devoted to lighting in French periodicals such as *Mon bureau* during the same decade, or the ergonomics handbook *The Measure of Man* by the American industrial designer Henry Dreyfuss (first published in 1960).[173] The novelty of the post-war "environmental" approach, as discussed by Bruyninckx, lay mainly in its attempt to incorporate subjective perspectives into theoretical frameworks, with workers being used "as meters to register [...] their experiences" of indoor climate and noise. While this offered a theoretical opportunity for the democratisation of expertise, office environment researchers failed to develop this potential, as doing so would have undermined their self-understanding as experts. Consequently, they continued to treat workplace comfort in a reductionist way, determining "ideal" threshold levels within which workers were believed to perform their tasks in the most focused manner. Such ideas were implemented in response to the constant need to "repair" the open office layout concept, whose inherent inadequacies – particularly regarding ambient noise – had been evident from the very outset. Moreover, as Bruyninckx notes, experts typically took complaints from users seriously only when they were voiced by executive workers.

The problematic position of low-ranking workers is further explored in **Amy Thomas**' contribution on workplace activism in post-war Britain. "Unlike housing", Thomas argues, "office design has rarely (if ever) been used as an infrastructure for social change; it has simply moved with the mode of production due to the continued necessity for productivity under capitalism". The foundations of office design indeed largely remained unchallenged during and after the 1960s, when the dogmatic nature of modernist principles came under attack in both architectural circles and society at large. This persistence can once again be understood as a result of the adaptability of both office management and office architecture, which effectively succeeded in absorbing criticism without fundamentally altering their core principles. A notable example of such criticism, explored by Thomas, emanated from the Women and Work Hazards group established in 1977. By operationalising the new concept of Sick Building Syndrome, this group of feminist workplace reformers challenged the widespread belief that administrative work was largely free of occupational health risks. Like Michelle Murphy, Thomas demonstrates how architectural and social analyses of the office can draw valuable insights from the field of environmental history: "Environmental activism [...] not only sought to raise awareness of the damaging effects of chemicals [or] oil spills [...] but also challenged the ways in which the scientific establishment was interconnected with political and economic power structures" – including those affecting administrative work. Although fundamental reforms were not achieved, new expert groups did manage to capitalise on workers' dissatisfaction. By the 1990s, Thomas argues, "well-being in the office became divided into two disciplinary conversations: the 'hard' science of comfort, involving the technicalities of light, heat, sound and air, which fell under the domain of architecture and building technology; and the 'soft' factors of employees' mental health, which resided in an imprecise and unstable coalition of psychology, self-help and management theory".

The role of new groups of experts also features prominently in **Bernd Holtwick**'s chapter on the rise of "screen work" in West Germany between the 1970s and mid-1990s. At the start of this period, the government initiated the "Humanisation of Working Life" programme, aimed at improving conditions across various sectors. Despite the ambitious goals implied in the programme's name, the government allowed the debate to be dominated by technical experts who viewed office work primarily through the lens of quantifiable ergonomics. These experts essentially treated electronic terminals as "typewriters with a screen", neglecting the broader implications of digitalisation. That such implications were nevertheless significant has been demonstrated by earlier historians of the office. In 1982, Hans-Joachim Fritz, for instance, already noted that the computerised automation of administrative tasks had long been a pipe dream for managers, who sought to reduce reliance on employees. While complete independence was obviously never realised, the introduction of electronic terminals did create – as Adrian Forty observed in 1986 – a new category of office tasks characterised by monotonous data entry.[174] In Holtwick's narrative, the 1996 enactment of a screen work regulation marked the conclusion of the German debate by establishing a legal, updatable repository of norms and regulations that determined which conditions were "ergonomic" and therefore desirable. Through this repository, "the experiences and assessments of the workers themselves became less important"; feedback from below and processes of workplace negotiation were effectively sidelined in favour of "alleged scientific neutrality and objectivity", which "disciplined the workers 'for their own good'". Yet Holtwick ends on a positive note, noting that the personal computer, as it developed in the 1990s, contributed to a partial flattening of office hierarchies. Its multifunctional capabilities made typing and data entry part of the tasks performed at all levels, including upper management, while lower-ranking employees, in turn, generally gained access to more varied and complex roles.[175]

The next set of chapters shifts the focus from the office as an environment influencing health and well-being to a more explicit examination of managerial discourses surrounding offices, with an emphasis on the way administrative elites understood their own office use. **Petra Seitz**'s case study on the Herman Miller company offers a fresh perspective on the creators behind Action Office, a canonical product (with various iterations) that first appeared in the mid-1960s and played a significant role in the proliferation of the "cubicle". Marketed as a revolutionary design promising flexibility and efficiency, Action Office is interpreted by Seitz as a case of regrettable substitution, entrenching many of the long-standing problems of open-plan offices, including lack of privacy and personalisation. Paradoxically, Herman Miller acknowledged that "cubiclisation" often degraded working conditions by imposing sterile rigidity, but the company insisted that this degradation resulted from improper implementation rather than flaws in the original Action Office concept. Seitz exposes a deeper issue by investigating the managerial principles at Herman Miller itself. Her analysis reveals that the Action Office designers developed their understanding of office work through their experiences as high-ranking, relatively autonomous, middle-class men. Consequently, their design reflected the needs of this narrow demographic. As Seitz observes: "Herman Miller's white-collar employees may have been able to self-direct their work patterns and tasks, but other white-collar employees were expected to conform to and follow specific working patterns established by management." This disconnect between the designers' idealised vision and the realities of office hierarchies ultimately facilitated the transformation of Action Office into the rigid cubicle system. Seitz situates this failure within broader trends in capitalist labour relations, illustrating again how the ideological assumptions underpinning mid-century office design often obscured the practical needs and experiences of workers.[176]

The self-understanding of senior office workers is also central to the chapter by **Marco Ninno** on the office spaces of the European Commission (1950s-1970s). This case study examines the spatial and organisational challenges faced by a transnational institution with little precedent, where officials from diverse national backgrounds worked together under a shared administrative structure. A key question addressed is how the Commission sought to foster "cohabitation" among its multinational staff while maintaining administrative efficiency. Ninno shows that senior officials regarded private office rooms as central to their professional identity and status. These officials invested considerable effort into legitimising this preference, commissioning a report (1969) to explore potential links between office layouts and productivity. However, this justification clashed with dominant office planning theories, which favoured open-plan layouts to promote collaboration. Despite the absence of empirical evidence connecting private offices to greater efficiency, private spaces were ultimately allocated to senior officials, reflecting the Commission's hierarchical ethos. Ninno further incorporates perspectives "from below", particularly through letters and cartoons published in an employee periodical. These sources highlight the dissatisfaction of lower-ranking staff, who were often accommodated in shared offices. Their criticism brought attention to inequalities in spatial arrangements and frustrations with rigid hierarchies. By juxtaposing these viewpoints, Ninno emphasises the tensions between the Commission's attempts to project an elite identity through office design and the lived experiences of its broader workforce.

The volume's fourth part offers three essays which centralise visual sources. As suggested by photography theorist Elizabeth Edwards, a focus on photographs offers "a different scale of historical engagement", as it inserts "the telling detail that opens the imagination and informs thinking about scale, [such as] global versus local histories, network flows versus individual experience, societal versus experimental dynamics". Moreover, Edwards argues, photographs "provide a continual reminder of human experience".[177] With regard to the office, as we have seen above, the breadth of this experience is rarely retraceable in the abundant number of normative sources produced by architects and managers. Drawing on a wide selection of visuals – including photographs, artworks, architectural plans, technical specifications, cartoons and book covers – **Johan Lagae** and **Jens van de Maele**'s contribution explores governmental and commercial office cultures in post-war Belgian Congo. From the perspective of the architectural canon, this represents a doubly peripheral location: a "follower" of a minor "metropole" that is not known for any noteworthy innovation in office design or management. However, when considering the users' viewpoint, the colonial office reveals itself as a site of mediation par excellence, where Western views were adapted to the local context. An analysis of architectural drawings, for example, uncovers racial segregation patterns in post-war office buildings in Kinshasa. Lagae and Van de Maele highlight the need to understand these patterns within a broader spatial context that also considers the overall segregation dynamics of the colonial city. At the same time, mediating power was also exercised by the colonised. Numerous Belgian propaganda photographs depicted African clerks as "civilised" and "evolved" – terms rooted in colonial racism – and as having mastered all the skills of their lower- or middle-ranking Western counterparts: they operated tabulating machines, typewriters and telephones, thus fully contributing to the "bureaucratisation of the world".[178] While these images sought to affirm the colonisers' narrative of control and modernisation, they also veiled the true extent of the clerks' agency. In the offices of post-war colonies, this agency was perhaps even more pronounced than in Western offices, given the colonisers' reliance on a local workforce, the various opportunities for African clerks to assert themselves within a still unfolding terrain of power (also politically), and their ability to navigate between Western bureaucratic norms and their own cultural traditions. This in-betweenness allowed them to use their positions not only to facilitate colonial administration, but also to subvert it.

Government offices are also the focus of the subsequent short visual essays on Portugal and India. As Delphine Gardey argues, from the late 19th century onwards, the civil service in various countries became increasingly subject to "rational, mechanical and objective processes carried out by interchangeable personnel", with the "mechanisation of routines" anticipating the "technical mechanisation" later developed by architects, office layout planners and appliance companies.[179] Both essays show how efforts to impose this double "mechanisation" were continually reshaped by the material constraints of office spaces and the practices of their occupants. **Ana Mehnert Pascoal**'s contribution examines Portuguese government offices under the Estado Novo dictatorship (with a focus on the 1930-1960 period), during which the historic buildings on Lisbon's *Terreiro do Paço* served to project the regime's authority and link its governance to the nation's glorious past. Although these ministerial buildings embodied the centralised and hierarchical nature of the state, they also exposed the difficulties of working within outdated and restrictive spaces. Mehnert Pascoal's use of photography resonates with an approach taken earlier by archival scholars Barbara L. Craig and Heather MacNeil, who examined British civil service photographs from the first half of the 20th century to reveal tensions between the "ideology of efficiency" and the limitations of inherited buildings never designed for such purposes.[180] In the Portuguese case, rather than undermining the regime's authority, the permanent need for on-the-ground improvisation illustrates how the Estado Novo managed to reconcile its emphasis on heritage with logistical challenges.

Ruth Baumeister and **Shaun Fynn** explore a similar dynamic in Le Corbusier's Chandigarh office buildings, which were conceived as symbols of government order and progress. An iconic showpiece of modernism, the Chandigarh complex has in recent years been re-examined as both an exponent of and a countercurrent to modernisation, embodying tensions between supposedly universal ideals and the specificity of the local context.[181] This tension is reflected in Fynn's photographs from the early 2010s – commented on by Baumeister – which reveal interiors no longer dominated by the architect's ideals but by the pragmatic adaptations of their users. By tracing these adaptations, Baumeister and Fynn – just like Mehnert Pascoal – show how government offices are not static symbols of state power but evolving environments, whose occupants mediate daily between design ambitions and the practicalities of governance. Additionally, Baumeister highlights the problematic environmental impact of much 20th-century office architecture. Office interiors were often built – and subsequently routinely discarded during rounds of refurbishment – with little regard for sustainability, a phenomenon also discussed in Daniel Abramson's 2016 monograph on obsolescence in architecture.[182] Despite technological, managerial and economic shifts enabling the rise of working from home during and after the COVID-19 pandemic – a trend embedded in the "history of the present" and mentioned in various chapters in this volume – office buildings and the commuting infrastructure they depend on indeed continue to be significant contributors to environmental pollution and climate change.[183] Artificial intelligence, the defining emerging technology, will continue to reshape office work by altering the need for physical workplaces and office workers themselves – but whether these transformations will help address or instead set in motion social, economic and environmental problems remains to be seen.

The final contribution to the volume is an epilogue by **Martin Kohlrausch** and **Andreas Fickers**, who emphasise the office's centrality to 20th-century transformations in work, politics and technology. They explore two key dimensions: first, the office as a political space where bureaucratic power and violence underpinned major ideological and historical developments – from totalitarian regimes to liberal democracies; and second, the office as a socio-technical environment in which technologies such as the typewriter, filing cabinet and photocopier reshaped labour, gender roles and communication. Drawing on literary, architectural and media examples, they argue that the office was both a symbol of modern rationality and a site where its darker logics were enacted.

NOTES

1. Hannes Schwenger, 'Nachwort', in idem (ed.), Menschen im Büro: Von Kafka zu Martin Walser, Vierzig Geschichten (Munich, 1984), 266.
2. Kathy Marchand, In retrospectief: Herbestemmen van de Scryptioncollectie (Eindhoven, 2014), 9.
3. Ibid., 19-20.
4. 'Abschied nach 24 Jahren: Museum für historische Bürotechnik schließt seine Pforten' (via www.naunhof.de).
5. Revelatory, in this respect, is a 1992 statement by a cultural historian: "I anticipate that research on the material culture of the modern office will expand. For example, several museums have done computer exhibitions, and we now have a Computer Museum in Boston." See Thomas J. Schlereth, Cultural History and Material Culture: Everyday Life, Landscapes, Museums (Charlottesville, 1992), 145.
6. At least five major exhibitions have been organised, each accompanied by excellent catalogues: Paola Antonelli (ed.), Workspheres: Design and Contemporary Work Styles (New York, 2001); Donald Albrecht and Chrysanthe B. Broikos (eds.), On the Job: Design and the American Office (New York, 2000); Herbert Lachmayer and Eleonora Louis (eds.), Work & Culture: Büro, Inszenierung von Arbeit (Klagenfurt, 1998); Alain Guiheux (ed.), Lieux? de travail (Paris, 1986); Jean-Jacques Brisebarre (ed.), L'empire du bureau, 1900-2000 (Paris, 1984).
7. One example, the Museum of Business History and Technology in Wilmington, Delaware (established in 2001), is mentioned in Sheila Liming's 2020 essay on the history of the office. Liming mentions that "when I called to make an appointment, a rather sad-sounding voice informed me that it had closed". See Sheila Liming, Office (New York, 2020), 55. Regarding *virtual* office exhibitions: the 'Early Office Museum' (created between 2000 and 2016) was shut down over the course of 2024-2025, while the website of the 'Antique and Vintage Office Museum' (https://officemuseum.online), created in 2021, is still being updated as of 2025. On this matter, see also Alexandra Irimia and Jonathan Foster, 'Artministration', in Bureaucritics (newsletter, 2024; via bureaucritics.substack.com).
8. On this effect in the context of industrial history, see Regina Wonisch, 'Museum und Migration: Einleitung', in Regina Wonisch and Thomas Hübel (eds.), Museum und Migration: Konzepte, Kontexte, Kontroversen (Bielefeld, 2012), 14. On this theme, see also Stephen Mihm, 'Clerks, Classes and Conflicts: A Response to Michael Zakim's "The Business Clerk as Social Revolutionary"', in Journal of the Early Republic, 26 (2006), 608.
9. Élisabeth Pélegrin-Genel, L'angoisse de la plante verte sur le coin du bureau (Paris, 1994), 12.
10. Ibid., 10. For a similar statement, see Andreia Alves de Oliveira, 'The Politics of the Office: Space, Power and Photography', PhD thesis (University of Westminster), 2014, 195.
11. For the evaluation "dusty", see Marchand, In retrospectief, 9. On popular aversion to bureaucracy, see, for instance, Delphine Gardey, La dactylographe et l'expéditionnaire: Histoire des employés de bureau (Paris, 2001), 30-31.
12. On this relative absence, see Paul Katz, 'The Office Building Type: A Pragmatic Approach', in A. Eugene Kohn and Paul Katz (eds.), Building Type Basics for Office Buildings (New York, 2002), 25; Ulrich Keller, 'On the Pictures', in Gunther Sander (ed.), August Sander: Citizens of the Twentieth Century – Portrait Photographs, 1892-1952 (Cambridge, 1997), 47. For a broader analysis of the relation between art and bureaucracy, see Sven Spieker, The Big Archive: Art from Bureaucracy (Cambridge MA, 2008).
13. Alves de Oliveira, The Politics of the Office, 59.
14. See, for instance, Steven Ahlgren, The Office (London, 2022); Lars Tunbjörk, Office (Stockholm, 2002). Tunbjörk's work is also featured in Albrecht and Broikos, On the Job. For the description "unbearable ennui", see 'Pointless Jobs: The Unbearable Ennui of Office Life – In Pictures', in The Guardian, 11 Dec. 2024. Jan Banning's series *Bureaucratics*, which depicts administrators around the world at their desks, takes a somewhat different approach; while not devoid of absurdity, these photographs distinguish themselves by foregrounding individual personalities. See Jan Banning, Bureaucratics (Portland, 2009). For a more complete overview, see Irimia and Foster, Artministration.

15 Sabine Biebl, 'Von der Brutstätte des Bürgers zur Allegorie der Gesellschaft: Literarische Darstellungen des Büros bei Gustav Freytag, Robert Walser und Martin Kessel', in Gianenrico Bernasconi and Stefan Nellen (eds.), Das Büro: Zur Rationalisierung des Interieurs (Bielefeld, 2019), 157. Analyses of office novels are without a doubt the best-developed scholarly genre devoted to the history of office work. For other examples and commentaries, see the contribution by Nicola Bishop in the present volume.

16 Jesse Colautti, 'The Human Cost of Torture', in The Fulcrum, 11 Sept. 2014. The total number of interrogation rooms at Hohenschönhausen is said to have been around 120. See Deirdre Byrnes, 'Remembering at the Margins: Trauma, Memory Practices and the Recovery of Marginalised Voices at the Berlin-Hohenschönhausen Memorial', in Journal of Contemporary European Studies, 25/4 (2017), 456; Hubertus Knabe, 'Einführung', in idem (ed.), Gefangen in Hohenschönhausen: Stasi-Häftlinge berichten (Berlin, 2007), 13.

17 Grace Meloy, 'Circulation, Access, and Tourist Experience: Berlin's Center and Periphery as Case Study', BA thesis (University of Pittsburgh), 2014, 45.

18 From the mid-1960s onwards, the bureaucratic nature of this coercion process was reinforced by the Stasi's belief that its interrogation techniques were based on a "scientifically proven" understanding of human psychology. See Moritz Michels and Martin Wieser, 'From Hohenschönhausen to Guantanamo Bay: Psychology's Role in the Secret Services of the GDR and the United States', in Journal of the History of the Behavioral Sciences, 54 (2018), 51. On the interrogation rooms, see also Julia Spohr, In Haft bei der Staatssicherheit: Das Untersuchungsgefängnis Berlin-Hohenschönhausen, 1951-1989 (Göttingen, 2015), 279.

19 Reinhold Martin, The Organizational Complex: Architecture, Media, and Corporate Space (Cambridge MA, 2003), 3-4. See also Olga Touloumi, Assembly by Design: The United Nations and its Global Interior (Minneapolis, 2024), 221; Reinhold Martin, 'One or More', in Grey Room, 7 (2002).

20 In recent years, there has been a remarkable increase in the number of publications exploring the history of the office. Books that will be referenced further in this introductory chapter are Craig Robertson, The Filing Cabinet: A Vertical History of Information (Minneapolis, 2021); Annette Gigon, Mike Guyer and Arend Kölsch (eds.), Bürogebäude (Zürich, 2019); Bernasconi and Nellen, Das Büro. Other examples include Johan Jarlbrink and Charlie Järpvall (eds.), Deskbound Cultures (Lund, 2022), Grace Ong Yan, Building Brands. Corporations and Modern Architecture (London, 2020); Wim de Wit (ed.), Design for the Corporate World, 1950-1975 (London, 2017). This increase can be linked to a growing interest in bureaucracy as a broader historical phenomenon. With regard to the relationship between bureaucracy and architecture, see for instance Sven Sterken and Dennis Pohl, 'The Architecture of Global Governance: Paths of Approach', in Architectural Theory Review, 27/1 (2023); Ricardo Costa Agarez, Rika Devos and Fredie Floré, 'Introduction: The Puzzle of Architecture and Bureaucracy', in Architectural History, 65 (2022).

21 A starting point for an exploration of the heritagisation theme might be: John Schofield, 'Office Cultures and Corporate Memory: Some Archaeological Perspectives', in Archaeologies, 5/2 (2009).

22 For a critique of the evaluation of the office as "dry matter", see Annette Gigon and Mike Guyer, 'Bürogebäude – eine trockene Materie?', in Gigon, Guyer and Kölsch, Bürogebäude, 8-11.

23 For Star's conceptualisation of "boring things", see Mark Zachry, 'An Interview with Susan Leigh Star', in Technical Communication Quarterly, 17/4 (2008); Susan Leigh Star, 'The Ethnography of Infrastructure', in American Behavioral Scientist 43/3 (1999).

24 The title of the present volume is borrowed from the eponymous 1931 U.S. comedy-drama film, which was based on Alan Schultz's 1929 novel *Private Secretary*.

25 The "jungle" metaphor has been used in the context of European Union history, a domain facing a similar challenge of weak interdisciplinary integration. See Dimitris N. Chryssochoou, 'Theory Discourses and European Integration', in M. Peter van der Hoek (ed.), Handbook of Public Administration and Policy in the EU (Boca Raton, 2005), 47.

26 On the notions of composite phenomenon and assemblage, see Helena Mattsson and Sven-Olov Wallenstein, 'Introduction', in idem (eds.), Swedish Modernism: Architecture, Consumption and the Welfare State (London, 2010), 19. On the transdisciplinary nature of the office building in particular, see for instance Francis Duffy, 'Office Buildings and Organisational Change', in Anthony D. King

(ed.), Buildings and Society: Essays on the Social Development of the Built Environment (London, 1980), 141.

[27] Walter Benjamin, Gesammelte Schriften Vol. V/1 (ed. by Rolf Tiedemann) (Frankfurt/M., 1982), 52 and 53 (citation). This passage has also been mentioned by Gianenrico Bernasconi and Stefan Nellen, 'Einleitung', in idem, Das Büro, 11-12; Soline Nivet, 'Office Story: A Century of Architecture', in Alexandre Labasse (ed.), Work in Process: New Offices, New Practices (Paris, 2012), 18; Penny Sparke, The Modern Interior (London, 2008), 129; Katherine Schonfield, Walls Have Feelings: Architecture, Film and the City (London, 2000), 77. For another take by Benjamin on bureaucracy, see his comments on Siegfried Kracauer's seminal 1930 essay on white-collar work in Weimar Germany: Walter Benjamin, '"An outsider attracts attention": On The Salaried Masses by S. Kracauer', in Siegfried Kracauer, The Salaried Masses: Duty and Distraction in Weimar Germany (London, 1998). On the domestic nature of the 19th-century office, see also Lance Knobel, Office Furniture: Twentieth-Century Design (New York, 1987), 7-8.

[28] Cited by Friedrich Kittler, 'Die Herrschaft der Schreibtische', in Lachmayer and Louis, Work & Culture, 38-42, here 39.

[29] Georges Friedmann, La crise du progrès: Esquisse d'histoire des idées, 1895-1935 (Paris, 1936), 57.

[30] Francis Duffy, 'The Unstable Agenda', in idem (ed. by Patrick Hannay), The Changing Workplace (London, 1992), 125. For similar statements, see for instance Ingrid Jeacle and Lee Parker, 'The "Problem" of the Office: Scientific Management, Governmentality and the Strategy of Efficiency', in Business History, 55/7 (2013), 1074; Katz, The Office Building Type, 25; Francis Duffy, The New Office (London, 1997), 14.

[31] For these terms, see Gustave-Nicolas Fischer, 'Le bureau, espace de la vie quotidienne', in Brisebarre, L'empire, 17.

[32] Élisabeth Pélegrin-Genel, The Office (Paris, 1996), 7; Bernasconi and Nellen, Einleitung, 9-10. See also Christopher Baldry, 'Space – The Final Frontier', in Sociology, 33/3 (1999).

[33] For the hardware/software analogy in relation to the office, see Delphine Gardey, Écrire, calculer, classer: Comment une révolution de papier a transformé les sociétés contemporaines, 1800-1940 (Paris, 2008), 164-165 and 253; Duffy, 'The Case for Bürolandschaft', in idem, The Changing Workplace, 13. On the metaphor in general, see for instance Andreas Fickers and Pascal Griset, Communicating Europe: Technologies, Information, Events (London, 2019), xviii and 7.

[34] James S. Dorson and Jasper Verlinden, 'Introduction: Management, Culture, Society', in idem (eds.), Fictions of Management: Efficiency and Control in American Literature and Culture (Heidelberg, 2019), 18.

[35] Gideon Haigh, The Office: A Hardworking History (Victoria, 2012), 10-11. On this matter, see also the chapter by Nicola Bishop in the present volume.

[36] For Duffy's comment, see Duffy, 'The Princeton Dissertation', in idem, The Changing Workplace, 85. In 1973, the anthropologist Bernard James for instance found that "for a hundred years, [...] the managerial literature [has] unrolled as a single great paean to the virtues of efficiency" – and it is clear that this managerial virtue did not dissipate in the decades that followed. See Bernard James, The Death of Progress (New York, 1973), 43. On the (illusion of) immobility with regard to office architecture, see also Liming, Office, 35; Arthur Rüegg, 'Mönchszelle oder Bürolandschaft? Der Faktor Mensch in der Bürogestaltung', in Gigon, Guyer and Kölsch, Bürogebäude, 39; Alan Delgado, The Enormous File: A Social History of the Office (London, 1979), 11.

[37] I owe the notion of "fixing expectations" to Stefan Krebs (University of Luxembourg), who shared this idea in conversation.

[38] Dorson and Verlinden, Introduction, 18.

[39] For the observation on this integration, see Hartmut Böhme, 'Das Büro als Welt – Die Welt im Büro', in Lachmayer and Louis, Work & Culture, 102. A similar observation has been made by Onno de Wit et al., 'Innovation Junctions: Office Technologies in the Netherlands', in Technology and Culture, 43/1 (2002), 70.

[40] On these technologies, see De Wit et al., Innovation Junctions.

[41] The environmental innovativeness of the Larkin Building is a central element in a classic text in architectural historiography: Reyner Banham, The Architecture of the Well-Tempered Environment

(London, 1969). On this innovativeness, see for instance also Iñaki Ábalos and Juan Herreros (ed. by Joan Ockman), Tower and Office: From Modernist Theory to Contemporary Practice (Cambridge MA, 2003), 180.

42 Christine Schnaithmann, 'Maschine, Kirche, Organismus: Frank Lloyd Wrights Larkin Administration Building', in Bernasconi and Nellen, Das Büro. On these transcendental aspects, see also, for instance, Jonathan Lipman, 'Consecrated Space: The Public Buildings of Frank Lloyd Wright', in Robert McCarter (ed.), Frank Lloyd Wright: A Primer on Architectural Principles (New York, 1991); Linda Stewart Gatter, 'The Office: An Analysis of the Evolution of a Workplace', MA thesis (Massachusetts Institute of Technology), 1982, 54.

43 On this family rhetoric, see Zeynep Çelik Alexander, 'The Larkin's Technologies of Trust', in Journal of the Society of Architectural Historians, 77/3 (2018), 315; Howard R. Stanger, 'From Factory to Family: The Creation of a Corporate Culture in the Larkin Company of Buffalo, New York', in The Business History Review, 74/3 (2000), 427; Jack Quinan, Frank Lloyd Wright's Larkin Building: Myth and Fact (Cambridge MA, 1989), 51; Gatter, The Office, 52-54.

44 Çelik Alexander, The Larkin's Technologies, 310.

45 On this fusion, see Stephen Grabow and Kent Spreckelmeyer, The Architecture of Use: Aesthetics and Function in Architectural Design (New York, 2015), 49. The fact that the Larkin Building cannot be considered a model was recognised at an early point; see Jürgen Joedicke, A History of Modern Architecture (New York, 1960), 35. On the Larkin Building as a *Gesamtkunstwerk*, see also Kenneth Frampton, Modern Architecture: A Critical History (London, 1985), 61-62.

46 Pélegrin-Genel, L'angoisse, 40. On the building not being representative, see also Gatter, The Office, 6 and 112.

47 Cited by Stephan Petermann, 'Centraal Beheer', in Ruth Baumeister, Stephan Petermann and Marieke van den Heuvel, Back to the Office: 50 Revolutionary Office Buildings and How They Sustained (Rotterdam, 2022), 390.

48 Nikolaus Pevsner, A History of Building Types (Princeton, 1997 [first ed. 1976]), 319. More recently, the abundance of titles on skyscraper history has also been highlighted in a 2021 talk by literature scholar Adrienne Brown, available on the YouTube channel of the Skyscraper Museum (New York City).

49 On Wright as a messianic figure, see James S. Russell, 'Form Follows Fad: The Troubled Love Affair of Architectural Style and Management Ideal', in Albrecht and Broikos, On the Job, 50.

50 This observation evidently applies to other architectural typologies as well. On this matter, see Charles Jencks, 'Canons in Crossfire: On the Importance of Critical Modernism', in William S. Saunders (ed.), Judging Architectural Value (Minneapolis, 2007), 59; David Leatherbarrow, 'What Goes Unnoticed: On the Canonical Quality of the PSFS Building', in Saunders, Judging Architectural Value, 25-29.

51 Henry-Russell Hitchcock, 'The Architecture of Bureaucracy and the Architecture of Genius', in Architectural Review, 101 (1947).

52 Instead, "the heroics were being performed in housing, projects of social purpose, public buildings, the replanning of cities and whole regions". See Patrick Hannay, 'Opening the Debate', in Duffy, The Changing Workplace, 1. A similar statement was made by the American architect Linda Stewart Gatter in 1982: "The architectural community, in general, seems fairly disinterested in contributing to a more thoughtful investigation of the organization of space in the office." See Gatter, The Office, 122.

53 Francis Duffy and Colin Cave, 'Bürolandschaft Revisited', in Duffy, The Changing Workplace, 66.

54 Amy Thomas, 'Prejudice and Pragmatism', in Grey Room, 71 (2018), 89.

55 On the historical conceptualisation of high-profile experts as "geniuses", see also Martin Kohlrausch, 'The Social Promise of Scientific Progress: Technical Experts and the Quest for Authority', in Eva Giloi et al. (eds.), Staging Authority: Presentation and Power in Nineteenth-Century Europe (Berlin, 2022), 94.

56 Nicholas Adams, Gordon Bunshaft and SOM: Building Corporate Modernism (New Haven, 2019), 252. For another example of an alternative to this binary, see David L. Salomon, 'Divided Responsibilities: Minoru Yamasaki, Architectural Authorship, and the World Trade Center', in Grey Room, 7 (2002), 87-88.

57 The expression "geniuses within the bureaucracy" comes from a review of Adams' book: Murray Fraser, 'Review of Gordon Bunshaft and SOM [...]', in Architectural History, 64 (2021), 434.
58 Erik Sigge, 'Bureaucratic Reforms as Triggers of Experimental Design: KBS and Public Building in Sweden, 1963-74', in Architectural History, 65 (2022), 124-125.
59 Cited by ibid., 126. On the inherent difficulty of representing welfare state ideals through administrative architecture, see also Daniel M. Abramson, 'Representing the American Welfare State', in Grey Room, 78 (2020).
60 On Benjamin's conception, see Mattsson and Wallenstein, Introduction, 10.
61 For an example of such a judgment, see a popularising book by a British architectural historian: Dan Cruickshank, Around the World in 80 Treasures (London, 2005), 51.
62 From a 1994 interview with Koolhaas: Hans van Dijk, 'The Architect is Obliged to be an Honorable Man', in Christophe Van Gerrewey (ed.), OMA/Rem Koolhaas: A Critical Reader from Delirious New York to S,M,L,XL (Basel, 2019), 336. See also Rem Koolhaas, 'Typical Plan', in Jeannette Kuo (ed.), A-Typical Plan: Projects and Essays on Identity, Flexibility, and Atmosphere in the Office Building (Zurich, 2013). On the notion of the programmatical void, see also a recent comment by Sheila Liming: "[...] [The] structural components that define [the office] amount to little more than walls designating a space apart. It doesn't matter what happens within that space. What matters is that the office exists to contain and consecrate whatever *might* happen." See Liming, Office, 36. On geographical variations in office design, see for instance Juriaan van Meel, The European Office: Office Design and National Context (Rotterdam, 2000).
63 On urban conflicts resulting from office district development, see for instance Jeroen van den Biggelaar, De lelijke jaren zeventig: Moderne architectuur, publieke perceptie en vroegtijdige sloop van vier prestigieuze projecten (Houten, 2018), 9-14; Dirk Schubert, 'Opposition, Participation and Community-Driven Planning Theories', in Carola Hein (ed.), The Routledge Handbook of Planning History (New York, 2018), 406-407.
64 Böhme, Das Büro, 98.
65 Michel Foucault, Surveiller et punir (Paris, 1975).
66 Delgado, The Enormous File, 7. Together with Pevsner's scattered observations on offices (1976), a rare precedent to Delgado's book is a short historical article in a 1976 book on office interior planning: Stephen Mullin, 'Some Notes on an Activity', in Francis Duffy, Colin Cave and John Worthington (eds.), Planning Office Space (London, 1976).
67 Delgado, The Enormous File, 96.
68 Duffy, 'Office Buildings and Organisational Change', 141.
69 Baldry emphasised the "remarkably synchronous development" of "the office *building* [...], the office *space*, and office *work* within that space". Albrecht and Broikos characterised offices as embodiments of the synthesis between "business management, information systems and construction technologies". Murphy's study on Sick Building Syndrome in offices used the notion of "assemblage" to describe "the historically specific patterns through which buildings and bodies were connected [...] to each other and to the objects and practices around them". Finally, Gardey defined the office as a "technical-organisational complex" characterised by "a mix of intellectual and material techniques that organises, weaves together and redefines the practices and content of numerous industrial, administrative and commercial activities". As mentioned above, Fischer pleaded for a research perspective on the office as both a "spatial system" and a "social structure". Fritz's views are discussed below. See Fischer, 'Le bureau', 17; Christopher Baldry, 'The Social Construction of Office Space', in International Labour Review, 136/3 (1997), 366; Donald Albrecht and Chrysanthe B. Broikos, 'Introduction', in idem, On the Job, 17; Michelle Murphy, Sick Building Syndrome and the Problem of Uncertainty: Environmental Politics, Technoscience and Women Workers (Durham, 2006), 12; Gardey, Écrire, 164-165. Similar frameworks also informed recent edited volumes: Bernasconi and Nellen, Einleitung, 10; Rüegg, Mönchszelle.
70 Duffy made these observations in relation to the Larkin Building. See Duffy, 'Office Buildings and Organisational Change', 147. Petra Seitz has argued that Duffy considered technology to be the main driving force behind the development of the office building typology. See Petra Seitz, 'Where Do You Cry in an Open Plan Office? A Historiography of Interior Office Design', unpublished paper

(2019), 12. On Duffy being uninterested in "issues of power", see also Johanna Hofbauer, 'Bodies in a Landscape: On Office Design and Organization', in John Hassard, Ruth Holliday and Hugh Willmott (eds.), Body and Organization (London, 2000), 167.

71 Hans-Joachim Fritz, Menschen in Büroarbeitsräumen: Über langfristige Strukturwandlungen büroräumlicher Arbeitsbedingungen mit einem Vergleich von Klein- und Großraumbüros (Munich, 1982). Fritz's monograph is based on a doctoral thesis defended at the University of Hannover. Interestingly, also in 1982, architect Linda Stewart Gatter completed an MA thesis at the MIT on the history of office spaces, in which she likewise applied Foucault's theories. The novelty of these ideas is evident, since both Fritz and Gatter frequently misspell Foucault's name as "Foucoult". See Gatter, The Office. The appearance of Fritz's book in 1982 can serve to relativise the Anglocentric viewpoint expressed in a recent review article, which argued that all histories of office cultures must be indebted to Adrian Forty's 1986 monograph *Objects of Desire*. This review article also ignored French literature, such as the aforementioned exhibition catalogues *Lieux? de travail* (1986) and *L'empire du bureau* (1984). See Robert Gordon-Fogelson, 'Review of Open Plan […]', in Journal of Design History, 35/4 (2022), 442.

72 Long-term perspectives did characterise popular history books on the office: Haigh, The Office; Élisabeth Pélegrin-Genel, The Office (Paris, 1996). Another example – a scholarly work written by a real estate consultant – appeared just as the manuscript for the present volume was being submitted to the publisher: Rob Harris, A History of the Office and Office Work: From Castle to Condominium (Abingdon, 2025).

73 Fritz, Menschen, 146 and 13.

74 For general comparisons between Foucault's and Elias' theories, see Dennis Smith, 'The Civilizing Process and The History of Sexuality: Comparing Norbert Elias and Michel Foucault', in Theory and Society, 28/1 (1999); Robert van Krieken, 'The Organisation of the Soul: Elias and Foucault on Discipline and the Self', in European Journal of Sociology, 31/2 (1990).

75 Fritz, Menschen, 14. For a related interpretation, see Ronn M. Daniel, 'Taylorizing the Modern Interior: Counter-Origins', in Jo Ann Asher Thompson and Nancy H. Blossom (eds.), The Handbook of Interior Design (Chichester, 2015), 66.

76 Fritz, Menschen, 61. On Weber's theories as a means for understanding the increasing importance of discipline, see also Jens Steffek, International Organization as Technocratic Utopia (Oxford, 2021), 23-33; Vicente Berdayes, 'Traditional Management Theory as Panoptic Discourse: Language and the Constitution of Somatic Flows', in Culture and Organization, 8/1 (2002), 36-38; Philipp Sarasin, 'Die Rationalisierung des Körpers: Über "Scientific Management" und "biologische Rationalisierung"', in Michael Jeismann (ed.), Obsessionen: Beherrschende Gedanken im wissenschaftlichen Zeitalter (Frankfurt/M., 1995), 81.

77 Fritz, Menschen, 98.

78 An incomplete overview: Arend Kölsch, '"Ich bin du": Bürogebäude und Transparenz', in Gigon, Guyer and Kölsch, Bürogebäude, 53; Pascal Dibie, Ethnologie du bureau: Brève histoire d'une humanité assise (Paris, 2020), 200; Liming, Office, 27 and 30; Lena Christolova, 'Ein Mann der Masse: Der Büroangestellte im Film The Crowd von King Vidor (1928)', in Bernasconi and Nellen, Das Büro, 182, 188 and 191; Imma Forino, 'Die Despotie des Büros: Innenräume und Einrichtungen, 1880-1960', in Bernasconi and Nellen, Das Büro, 43-44; Jens van de Maele, 'Gläserne Zwischenwände für effektive Kontrollen: Das belgische Regierungsbüro in der Zwischenkriegszeit, in Bernasconi and Nellen, Das Büro, 106-107; Élisabeth Pélegrin-Genel, Comment (se) sauver (de) l'open-space? Décrypter nos espaces de travail (Marseille, 2016), 17; Nikil Saval, Cubed: A Secret History of the Workplace (New York, 2014), 9; Andreas Rumpfhuber, Architektur immaterieller Arbeit (Vienna, 2013), 42 and 58; Christine Schnaithmann, 'Das Schreibtischproblem: Amerikanische Büroorganisation um 1920', in Lars Bluma and Karsten Uhl (eds.), Kontrollierte Arbeit – disziplinierte Körper? Zur Sozial- und Kulturgeschichte der Industriearbeit im 19. und 20. Jahrhundert (Bielefeld, 2012), 324, 330, 336 and 348-349; Dale Bradley, 'Dimensions Vary: Technology, Space, and Power in the 20th Century Office', in Topia, 11 (2004), 71; Graham Thompson, Male Sexuality under Surveillance: The Office in American Literature (Iowa City, 2003), xiii-xiv, 7, 24, 50, 111, 135, 139 and 183; Berdayes, Traditional Management; Hofbauer, Bodies in a Landscape, 174-175; Johanna Hofbauer, 'Raum als geronnenes

Denken: Büroorganisation vom Fabriksmodell zur Kulturlandschaft', in Lachmayer and Louis, Work & Culture, 304-306; Daphne Spain, Gendered Spaces (Chapel Hill, 1992), 218, 220 and 222; Alain Guiheux, 'Neutralité', in idem, Lieux, 24.

[79] The notion of the information panopticon was developed in a sociological study: Shoshana Zuboff, In the Age of the Smart Machine: The Future of Work and Power (New York, 1988), 315-361. It has subsequently been used in other explorations of office cultures and office history; see for instance Karen Dale and Gibson Burrell, The Spaces of Organization and the Organization of Space: Power, Identity and Materiality at Work (Basingstoke, 2008), 206; Murphy, Sick Building Syndrome, 55. On control exerted through computer systems, see also for instance Margaret L. Hedstrom, 'Beyond Feminisation: Clerical Workers in the United States from the 1920s through the 1960s', in Gregory Anderson (ed.), The White-Blouse Revolution: Female Office Workers since 1870 (Manchester, 1988), 160.

[80] Dirk van Laak, 'Infrastrukturen und Macht', in François Duceppe-Lamarre and Jens Ivo Engels (eds.), Umwelt und Herrschaft in der Geschichte (Munich, 2008), 108.

[81] For this reason, the "flexibility" of open-plan designs is only a hypothetical quality. See Ábalos and Herreros, Tower and Office, 186. On the limits to flexibility, see also Jennifer Kaufmann-Buhler, Open Plan: A Design History of the American Office (London, 2021), 39-40 and 49.

[82] On the notion of office work being a black box in itself, see Pélegrin-Genel, Comment (se) sauver, 18. This notion relates to the understanding of "blackboxing" in science and technology studies, as described for instance in an article on the history of German unemployment agencies: "Once a building has been constructed, a 'black box' has been created that defines the social relationships, political interests and compromises that have been incorporated into the planning. Buildings can now control social behaviour in a way that users are not always aware of [...]." See Thomas Buchner, 'Orte der Produktion von Arbeitsmarkt: Arbeitsämter in Deutschland, 1890-1933', in Peter Becker (ed.), Sprachvollzug im Amt: Kommunikation und Verwaltung im Europa des 19. und 20. Jahrhunderts (Bielefeld, 2011), 313.

[83] In the words of Stephen Mihm: "Clerks didn't produce anything – which is not the same as saying that they didn't work. A clerk had, as [Michael] Zakim notes, 'no tangible product to show for all his long hours on the job' – a curious condition of 'strenuous idleness' that flew in the face of the labor theory of value." See Mihm, Clerks, 608. On this matter, see also Jennifer Kaufmann-Buhler, 'Diversionary Tactics at Work: Making Meaning through Misuse', in Jennifer Kaufmann-Buhler, Victoria Rose Pass and Christopher S. Wilson (eds.), Design History Beyond the Canon (London, 2023), 38.

[84] Rainer Paris, 'Warten auf Amtsfluren', in Kölner Zeitschrift für Soziologie und Sozialpsychologie, 53/4 (2001), 717. Observations from the field of organisation studies illustrate this as well: "A central assumption of work, reflected in organizational rhetoric, is that when the employee is 'at their desk' they are involved in productive work." See Gibson Burrell and Karen Dale, 'Desk', in Timon Beyes, Robin Holt and Claus Pias (eds.), The Oxford Handbook of Media, Technology and Organization Studies (Oxford, 2020), 207. See also a recent cultural analysis of office work that discusses this notion of "presenteeism": Julia Hobsbawm, The Nowhere Office: Reinventing Work and the Workplace of the Future (London, 2022), 22-25 and 136-137.

[85] Thompson, Male Sexuality, 5; Nicola Bishop, Lower-Middle-Class Nation: The White-Collar Worker in British Popular Culture (London, 2021), 66. See also Alves de Oliveira, The Politics of the Office, 138.

[86] Cited by Thompson, Male Sexuality, 5.

[87] Bishop, Lower-Middle-Class Nation, 32 and 65 (citation).

[88] Foucault, Surveiller, 299. For observations on factories, see for instance 144 and 176.

[89] On being overused, see David Adler, 'Beyond Strategy and Tactics: On the Micropolitics of Organisational Aesthetics', in Yannik Porché, Ronny Scholz and Jaspal Naveel Singh (eds.), Institutionality: Studies of Discursive and Material (Re-)Ordering (Cham, 2022), 118. For Anderson's evaluation, see Perry Anderson, The Origins of Postmodernity (London, 1998), 120. An almost caricatural condemnation of Foucault – which also cites Anderson – is offered in a "handbook" of management history: Bradley Bowden, 'Paul-Michel Foucault: Prophet and Paradox', in idem et al. (eds.), The Palgrave Handbook of Management History (Cham, 2020).

90 André Patrão, 'Foucault's Relation with Architecture: The Interest of his Disinterest', in Architecture and Culture, 10/2 (2022), 220. For a similar view, see H. Horatio Joyce and Edward Gillin, 'Experiencing Architecture in the Nineteenth Century', in idem (eds.), Experiencing Architecture in the Nineteenth Century: Buildings and Society in the Modern Age (London, 2019), 3-4.
91 On the mediation of Bentham's ideas by Foucault, see for instance Gary Browning, A History of Modern Political Thought: The Question of Interpretation (Oxford, 2016), 114; Anne Brunon-Ernst, 'Deconstructing Panopticism into the Plural Panopticons', in idem (ed.), Beyond Foucault: New Perspectives on Bentham's Panopticon (Farnham, 2012); Cyprian Blamires, The French Revolution and the Creation of Benthamism (Basingstoke, 2008), 3, 22-23 and 30. On the reception history of the panopticon, see Roy Boyne, 'Post-Panopticism', in Economy and Society, 29/2 (2000), 292-294.
92 I have discussed Bentham's ministerial office plans more extensively elsewhere: Jens van de Maele, 'From Bentham to Guadet', in International Journal for History, Culture and Modernity, 7/1 (2019), 674-677. On *Constitutional Code*, see for instance Guillaume Tusseau, 'From the Penitentiary to the Political Panoptic Paradigm', in Brunon-Ernst, Beyond Foucault; Frederick Rosen, Jeremy Bentham and Representative Democracy: A Study of the Constitutional Code (Oxford, 1983).
93 Jeremy Bentham (ed. by F. Rosen and J.H. Burns), Constitutional Code (Vol. 1) (Oxford, 1983), 442-443.
94 Ibid., 445.
95 Blamires, The French Revolution, 35. Likewise, Bentham has been called a progenitor of Taylorism; see for instance Alan McKinlay and Ken Starkey, 'Managing Foucault: Foucault, Management and Organization Theory', in idem (eds.), Foucault, Management and Organization Theory: From Panopticon to Technologies of Self (London, 1998), 4. On open office ideas in the mid-19th century, see Pedro Guedes, 'Free Plan for the 1850s: Forgotten Imagined Architectures from Mid-Century', in Architectural History, 57 (2014).
96 On the notion of regimes in offices, see for instance Murphy, Sick Building Syndrome, 36; Thompson, Male Sexuality, 7; J. van den Ende, 'Kantoortechnologie in de twintigste eeuw', in J.W. Schot et al. (eds.), Techniek in Nederland in de twintigste eeuw (Vol. 1) (Zutphen, 1998), 334-336.
97 Paris, Warten, 717; Thompson, Male Sexuality, 7. Foucault's strong focus on prison life has also been criticised by literature scholar Alexander Welsh: "We do not think about [prisons] unless we have to. This neglect or oblivion of the prison, in fact, is what makes Foucault's vision of incarceration as the condition of modern life seem so strained. If one were to place at the center of consciousness the workplace, or better still the housing of the population, one would begin to approach better grounds for social theorizing." See Alexander Welsh, 'Review of Imagining the Penitentiary [...]', in Eighteenth-Century Studies, 21/3 (1988), 378.
98 Alan McKinlay and Robbie Guerriero Wilson, '"Small acts of cunning": Bureaucracy, Inspection and Career, c. 1890-1914', in Critical Perspectives on Accounting, 17 (2006), 671. See also Bishop, Lower-Middle-Class Nation, 65.
99 For these negative evaluations, see the following article from the field of managerial theory: Chris Baldry, Peter Bain and Phil Taylor, '"Bright satanic offices": Intensification, Control and Team Taylorism', in Paul Thompson and Chris Warhurst (eds.), Workplaces of the Future (Houndmills, 1998), 163 and 182. For the notion of glamour, see Murphy, Sick Building Syndrome, 39.
100 John F. Pile, Open Office Planning: A Handbook for Interior Designers and Architects (New York, 1978), 143. For a similar view, see Kaufmann-Buhler, Diversionary Tactics, 45. On Pile, see Kaufmann-Buhler, Open Plan, 175.
101 Martin Albrow, Do Organizations Have Feelings? (London, 1997), 5.
102 Francisca de Haan, Gender and the Politics of Office Work: The Netherlands 1860-1940 (Amsterdam, 1998), 150.
103 Ibid., 151.
104 Murphy, Sick Building Syndrome, 39-40.
105 McKinley and Guerriero Wilson, Small acts, 671.
106 Michel Foucault, The History of Sexuality (Vol. 1: An Introduction) (New York, 1978), 86. See also Kim Dovey, Framing Places: Mediating Power in Built Form (London, 2001), 13.
107 On the notion of codes of visibility, see Thompson, Male Sexuality, 7.

108 On the notion of sideways glances, see Sara Ahmed, What's the Use? On the Uses of Use (Durham, 2019), 122. On the polycentricity of surveillance in offices, see also Jens van de Maele, Architectures of Bureaucracy: The Politics of Government Office Buildings in Interwar Belgium (Berlin, 2025), 52, 106 and 161-163; Bishop, Lower-Middle-Class Nation, 65; Forino, Die Despotie, 43-44; Zuboff, In the Age, 351; Fritz, Menschen, 83 and 136. On polycentricity as a general architectural principle, see for instance Anna Vemer Andrzejewski, Building Power: Architecture and Surveillance in Victorian America (Knoxville, 2008), 3-5 and 89-95.

109 Julie Berebitsky, Sex and the Office: A History of Gender, Power, and Desire (New Haven, 2012), 15. See also Robertson, The Filing Cabinet, 199-203.

110 On the notion of gaze-ability, see Varda Wasserman, 'The Gendered Aesthetics of the Physical Environment of Work', in Oluremi B. Ayoko and Neal M. Ashkanasy (eds.), Organizational Behaviour and the Physical Environment (London, 2019), 189.

111 Vemer Andrzejewski, Building Power, 5.

112 On silence as a component of office regimes, see for instance Van de Maele, Architectures, 52; Adrian Forty, Objects of Desire: Design and Society from Wedgwood to IBM (New York, 1986), 126.

113 Patrick Joyce, The Rule of Freedom: Liberalism and the Modern City (London, 2003), 148. See also Van de Maele, Architectures, 52-53; Jens van de Maele, 'The Twentieth-Century Ministerial Office Building as a Laboratory of Government', in Moderne Stadtgeschichte, 2 (2021), 158; Clare Copley, Nazi Buildings, Cold War Traces and Governmentality in Post-Unification Berlin (London, 2020), 26.

114 John C. Wood and Michael C. Wood, 'Introduction', in idem (eds.), Henri Fayol: Critical Evaluations in Business and Management (Vol. 1) (London, 2002), 1 and 5. Fayol's principal work is *Administration industrielle et générale* (1916). On the book's reception in the Anglo-Saxon world, see also Nancy Harding, The Social Construction of Management: Texts and Identities (London, 2003), 117. On the fact that Fayol's work is barely known outside the sphere of management "insiders", see Wolfgang Seibel, Verwaltung Verstehen: Eine theoriegeschichtliche Einführung (Berlin, 2017), 29. On the general rise of managerial thought from the 1910s onward, see Marshall W. Meyer, William Stevenson and Stephen Webster, Limits to Bureaucratic Growth (Berlin, 1985), 14-15.

115 For an introduction to Fayol's surveillance ideas, see Van de Maele, Architectures, 34-39.

116 Spain, Gendered Spaces, 215-217.

117 Fayol's principal work was only published in German twelve years after the original: Henri Fayol, Allgemeine und industrielle Verwaltung (Munich, 1929).

118 Fritz, Menschen, 83 (citation) and 136. Paradoxically, managerial literature does not play an important role in Fritz's narrative; source-wise, his account is largely based on novels (and, in a final ethnographic chapter, on personal observations).

119 Forty, Objects; Gardey, Écrire; Gardey, La dactylographe; Murphy, Sick Building Syndrome; Baumeister, Petermann and Van den Heuvel, Back to the Office.

120 Kaufmann-Buhler, Diversionary Tactics, 35.

121 Kaufmann-Buhler, Open Plan, 9-10.

122 Kaufmann-Buhler, Diversionary Tactics, 43.

123 Kenny Cupers, 'Introduction', in idem (ed.), Use Matters: An Alternative History of Architecture (Abingdon, 2013), 1.

124 On being under-explored, see ibid. Likewise, the academic field of organisation studies has "tended largely to ignore the humdrum, the everyday experiences of people working in organizations". See Sierk Ybema et al., 'Studying Everyday Organizational Life', in idem (eds.), Organizational Ethnography: Studying the Complexities of Everyday Life (Los Angeles, 2009), 1.

125 Thomas Hine, 'Office Intrigues: The Interior Life of Corporate Culture', in Albrecht and Broikos, On the Job, 135. On being unknowable, see Cupers, Introduction, 1.

126 Kaufmann-Buhler, Open Plan, 37 (citation); Kaufmann-Buhler, Diversionary Tactics, 37. On this inhibition, see for instance also Geert Dewulf and Juriaan van Meel, 'User Participation and the Role of Information and Communication Technology', in Journal of Corporate Real Estate, 4/3 (2002), 238.

127 Francis Duffy, 'Six of the Past', in The Changing Workplace, 129 (marginal note).

128 Federico Maria Butera, 'Envelope and Mechanical Systems in 20th-Century Building Design: A History of Masters and Servants', in Franz Graf and Giulia Marino (eds.), Building Environment and

Interior Comfort in 20th-Century Architecture: Understanding Issues and Developing Conservation Strategies (Lausanne, 2016), 134.

129 That architecture came to strongly depend on multiple specialisations was of course not a new phenomenon: the major new typologies which emerged in the second half of the 19th century, such as university laboratories, hospitals and stations, were typically shaped through close interactions between various experts. The novelty of Taylorism rather lay in its combination of scientific pretence with societal claims extending far beyond the realm of corporate management. On the importance of teamwork for the development of 19th-century typologies, see Sieger Vreeling, Geen stijl: Een rijkere architectuurgeschiedenis (Hilversum, 2022). On the cultural innovativeness of Taylorism, see for instance Alan McKinlay and James Wilson, '"All they lose is the scream": Foucault, Ford and Mass Production', in Management & Organizational History, 7/1 (2012), 47; Philipp Sarasin, Geschichtswissenschaft und Diskursanalyse (Frankfurt/M., 2003), 64.

130 See for instance Kim England and Kate Boyer, 'Women's Work: The Feminization and Shifting Meanings of Clerical Work', in Journal of Social History, 43/2 (2009); Gardey, Écrire, 110; Robbie Guerriero Wilson, Disillusionment or New Opportunities? The Changing Nature of Work in Offices, Glasgow 1880-1914 (Aldershot, 1998), 10-11; Forty, Objects, 124, 132-133 and 142; Fritz, Menschen, 16, 96 and 128-129; Graham S. Lowe, 'Women, Work and the Office: The Feminization of Clerical Occupations in Canada, 1901-1931', in Canadian Journal of Sociology, 5/4 (1980), 371.

131 De Wit et al., Innovation Junctions.

132 On the last two professions, see respectively Jennifer Kaufmann-Buhler, 'Designing for Maintenance: Plant Care Technology in the Office', in Technology and Culture, 63/4 (2022); Louise A. Mozingo, Pastoral Capitalism: A History of Suburban Corporate Landscapes (Cambridge MA, 2011).

133 On these core features, see for instance Francis Duffy, The New Office (London, 1997), 17. On the notion of technologies becoming locked in, see Helga Nowotny, 'The Quest for Innovation and Cultures of Technology', in idem (ed.), Cultures of Technology and the Quest for Innovation (New York, 2006), 6.

134 Duffy, The New Office, 17.

135 On the notion of Taylorism as a horizon of expectations that did not necessarily align with practical implementation, see for instance Gardey, Écrire, 110; Arthur F. McEvoy, 'Working Environments: An Ecological Approach to Industrial Health and Safety', in Technology and Culture, 36/2 (1995), 154-155; Margery Davies, Women's Place is at the Typewriter: Office Work and Office Workers, 1870-1930 (Pennsylvania, 1984), 107; Richard Edwards, Contested Terrain: The Transformation of the Workplace in the Twentieth Century (New York, 1979), 98.

136 On the notion of internal logic and rationality, see Van Laak, Infrastrukturen, 109. On the notion of winners and losers in sociotechnical systems, see Nowotny, The Quest, 6.

137 The Quickborner Team's first important commission was an office interior for the Bertelsmann company in Gütersloh, West Germany (1960-1961). See Joseph L. Clarke, 'Too Much Information: Noise and Communication in an Open Office', in Journal of the Society of Architectural Historians, 82/4 (2023), 452; Andreas Rumpfhuber, 'In Praise of Cybernetics: Office Landscaping and the (Self-)Conditioning of Workers', in Footprint, 25 (2019), 92; Andreas Rumpfhuber, 'The Incorporation of Dissent: Bürolandschaft's Legacy', in Harvard Design Magazine, 46 (2018), 5.

138 On the cybernetic dimension, see Joseph L. Clarke, 'The Art of Work: "Bürolandschaft" and the Aesthetics of Computation', in Nathalie Bredella, Chris Dähne and Frederike Lausch (eds.), Utopia Computer: The "New" in Architecture? (Berlin, 2023); Clarke, Too Much Information; Forino, Die Despotie, 59-60; Rumpfhuber, In Praise; Rumpfhuber, The Incorporation; Anne Kockelkorn, 'Bürolandschaft: Eine vergessene Reformstrategie der deutschen Nachkriegsmoderne', in Arch+, 186-187 (2008). On the innovation claims, see also Kaufmann-Buhler, Open Plan, 29-30.

139 Pile, Open Office Planning, 144.

140 Rumpfhuber, The Incorporation, 7 and 12.

141 Clarke, Too Much Information, 452 (citation) and 454.

142 Ábalos and Herreros, Tower and Office, 150; Kaufmann-Buhler, Open Plan, 26 and 167. On this continuity, see also Jeremy Myerson and Philip Ross, Unworking: The Reinvention of the Modern Office (London, 2022), 29.

143 Peter Blake, Form Follows Fiasco: Why Modern Architecture Hasn't Worked (Boston, 1974), 36. Organisational psychologists have pointed to the fact that the office landscape model generally "[decreased] satisfaction with the workspace and the job [...], [decreased] the amount of interaction within a firm [...] and [decreased] employee motivation". See Scott Taylor and André Spicer, 'Time for Space: A Narrative Review of Research on Organizational Spaces', in International Journal of Management Reviews, 9/4 (2007), 328.

144 On Fayol, see for instance Seibel, Verwaltung verstehen, 55-56. On Leffingwell, see for instance Van de Maele, Architectures, 45-49. On the human relations school, see for instance Forty, Objects, 147; Bevis Fuller, 'Bürolandschaft: A Science of Office Design?', in Duffy, Cave and Worthington, Planning Office Space, 66. For a similar analysis that traces reportedly new tendencies from the early 21st century back to innovations from the 1960s and 1970s, see Juriaan van Meel, 'The Origins of New Ways of Working: Office Concepts in the 1970s', in Facilities, 29/9-10 (2011).

145 It appears that the office landscape model indeed provided the impetus for many European countries to finally adopt the large open office as the dominant mode of organisation. While this model had already been firmly established in the U.S. prior to the 1960s, Europeans had long continued to use and build smaller rooms. See for instance Joeri Bruyninckx's contribution to this volume, which cites a British survey from the mid-1960s making mention of a preponderance of "small-size rooms (for single or double occupancy)".

146 See for instance Kurd Alsleben et al., Bürohaus als Großraum (Hamburg, 1961), 127.

147 Rumpfhuber, The Incorporation, 7.

148 Forty, Objects, 147-148. On the cost-efficiency, see Kaufmann-Buhler, Open Plan, 166-167.

149 On the notion of calming anxieties, see Forty, Objects, 120.

150 On the concept, see Martin Conway, Western Europe's Democratic Age, 1945-1968 (Princeton, 2020), 216-217. For a related political-historical analysis of the *Bürolandschaft*, which links the model to "liberal pragmatism" and "a liberal response to the rigid bureaucracies of totalitarian governments", see Clarke, The Art of Work; Clarke, Too Much Information, 452.

151 Kracauer, The Salaried Masses, 75-76.

152 This evaluation has been offered by management scholars Jana Costas and Christopher Grey regarding classic Taylorism at the time of its first appearance; it also applies well to the *Bürolandschaft*. See Jana Costas and Christopher Grey, Secrecy at Work: The Hidden Architecture of Organizational Life (Stanford, 2016), 64.

153 Pile, Open Office Planning, 120. For the qualification "chaotic", see Spain, Gendered Spaces, 220.

154 Clarke, The Art of Work, 104.

155 Peter Gay, Modernism: The Lure of Heresy: From Baudelaire to Beckett and Beyond (London, 2007).

156 Clarke, Too Much Information, 454.

157 Knobel made the remark in relation to the Quickborner Team; see Knobel, Office Furniture, 61. On the notion of expertise as a performative activity, see Joris Vandendriessche, Evert Peeters and Kaat Wils (eds.), Scientists' Expertise as Performance (Abingdon, 2015).

158 This rhetorical creation of the inefficiency of established practices has also been observed in relation to Taylorism; see Dirk van Laak, Weiße Elefanten: Anspruch und Scheitern technischer Großprojekte im 20. Jahrhundert (Stuttgart, 1999), 41.

159 On the notion of a contested terrain, see Baldry, Space, 536.

160 On the Foucauldian notion of microphysics, see for instance Ceri Sullivan, Literature in the Public Service: Sublime Bureaucracy (Houndmills, 2013), 16; Murphy, Sick Building Syndrome, 36. On De Certeau, see for instance Sullivan, Literature, 16; Dovey, Framing Places, 47. On Lefebvre, see for instance Dovey, Framing Places, 46-47. For an introduction to the STS perspective on users, see Nelly Oudshoorn, 'Placing Users and Nonusers at the Heart of Technology', in Todd L. Pittinsky (ed.), Science, Technology, and Society: New Perspectives and Directions (Cambridge, 2019).

161 This definition by sociologist Andrew Sayer has been cited by Steven High, Lachlan MacKinnon and Andrew Perchard, 'Introduction', in idem (eds.), The Deindustrialized World: Confronting Ruination in Postindustrial Places (Vancouver, 2017), 5. On the notion of moral economy, see also Jim Phillips, 'Deindustrialization and the Moral Economy of the Scottish Coalfields, 1947 to 1991', in International Labor and Working-Class History, 84 (2013); Jefferson Cowie and Joseph Heathcott,

'Introduction: The Meanings of Deindustrialization', in idem (eds.), Beyond the Ruins: The Meanings of Deindustrialization (Ithaca, 2003), 13. On working class history being better researched than clerical class history, see Mihm, Clerks, 608; Guerriero Wilson, Disillusionment, 298.

[162] Gérard Noiriel, 'Défendre l'usine secrète', in Travail: Bulletin de l'Association d'enquête et de recherche sur l'organisation du travail, 4 (1984).

[163] On the notion of technologies being dependent on the existence of stable social relations, see Wiebe E. Bijker and John Law, 'Introduction', in idem (eds.), Shaping Technology/Building Society: Studies in Sociotechnical Change (Cambridge MA, 1997), 10. A concern with informal practices has also appeared in Kaufmann-Buhler's account of office workers who "misused" their equipment and environments to personal ends, though her focus lay on individual acts of adaptation rather than on the socially negotiated norms that, for Noiriel, underpinned such behaviours. See Kaufmann-Buhler, Diversionary Tactics.

[164] To date, the notion of "regrettable substitution" has mainly been used in the environmental sciences, where it refers to the introduction of harmful chemical components in the environment as replacements for similarly harmful substances. See for instance Laura D. Scherer et al., 'The Psychology of "Regrettable Substitutions": Examining Consumer Judgements of Bisphenol A and its Alternatives', in Health, Risk & Society, 16/7-8 (2014). On the history of repair and maintenance as a burgeoning area of research, see for instance Stefan Krebs and Heike Weber (eds.), The Persistence of Technology: Histories of Repair, Reuse and Disposal (Bielefeld, 2021).

[165] Susan Leigh Star and Anselm Stauss, 'Layers of Silence, Arenas of Voice: The Ecology of Visible and Invisible Work', in Computer Supported Cooperative Work, 8 (1999), 20.

[166] Florian Idenburg and LeeAnn Suen, The Office of Good Intentions: Human(s) Work (Cologne, 2022). On maintenance personnel, see also Kaufmann-Buhler, Open Plan, 159-160; Judy Wajcman, '"Fitter, happier, more productive": Optimising Time with Technology', in Vera King, Benigna Gerisch and Hartmut Rosa (eds.), Lost in Perfection: Impacts of Optimisation on Culture and Psyche (London, 2019), 56; Winifred R. Poster, Marion Crain and Miriam A. Cherry, 'Introduction: Conceptualizing Invisible Labor', in idem (eds.), Invisible Labor: Hidden Work in the Contemporary World (Oakland, 2016), 11.

[167] Historian Jonathan Voges has argued that since the same decade, office work has also been subject to a gradual, cultural "postmodern deconstruction". See Jonathan Voges, 'Review of Das Büro [...]', in Zeitschrift für Unternehmensgeschichte, 66/1 (2021), 155. The rise of working from home was already predicted in the 1986 exhibition catalogue Lieux? de travail, precisely as a result of ongoing digitalisation. See Yves Lasfargue, 'Scénarios pour 2005: Mutations technologiques dans le tertiaire et le secondaire', in Alain Guiheux (ed.), Lieux? de travail (Paris, 1986).

[168] For Gardey's call, see Delphine Gardey, 'Culture of Gender, and Culture of Technology: The Gendering of Things in France's Office Spaces between 1890 and 1930', in Helga Nowotny (ed.), Cultures of Technology (New York, 2006), 74.

[169] On film, see for instance Merrill Schleier, Skyscraper Cinema: Architecture and Gender in American Film (Minneapolis, 2009). On television, see for instance Haigh, The Office, 9-10. Much potential for exploration remains regarding publicity, comics and cartoons. On the latter two, see for instance Berebitsky, Sex and the Office. On advertisements, see for instance Idenburg and Suen, The Office, 156 and 249-264; Gianenrico Bernasconi, 'Performance, fatigue et style de vie: Ovomaltine et le travail au bureau au début du XXe siècle', in Food & History, 14/2-3 (2016).

[170] The foundational text on the history of air-conditioning is Banham, The Architecture. For more recent observations, see Daniel A. Barber, Modern Architecture and Climate: Design Before Air Conditioning (Princeton, 2020); Marsha E. Ackermann, Cool Comfort: America's Romance with Air-Conditioning (Washington D.C., 2010); Ábalos and Herreros, Tower and Office, 193; Martin, The Organizational Complex, 89.

[171] Concerning normative ideas on (female) clothing in the social history of the office, see also for instance Nicole Robertson, 'Women at Work: Activism, Feminism and the Rise of the Female Office Worker during the First World War and its Immediate Aftermath', in Keith Laybourn and John Shepherd (eds.), Labour and Working-Class Lives: Essays to Celebrate the Life and Work of Chris Wrigley (Manchester, 2017); Schonfield, Walls Have Feelings, 93-105; De Haan, Gender, 144-150.

172 For this study, see Christopher R. Henke and Benjamin Sims, Repairing Infrastructures: The Maintenance of Materiality and Power (London, 2020), 40.
173 On Neufert, see Gernot Weckherlin, BEL: Zur Systematik des architektonischen Wissens am Beispiel von Ernst Neuferts Bauentwurfslehre (Tübingen, 2017). On the French example, see Gardey, Écrire, 253. On Dreyfuss, see John Harwood, The Interface: IBM and the Transformation of Corporate Design, 1945-1976 (Minneapolis, 2011), 94-99; Russell Flinchum, Henry Dreyfuss, Industrial Designer: The Man in the Brown Suit (New York, 1997).
174 Fritz, Menschen, 133; Adrian Forty, Objects, 141.
175 On this shift, see also Thomas Haigh, 'Remembering the Office of the Future: The Origins of Word Processing and Office Automation', in IEEE Annals of the History of Computing, Oct.-Dec. 2006, 26.
176 For another critique of Action Office through the lens of labour relations, see Renyi Hong, 'Office Interiors and the Fantasy of Information Work', in tripleC, 15/2 (2017), 540-562, here 556.
177 Elizabeth Edwards, Photographs and the Practice of History: A Short Primer (London, 2022), 49-50.
178 Bruno Rizzi's 1939 theory of the "bureaucratisation of the world" described the rise of a new bureaucratic ruling class across capitalist, fascist and communist regimes. This framework can be extended to colonial contexts, where local clerks operated within this emerging global order. See Bruno Rizzi, The Bureaucratization of the World (New York, 1985).
179 Delphine Gardey, 'Nachwort: "Espèces d'espaces", Raumarten – Soziale, technische und politike Aspekte', in Gianenrico Bernasconi and Stefan Nellen (eds.), Das Büro: Zur Rationalisierung des Interieurs (Bielefeld, 2019), 279.
180 Barbara L. Craig and Heather MacNeil, 'Records Making, Office Machines, and Workers in Historical Contexts: Five Photographs of Offices in the British Civil Service c. 1919 and 1947', in Journal of the Society of Archivists, 32/2 (2011), 210.
181 For a prominent example, see Tom Avermaete and Maristella Casciato, Casablanca Chandigarh: A Report on Modernization (Montreal, 2014). The terms exponent and countercurrent are mentioned on the book's back cover.
182 Daniel M. Abramson, Obsolescence: An Architectural History (Chicago, 2016) (on office buildings, see 16-37 in particular). See also Amy Thomas, 'The Political Economy of Flexibility: Deregulation and the Transformation of Corporate Space in the Postwar City of London', in Kenny Cupers, Helena Mattsson and Catharina Gabrielsson (eds.), Neoliberalism on the Ground: Architecture and Transformations from 1960 to the Present (Pittsburgh, 2020). For a discussion of the environmental impact of construction materials in general, see Adrian Forty, Concrete and Culture: A Material History (London, 2012), 69-77.
183 I borrow the notion of "history of the present" from Timothy Garton Ash, History of the Present: Essays, Sketches and Dispatches from Europe in the 1990s (New York, 1999). On the environmental impact, see Raphaël Ménard, 'Don Draper, the Car and the Climate', in Labasse, Work in Process.

BIBLIOGRAPHY

Iñaki Ábalos and Juan Herreros (ed. by Joan Ockman), Tower and Office: From Modernist Theory to Contemporary Practice (Cambridge MA, 2003).
Daniel M. Abramson, Obsolescence: An Architectural History (Chicago, 2016).
Daniel M. Abramson, 'Representing the American Welfare State', in Grey Room, 78 (2020), 96-123.
Marsha E. Ackermann, Cool Comfort: America's Romance with Air-Conditioning (Washington D.C., 2010).
Nicholas Adams, Gordon Bunshaft and SOM: Building Corporate Modernism (New Haven, 2019).
David Adler, 'Beyond Strategy and Tactics: On the Micropolitics of Organisational Aesthetics', in Yannik Porché, Ronny Scholz and Jaspal Naveel Singh (eds.), Institutionality: Studies of Discursive and Material (Re-)Ordering (Cham, 2022), 115-139.
Ricardo Costa Agarez, Rika Devos and Fredie Floré, 'Introduction: The Puzzle of Architecture and Bureaucracy', in Architectural History, 65 (2022), 1-20.
Steven Ahlgren, The Office (London, 2022).

Sara Ahmed, What's the Use? On the Uses of Use (Durham, 2019).
Martin Albrow, Do Organizations Have Feelings? (London, 1997).
Zeynep Çelik Alexander, 'The Larkin's Technologies of Trust', in Journal of the Society of Architectural Historians, 77/3 (2018), 300-318.
Donald Albrecht and Chrysanthe B. Broikos (eds.), On the Job: Design and the American Office (New York, 2000).
Donald Albrecht and Chrysanthe B. Broikos, 'Introduction', in idem (eds.), On the Job: Design and the American Office (New York, 2000), 17-29.
Kurd Alsleben et al., Bürohaus als Großraum (Hamburg, 1961).
Perry Anderson, The Origins of Postmodernity (London, 1998).
Anna Vemer Andrzejewski, Building Power: Architecture and Surveillance in Victorian America (Knoxville, 2008).
Paola Antonelli (ed.), Workspheres: Design and Contemporary Work Styles (New York, 2001).
Tom Avermaete and Maristella Casciato, Casablanca Chandigarh: A Report on Modernization (Montreal, 2014).
Christopher Baldry, 'The Social Construction of Office Space', in International Labour Review, 136/3 (1997), 365-378.
Christopher Baldry, 'Space – The Final Frontier', in Sociology, 33/3 (1999), 535-553.
Chris Baldry, Peter Bain and Phil Taylor, '"Bright satanic offices": Intensification, Control and Team Taylorism', in Paul Thompson and Chris Warhurst (eds.), Workplaces of the Future (Houndmills, 1998), 163-183.
Reyner Banham, The Architecture of the Well-Tempered Environment (London, 1969).
Jan Banning, Bureaucratics (Portland, 2009).
Daniel A. Barber, Modern Architecture and Climate: Design Before Air Conditioning (Princeton, 2020).
Walter Benjamin, Gesammelte Schriften Vol. V/1 (ed. by Rolf Tiedemann) (Frankfurt/M., 1982).
Walter Benjamin, '"An outsider attracts attention": On The Salaried Masses by S. Kracauer', in Siegfried Kracauer, The Salaried Masses: Duty and Distraction in Weimar Germany (London, 1998), 109-114.
Jeremy Bentham (ed. by F. Rosen and J.H. Burns), Constitutional Code (Vol. 1) (Oxford, 1983).
Vicente Berdayes, 'Traditional Management Theory as Panoptic Discourse: Language and the Constitution of Somatic Flows', in Culture and Organization, 8/1 (2002), 35-49.
Julie Berebitsky, Sex and the Office: A History of Gender, Power, and Desire (New Haven, 2012).
Gianenrico Bernasconi, 'Performance, fatigue et style de vie: Ovomaltine et le travail au bureau au début du XXe siècle', in Food & History, 14/2-3 (2016), 77-104.
Gianenrico Bernasconi and Stefan Nellen (eds.), Das Büro: Zur rationalisierung des Interieurs (Bielefeld, 2019).
Gianenrico Bernasconi and Stefan Nellen, 'Einleitung', in idem (eds.), Das Büro: Zur Rationalisierung des Interieurs (Bielefeld, 2019), 9-26.
Sabine Biebl, 'Von der Brutstätte des Bürgers zur Allegorie der Gesellschaft: Literarische Darstellungen des Büros bei Gustav Freytag, Robert Walser und Martin Kessel', in Gianenrico Bernasconi and Stefan Nellen (eds.), Das Büro: Zur Rationalisierung des Interieurs (Bielefeld, 2019), 157-174.
Jeroen van den Biggelaar, De lelijke jaren zeventig: Moderne architectuur, publieke perceptie en vroegtijdige sloop van vier prestigieuze projecten (Houten, 2018).
Wiebe E. Bijker and John Law, 'Introduction', idem (eds.), Shaping Technology/Building Society: Studies in Sociotechnical Change (Cambridge MA, 1997), 1-16.
Nicola Bishop, Lower-Middle-Class Nation: The White-Collar Worker in British Popular Culture (London, 2021).
Peter Blake, Form Follows Fiasco: Why Modern Architecture Hasn't Worked (Boston, 1974).
Cyprian Blamires, The French Revolution and the Creation of Benthamism (Basingstoke, 2008).
Hartmut Böhme, 'Das Büro als Welt – Die Welt im Büro', in Herbert Lachmayer and Eleonora Louis (eds.), Work & Culture: Büro, Inszenierung von Arbeit (Klagenfurt, 1998), 95-103.
Bradley Bowden, 'Paul-Michel Foucault: Prophet and Paradox', in idem et al. (eds.), The Palgrave Handbook of Management History (Cham, 2020), 671-697.
Roy Boyne, 'Post-Panopticism', in Economy and Society, 29/2 (2000), 285-307.

Dale Bradley, 'Dimensions Vary: Technology, Space, and Power in the 20th Century Office', in Topia, 11 (2004), 67-82.
Jean-Jacques Brisebarre (ed.), L'empire du bureau, 1900-2000 (Paris, 1984).
Gary Browning, A History of Modern Political Thought: The Question of Interpretation (Oxford, 2016).
Anne Brunon-Ernst, 'Deconstructing Panopticism into the Plural Panopticons', in idem (ed.), Beyond Foucault: New Perspectives on Bentham's Panopticon (Farnham, 2012), 17-41.
Thomas Buchner, 'Orte der Produktion von Arbeitsmarkt: Arbeitsämter in Deutschland, 1890-1933', in Peter Becker (ed.), Sprachvollzug im Amt: Kommunikation und Verwaltung im Europa des 19. und 20. Jahrhunderts (Bielefeld, 2011), 305-334.
Gibson Burrell and Karen Dale, 'Desk', in Timon Beyes, Robin Holt and Claus Pias (eds.), The Oxford Handbook of Media, Technology and Organization Studies (Oxford, 2020), 202-213.
Federico Maria Butera, 'Envelope and Mechanical Systems in 20th-Century Building Design: A History of Masters and Servants', in Franz Graf and Giulia Marino (eds.), Building Environment and Interior Comfort in 20th-Century Architecture: Understanding Issues and Developing Conservation Strategies (Lausanne, 2016), 127-138.
Deirdre Byrnes, 'Remembering at the Margins: Trauma, Memory Practices, and the Recovery of Marginalised Voices at the Berlin-Hohenschönhausen Memorial', in Journal of Contemporary European Studies, 25/4 (2017), 455-469.
Lena Christolova, 'Ein Mann der Masse: Der Büroangestellte im Film The Crown von King Vidor (1928)', in Gianenrico Bernasconi and Stefan Nellen (eds.), Das Büro: Zur Rationalisierung des Interieurs (Bielefeld, 2019), 175-192.
Dimitris N. Chryssochoou, 'Theory Discourses and European Integration', in M. Peter van der Hoek (ed.), Handbook of Public Administration and Policy in the EU (Boca Raton, 2005), 29-51.
Joseph L. Clarke, 'The Art of Work: "Bürolandschaft" and the Aesthetics of Computation', in Nathalie Bredella, Chris Dähne and Frederike Lausch (eds.), Utopia Computer: The "New" in Architecture? (Berlin, 2023), 103-121.
Joseph L. Clarke, 'Too Much Information: Noise and Communication in an Open Office', in Journal of the Society of Architectural Historians, 82/4 (2023), 449-466.
Jesse Colautti, 'The Human Cost of Torture', in The Fulcrum, 11 Sept. 2014.
Martin Conway, Western Europe's Democratic Age, 1945-1968 (Princeton, 2020).
Clare Copley, Nazi Buildings, Cold War Traces and Governmentality in Post-Unification Berlin (London, 2020).
Jana Costas and Christopher Grey, Secrecy at Work: The Hidden Architecture of Organizational Life (Stanford, 2016).
Jefferson Cowie and Joseph Heathcott, 'Introduction: The Meanings of Deindustrialization', in idem (eds.), Beyond the Ruins: The Meanings of Deindustrialization (Ithaca, 2003), 1-18.
Barbara L. Craig and Heather MacNeil, 'Records Making, Office Machines, and Workers in Historical Contexts: Five Photographs of Offices in the British Civil Service c. 1919 and 1947', in Journal of the Society of Archivists, 32/2 (2011), 205-220.
Dan Cruickshank, Around the World in 80 Treasures (London, 2005).
Kenny Cupers, 'Introduction', in idem (ed.), Use Matters: An Alternative History of Architecture (Abingdon, 2013), 1-14.
Karen Dale and Gibson Burrell, The Spaces of Organization and the Organization of Space: Power, Identity and Materiality at Work (Basingstoke, 2008).
Ronn M. Daniel, 'Taylorizing the Modern Interior: Counter-Origins', in Jo Ann Asher Thompson and Nancy H. Blossom (eds.), The Handbook of Interior Design (Chichester, 2015), 58-69.
Margery Davies, Women's Place is at the Typewriter: Office Work and Office Workers, 1870-1930 (Pennsylvania, 1984).
Alan Delgado, The Enormous File: A Social History of the Office (London, 1979).
Geert Dewulf and Juriaan van Meel, 'User Participation and the Role of Information and Communication Technology', in Journal of Corporate Real Estate, 4/3 (2002), 237-248.
Pascal Dibie, Ethnologie du bureau: Brève histoire d'une humanité assise (Paris, 2020).

Hans van Dijk, 'The Architect is Obliged to be an Honorable Man', in Christophe Van Gerrewey (ed.), OMA/Rem Koolhaas: A Critical Reader from Delirious New York to S,M,L,XL (Basel, 2019), 335-339.
James S. Dorson and Jasper Verlinden, 'Introduction: Management, Culture, Society', in idem (eds.), Fictions of Management: Efficiency and Control in American Literature and Culture (Heidelberg, 2019), 7-30.
Kim Dovey, Framing Places: Mediating Power in Built Form (London, 2001).
Francis Duffy, 'Office Buildings and Organisational Change', in Anthony D. King (ed.), Buildings and Society: Essays on the Social Development of the Built Environment (London, 1980), 140-157.
Francis Duffy, 'The Case for Bürolandschaft', in idem (ed. by Patrick Hannay), The Changing Workplace (London, 1992), 6-23.
Francis Duffy, 'The Princeton Dissertation', in idem (ed. by Patrick Hannay), The Changing Workplace (London, 1992), 79-95.
Francis Duffy, 'The Unstable Agenda', in idem (ed. by Patrick Hannay), The Changing Workplace (London, 1992), 121-128.
Francis Duffy, 'Six of the Past', in idem (ed. by Patrick Hannay), The Changing Workplace (London, 1992), 129-142.
Francis Duffy, The New Office (London, 1997).
Francis Duffy and Colin Cave, 'Bürolandschaft Revisited', in idem (ed. by Patrick Hannay), The Changing Workplace (London, 1992), 65-78.
Elizabeth Edwards, Photographs and the Practice of History: A Short Primer (London, 2022).
Richard Edwards, Contested Terrain: The Transformation of the Workplace in the Twentieth Century (New York, 1979).
J. van den Ende, 'Kantoortechnologie in de twintigste eeuw', in J.W. Schot et al. (eds.), Techniek in Nederland in de twintigste eeuw (Vol. 1) (Zutphen, 1998), 328-339.
Kim England and Kate Boyer, 'Women's Work: The Feminization and Shifting Meanings of Clerical Work', in Journal of Social History, 43/2 (2009), 307-340.
Henri Fayol, Allgemeine und industrielle Verwaltung (Munich, 1929).
Andreas Fickers and Pascal Griset, Communicating Europe: Technologies, Information, Events (London, 2019).
Gustave-Nicolas Fischer, 'Le bureau, espace de la vie quotidienne', in Jean-Jacques Brisebarre (ed.), L'empire du bureau, 1900-2000 (Paris, 1984), 16-34.
Russell Flinchum, Henry Dreyfuss, Industrial Designer: The Man in the Brown Suit (New York, 1997).
Imma Forino, 'Die Despotie des Büros: Innenräume und Einrichtungen, 1880-1960', in Gianenrico Bernasconi and Stefan Nellen (eds.), Das Büro: Zur Rationalisierung des Interieurs (Bielefeld, 2019), 27-68.
Adrian Forty, Objects of Desire: Design and Society from Wedgwood to IBM (New York, 1986).
Adrian Forty, Concrete and Culture: A Material History (London, 2012).
Michel Foucault, Surveiller et punir (Paris, 1975).
Michel Foucault, The History of Sexuality (Volume 1: An Introduction) (New York, 1978).
Kenneth Frampton, Modern Architecture: A Critical History (London, 1985).
Murray Fraser, 'Review of Gordon Bunshaft and SOM [...]', in Architectural History, 64 (2021), 433-435.
Georges Friedmann, La crise du progrès: Esquisse d'histoire des idées, 1895-1935 (Paris, 1936).
Hans-Joachim Fritz, Menschen in Büroarbeitsräumen: Über langfristige Strukturwandlungen büroräumlicher Arbeitsbedingungen mit einem Vergleich von Klein- und Großraumbüros (Munich, 1982).
Bevis Fuller, 'Bürolandschaft: A Science of Office Design?', in Francis Duffy, Colin Cave and John Worthington (eds.), Planning Office Space (London, 1976), 61-67.
Delphine Gardey, La dactylographe et l'expéditionnaire: Histoire des employés de bureau (Paris, 2001).
Delphine Gardey, 'Culture of Gender, and Culture of Technology: The Gendering of Things in France's Office Spaces between 1890 and 1930', in Helga Nowotny (ed.), Cultures of Technology (New York, 2006), 73-94.
Delphine Gardey, Écrire, calculer, classer: Comment une révolution de papier a transformé les sociétés contemporaines, 1800-1940 (Paris, 2008).

Delphine Gardey, 'Nachwort: "Espèces d'espaces", Raumarten – Soziale, technische und politike Aspekte', in Gianenrico Bernasconi and Stefan Nellen (eds.), Das Büro: Zur Rationalisierung des Interieurs (Bielefeld, 2019), 277-286.
Timothy Garton Ash, History of the Present: Essays, Sketches and Dispatches from Europe in the 1990s (New York, 1999).
Linda Stewart Gatter, 'The Office: An Analysis of the Evolution of a Workplace', MA thesis (Massachusetts Institute of Technology), 1982.
Peter Gay, Modernism: The Lure of Heresy: From Baudelaire to Beckett and Beyond (London, 2007).
Annette Gigon, Mike Guyer and Arend Kölsch (eds.), Bürogebäude (Zürich, 2019).
Annette Gigon and Mike Guyer, 'Bürogebäude – eine trockene Materie?', in Annette Gigon, Mike Guyer and Arend Kölsch (eds.), Bürogebäude (Zürich, 2019), 8-11.
Robert Gordon-Fogelson, 'Review of Open Plan [...]', in Journal of Design History, 35/4 (2022), 439-442.
Stephen Grabow and Kent Spreckelmeyer, The Architecture of Use: Aesthetics and Function in Architectural Design (New York, 2015).
Pedro Guedes, 'Free Plan for the 1850s: Forgotten Imagined Architectures from Mid-Century', in Architectural History, 57 (2014), 239-275.
Alain Guiheux (ed.), Lieux? de travail (Paris, 1986).
Alain Guiheux, 'Neutralité', in idem (ed.), Lieux? de travail (Paris, 1986), 15-27.
Francisca de Haan, Gender and the Politics of Office Work: The Netherlands 1860-1940 (Amsterdam, 1998).
Gideon Haigh, The Office: A Hardworking History (Victoria, 2012).
Thomas Haigh, 'Remembering the Office of the Future: The Origins of Word Processing and Office Automation', in IEEE Annals of the History of Computing, Oct.-Dec. 2006, 6-31.
Patrick Hannay, 'Opening the Debate', in Francis Duffy (ed.), The Changing Workplace (London, 1992), 1-6.
Nancy Harding, The Social Construction of Management: Texts and Identities (London, 2003).
Rob Harris, A History of the Office and Office Work: From Castle to Condominium (Abingdon, 2025).
John Harwood, The Interface: IBM and the Transformation of Corporate Design, 1945-1976 (Minneapolis, 2011).
Margaret L. Hedstrom, 'Beyond Feminisation: Clerical Workers in the United States from the 1920s through the 1960s', in Gregory Anderson (ed.), The White-Blouse Revolution: Female Office Workers since 1870 (Manchester, 1988), 143-169.
Christopher R. Henke and Benjamin Sims, Repairing Infrastructures: The Maintenance of Materiality and Power (London, 2020).
Steven High, Lachlan MacKinnon and Andrew Perchard, 'Introduction', in idem (eds.), The Deindustrialized World: Confronting Ruination in Postindustrial Places (Vancouver, 2017), 3-24.
Henry-Russell Hitchcock, 'The Architecture of Bureaucracy and the Architecture of Genius', in Architectural Review, 101 (1947), 3-6.
Thomas Hine, 'Office Intrigues: The Interior Life of Corporate Culture', in Donald Albrecht and Chrysanthe Broikos (eds.), On the Job: Design and the American Office (New York, 2000), 128-143.
Julia Hobsbawm, The Nowhere Office: Reinventing Work and the Workplace of the Future (London, 2022).
Johanna Hofbauer, 'Raum als geronnenes Denken: Büroorganisation vom Fabriksmodell zur Kulturlandschaft', in Herbert Lachmayer and Eleonora Louis (eds.), Work & Culture: Büro, Inszenierung von Arbeit (Klagenfurt, 1998), 303-309.
Johanna Hofbauer, 'Bodies in a Landscape: On Office Design and Organization', in John Hassard, Ruth Holliday and Hugh Willmott (eds.), Body and Organization (London, 2000), 166-191.
Renyi Hong, 'Office Interiors and the Fantasy of Information Work', in tripleC, 15/2 (2017), 540-562.
Florian Idenburg and LeeAnn Suen, The Office of Good Intentions: Human(s) Work (Cologne, 2022).
Alexandra Irimia and Jonathan Foster, 'Artministration', in Bureaucritics (newsletter, 2024; via bureaucritics.substack.com).
Bernard James, The Death of Progress (New York, 1973).
Johan Jarlbrink and Charlie Järpvall (eds.), Deskbound Cultures (Lund, 2022).

Ingrid Jeacle and Lee Parker, 'The "Problem" of the Office: Scientific Management, Governmentality and the Strategy of Efficiency', in Business History, 55/7 (2013), 1074-1099.
Charles Jencks, 'Canons in Crossfire: On the Importance of Critical Modernism', in William S. Saunders (ed.), Judging Architectural Value (Minneapolis, 2007), 52-65.
Jürgen Joedicke, A History of Modern Architecture (New York, 1960).
H. Horatio Joyce and Edward Gillin, 'Experiencing Architecture in the Nineteenth Century', in idem (eds.), Experiencing Architecture in the Nineteenth Century: Buildings and Society in the Modern Age (London, 2019), 1-11.
Patrick Joyce, The Rule of Freedom: Liberalism and the Modern City (London, 2003).
Paul Katz, 'The Office Building Type: A Pragmatic Approach', in A. Eugene Kohn and Paul Katz (eds.), Building Type Basics for Office Buildings (New York, 2002), 25-56.
Jennifer Kaufmann-Buhler, Open Plan: A Design History of the American Office (London, 2021).
Jennifer Kaufmann-Buhler, 'Designing for Maintenance: Plant Care Technology in the Office', in Technology and Culture, 63/4 (2022), 1033-1056.
Jennifer Kaufmann-Buhler, 'Diversionary Tactics at Work: Making Meaning through Misuse', in Jennifer Kaufmann-Buhler, Victoria Rose Pass and Christopher S. Wilson (eds.), Design History Beyond the Canon (London, 2023), 35-48.
Ulrich Keller, 'On the Pictures', in Gunther Sander (ed.), August Sander: Citizens of the Twentieth Century – Portrait Photographs, 1892-1952 (Cambridge, 1997), 43-52.
Friedrich Kittler, 'Die Herrschaft der Schreibtische', in Herbert Lachmayer and Eleonora Louis (eds.), Work & Culture: Büro, Inszenierung von Arbeit (Klagenfurt, 1998), 38-42.
Hubertus Knabe, 'Einführung', in idem (ed.), Gefangen in Hohenschönhausen: Stasi-Häftlinge berichten (Berlin, 2007), 7-20.
Lance Knobel, Office Furniture: Twentieth-Century Design (New York, 1987).
Anne Kockelkorn, 'Bürolandschaft: Eine vergessene Reformstrategie der deutschen Nachkriegsmoderne', in Arch+, 186-187 (2008), 6-7.
Martin Kohlrausch, 'The Social Promise of Scientific Progress: Technical Experts and the Quest for Authority', in Eva Giloi et al. (eds.), Staging Authority: Presentation and Power in Nineteenth-Century Europe (Berlin, 2022), 91-124.
Arend Kölsch, '"Ich bin du". Bürogebäude und Transparenz', in Annette Gigon, Mike Guyer and Arend Kölsch (eds.), Bürogebäude (Zürich, 2019), 52-61.
Rem Koolhaas, 'Typical Plan', in Jeannette Kuo (ed.), A-Typical Plan: Projects and Essays on Identity, Flexibility, and Atmosphere in the Office Building (Zurich, 2013), 128-143.
Siegfried Kracauer, The Salaried Masses: Duty and Distraction in Weimar Germany (London, 1998).
Stefan Krebs and Heike Weber (eds.), The Persistence of Technology: Histories of Repair, Reuse and Disposal (Bielefeld, 2021).
Robert van Krieken, 'The Organisation of the Soul: Elias and Foucault on Discipline and the Self', in European Journal of Sociology, 31/2 (1990), 353-371.
Dirk van Laak, 'Infrastrukturen und Macht', in François Duceppe-Lamarre and Jens Ivo Engels (eds.), Umwelt und Herrschaft in der Geschichte (Munich, 2008), 106-114.
Dirk van Laak, Weiße Elefanten: Anspruch und Scheitern technischer Großprojekte im 20. Jahrhundert (Stuttgart, 1999).
Herbert Lachmayer and Eleonora Louis (eds.), Work & Culture: Büro, Inszenierung von Arbeit (Klagenfurt, 1998).
Yves Lasfargue, 'Scénarios pour 2005: Mutations technologiques dans le tertiaire et le secondaire', in Alain Guiheux (ed.), Lieux? de travail (Paris, 1986), 49-55.
David Leatherbarrow, 'What Goes Unnoticed: On the Canonical Quality of the PSFS Building', in William S. Saunders (ed.), Judging Architectural Value (Minneapolis, 2007), 24-37.
Sheila Liming, Office (New York, 2020).
Jonathan Lipman, 'Consecrated Space: The Public Buildings of Frank Lloyd Wright', in Robert McCarter (ed.), Frank Lloyd Wright: A Primer on Architectural Principles (New York, 1991), 193-217.
Graham S. Lowe, 'Women, Work and the Office: The Feminization of Clerical Occupations in Canada, 1901-1931', in Canadian Journal of Sociology, 5/4 (1980), 361-381.

Jens van de Maele, 'From Bentham to Guadet', in International Journal for History, Culture and Modernity, 7/1 (2019), 673-685.

Jens van de Maele, 'Gläserne Zwischenwände für effektive Kontrollen: Das belgische Regierungsbüro in der Zwischenkriegszeit, in Gianenrico Bernasconi and Stefan Nellen (eds.), Das Büro: Zur Rationalisierung des Interieurs (Bielefeld, 2019), 89-108.

Jens van de Maele, 'The Twentieth-Century Ministerial Office Building as a Laboratory of Government', in Moderne Stadtgeschichte, 2 (2021), 147-166.

Jens van de Maele, Architectures of Bureaucracy: The Politics of Government Office Buildings in Interwar Belgium (Berlin, 2025).

Kathy Marchand, In retrospectief: Herbestemmen van de Scryptioncollectie (Eindhoven, 2014).

Helena Mattsson and Sven-Olov Wallenstein, 'Introduction', in idem (eds.), Swedish Modernism: Architecture, Consumption and the Welfare State (London, 2010), 6-33.

Reinhold Martin, 'One or More', in Grey Room, 7 (2002), 114-123.

Reinhold Martin, The Organizational Complex: Architecture, Media, and Corporate Space (Cambridge MA, 2003).

Arthur F. McEvoy, 'Working Environments: An Ecological Approach to Industrial Health and Safety', in Technology and Culture, 36/2 (1995), 145-173.

Alan McKinlay and Ken Starkey, 'Managing Foucault: Foucault, Management and Organization Theory', in idem (eds.), Foucault, Management and Organization Theory: From Panopticon to Technologies of Self (London, 1998), 1-13.

Alan McKinlay and James Wilson, '"All they lose is the scream": Foucault, Ford and Mass Production', in Management & Organizational History, 7/1 (2012), 45-60.

Alan McKinlay and Robbie Guerriero Wilson, '"Small acts of cunning": Bureaucracy, Inspection and Career, c. 1890-1914', in Critical Perspectives on Accounting, 17 (2006), 657-678.

Juriaan van Meel, The European Office: Office Design and National Context (Rotterdam, 2000).

Juriaan van Meel, 'The Origins of New Ways of Working: Office Concepts in the 1970s', in Facilities, 29/9-10 (2011), 357-367.

Grace Meloy, 'Circulation, Access, and Tourist Experience: Berlin's Center and Periphery as Case Study', BA thesis (University of Pittsburgh), 2014.

Raphaël Ménard, 'Don Draper, the Car and the Climate', in Alexandre Labasse (ed.), Work in Process: New Offices, New Practices (Paris, 2012), 235-264.

Marshall W. Meyer, William Stevenson and Stephen Webster, Limits to Bureaucratic Growth (Berlin, 1985).

Moritz Michels and Martin Wieser, 'From Hohenschönhausen to Guantanamo Bay: Psychology's Role in the Secret Services of the GDR and the United States', in Journal of the History of the Behavioral Sciences, 54 (2018), 43-61.

Stephen Mihm, 'Clerks, Classes and Conflicts: A Response to Michael Zakim's "The Business Clerk as Social Revolutionary"', in Journal of the Early Republic, 26 (2006), 605-615.

Stephen Mullin, 'Some Notes on an Activity', in Francis Duffy, Colin Cave and John Worthington (eds.), Planning Office Space (London, 1976), 16-21.

Louise A. Mozingo, Pastoral Capitalism: A History of Suburban Corporate Landscapes (Cambridge MA, 2011).

Michelle Murphy, Sick Building Syndrome and the Problem of Uncertainty: Environmental Politics, Technoscience and Women Workers (Durham, 2006).

Jeremy Myerson and Philip Ross, Unworking: The Reinvention of the Modern Office (London, 2022).

Soline Nivet, 'Office Story: A Century of Architecture', in Alexandre Labasse (ed.), Work in Process: New Offices, New Practices (Paris, 2012), 15-50.

Gérard Noiriel, 'Défendre l'usine secrète', in Travail: Bulletin de l'Association d'enquête et de recherche sur l'organisation du travail, 4 (1984), 18-24.

Helga Nowotny, 'The Quest for Innovation and Cultures of Technology', in idem (ed.), Cultures of Technology and the Quest for Innovation (New York, 2006), 1-26.

Andreia Alves de Oliveira, 'The Politics of the Office: Space, Power and Photography', PhD thesis (University of Westminster), 2014.

Nelly Oudshoorn, 'Placing Users and Nonusers at the Heart of Technology', in Todd L. Pittinsky (ed.), Science, Technology, and Society: New Perspectives and Directions (Cambridge, 2019), 163-175.

Rainer Paris, 'Warten auf Amtsfluren', in Kölner Zeitschrift für Soziologie und Sozialpsychologie, 53/4 (2001), 705-733.

André Patrão, 'Foucault's Relation with Architecture: The Interest of his Disinterest', in Architecture and Culture, 10/2 (2022), 207-225.

Élisabeth Pélegrin-Genel, L'angoisse de la plante verte sur le coin du bureau (Paris, 1994).

Élisabeth Pélegrin-Genel, The Office (Paris, 1996).

Élisabeth Pélegrin-Genel, Comment (se) sauver (de) l'open-space? Décrypter nos espaces de travail (Marseille, 2016).

Stephan Petermann, 'Centraal Beheer', in Ruth Baumeister, Stephan Petermann and Marieke van den Heuvel, Back to the Office: 50 Revolutionary Office Buildings and How They Sustained (Rotterdam, 2022), 388-399.

Nikolaus Pevsner, A History of Building Types (Princeton, 1997).

Jim Phillips, 'Deindustrialization and the Moral Economy of the Scottish Coalfields, 1947 to 1991', in International Labor and Working-Class History, 84 (2013), 99-115.

John F. Pile, Open Office Planning: A Handbook for Interior Designers and Architects (New York, 1978).

Winifred R. Poster, Marion Crain and Miriam A. Cherry, 'Introduction: Conceptualizing Invisible Labor', in idem (eds.), Invisible Labor: Hidden Work in the Contemporary World (Oakland, 2016), 3-27.

Jack Quinan, Frank Lloyd Wright's Larkin Building: Myth and Fact (Cambridge MA, 1989).

Bruno Rizzi, The Bureaucratization of the World (New York, 1985).

Craig Robertson, The Filing Cabinet: A Vertical History of Information (Minneapolis, 2021).

Nicole Robertson, 'Women at Work: Activism, Feminism and the Rise of the Female Office Worker during the First World War and its Immediate Aftermath', in Keith Laybourn and John Shepherd (eds.), Labour and Working-Class Lives: Essays to Celebrate the Life and Work of Chris Wrigley (Manchester, 2017), 172-193.

Frederick Rosen, Jeremy Bentham and Representative Democracy: A Study of the Constitutional Code (Oxford, 1983).

Arthur Rüegg, 'Mönchszelle oder Bürolandschaft? Der Faktor Mensch in der Bürogestaltung', in Annette Gigon, Mike Guyer and Arend Kölsch (eds.), Bürogebäude (Zürich, 2019), 36-43.

Andreas Rumpfhuber, Architektur immaterieller Arbeit (Vienna, 2013).

Andreas Rumpfhuber, 'The Incorporation of Dissent: Bürolandschaft's Legacy', in Harvard Design Magazine, 46 (2018), 4-12.

Andreas Rumpfhuber, 'In Praise of Cybernetics: Office Landscaping and the (Self-)Conditioning of Workers', in Footprint, 25 (2019), 85-100.

James S. Russell, 'Form Follows Fad: The Troubled Love Affair of Architectural Style and Management Ideal', in Donald Albrecht and Chrysanthe B. Broikos (eds.), On the Job: Design and the American Office (New York, 2000), 48-73.

David L. Salomon, 'Divided Responsibilities: Minoru Yamasaki, Architectural Authorship, and the World Trade Center', in Grey Room, 7 (2002), 86-95.

Philipp Sarasin, 'Die Rationalisierung des Körpers: Über "Scientific Management" und "biologische Rationalisierung"', in Michael Jeismann (ed.), Obsessionen: Beherrschende Gedanken im wissenschaftlichen Zeitalter (Frankfurt/M., 1995), 78-115.

Philipp Sarasin, Geschichtswissenschaft und Diskursanalyse (Frankfurt/M., 2003).

Nikil Saval, Cubed: A Secret History of the Workplace (New York, 2014).

Laura D. Scherer et al., 'The Psychology of "Regrettable Substitutions": Examining Consumer Judgements of Bisphenol A and its Alternatives', in Health, Risk & Society, 16/7-8 (2014), 649-666.

Merrill Schleier, Skyscraper Cinema: Architecture and Gender in American Film (Minneapolis, 2009).

Thomas J. Schlereth, Cultural History and Material Culture: Everyday Life, Landscapes, Museums (Charlottesville, 1992), 145.

Christine Schnaithmann, 'Das Schreibtischproblem: Amerikanische Büroorganisation um 1920', in Lars Bluma and Karsten Uhl (eds.), Kontrollierte Arbeit – disziplinierte Körper? Zur Sozial- und Kulturgeschichte der Industriearbeit im 19. und 20. Jahrhundert (Bielefeld, 2012), 323-357.

Christine Schnaithmann, 'Maschine, Kirche, Organismus: Frank Lloyd Wrights Larkin Administration Building', in Gianenrico Bernasconi and Stefan Nellen (eds.), Das Büro: Zur Rationalisierung des Interieurs (Bielefeld, 2019), 69-88.

John Schofield, 'Office Cultures and Corporate Memory: Some Archaeological Perspectives', in Archaeologies, 5/2 (2009), 293-305.

Katherine Schonfield, Walls Have Feelings: Architecture, Film and the City (London, 2000).

Dirk Schubert, 'Opposition, Participation and Community-Driven Planning Theories', in Carola Hein (ed.), The Routledge Handbook of Planning History (New York, 2018), 402-416.

Hannes Schwenger, 'Nachwort', in idem (ed.), Menschen im Büro: Von Kafka zu Martin Walser, Vierzig Geschichten (Munich, 1984), 266-268.

Petra Seitz, 'Where Do You Cry in an Open Plan Office? A Historiography of Interior Office Design', unpublished paper (2019) (via www.academia.edu).

Wolfgang Seibel, Verwaltung Verstehen: Eine theoriegeschichtliche Einführung (Berlin, 2017).

Erik Sigge, 'Bureaucratic Reforms as Triggers of Experimental Design: KBS and Public Building in Sweden, 1963-74', in Architectural History, 65 (2022), 123-142.

Dennis Smith, 'The Civilizing Process and The History of Sexuality: Comparing Norbert Elias and Michel Foucault', in Theory and Society, 28/1 (1999), 79-100.

Daphne Spain, Gendered Spaces (Chapel Hill, 1992).

Penny Sparke, The Modern Interior (London, 2008).

Sven Spieker, The Big Archive: Art from Bureaucracy (Cambridge MA, 2008).

Julia Spohr, In Haft bei der Staatssicherheit: Das Untersuchungsgefängnis Berlin-Hohenschönhausen, 1951-1989 (Göttingen, 2015).

Susan Leigh Star, 'The Ethnography of Infrastructure', in American Behavioral Scientist 43/3 (1999), 377-391.

Susan Leigh Star and Anselm Stauss, 'Layers of Silence, Arenas of Voice: The Ecology of Visible and Invisible Work', in Computer Supported Cooperative Work, 8 (1999), 9-30.

Jens Steffek, International Organization as Technocratic Utopia (Oxford, 2021).

Sven Sterken and Dennis Pohl, 'The Architecture of Global Governance: Paths of Approach', in Architectural Theory Review, 27/1 (2023), 1-18.

Howard R. Stanger, 'From Factory to Family: The Creation of a Corporate Culture in the Larkin Company of Buffalo, New York', in The Business History Review, 74/3 (2000), 407-433.

Ceri Sullivan, Literature in the Public Service: Sublime Bureaucracy (Houndmills, 2013).

Scott Taylor and André Spicer, 'Time for Space: A Narrative Review of Research on Organizational Spaces', in International Journal of Management Reviews, 9/4 (2007), 325-346.

Amy Thomas, 'Prejudice and Pragmatism', in Grey Room, 71 (2018), 88-115.

Amy Thomas, 'The Political Economy of Flexibility: Deregulation and the Transformation of Corporate Space in the Postwar City of London', in Kenny Cupers, Helena Mattsson and Catharina Gabrielsson (eds.), Neoliberalism on the Ground: Architecture and Transformations from 1960 to the Present (Pittsburgh, 2020), 127-150.

Graham Thompson, Male Sexuality under Surveillance: The Office in American Literature (Iowa City, 2003).

Olga Touloumi, Assembly by Design: The United Nations and its Global Interior (Minneapolis, 2024).

Lars Tunbjörk, Office (Stockholm, 2002).

Guillaume Tusseau, 'From the Penitentiary to the Political Panoptic Paradigm', in Anne Brunon-Ernst (ed.), Beyond Foucault: New Perspectives on Bentham's Panopticon (Farnham, 2012), 115-140.

Joris Vandendriessche, Evert Peeters and Kaat Wils (eds.), Scientists' Expertise as Performance (Abingdon, 2015).

Jonathan Voges, 'Review of Das Büro [...]', in Zeitschrift für Unternehmensgeschichte, 66/1 (2021), 154-156.

Sieger Vreeling, Geen stijl: Een rijkere architectuurgeschiedenis (Hilversum, 2022).

Judy Wajcman, '"Fitter, happier, more productive": Optimising Time with Technology', in Vera King, Benigna Gerisch and Hartmut Rosa (eds.), Lost in Perfection: Impacts of Optimisation on Culture and Psyche (London, 2019), 51-60.

Varda Wasserman, 'The Gendered Aesthetics of the Physical Environment of Work', in Oluremi B. Ayoko and Neal M. Ashkanasy (eds.), Organizational Behaviour and the Physical Environment (London, 2019), 185-199.

Gernot Weckherlin, BEL: Zur Systematik des architektonischen Wissens am Beispiel von Ernst Neuferts Bauentwurfslehre (Tübingen, 2017).

Alexander Welsh, 'Review of Imagining the Penitentiary [...]', in Eighteenth-Century Studies, 21/3 (1988), 373-378.

Robbie Guerriero Wilson, Disillusionment or New Opportunities? The Changing Nature of Work in Offices, Glasgow 1880-1914 (Aldershot, 1998).

Wim de Wit (ed.), Design for the Corporate World, 1950-1975 (London, 2017).

Onno de Wit et al., 'Innovation Junctions: Office Technologies in the Netherlands', in Technology and Culture, 43/1 (2002), 50-72.

Regina Wonisch, 'Museum und Migration: Einleitung', in Regina Wonisch and Thomas Hübel (eds.), Museum und Migration: Konzepte, Kontexte, Kontroversen (Bielefeld, 2012), 9-32.

John C. Wood and Michael C. Wood, 'Introduction', in idem (eds.), Henri Fayol: Critical Evaluations in Business and Management (Vol. 1) (London, 2002), 1-10.

Grace Ong Yan, Building Brands: Corporations and Modern Architecture (London, 2020).

Sierk Ybema et al., 'Studying Everyday Organizational Life', in idem (eds.), Organizational Ethnography: Studying the Complexities of Everyday Life (Los Angeles, 2009), 1-20.

Mark Zachry, 'An Interview with Susan Leigh Star', in Technical Communication Quarterly, 17/4 (2008), 435-454.

Shoshana Zuboff, In the Age of the Smart Machine: The Future of Work and Power (New York, 1988).

PART 1
CATEGORIES AND REPRESENTATIONS OF OFFICE USERS

Chapter 1
What's the Use? The Users and Usability of the Filing Cabinet

Craig Robertson

INTRODUCTION

The filing cabinet, an American invention, rapidly transformed the storage and circulation of paper and information in offices in the early 20th century (Fig. 1.1.). It was one of a number of new office technologies that signalled the emergence of the modern office as a site of efficiency. I examined its history in a recently published monograph.[1] The purpose of that history was to use textual and visual sources to reconstruct how the filing cabinet was understood in the context of the modern office: what made the filing cabinet possible and what did the filing cabinet make possible? In one sense, it is my take on Taylorism-influenced ideologies of efficiency; my intervention is to argue that those ideologies contributed to a reconceptualisation of information. In another sense, it is a history informed by the focus on materiality and infrastructure in my academic home of media studies. However, neither of these frameworks pushed me to prioritise the experience of users. When I did discuss use, the combination of my theoretical framework and the limitations of my sources made it an analysis of the "ideal file clerk" created in the prescriptive literature. This chapter provides the opportunity to re-read my sources and to think more critically about what they say about the users of the filing cabinet.

By shifting my focus from the object in use to those engaging with it, I aim to explore what their perspectives reveal about the value of *user* as an analytic category, rather than concentrating on the filing cabinet as a material object. My title, which I borrow from Sara Ahmed's book on use, is intended to capture this change in focus and to highlight the question of how something is used.[2] However, I also intend it to convey an element of its more common meaning – the uselessness of something. As a title, it signals

Fig. 1.1. A common four-drawer filing cabinet featured in a promotional brochure by Globe-Wernicke, with drawers sized to hold letters and similarly sized documents. (Steel Filing Cabinets, 1931. Trade Catalogue Collection, Hagley Museum and Library, Wilmington, Delaware.)

that a historical examination of users, while valuable, requires some important caveats. The experiences of many users do not make it into archives; this is especially true of women office workers in the early 20th century, whose rare archival appearances tend to be as data points in surveys of workers rather than in their own words. When users' words are found in archives, it necessitates caution, not celebration. The so-called "actual" users that researchers find in archives are always mediated; their subjective experiences are expressed and recorded within complex ideological formations.

To reflect on the use and usability of the filing cabinet, this chapter is divided into two sections. In the first section, I briefly discuss the emergence of the filing cabinet in the United States in the early decades of the 20th century to explain how it was represented as a useful technology. It was celebrated as an original invention, but despite (or because of) its novelty, the filing cabinet was quickly seen to have value. It became useful because specific people in specific situations found it useful. It had value because of the way it stored paper, and because, in the name of efficiency, it made storage a problem of retrieval. In the second section, I focus on the people who used it. However, because of the very limited subjective descriptions of actual user experiences in historical sources, my analysis centres on the relationship between the categories of use and the types of users constructed in sources that document historically specific relations of power. That is, I highlight different moments of use (selling, indexing, instructing, learning and filing), with each moment having a different user with a different relationship to the act of use.

THE USABILITY OF THE FILING CABINET

The filing cabinet was invented in the United States in the 1890s. The most popular origin story attributes it to the Library Bureau, a company founded by the racist and misogynist Melville (or Melvil) Dewey of the Dewey Decimal System. In 1893, the secretary of a charity organisation asked the company to design something similar to their new library card catalogues, but larger, to store sheets of paper. However, it was not until the turn of the century that the Library Bureau (along with other office furniture companies) started to market filing cabinets. In less than a decade, they were on their way to becoming pervasive in American offices of all sizes.[3] The filing cabinet was an innovative storage technology because it allowed loose paper to be stored on its edge. Loose paper cannot stand on its edge on its own; it needs support. A filing cabinet provided that support through follower blocks, folders and specially designed drawers. Critically, it allowed paper to stand on its edge but retain its looseness as an individual sheet – unlike a book, which stored paper as pages, binding them into a fixed place.

Storing paper on its long edge had two important advantages. It is easier to retrieve a piece of paper standing on its edge in a filing cabinet than from within a pile of papers (storing paper on its edge was called vertical filing in contrast to flat, horizontal piles). Second, it can be easier to find a particular sheet of paper. Loose paper can be grouped together in a folder with other relevant pieces of paper regardless of when they were created. In a vertical filing cabinet, subject trumped chronology. As this suggests, the innovation of storing loose paper on its long edge moved from gimmick to useful because paper was the preferred medium to record and store information at the turn of the 20th century. The filing cabinet helped make pervasive the idea that information was discrete and instrumental, a thing that had presence in the world.[4] The filing cabinet did not invent this conception of information, but it provided a way to make sense of it, including a set of tools still used today as concepts that shape how information is encountered: file, folder, tab. A quote from a 1912 issue of a magazine called *Machinery* gives a sense of what was new about information and what made it distinct from knowledge: "Not only does scientific management depend upon information, but this information is carefully and systematically collected; once obtained, [it] is classified and digested until it is instantly available whenever a problem is presented to the management."[5] The filing cabinet turned knowledge into something instrumental and more useful: information.

Information emerged from knowledge through increased specificity: it was carefully and systematically collected, then classified and finally rendered instantly available. Its particularity granted it a facticity. Inside a filing cabinet, a file drawer showcased this understanding of information. It identified loose sheets of paper via a system of folders, guide cards and tabs to make classifications highly visible; a piece of paper or a manila folder of sheets could be extracted so the user had all the available information on a particular customer or product. The attraction of the filing cabinet to the 20th-century business imagination lay in how quickly it allowed hands to get to that information. In an environment besotted with the idea of efficiency, classification was defined as a temporal problem as well as a spatial problem; storage became a matter of retrieval. Advertisements claimed that a filing cabinet allowed a user to find papers "at a moment's notice" or "almost instantaneously".[6]

In the spirit of the times, these assertions were quickly quantified. According to a solicited letter from a satisfied customer, "almost instantaneously" translated to twenty seconds to find one letter and ninety seconds to file five folders.[7] In the 1930s, an advertising agency president noted that "information does not rot in our files, it is continuously shuttling back and forth between file and everyday business use". Claiming that "within a few minutes" a clerk could retrieve sales presentations from thirty different companies in thirty different fields, he concluded that "thus our file lives".[8] In focusing on retrieval, filing cabinets challenged the concept of storage. The "living" documents contrasted with older forms of paper storage that hid papers in drawers or pigeon-holes or left them lying flat in piles, leaving their contents "dead". "Shuttling back and forth between file and everyday business use" signals how the vertical filing cabinet facilitated the flow of information; during the interwar period, the notion of "workflow" indeed began to influence the design and organisation of offices.[9] This emphasis on workflow highlighted the continuous movement of documents and personnel, with the aim of enhancing productivity through greater efficiency. As one office manager remarked, "every time a piece of paper stops, a dollar is resting".[10] Within this framework, the filing cabinet became indispensable, as the rapid retrieval of paper was understood within the collective flow of people, paper and work (Fig. 1.2.).

The primary function of the modern office thus became the organisation of objects, people and tasks. As with other office technologies developed in the early 20th century, the filing cabinet was designed with a heightened sensitivity to the bodies and motions of the assumed

Fig. 1.2. A file drawer in a promotional brochure by Shaw-Walker showcases a complex system of folders and tabs designed to enable the filing and retrieval of information. (How to File Letters and Cards, 1920. Trade Catalogue Collection, Hagley Museum and Library, Wilmington, Delaware.)

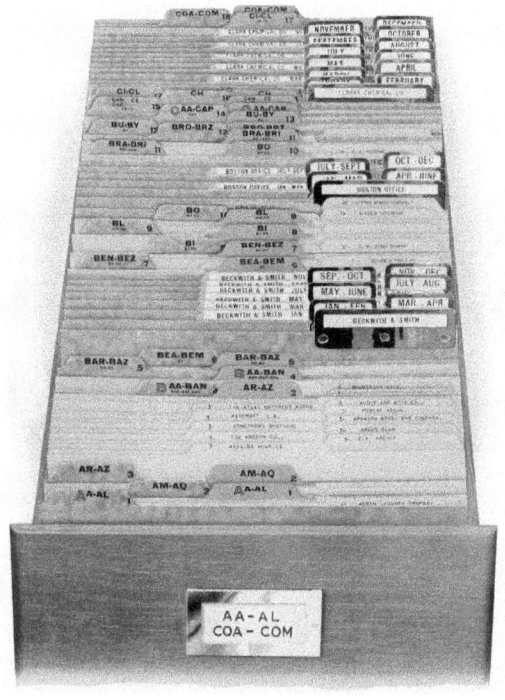

user. According to a trade catalogue, a regular filing cabinet was four drawers high because that is "about as high as an ordinary girl can work to advantage". Similarly, a drawer was only 27 inches (68.5 cm) long because it could be pulled "by the file clerk as an arm operation". Any longer and filing would become a "walking operation" as the user would have to move to the side of the drawer to reach files at the rear.[11] A filing cabinet was initially designed with a woman's body in mind because dominant ideas of gender suggested that women had naturally nimble fingers and an affinity for repetitive work, which meant they were ideally suited to once again be employed to assist men. Images used to promote office equipment presented filing as manual labour distinct from thought or so-called mental work.[12] Occasionally, images of drawers also included hands. When close-ups of drawers were necessary to show the guides and tabs, it was not possible to show the body attached to the hands. The result was an image of gendered but disembodied hands that not only pointed out how filing equipment functioned, but also represented the ideal relationship of labour and technology that underpinned efficiency in an office. A disembodied hand highlighted a filing cabinet as a machine to be operated on – not a machine to think with. Therefore, the visual use of disembodied hands established filing as manual labour. It emphasised this by *not* showing a connection to the body and mind. In filing, the processes of choice and deliberation (thinking) were transferred to the predetermined pathways of tabs; as one advertisement put it, tabs were "the intellect of the filing machine".[13] Or put another way, the filing cabinet housed an "automatic memory".[14] Therefore, the ideal users of the filing cabinet did work that required neither thought nor interpretation and did not directly produce knowledge – they used their hands, not their minds. This fitted within the redefinition of office work as machine work centred on the recording and circulation of information on paper; a redefinition that, by articulating deskilling and feminisation, opened the way for women to work in offices.

THE USERS OF THE FILING CABINET

According to the Oxford English Dictionary, "to use" is to take hold of or deploy something as a means of accomplishing or achieving a goal. A user is most commonly a person who uses or operates something, and it is this relationship that distinguishes the categories "user" and "worker". To identify users is to create a distinct group of people who use or interact with a technology. For example, Ahmed argues that usefulness must reside within the user.[15] The status of different filing cabinet users highlights how specific skills and tasks constituted them as users. Often, in defining one group of users, sources defined other groups in a hierarchical relationship based around the intersection of gender and class. In this section I explore what these differing statuses suggest about user, use and usefulness as both social categories and categories of analysis. Technologies emerge from and are used in specific historical contexts shaped by dynamics of power; in this instance the driving force was dominant economic ideas, particularly a gendered conception of efficiency. Linking filing cabinet users with gender and efficiency illustrates that, from a social perspective, different users have different degrees of agency, and this in turn offers a more nuanced understanding of use as a category of analysis. I examine the available historical sources to argue for a more expansive understanding of users inspired by Andreas Fickers and Annie van den Oever.[16] As their work shows, this allows us to better understand the social and cultural role of technologies. While their approach and taxonomy of media users has shaped my analysis, the categories of users I discuss below are not offered as "ideal types", as their project required. Rather, they are categories that allow me to explore the users of one technology (the filing cabinet) in such a way as to consider the social and cultural role of users and use. Different users found the filing cabinet useful in different ways:

Fig. 1.3. *The LB File*, the Library Bureau's monthly company magazine, primarily featured reports of successful sales. (Courtesy of the Herkimer County Historical Society, New York.)

it allowed them to practise or create expertise, to be a professional, to be paid. They also had different relationships to the act of use: they were expert users, valuable users, enthusiastic users, clerical users or distracted users.

In promoting their products, office equipment manufacturers claimed the position of *expert users* for themselves, manifested in certain employees. The Library Bureau, the company identified with inventing the filing cabinet, provides a good example of this. Founded in 1873, it became a mid-level library and office equipment manufacturer by the 1920s. In 1926, Remington Rand bought it as they sought to dominate the American market and make inroads into the European one. Like similar companies, the Library Bureau had multiple publications, including yearly catalogues, brochures and pamphlets for specific products. Appearing in the 1910s and 1920s, *The LB File* was a twenty-page monthly in-house magazine (Fig. 1.3.). It highlighted the work of salesmen who uncritically embraced dominant ideas about the filing cabinet as a machine with an automatic memory that could be easily operated without thought. Much of the magazine detailed successful "installations": sales that involved the purchase of multiple types of filing technologies. These brief articles used the authority of the company to position its salesmen as expert users.

A Library Bureau salesman was an expert user based on his knowledge of the product. He – and the company he represented – defined usefulness according to dominant managerial values and discourses, suggesting that it resided in the expert's knowledge rather than in the users' experience. The salesman sold the filing cabinet by showing how it could make a business more efficient. This involved selling a range of company products to create a system for filing. According to *The LB File*, an installation could involve one or more of the following: filing cabinets for different types of paper (e.g. correspondence and invoices), standardised forms and folders, an index system (alphabetical, numerical, etc.), and a system for getting rid of old records. Efficiency provided the framework for assessing which of these needed to be included in an installation. The American LaFrance Fire Engine Company had a typical Library Bureau central file installation. While it had previously used eight separate departmental files, the installation replaced these with a central file department; selling centralisation as efficiency involved the company buying thirty new filing cabinets. Twenty were for correspondence, with the bottom two drawers of each cabinet kept empty to accommodate expansion (more frequently, a four-drawer cabinet was split using the "two-period plan", with the top two drawers for current files and the bottom two drawers for files from the previous year). The ten cabinets assigned to store invoice folders replaced a system of loose-leaf binders that had been stacked on shelves in a vault. The complete order included smaller units for documents, a cabinet for cheques, a cupboard, tabulating units, two 125-division Automatic Indexes for correspondence (one for transferred material), several 25-division and 60-division Direct Alphabetic indexes for smaller papers, reinforced folders, pressboard expansion fastener folders, sorter trays and guides, letter trays as well as other unlisted supplies.[17] *The LB File* also recorded installations carried out by the company's Indexing Service. Created in 1915, its goal was to prevent usage failure and therefore the loss of current customers (and through bad reputation, future customers). The Indexing Service sought to avert failure through the work of trained women who were presented as another kind of expert user. In 1922, seven years after the Indexing Service was established, it employed forty permanent "indexers". That year, with 700 clients seeking assistance, the Library Bureau hired thirty on-call indexers as the division generated $3.23 million of business in today's U.S. dollars.[18]

Indexers determined the best system and the necessary equipment and supplies to realise it. They also typed up labels and transferred existing files into drawers and folders. This work could take considerable time. An installation at the Department of Public Welfare in Harrisburg, Pennsylvania required the work of three women: Mrs. Smith spent three months on the general file, Miss Kinney spent five months on the business library and Miss Young spent one month on transfer files. The success of that installation saw the neighbouring Department of Public Instruction hire the Indexing Service. A two-week analysis of the existing system in its Bureau of Instruction led to a report which resulted in an order for four operators to combine eleven separate files into a 500-division Automatic Index, a job that was expected to take eighteen weeks. A second report for all the bureaus in the department produced an order for a central file and a business library.[19] Indexers also did smaller jobs, such as dividing existing files following an inspection. As a result of a Library Bureau report, the Los Angeles office of Aetna Life Insurance hired two indexers to "separate vital information into folders filed by policy number from non-essential correspondence". The latter was to be filed in an eighty-division Automatic Index along with general office correspondence.[20] The description of their work identifies the indexers as a specific type of expert user, shaped by the gendered nature of their tasks which simultaneously granted and denied them expertise. Female indexers focused on organisation within filing cabinets, and were distinguished from male salesmen, who were seen as having a broader grasp of office technologies, including their mechanics.

The women's role emphasised an overlooked aspect of filing: the intellectual labour involved in creating and implementing classification systems that enabled clerks to efficiently file and retrieve documents. As expert users, these women created the "automatic memory" that advertising attributed to the filing cabinet. While the Library Bureau promoted their expertise, the greater promotion it gave to the filing cabinet as a machine made their work invisible. As the disembodied hand devalued the usefulness of file clerks, automatic memory performed a similar function for indexers. Most indexers experienced this double erasure as they were former file clerks. While their experience produced anecdotal evidence based on personal instances rather than aggregated data from technical test reports, indexers did ground their expertise in claims of empirical and scientific assessment. The indexers' work reflected the broader professionalisation of librarianship, particularly in business libraries, and, within the world of the Indexing Service and its customers, challenged prevailing office management literature that downplayed the need for specialised training in filing.

Training in filing was available to some women. However, rather than conferring expertise, this training was intended to create use value. It made young women useful by instructing them how to quickly file and retrieve papers; the emphasis was on physical dexterity more than mental dexterity. From the perspective of office managers, these women were *valuable users*: education techniques directed them towards useful ends.[21] Filing was a potential subject within the commercial education curriculum that emerged as part of a shift to vocational education in the early 20th century. The Library Bureau was one of the few office equipment companies to supply materials for instructing filing in high schools. By the 1920s, it had sold its training tools to more than 250 schools, integrating filing instruction into the two- and four-year commercial courses offered by many institutions; the company's Educational Division also ran a handful of filing schools and a distance learning programme. Students practised filing at their desks using small boxes designed as miniature file drawers. These boxes held four-by-six-inch sheets of paper, scaled-down versions of real business documents, including incoming and outgoing letters and carbon copies – complete with typos and errors that occasionally frustrated teachers. Each set included seventy-five sample letters, forty-two guide cards matching the standard layout of a full-size filing drawer, alphabetical index sections, state and town guides, and various blank and cross-reference cards. These materials simulated real filing tasks, allowing students to engage with the mechanics and logic of classification.[22] In longer courses, students used the same set of correspondence to practise different types of alphabetical systems, a geographical system or, very occasionally, a subject system. Library Bureau salesmen pitched the idea that "by treating this correspondence from various angles, the student develops a sense of classification and is made to realize the importance of accuracy".[23] According to this argument, by prioritising rationality and procedure, classification was the gateway to understanding "system", which was central to the organisation of work and production. In this way the successful graduates of these courses became valuable users: through their education they made themselves useful – in this instance being beneficial or profitable. Their training did not remove them from the parameters of the ideal worker found in office management literature. The value of the valuable user was their efficiency: they used filing cabinets to file and retrieve papers in a timely manner (Fig. 1.4.).

A sub-group of valuable users tried to make filing a profession, based around the idea of a "file executive". I label them *enthusiastic users*. They constituted a minority of the people who used filing cabinets in offices, but they are the only group who left an archival trace in their own words, albeit heavily mediated by ideas of efficiency, gender and professionalisation. Enthusiastic users cannot be identified as professional users because their professionalisation campaign failed. This campaign appears in two

Fig. 1.4. A 1923 promotional photo showing students at Lowell High School (Massachusetts) practicing filing with equipment produced by the Library Bureau. The company introduced miniature filing equipment to allow high school students to practise filing at their own desks instead of waiting in line to use full-size cabinets. (Author's collection.)

sources: *Filing*, a magazine which began publication in 1918 and appeared ten times a year for four years until it abruptly stopped publication in 1922, and *The File*, a ten-page monthly bulletin published by the New York Filing Association after the demise of *Filing*. The two male editors of *Filing* presented the magazine as a broker for information on filing and a precursor to the formation of a national filing association, which would lay the groundwork to professionalise filing. Neither happened, but from 1920, *Filing* included a column that reported the activities of filing associations that had formed in several large cities. Although membership in most associations struggled to reach a hundred, the associations continued to exist until at least the 1940s. Filing associations typically held monthly meetings that featured one or two invited speakers. Most of the speakers were women who discussed filing practices at their places of work. Common problems provided additional topics for discussion: in 1921, the Chicago association reported a "lively discussion" on transfer files, with the participation of twenty of the sixty people in attendance. Other issues covered at association meetings related to the quality of work. "Personality" was a recurring topic across associations in the 1920s and

1930s. A favourite speaker at the New York Filing Association delivered a talk entitled "I Like My Job" in 1921, and in a speech the following year, she stated that "personality, brain power and interest are assets to success, when combined with observation". By the 1930s, most associations were beginning to broaden the topics addressed at meetings to include such things as fashion and home decorating advice.[24]

The shift in focus away from office work acknowledged that filing was not going to be a profession. In other words, it is an example of how expert discourse constrains users.[25] The campaign to professionalise filing was a discursive struggle for a group's identity. The association members failed to displace the dominant idea that filing involved nothing more than putting papers away and retrieving them on demand. They failed to convince people that their usefulness was located in their minds rather than their hands. The idea of filing as unskilled manual labour had quickly created a homogeneous *clerical user* who could do their work guided by a machine. However, the call to recognise filing as a profession came from the world of the office, in which filing cabinet users were not a homogeneous group. While gender provided some homogeneity, class intersecting with race and ethnicity created diversity among users. White middle-class women populated filing cabinet associations, and their campaign was in part an expression of the collapsing of identity into work that made professions the basis of a still-developing middle-class identity. The professionalisation movement also challenged the gendered expertise of office management literature. Many of the key figures in file associations wrote books on filing, which established them as expert users in their own world, while the office management books written by men with a broader brief spoke to a wider world of male readers.

In contrast to enthusiastic users, the largest group of filing cabinet users was indeed clerical users. These were users defined in relationship to their employment rather than their expertise or attitude. Their usefulness was in their hands: they epitomised the user represented in office management literature as requiring no skills other than the basic literacy needed to file and retrieve letters. Clerical users were useful to employers because they assisted men in offices and, as women, they could be paid less than men in junior positions. They are found in a range of sources, although not in their own words. Census data and surveys performed by religious groups and the Department of Labour's Women's Bureau in the 1920s and 1930s identified the typical female office worker as a woman in her mid-twenties; half of them had begun office work before they turned seventeen. Regardless of job title, clerks were expected to have some high school education, but there was no expectation that they would have completed high school. They tended to be lower-class young women, many the children of immigrants with aspirations to be part of the middle-class. On average, they earned $25 ($450 today) per week, but file clerks earned considerably less than that.[26] One survey referred to the position of file clerk as a "beginning job".[27] Only 5 percent of clerical workers were designated as specialised file clerks; the two largest categories of female office workers, each comprising one-third of workers, were "general clerk" and "stenographer".[28] General clerks almost certainly filed, and I categorise all these workers as clerical users. Despite the focus in office management literature on large offices with specialised clerical positions, most women worked in small offices with fewer than twenty-five employees where all female clerical workers did filing work.

If to use is "to take hold of or deploy something as a means of accomplishing or achieving something", these women used clerical employment to make money for themselves and their family and possibly to gain middle-class status or a husband. The author of one of the most detailed 1920s surveys of women office workers concluded that young female workers possessed a "sublime faith in early marriage", and she recommended that they be given "vocational training for marriage".[29] Faith in marriage encouraged young women to accept the short-term nature of work, which, according to the survey author, was one reason for the lack of unionisation in clerical roles. Society promoted the idea that a woman's greatest value lay in becoming a wife, positioning the office as an ideal environment for meeting a potential husband.[30] Within this context, popular culture and advice literature aimed at working women often portrayed the clerk as a *distracted user*. An experienced female office manager captured employers' concerns about the priority young women gave to socialising in the city when she instructed file clerks to "leave fine clothes, the theatre, pleasant parties, Tom, Dick and Harry, at home". This was necessary because "important tasks cannot be accomplished with your hands while unimportant details fill your head". Put differently: "You cannot file 'Amusement' under 'Work', [since] they are at the extremes of the alphabet."[31] Thus, a clerical user would misfile if she failed to compartmentalise and keep her personal concerns and work duties in their proper place and order. Instructions to "leave fine clothes […] at home" to avoid distraction originated in the somewhat novel proximity and behaviour of men and women in the relatively public space of the office.

Clothes became a site of struggle, a sign to an employer that clerical users could lose their usefulness in the office. Debates over "transparent flimsies in blouse and hose, and the high-healed [sic] unhygienic pumps" positioned younger women against older women in offices.[32] In most offices, dress codes were little more than series of suggestions regarding styles considered appropriate and inappropriate. In the late 1930s, the Transcription Supervisors Association told high school girls interested in office work that it was acceptable to dress in ways that were "modish and becoming but not rakish or bizarre". They also informed the "girls" that "unobtrusive jewellery and straight heels on polished shoes are recommended, and fragmentary heels and toes are [...] akin [to] poor taste".[33] These choices were important for clerical users who saw the office as a site to claim middle-class identity (and possibly a husband, as previously mentioned). Other advice addressed young women exclusively as clerical users. Responding to the need for clothing that did not restrict arm movement, a Library Bureau booklet targeting potential file clerks suggested that "the loose Russian blouse or Norfolk jacket worn outside the skirt is neat and comfortable and does not expose you to the possibility of its working loose untidily, as sometimes happens with the best-behaved of shirt-waists".[34] One newspaper columnist went so far as to attribute the demise of the corset to the "loose-fitting sensible style" of "business-women whose office day usually consists in bending over a desk, playing the typewriter keys or stooping over filing cabinets".[35] Clerical users also had to navigate the expectations of the men who hired them, who saw their presence as providing another kind of usefulness in the office. The male manager of an employment service believed women were hired to "add to the general attractiveness of the office".[36]

EPILOGUE

The filing cabinet's innovation came from the way in which existing technologies were utilised to allow unbound loose paper to stand tall on its long edge. However, originality only gets an invention so far: it must have value, and it must be useful. The filing cabinet was useful because it emerged from ideas of efficiency and the division of labour: it put information at one's fingertips (a phrase that came into use in the early 20th century). Its usefulness, however, depended on users, specific groups of people with different relationships to use. Designers and manufacturers inscribed ideal use in the filing cabinet, which, along with how-to literature, configured an ideal everyday user. Actual everyday users, whether valuable users, enthusiastic users or clerical users, had no direct involvement in the design of filing cabinets, but with different degrees of agency they positioned themselves as specific types of users. Highlighting their experiences from historical sources helps us think critically about categories of use and user.

As I have implicitly argued, focusing on users does not automatically centre control or agency. However, users can voice their rejection of ideal use practices through intentional misuse, inverting the idea that design completely controls actions. The historical record provides tantalising glimpses of this from filing cabinet users. Misuse offers another way to think about the categories of use and user. Patents occasionally indicate instances of misuse and the existence of an indirect relationship between filing cabinet users and manufacturers and office designers. Inventors occasionally present their innovations as a response to unanticipated practices of use. For example, tabs began as projections cut away from the back of manila folders or cardstock glued to the back of a folder or guide card. However, problems arose because operators used tabs as handles to remove folders. In this "misuse", paper tabs absorbed moisture. The first attempts to prevent this, celluloid tabs, resulted in injury to an operator's fingers as the tabs bent, curled or cracked from continued handling. Tabs were redesigned using different methods to attach the celluloid more securely so they could be used as handles without injuring the worker or becoming unreadable.[37] In 1939, an office equipment company representative candidly told a meeting of the New York Filing Association that "for every one organization where efficient control of records exists there are hundreds sadly lacking on this score".[38] Rather than store paper inefficiently, other clerical users turned filing cabinets into surrogate wardrobes, lockers and wastepaper baskets.

Another example of misuse comes from a 1921 comic strip, which recounts an attempt by a file clerk to obtain a pay rise (Fig. 1.5.).[39] When his boss refuses the increase, the clerk empties the filing cabinet drawers in a fit of anger, scattering paper on the floor as he prepares to quit. While he is doing this, his boss changes his mind. The clerk gets his pay rise, but now he must deal with the mess of files he has created. This comic stood out to me, not only because the clerk was male, but because when the boss makes the decision to increase the file clerk's pay, he identifies the man as "Mr Google". The coincidence of the name Google being associated with access to information is uncanny to say the least. The fact that the image I found online was from an issue of *Filing* marked as "digitized by Google" made it even weirder. *Filing* had reprinted it from one of the most popular cartoon strips of the 1920s – a nationally syndicated cartoon about the "hen-pecked" Barney Google, who only ever spent that one week working in an office. In the early 1920s, even a brief stint as a file clerk would have reinforced his lowly masculine status. By this point, male clerical users had become obsolete; they had fallen out of use with the feminisation of the office.

Fig. 1.5. Reprinted in an issue of *Filing*, this 1921 cartoon about a male file clerk's ultimately successful attempt to get a pay rise features one of the most popular comic characters of the 1920s, Barney Google. (Google Books.)

Prescriptive literature presented the filing cabinet as a machine: it provided an organisation with an automatic memory and would only malfunction through misuse. This belief stemmed from the dominant view in the machine age that attributed the fault for misuse or misfiling to the file clerk's fallibility. Following this logic, the unreliable user lurked in all non-expert users. Like a version of the Hulk, when Mr. Google got angry, his unreliable user emerged to misuse a machine that, as a mild-mannered clerical user, he operated efficiently. Albeit in the excessive manner befitting a comic strip, Barney Google's bad day at the office shows misfiling to be an example of what Victoria Olwell calls "bodily malfunction", in the sense that it punctures the fiction that a filing cabinet is automatic. As a form of misuse and error, it draws attention to the fact that filing depends on users; it is not an abstract system. As Olwell argues, "the cloak of invisibility covering the body drops away [...] the moment that body makes a mistake".[40] Outside the low-level masculinity of Mr. Google, misfiling was usually associated with a very particular type of body (and mind, albeit a distracted one): that of a young woman, a body dressed to be a certain type of user. As the clerical user distracted by Tom, Dick and Harry illustrated, age and sexuality could override gender in explaining the failure of the innate dexterity and sense of order typically cited when presenting women as ideal users of the filing cabinet.

In terms of the arguments of this chapter, the "cloak of invisibility" is the naturalisation of the power relations through which technologies create use and categories of users, each with different degrees of agency. To study users is to study a distinct group of people who interact with a technology. A technology and its users emerge from specific historical contexts shaped by social dynamics of power. The plural is critical: a technology has different kinds of users, granted different degrees of status and visibility. Expert users are generally visible, their use occurring outside the daily functioning of a technology. However, that is not always the case. The Library Bureau's indexers remained largely invisible, existing only in the company's sales literature – although a version of their expertise shaped the campaign to professionalise filing. But this type of expert user was not found in the dozens of books about office management written by men in the interwar period who expounded the role of office equipment in creating efficiency in the office. As with all groups of users associated with the filing cabinet, gender and class intersected in different ways (along with age and race) to create space not only for expert users but also for valuable users, enthusiastic users and clerical users. Use is always situated in time and space; therefore, users are always situated in time and space. To study use and users in the history of the office is to shed light on the uneven distribution of use in the office.

NOTES

1. Craig Robertson, The Filing Cabinet: A Vertical History of Information (Minneapolis, 2021).
2. Sara Ahmed, What's the Use? On the Uses of Use (Durham, 2019).
3. Robertson, The Filing Cabinet, 8-9.
4. Geoffrey Nunberg, 'Farewell to the Information Age', in idem (ed.), The Future of the Book (Berkeley, 1996), 116.
5. Forrest E. Cardullo, 'Industrial Administration and Scientific Management, 1', in Machinery (July 1912), 846.
6. Cited by Robertson, The Filing Cabinet, 173.
7. Ibid.
8. John F. Arndt, 'Making a File Drawer Live', in The File (Feb. 1936), 10.
9. Robertson, The Filing Cabinet, 47.
10. Louis Carlisle Walker, The Office and Tomorrow's Business (New York, 1930), 47.
11. Built Like a Skyscraper (Muskegon, 1927), 6.
12. Robertson, The Filing Cabinet, 183, 187 and 192.
13. Cited by ibid., 173.
14. Ethel Scholfield, Filing Department Operation and Control (New York, 1923), 4.
15. Ahmed, What's the Use?, 95.
16. Andreas Fickers and Annie van den Oever, Doing Experimental Media Archaeology: Theory (Berlin, 2022), 30-38.
17. W.J. Mills, 'Old Idea, Presented in New Way: Lands Order', in The LB File (April 1924), 66-67.
18. E.A. Dunn, 'Indexing Service', in The LB File (March 1923), 15; 'Sales Meeting at Chicago: Interesting Address by Mr Canham', in The LB File (May 1921), 8.
19. 'Analysis Brings 5 Contracts', in The LB File (July-Sept. 1924), 127.
20. 'Aetna Life Files Reorganized by Service Dept', in The LB File (Oct. 1924), 132.
21. Ahmed, What's the Use?, 10.
22. Robertson, The Filing Cabinet, 211.
23. Herkimer County Historical Society (New York), Library Bureau, 'Salesmen's Help', 7.
24. 'Filing Association Reports', in The File (Nov. 1933), 3; Ethel G. Armstrong, 'New York Association', in Filing and Office Management (April 1922), 116; Catherine McNulty, 'Warren Filing Association', in Filing (Jan. 1921), 718.
25. Nelly Oudshoorn and Trevor Pinch, 'Introduction: How Users and Non-Users Matter', in idem (eds.), How Users Matter: The Co-Construction of Users and Technology (Cambridge MA, 2005), 5-6.
26. A.M. Edwards, Sixteenth Census of the United States 1940 – Population: Comparative Occupation Statistics for the United States, 1870 to 1940 (Washington D.C., 1943), 113 and 121; Ethel Erickson, The Employment of Women in Offices (Washington D.C., 1934).
27. Erickson, The Employment, 6.
28. Edwards, Sixteenth Census, 113 and 121.
29. Ruth Shonle Cavan, Business Girls: A Study of Their Interests and Problems (Chicago, 1929), 48.
30. Lisa Fine, The Souls of the Skyscraper: Female Clerical Workers in Chicago, 1870-1930 (Philadelphia, 1990), 6-75 and 140-151.
31. Elizabeth King McDowall, 'The Requisites of a Good File Clerk', in Filing (March 1921), 760.
32. Sharon Hartman Strom, Beyond the Typewriter: Gender, Class, and the Origins of Modern American Office Work, 1900-1930 (Urbana, 1992), 371.
33. Anne Petersen, 'Office Girls Get Personality Tips', in The File (Jan. 1938), 4.

[34] Filing as a Profession for Women (Cambridge MA, 1919), 45.
[35] 'Beauty Chats: The Decline of the Corset', in Charlotte News (20 Aug. 1922), 15.
[36] Frances Maule, 'Women are so Personal', in Independent Women (Sept. 1934), 280.
[37] W.B. Mehl, Catalogue Card, U.S. Patent 968,065, filed 26 Aug. 1908 and issued 23 Aug. 1910; G.H. Dawson, Index Tab, U.S. Patent 1,511,268, filed 21 Feb. 1923 and issued 14 Oct. 1924.
[38] Arthur Frey, 'Filing as a Profession', in The File (June 1939), 1.
[39] 'Barney, the File Clerk, Gets Fired: Will He Get the Raise?', in Filing and Office Management (July 1921), 42-43.
[40] Victoria Olwell, 'The Body Types: Corporeal Documents and Body Politics, circa 1900', in Leah Price and Pamela Thurschwell (eds.), Literary Secretaries/Secretarial Culture (Aldershot, 2005), 50.

BIBLIOGRAPHY

Sara Ahmed, What's the Use? On the Uses of Use (Durham, 2019).
Ethel G. Armstrong, 'New York Association', in Filing and Office Management (April 1922).
John F. Arndt, 'Making a File Drawer Live', in The File (Feb. 1936).
Forrest E. Cardullo, 'Industrial Administration and Scientific Management, 1', in Machinery (July 1912).
Ruth Shonle Cavan, Business Girls: A Study of Their Interests and Problems (Chicago, 1929).
E.A. Dunn, 'Indexing Service', in The LB File (March 1923).
A.M. Edwards, Sixteenth Census of the United States 1940 – Population: Comparative Occupation Statistics for the United States, 1870 to 1940 (Washington D.C., 1943).
Ethel Erickson, The Employment of Women in Offices (Washington D.C., 1934).
Andreas Fickers and Annie van den Oever, Doing Experimental Media Archaeology: Theory (Berlin, 2022).
Lisa Fine, The Souls of the Skyscraper: Female Clerical Workers in Chicago, 1870-1930 (Philadelphia, 1990).
Arthur Frey, 'Filing as a Profession', in The File (June 1939).
Frances Maule, 'Women Are So Personal', in Independent Women (Sept. 1934).
Elizabeth King McDowall, 'The Requisites of a Good File Clerk', in Filing (March 1921).
Catherine McNulty, 'Warren Filing Association', in Filing (Jan. 1921).
W.J. Mills, 'Old Idea, Presented in New Way: Lands Order', in The LB File (April 1924).
Geoffrey Nunberg, 'Farewell to the Information Age', in idem (ed.), The Future of the Book (Berkeley, 1996), 103-138.
Victoria Olwell, 'The Body Types: Corporeal Documents and Body Politics, circa 1900', in Leah Price and Pamela Thurschwell (eds.), Literary Secretaries/Secretarial Culture (Aldershot, 2005), 48-62.
Nelly Oudshoorn and Trevor Pinch, 'Introduction: How Users and Non-Users Matter', in idem (eds.), How Users Matter: The Co-Construction of Users and Technology (Cambridge MA, 2005), 1-25.
Anne Petersen, 'Office Girls Get Personality Tips', in The File (Jan. 1938).
Craig Robertson, The Filing Cabinet: A Vertical History of Information (Minneapolis, 2021).
Ethel Scholfield, Filing Department Operation and Control (New York, 1923).
Sharon Hartman Strom, Beyond the Typewriter: Gender, Class, and the Origins of Modern American Office Work, 1900- 1930 (Urbana, 1992).
Louis Carlisle Walker, The Office and Tomorrow's Business (New York, 1930).
Olivier Zunz, Making America Corporate, 1870-1920 (Chicago, 1992).

Chapter 2
The Office in Popular Culture, or the "Plight of the Clerk"

Nicola Bishop

INTRODUCTION

> Put the key of despair into the lock of apathy. Turn the knob of mediocrity slowly and open the gates of despondency – welcome to a day in the average office.[1]

In a line memorably delivered by comedian Ricky Gervais in *The Office* (2001-2003), anarchic manager David Brent captures the essence of attitudes towards office life. A mockumentary show that ran for just two seasons in the U.K. (plus two Christmas specials) before Greg Daniels adapted it for the United States where it ran successfully for nine seasons, *The Office* is still considered one of the most iconic television programmes of the early 21st century. Indeed, Christopher Olsen and CarrieLynn Reinhard have suggested that *The Office* "changed the face of television production for years to come".[2] A key part of its success was the use of a real office building as a set and the accompanying attention to the authenticity of the uses and users of the office space, giving viewers scenes that were so familiar for many: the "average office". *The Office* struck a chord because it drew on a scenario and setting that Ingrid Jeacle and Lee Parker refer to as a "ubiquitous feature of daily life",[3] while simultaneously entering a ready-made market of fictional depictions from across the 19th, 20th and 21st centuries of the office – and by extension office work and office workers – as intrinsically dull, boring and uninspiring. From their earliest literary incarnations, office spaces were written about as environments that could stifle individuality, redirect energy to obscure or meaningless ends or simply grind down their inhabitants. Examining these depictions offers an important contextual lens through which to understand broader histories of office buildings and office culture, as well as contemporary attitudes that frame the wider backdrop to any research in the field. The pervasive and persistent rendering of this environment as a negative cultural space through multiple media has certainly had an impact on various aspects of office life, from scholarship, policy and employment to health and well-being.

Fictional representations that chart the office space and offer a reading of the lives of those within date back to the very beginnings of the office. In 1825, Charles Lamb wrote: "I am grown to my desk as it were; and the wood had entered my soul",[4] demonstrating the type of deep and often obsessive relationship with the labour of bureaucracy that many later depictions would return to. Charles Dickens, most famous as the author of the working-class experience, of factories, workhouses and poor houses, was equally negative about the office in his many novels, particularly those "dismal little cells" housing the clerks that were involved in the grinding mill of the growing bureaucracy.[5] Dickens's Ebenezer Scrooge, famous from the many adaptations of *A Christmas Carol* (1843), is, like David Brent, an example of the typically problematic manager so often represented in fictional depictions; using his meagre power to further his own ends, to perpetuate problematic personal agendas or to undermine the purpose of the work that should take place within the office space. At the same time, Bob Cratchit is the "typically" enfeebled, ill-treated clerk who has little choice but to continue in his employment due to his financial and social status. Equally numerous in British literary portrayals are clerks who sat at their desks dreaming of escaping the walls of the office – of making a living from writing rather than copying. In the late 19th and early 20th centuries, aspirational figures who had made the transition wrote often about their journey from desk ledger to authorship. Writers like Arnold Bennett, Shan Bullock, P.G. Wodehouse, even T.S. Eliot, all penned narratives about the clerical lives that they inhabited before moving into more literary pursuits, showcasing not only the appetite for this path but the potential for people to succeed. Indeed, Bennett wrote a series of instructional essays (1901-1903) that told aspiring writers exactly how to follow in his footsteps. As Scott Banville has discussed, "authorship as a transformative occupation for lower-middle-class men becomes a common Victorian literary trope".[6] It continues beyond this into the Edwardian period but is also evident in more contemporary literature (see George Orwell's *Keep the Aspidistra Flying* from 1936 and Julian Barnes's *Metroland* from 1980).

Later in the 20th century, this association met the development of film and television. Capturing the essence of the white-collar workplace became a key aspect of many productions, with films such as *The Rebel* (1961), *Mary Poppins* (1964), *Girl from Rio* (2001), *Bridget Jones's Diary* (2001) and more recently *Living* (2022), and television shows like *The Fall and Rise of Reginald Perrin* (1976-1979), *Ever Decreasing Circles* (1984-1989), *The Office* and *The IT Crowd* (2006-2013) using the office as a backdrop. In addition to television series that focus on the office environment explicitly, there are also prominent office workers in a much wider range of situations, like Captain Mainwaring in *Dad's Army* (1968-1977), Richard Bucket in *Keeping Up Appearances* (1990-1995), Gary Strang in *Men Behaving Badly* (1992-1999) and Mr. Brown in the two Paddington films (2014, 2017), all of whom carry a certain set of characteristics and stereotypes linked to their employment. Part of the context for understanding the office as a site rich in cultural meaning comes from the historic status of those who inhabited it. The clerk has long been seen as a comedic figure in representational terms, from the mocking tone of T.W.H. Crosland's *The Suburbans* (1905) (in which he referred to suburban clerks as being "browbeaten" at the office)[7] to music hall songs,[8] George and Weedon Grossmith's pompous fictional diarist Charles Pooter and bank clerk Private Pike's dependency on his mother in *Dad's Army*. In Britain, as in many other countries, this rested on the class status of this newly white-collar worker, who did not fit into straightforward understandings of either working-class identity (despite being a paid labourer rather than a business- or landowner) or a middle-class identity. Levels of education, literacy, expectations of formal dress, white-collar rather than manual conditions of work, income level and the ability to afford to live in the new suburbs, all complicated the status of the clerk and the newly growing petty bourgeoisie rested uneasily between the more established class categories. As E.M. Forster wrote in *Howards End* (1910) of his intellectually eager yet down-at-heel clerk, Leonard Bast:

> [...] the angel of Democracy had arisen, enshadowing the classes with leathern wings, and proclaiming, "All men are equal – all men, that is to say, who possess umbrellas", and so [Leonard] was obliged to assert gentility, lest he slipped into the abyss where nothing counts, and the statements of Democracy are inaudible.[9]

Being lower middle class traps Leonard Bast in an untenable situation; he has neither the means to remain respectable nor the options to find himself in a better position. Instead, he becomes an object of pity for the middle-class Schlegel family, suffering from their well-intentioned but naive interventions.

Although women began working in offices from 1870 onwards,[10] representations in popular culture have tended to focus on men like Leonard Bast. The Dickensian clerk of Victorian culture was pervasive, and the association between masculinity, white-collar labour and a series of issues that were perceived as affecting the population (poor health, sedentary bodies, and in the face of the Second Boer War, an ill-equipped potential army) became culturally ingrained. As Michelle Johansen has argued, "it was broadly accepted that lower-middle-class occupations offered few opportunities for masculine self-realisation".[11] In response to this, caricatures soon developed that captured what many critics and commentators saw as the "everyman" of these problems: the clerk. In *Sketches by Boz* (1837), for instance, Dickens draws attention to the "tall, thin, pale person, in a black coat, scanty grey trousers, little pinched-up gaiters, and brown beaver gloves" who walks "up and down before the little patch of grass on which the chairs are placed for hire, not as if he were doing it for pleasure or recreation, but as if it were a matter of compulsion".[12] The sartorial choices here betray the clerk's lack of funds, while the formality of dress highlights the tension between low wages and high standards that plagued the lower-middle-class white-collar worker. Dickens's clerk is thin (malnourished), pale (indoors too much) and unsure of how to behave on the grass or to enjoy his hours outside work, which Dickens uses to draw attention to the type of "dingy little back office into which he walks every morning".[13]

This chapter focuses on fictional representations like these of the office in British popular culture, exploring a variety of depictions from the mid-Victorian period to the early 21st century and arguing that, as a cultural phenomenon, the office is almost universally shown in a negative light. It will look at the ways in which authors, filmmakers and television writers have responded to organisational changes, administrative practices and architectural culture to show how the office and office users have become a wider metaphor for the mundane aspects of everyday life.

HISTORIOGRAPHY

Studies of office work have often focused on the economic, architectural, organisational or administrative histories of these spaces, which provide a rich exploration of the structures and systems of bureaucracy and white-collar labour. Likewise, scholarship discussing the office worker has focused on the economic status of this figure and the effects of the rapid expansion of administration at the end of the 19th century on the identity of clerical workers, before the later developments of mechanisation, Taylorist principles and technological advancements, and the arrival of typists, secretaries and administrators. Much of this research has centred on the class status of the Victorian and Edwardian clerk, and there are ongoing, if infrequent, contributions to a debate about the concept of a "lower middle class" that includes a wide – and ever-increasing – subsection of society which sits between the traditional middle and working classes, and which closely subscribes to the socio-economic status of the white-collar office worker.[14] However, as Rita Felski pointed out, "being lower-middle-class is a singularly boring identity", and this impression has certainly resulted in far fewer critical studies than have been written about the working class.[15] Stephen Mihm also observed that many "deskbound academics" actually have the same insecurities as lower-middle-class clerks themselves, particularly when it comes to discussing the implications of participating in non-manual labour, and this may also be a factor in the reluctance to engage with lower-middle-class issues and white-collar work in particular.[16] The work that has been done has largely focused on the position of the clerk within a Marxist framework, aiming to make sense of a petty bourgeoisie that was overlooked in Karl Marx's stratification of class hierarchies.

As a result, between the 1930s and the present day, scholars such as F.D. Klingender, David Lockwood, Michel Crozier, Gregory Anderson, Geoffrey Crossick, Ross McKibbin, and more recently Michael Heller and Dan Evans have written informative studies on the impact of changes to white-collar workers across the 19th and early 20th centuries, arguing that clerks became either part of the proletariat because of poor working conditions, real wages and societal expectations, or part of the middle classes through standards of living and the ability to improve their situation and education.[17] Meta Zimmeck, Graham Lowe, Gregory Anderson, Julie Berebitsky, Helen Glew and Nicole Robertson have also explored the gendered makeup of this administrative class of worker, analysing the implications of increasing numbers of female workers in the industry and the impact this had on the position of male clerks.[18] These various histories have sometimes reiterated stereotypes and popular cultural representations, and occasionally explored the underlying accuracy of assessments made by novelists, social commentators and cartoonists, but such cultural depictions have not been explored in depth as frequently as the economic status of the white-collar worker. John Carey began a conversation about the *cultural* significance of office workers in *The Intellectuals and the Masses* (1992) that was picked up by Jonathan Rose in a chapter in his seminal work *The Intellectual Life of the British Working Classes* (2001). Carey suggested that the impression of office work – and by extension those who engaged in it – as degrading and mind-numbing was flawed; it was an impression created by "intellectuals" to maintain distance between them and the self-educated clerks who were getting too close for comfort.[19] Evidence to the contrary, Carey proposes, was the wide range of literary texts produced by those who were participating in this labour. Likewise, Rose has argued that engagement with literary culture from within the "masses" demonstrates the intellectual interest and literary capabilities of the "Leonard Basts". When looking at autobiographies for evidence of this, Rose acknowledges that there is a potential bias, suggesting that "those clerks who did leave behind literary works probably also had the drive and imagination to rise above the kind of office routine that would have anaesthetised others".[20] Like the novelists, poets and scriptwriters who came from offices, autobiographers are self-selectively those who are striving creatively beyond their nine-to-five labour.

As Rose argues, many of those Bastian authors went on to write non-fiction and novels that were far more popular at the time than those written by the intelligentsia (even though they have remained stubbornly outside of the canon). Crucially, however, many of those same clerks-turned-authors went on to produce novels that captured and lamented the monotony of their former existence – for instance, the novels of Shan Bullock, Arnold Bennett, Frank Swinnerton and Edwin Pugh. As a result, as Jeremy Lewis put it in his collection of literary quotations about office life: "Not all clerks, it goes without saying, are figures of pathos, though this is how the literary world loves to see them".[21] While Carey is right that office workers should not be collectively assumed to hate their work, it is nonetheless important to scrutinise the cultural phenomenon that surrounds the office environment and its overwhelmingly negative portrayal, coming from writers who are writing from lived experience. Jonathan Wild revisited Carey's ideas in his important monograph on the literary life of this class, with *The Rise of the Office Clerk in Literary Culture, 1880-1939* (2006). Wild talks about the dominant late-Victorian image of the "'quarter-educated' board school clerk feebly sipping culture while shackled to an office desk" which pervaded literary culture at the time.[22] While he argues that there is a shift away from this wholly negative portrayal at various points before the Second World War, Wild also suggests that the term "clerk" and the assumptions that by this point dogged the idea of clerical work did much to prevent a complete rethink. Certainly, there are traces of this board school clerk character in *The Office*'s Tim, who wants to go to university at the age of thirty but finds himself unable to break away from a job he hates at the paper company Wernham Hogg.

The first study to look at the distinctive representations of office workers in literature by authors such as George Gissing, Arnold Bennett, Frank Swinnerton, Edwin Pugh and Walter Besant, as well as long-neglected work by Rudolf Dircks, Herbert Tremaine and writers who published anonymously about their experiences as clerks, Wild's work inspired the investigation of class, culture and the clerk that led to my own study *Lower-Middle-Class Nation: The White-Collar Worker in British Popular Culture* (2021), an exploration of the lower middle class in representations that included print and screen media and continued the cultural cartography of depictions up to the present time. Within that study, I argue that there is a universality to the negative portrayals of office spaces, in terms of architectural design and decor, categories of tasks and labour, and the characters and personalities of those within, that remains surprisingly consistent from the mid-Victorian period to today. More broadly, I also suggest that there is something universal about the perceived plight of the office worker in 21st-century society that brings us together as a society. Aside from these more specific examples focusing on the office worker in popular culture, the development of the field of middlebrow studies (which often includes the type of literature that was widely assumed to be read, and was often also written, by former clerks, typists and secretaries) means there is a growing understanding of this area.[23] Studies specific to literary interpretations of the office worker in middlebrow culture include A. James Hammerton's articles on Charles and Weedon Grossmith's *The Diary of a Nobody* (1892),[24] Richard Higgins's work on clerks in H.G. Wells's novels,[25] Lena Wånggren's mention of the popular motif of the New Woman typist in fin-de-siècle literature,[26] and Erica van Boven's recent work which demonstrates how lower-middle-class office workers, teachers, civil servants and journalists were referred to as "the common reader" by publishers across Europe.[27]

Within the fields of literary criticism, history, architecture, organisational and business studies, there are further pockets of research into the significance of cultural attitudes towards the office environment and the office worker. As Leah Price and Pamela Thurschwell indicated in *Literary Secretaries/Secretarial Culture* (2005), there is a literary preconception about "deskbound clerks in dead-end jobs" that resurfaces across a wide chronology.[28] Likewise, Carl Rhodes and Robert Westwood talk about the ways that popular culture frequently showcases representations that are "explicitly critical of work and its organization",[29] while Alexia Panayiotou writes about this as a distinctly gendered issue: "Popular culture is imbued with images of managers, employees and organizations from the novels we read to the music we listen to, daily life is filled with images of blue collar heroes, ruthless bosses and bored office workers – typically male".[30] Francis Duffy reinforces this point when he discusses the legacy of the Victorian male clerk. For Duffy, the Grossmiths' Charles Pooter, the anti-hero of *Diary of a Nobody*, remains a formidable "ghost" while "the office buildings which were designed to meet [the clerks'] need and foster their fantasy still exist".[31] In this sense, Scott Banville's conceptualisation of "remediation", or the process by which popular cultural expressions transcend a particular moment, intertextually informing and shaping future impressions, is hugely significant. Banville compares contemporary sitcoms with Victorian music hall acts and traces the multiplicity of interrelated tropes and types, arguing that "all of these cultural forms have one thing in common, the goal of representing the lived experiences of ourselves and others to both ourselves and those others".[32] A palimpsest is created of cultural attitudes that are embedded to create a long-lasting and surprisingly coherent perception of office life.

The office as a space is once more at the forefront of critical debate as the legacy of the COVID-19 pandemic has forced a global rethink about the fundamental practice of working collectively in a designated space. Very recent scholarship on office work has therefore focused on mental health and wellbeing and on the logistical, psychological, environmental and systematic challenges that the office faces.[33] In this regard, the long-standing, deeply embedded cultural impressions of offices and office work discussed as part of this chapter may yet still impact the arguments that are had about the return to the office, or further support a revolution in home working.

METHODOLOGY

There is a wide catalogue of fictional examples of the office and office worker available to the historian, which demonstrates the social, economic and representative continuities that are woven across the last two centuries. Many of the traits ascribed to Victorian clerks – pedantry, caution, fussiness, inactivity, dullness – continue to be part of comical outlines of contemporary bureaucrats and administrators. As a result of this, a particular series of temperamental behaviours and physical characteristics remain frequently invoked. See, for example, the assumption that male office workers are short in stature and are likely to experience premature hair loss or have boring personalities (more on which later). At the same time, the environments that clerks work in are presumed to either suit or shape these behaviours – offices abound that are characterised by rigid expectations or monotonous tasks, and that are architecturally stifling, unwelcoming or ill-suited for their purposes. Understanding these representations is key in conceptualising why certain traits and assumptions are commonly made about the office as a space, its administrative occupants and the place that work more widely holds within our lives. Alongside the empirical data about office management, administrative history and records of companies, architectural firms and office suppliers, these sources are a valuable way of exploring the tensions between intention and perception. They also help us to understand how the office is often seen as synonymous with the practices of everyday life and yet can frequently be chronically understudied – which is remarkable given the place it holds in modern society. Those long-standing prejudices against office work, bureaucracy, administration and the people who engage with it professionally remain deeply entrenched.

Studying and understanding Victorian novels or contemporary office-based sitcoms offers a way into the wider representational framework through which scholars (and society) encounter both users and uses of the office, helping to dissect the recurring tropes and to explore the relationship between society and art. Certainly, historical imagination owes much to the work of writers like Dickens; as Sigurd O. Schmidt argues, people's perception of the past is more likely shaped by fiction than it is by the work of historians.[34] Likewise, television is even more pervasive, reaching much wider audiences and, as Andrew Crisell suggests, "[acting] as a kind of mirror on, or relay mechanism of, events in the outside world", from which we can draw conclusions about the ways in which particular moments in society can be reflected in popular shows.[35] This does not mean that literature, film or television should be used without caution; Allan Pasco's work on the role and use of literature as a historical source raises valid warnings about the fact that "reality is never pure, simple, or linear" and suggests we should avoid the "mimetic fallacy" of assuming that cultural artefacts have "a one-to-one relationship with reality".[36] What is clear is that there is a predilection for those working in offices to explore this environment, particularly through creative writing discussing the white-collar condition. This means that many of the multimedia illustrations of office life come from the imaginations of those who are time served. As Paul Jordan has explored, the connection between the clerk and the author is long established, in part because the early practice of being a "scribe" placed the office worker precariously between the "creative" and the "routine".[37] For the young men who first arrived in London at the end of the 19th century, coming from their board school educations, eager to stand out in the clerical crowd and aware that self-education was a potential pathway to future social mobility, writing was increasingly a way to achieve some of these aims.

London was a very visible centre of publishing as well as of administration, and the parallel growth of various charitable and social enterprises that prioritised the cultural development of this new and vast demographic – partly as a philanthropic urge but equally as a mechanism to prevent less salubrious occupations – put scholarly pursuits high on the agenda. The new free public libraries, enabled by the 1850 Public Libraries Act, as Michelle Johansen explains, saw many enthusiastic "upper-working and lower-middle class readers seeking out instructional and productive leisure opportunities",[38] as did organisations such as the Young Men's Christian Association (YMCA).[39] Jerome Bjelopera and Timothy Alborn both comment that an additional benefit of these extra-curricular clubs and activities was to avert office workers' attention from the increasingly mechanised direction that their professional lives were heading in; as Alborn argues, they offered a "solidification of friendships to compensate for increasingly impersonal offices".[40] Literary examples at this time commonly contain the clerk-who-wants-to-be-a-writer trope. Richard Larch in Arnold Bennett's *A Man from the North* (1898) and the first-person narrator in Edwin Pugh's *The Broken Honeymoon* (1908) both take part in a punishing timetable of additional writing practices before and after a long day as a clerk in a bid to become an author. Felski, in her essay on the lower middle classes, calls this the "talisman that offers the promise, however opaque, of entry into a higher world".[41] Both Bennett and Pugh were clerks while they were developing as writers, as were many others,[42] which leads to a natural bias offering a negative rendition of office life and the prioritisation of authorship as an "escape". By extension, those who enjoyed their employment were much less likely to want to write about that experience, thereby further reinforcing negative attitudes.

Jeremy Lewis, editor of *The Chatto Book of Office Life* (1992), draws attention to the fact that aspiring writers were also more likely to find their way into writerly environments than jobs where numbers formed a larger part of the daily working experience. As he says: "Probably because most writers are more familiar with newspapers and old-fashioned publishing houses than with City solicitors or merchant bankers, and have grown up on a diet of Dickens, those offices that find their way into print tend to be dingy, decrepit places with dirty windows and scuffed carpets."[43] Those working in fields like banking, finance and accounting, where conditions were often much more genial (Alborn describes "palatial" offices in insurance),[44] were thus less likely to be authoring narratives about their working lives. At the same time, as Ceri Sullivan suggests, there is a form of Weberian "creative bureaucracy" that creates a freedom for experimentation and imagination once there is an "absence of friction produced by systematic regularity".[45] Instead, this contribution of bureaucracy is often undervalued because the lingering impression about office work (and by extension the office worker) is that it is "deeply dull".[46] In *Colin's Sandwich*, a 1980s sitcom about Colin, a would-be author stuck working in the complaints department of British Rail (in a role where photocopying endless customer complaints forms fills most of his working day), the protagonist makes a similar point: that "the nuts and bolts of the daily round" require true creativity in order to enable survival.[47] As he puts it, "anyone can hold down a glamorous job", but the routine work of bureaucracy leaves space for the imagination. Colin refers to Franz Kafka and Richard Adams (author of *Watership Down*, 1972) and their ability to "scribble" down novels whilst maintaining their white-collar jobs. These observations do not prevent Colin from being utterly miserable at work and frustrated by the lack of progress made on his journey to full-time authorship, but they situate routine work and creative pursuits as being compatible.

Equally, as Ali Haggett has argued, we should not dismiss the pervasiveness of some of the "themes [that] emerge with regularity in popular culture" about white-collar men who are dissatisfied, disengaged or deeply unhappy with their working lives, particularly given that discussions about these representations are often missing from "organised debates about men and psychological illness".[48] Negative impressions, even if they originate from a bias against office work, are pervasive and deeply ingrained. This has become particularly apparent across the 20th and 21st centuries as screenwriters have continued the representations begun by Victorian authors and positioned the office set as a stage on which to explore the mundanity of everyday – and particularly male – life. The TV Tropes Wiki (a website that catalogues recurring tropes across popular culture) mentions the "Soul-Crushing Desk Job" as a common sub-trope within what it terms the "Standard Office Setting", summarised as an often comic, sometimes tragic environment that involves generic paperwork and a hierarchy in which the management have substantially nicer offices than the workers, who endure "cubicles and the fluorescent lighting that never turns off".[49] Most examples in this trope come from male characters, from the office supplies salesman in the popular American sitcom *Friends* (who Phoebe rescues from committing suicide) to Jim Halpert in *The Office* (U.S.), who comments: "If this was my career, I'd have to throw myself under a train."[50]

This widespread, negative representation of offices, office workers and office work is culturally significant and deserves attention. Methodologically, the use of media and fictional sources offers a myriad of viewpoints that disseminate through society in multiple ways, reaching vast and varied audiences, many of whom compare what they see and read with their own experiences. In this sense, the source base proliferates, engaging in dialogue with other versions, stories and narratives, and forming a canon of workplace depictions which then forge further culturally attuned perspectives. As Gail Honeyman says in her 2017 novel *Eleanor Oliphant is Completely Fine*:

> In almost nine years, no one's ever asked what kind of office, or what sort of job I do there. I can't decide whether that's because I fit perfectly with their idea of what an office worker looks like, or whether people hear the phrase *work in an office* and automatically fill in the blanks themselves.[51]

OFFICE SPACES

If contemporary impressions of the office space have become characterised by strip lighting and shared desk spaces, the conditions in the earlier Victorian workplace were also markedly glum. In Dickens's *Dombey and Sons* (1848), the office is "enveloped in a studious gloom" and in *The Pickwick Papers* (1837) the clerks work in a "dark, mouldy, earth-smelling room".[52] Robert Thorne, in Shan Bullock's novel of the same name, has a "carpet [that] was thin and shabby" and a "hearthrug worn through in the middle"; the passages between offices are "long, narrow, gloomy".[53] In another of Bullock's novels (*Mr Ruby Jumps the Traces*, 1917) there is an office that is "small, poorly lighted by one window, and [that] needed cleaning".[54] The lack of good light pervades, with authors like Frank Swinnerton and Edwin Pugh similarly remarking on this feature, while later, in the mid-20th century, crime writer P.D. James would also comment on the "dusty and ill-lit rooms" that her office-working murderer occupies.[55] Another recurrent trope is the stuffiness caused by windows that leaked heat in cold weather while insufficiently opening in the warmer months to create a "dusty wilderness".[56] Later literary texts demonstrate the continuity of the trend: in Elizabeth Jane Howard's *After Julius* (1965), the office is described as "very small, permanently dirty, and either stuffy or freezing depending on the window".[57] Reginald Perrin's office in *The Fall and Rise of Reginald Perrin* by David Nobbs has a "threadbare green carpet" and the building is so poorly maintained that more letters fall from the exterior sign reading Sunshine Desserts each day.[58] These conditions are represented as shaping the mood of the occupants within. Each day Perrin leaves his suburban house to his wife's cheery instruction to "have a good day at the office" and he verbosely retorts that he "won't".[59] In 1989, in his autobiography, Irish television writer and dramatist Hugh Leonard referred to his civil service workplace as having "cheerlessness [...] too absolute to have been accidental; despair seemed to have been knowingly mixed in with the paint and ingrained in the dark wooden floor tiles".[60]

Even where expensive new office buildings feature, those constructed in steel and with vast glass-panelled rooms and swanky new technologies, they remain problematic for their users. In the sitcom *W1A*, set in a hybridised fictional/non-fictional world of BBC management and filmed in the flagship new building based in the titular London postcode, the office workers are constantly tripped up by the complex set of "innovative" technologised infrastructure systems – doors that refuse to unlock for meetings, iPads that "digitally handshake" and share confidential information with random nearby users, and networks that spew printouts from potentially any machine in the building without warning. The users of the office are all champions of creativity because they are forced to hot-desk (with the exception of the bosses who reinforce hierarchy with their own designated spaces), which results in constant battles for privacy and meeting rooms to host guests. In *Christie Malry's Own Double-Entry* (1973), by experimental novelist B.S. Johnson, Christie's journey into violent sadism is depicted as being in response to this type of environment at the bank where he works, as "the atmosphere was acrid with frustration, boredom and jealousy, black with acrimony, pettiness and bureaucracy".[61]

Johnson's story, as John Lanchester observes in the introduction to the Picador edition, takes the significance of the double-entry bookkeeping method of accounting and turns it into a "way of structuring and comprehending the world".[62] Shaped by the cold, heartless office space, he takes bureaucratic organisational method and pushes it to a darkly rational end point – handing out lethal punishments and penalties for minor infractions. While many clerks talk about how the changing methods and technologies in the office resulted in them becoming merely cogs in a machine, Malry pushes mechanisation to its post-human conclusion.

Johnson was not the only author to play with this trope: Nigel Williams's *The Wimbledon Poisoner* (1990) works on a similar premise, with the suburban, white-collar Henry Farr accidentally poisoning a large number of his community during a bodged attempt at murdering his wife. His office is described as follows:

> "Cupboard" would have been a better description. It was a room about eight to ten feet square, offering, as an estate agent with whom Henry was dealing had put it, "a superb prospect of a ventilator shaft". It was, like so many other things in Henry's life, more like a carefully calculated insult from the Almighty than anything else.[63]

As a pastiche of the suburban novel, Williams's character Henry is deliberately attempting to play up to cliché, calling himself a "dull wounded little man whose horizons were bounded by the daily journey to the office" and who sees personal injury in each of the predicaments that he faces.[64] Another character later refers to him as a "little man in a bowler hat",[65] which shows that there remained a long-lasting association between the behatted clerk of Dickensian culture and the late-20th-century office worker, even though office workers no longer wore such millinery by 1990. There is also consistent cross-referencing between Henry's occupation and his dullness, his suit wearing, his small office and his feelings of powerlessness. In the novel, Detective Inspector Rush aligns with others in the crime genre (like Agatha Christie in *The ABC Murders*, 1936) in assuming that the poisoner he seeks is a "drab little man, obscure, meek and mild, hen-pecked perhaps" and that he "thinks the world owes him something" because he does not find satisfaction in his work.[66] This presumption that the conditions of clerical labour are intrinsically damaging to the psyches of those who operate within the office is a widespread assumption in fiction and one that is often repeated across fictional forms.

OFFICE WORKERS

As mechanisation continued apace at the end of the 19th century and office workers increasingly became party to Frederick Winslow Taylor's methods of efficiency and control, the representations of male clerks as facing a period of emasculation at work that rendered them both poignantly and comically moulded by routine began to filter through literature, as we have seen. The daily tasks associated with office work – and particularly those drawn from the assumption that such work was mechanised, repetitive and intellectually unstimulating – saw the terms clerk, office worker, bureaucrat, paper-pusher and pen-pusher increasingly used as shorthand for a set of characteristics and personality traits. This included various assumptions about the size and physical stature of office workers. See for instance Victor Canning's eponymous character Mr. Finchley, who is described as "forty-five, short", H.G. Wells's Mr. Polly who is a "short, compact figure", Jimmy Perry and David Croft's Captain Mainwaring in *Dad's Army*, whose shortness is in contrast to his second in command in both the Home Guard and the bank (Sergeant Wilson), and David Brent, who in one episode of *The Office* wears heeled shoes.[67] Other concerns include hair loss: T.S. Eliot's clerk in *The Love Song of J. Alfred Prufrock* worries that women comment on "how his hair is growing thin", and the Grossmiths' Charles Pooter reduces his hair brushing on the advice of his hairdresser for fear of losing more.[68] R.F. Delderfield's Edgar Frith is described as "timid, hopelessly indecisive about everything and excessively dull", while Captain Darling in Ben Elton's *Blackadder Goes Forth* (1989) is a bureaucrat by nature, expressing enjoyment in an evening spent unloading a shipment of paperclips.[69] Many of these physical attributes were also central to the undermining of masculinity that went hand in hand with attitudes towards office work.

Some of this comedy came from the ways in which office workers were subject to what was seen as enhanced surveillance and control. In Bullock's 1907 novel *Robert Thorne* (based, in part, on his own experiences as a young clerk), Robert receives a copy of "office regulations" on his first day at the Tax Office, which outline the many "personal conditions of service" to which he is supposed to adhere.[70] In many offices, these covered not only behaviours at work itself but expectations in society more widely for those in the role. While Thorne is a serious character in Bullock's work – a young man starting out on the career ladder, who eventually sees the light and leaves the office for an outdoor life of farming in

New Zealand – he captures the angst felt by so many young clerks that working in an office is going to prevent him from becoming a "real" man. In one lament, he even refers to himself as a "miserable little pen-driver" and adds that the "real men" – the bricklayers and bus drivers – rightly look down on office workers like him.[71] In the same novel, the older clerks – Mr. Cherry and Mr. Hope – offer a glimpse of the internalisation of this bound rulebook. Mr Cherry spends "an hour every morning" getting ready for work: "Everything had its own place, green pencil beside red, and blue between red and black, scissors paired with paper knife, pins lying head to head, inkpots square to the fraction of an inch".[72] Mr. Cherry is a personification of the Taylorist principle that had gained popularity at this point; everything is set out and ready to be used. Likewise, Mr. Hope is presented as being "before everything, in everything, [...] an official" – his personality is fundamentally shaped by the processes undertaken in his role. The poignancy of Mr. Hope's retirement and the character's utter desolation at a future in which he is no longer working at the Tax Office capture the recurring trope of the office worker as a bureaucrat in personality, character, behaviour and mindset:

> He lived for the office. It had his heart, filled his thoughts. Through the most of thirty years he had slaved devotedly; had shaped himself and been shaped into an almost perfect part of the machine. He never made a mistake. [...] He was order itself. Like a planet he moved in eternal routine.[73]

Other clerks are presented in this way on the date that they too leave service. In fact, the retirement of the office worker figure is an established moment across a wide range of cultural examples: Mr. Josser in Norman Collins's *London Belongs to Me* (1945), Herbert Norman Smeeth in J.B. Priestley's *Angel Pavement* (1930) and Bill Tidyman in *Ever Decreasing Circles* (1984). Retirement (and redundancy, seen as an even crueller practice for the office worker character) even forms the basis of *The Legacy of Reginald Perrin* (1996), a television series made without the titular character after Leonard Rossiter's death, which explores Reginald's friends/family as they find themselves ousted from various white-collar jobs because of their age. The first series of *The Office* is similarly predicated on the existential threat to the Slough branch and what would happen to the characters within.

This conflation of character and profession is unique to the office worker: in literature from the late 19th century through to the present day, there is, as Georg Lukács put it, an assumption of a "rational mechanisation [that] extends right into the worker's 'soul'".[74] Office types are much more likely to be used as a shorthand that implies rigidity, pedantry, method and a lack of humanity than those who work in the factory environments for which rationalisation was originally intended. Indeed, office workers are frequently depicted as "cogs" in the machine of bureaucracy: Robert Thorne calls himself "like a machine, grinding out its daily portion, mechanically turning pages with cold grimed fingers", while Bennett's Richard Larch talks about being "part of a business machine".[75] These machine clerks embody their function, blurring the divide between office work and office worker. In his reference to aged clerk Mr. Josser as little more than a walking set of ledgers in *London Belongs To Me*, Norman Collins evoked the anonymous contributor to the *International Labour Review* of 1936, who commented that "the invoice clerk who now works a book-keeping machine all day is nothing but an impersonal unit".[76] Later still, in the popular suburban sitcom *The Good Life* (1975-1978), the first episode sees Tom quit his stable office job and dive into the world of backyard self-sufficiency because he is merely a "grotty little cog in a great whacking machine".[77] In Keith Waterhouse's *Office Life* (1978), the main character Clement Gryce is wryly aware of the wider assumption that clerical types are shaped so deeply by their work behaviours that they struggle to exist without them:

> That he led any kind of life beyond the office he was fuzzily aware of, in a sleepwalking kind of way, only while he was leading it. He had found in all his previous billets that once he had hung up his mackintosh and got his feet firmly beneath his own desk, the outside world evaporated, like the waking memory of a dream.[78]

This lack of awareness of the "outside world" illustrates what would be understood, in more contemporary terminology, as a poor work-life balance that brought with it various issues around ill health for these fictional office workers. In many such instances in literature, clerks are depicted as not being particularly healthy specimens: George Gissing has a clerk in *The Odd Women* (1893) who is "trembling and bloodless", Mr. Meggs (one of P.G. Wodehouse's clerks from 1917) is "a chronic dyspeptic", D.H. Lawrence refers to one of his white-collar characters as "old [and] decaying" in *Sons and Lovers* (1913), R.F. Delderfield depicts his character Harold Goodbeer, a solicitor's clerk in *The Dreaming Suburb*, as "physically frail [...] fussy, pedantic, and inclined to be pompous".[79] Even without any specific physical ailment, George Orwell's Gordon Comstock, in *Keep the Aspidistra Flying* (1936), is "a small frail figure" worryingly described as "rather moth eaten", and the narrator "J" in Jerome K. Jerome's *Three Men in a Boat* (1889) is a susceptible hypochondriac who finds himself experiencing any symptoms that he reads about, including typhoid fever, Bright's disease, cholera and diphtheria.[80] In *Angel Pavement* (1930), J.B. Priestley diagnosed the issues behind this when describing one of the clerks in the office:

> He was obviously neither sick nor starved, yet something about his appearance, a total lack of colour and bloom, a slight pastiness and spottiness, the faint grey film that seemed to cover and subdue him, suggested that all the food he ate was wrong, all the rooms he sat in, beds he slept in and clothes he wore, were wrong, and that he lived in a world without sun and clean rain and wandering sweet air.[81]

This type of ill-health was not just rendered in literary portrayals. Anderson suggests that tuberculosis (commonly known as consumption at the time) was a serious condition among clerks "due to the damp and draughty conditions, inadequate sanitation and especially overcrowding".[82] His research shows that tuberculosis was the most common cause of death for those in the Liverpool Clerks' Association death insurance scheme, and while white-collar workers were not subject to the levels of dust that many manual labourers encountered during the course of their work, the close proximity of workers and general overcrowding meant that disease spread easily. Other less dangerous but nonetheless concerning illnesses ascribed to clerks included what Michael Zakim refers to as "desk diseases": "giddiness, liver problems, bladder and urinary infections, a swimming of the head, deafness, stomach and bowel disorders, piles and strictures".[83]

The rise of institutions like the YMCA in Britain provided opportunities for young office workers who spent many of their working hours in poor conditions, to engage in physical development. Rambling societies became very popular in the first half of the 20th century, giving office workers the chance to escape the city on weekends and Bank Holidays and to put their white-collar bodies to the test on long walks in the countryside. This too made its way into fiction, as early as in 1859, when Thomas Hughes wrote his *The Scouring of the White Horse: or, the Long Vacation of a London Clerk*. Later novels like H.G. Wells's *Love and Mr Lewisham* (1899) and *The Wheels of Chance* (1896), Canning's *Mr. Finchley Discovers His England* and Francis Brett Young's *Mr. Lucton's Freedom* (1940) continued this narrative of the office worker emerging from a two-week vacation as a newly vigorous, energised and masculine specimen. Even more interesting are the ways in which this office-walking rambler tapped into particular constructions of identity that channelled a nostalgic rural nationalism and connected urban white-collar workers with their "yeoman" forebears – something Rose suggests hints also at a "nostalgia for a rigid social hierarchy".[84] What this trend demonstrated was a belief in the premise that, freed of the office, the clerk could become a different kind of person: outside the class structures that imperilled their financial and social existence, the office worker would become brave, adventurous, even more manly. And yet so many of these escapes reluctantly only take place in the brief holiday periods that the office worker is granted before the inevitable return to the desk. In a modern rendition of this, in *The Office*, Tim tries to quit the job he hates at Wernham Hogg and vows to go to university to follow a different path. After David Brent offers him a meagre pay rise, he capitulates and rescinds his resignation, and, in the script, the stage directions poignantly point to "Tim back in the office, still trapped behind his desk".[85]

CONCLUSION

From the interiors of crumbling Dickensian cellar spaces depicted in novels to the inadequacies of modern workplaces equipped with Kafka-esque technologies shown on screen, the office environment continues to be presented as grinding down its weary inhabitants. More even than the specific issues raised by authors, television writers and filmmakers regarding daily irritations, unsociable behaviours, environmental challenges and poor management, the key impression from multiple media is of a general negativity of experience. Without question, assumptions are drawn from the four-word phrase "work in an office" about the nature of the architectural space (in terms of design, interior and even mood), the activities the users within are occupied with and, by extension, the type of person that they are. The wide array of literary and media representations examined have demonstrated that there is a certain power to the ways in which the office – and office workers and office work – are portrayed, one that is long-lasting, surprisingly stable and largely uncritically replicated across forms. What is less commonly commented on is the fact that users of the office space are particularly vocal in exploring their own status and in offering critical and creative responses to their experiences. Abigail

Schoneboom has linked the more recent proliferation of office-based work bloggers to this "rich, legitimizing tradition" of "intellectual clerkdom" through her ethnographical approach to the long canon of office workers who wrote about their working lives and who, she argues, helped shape a literary culture that is still present today.[86] While certain stereotypes persist and can cause unreflective imprints on the ways in which the office is encountered – resulting in generalisations about peoples' impressions and experiences – there is merit in understanding how these function, how they have developed over the course of the last two hundred years and how they feed into inferences that continue to be made. This is important because, as Rose, Felski and Schoneboom point out, if we ignore the ways in which office workers are rendered "subhuman, machine-like, dead inside" – as the Edwardian clerk so often was – then we subconsciously reinforce the assumption that "middlebrow" culture is not worth studying.[87]

And yet, office cultures – made up more broadly of the architectural and interior design, the collective, individual and managerial practices and behaviours of those working within and the resultant experiences of office users – across such a vast range of global industries and employers affect or are relevant to so many of us. In Germany, for instance, the proportion of the population working in offices is reportedly around fifty percent; in the United States, thirteen out of every hundred people are employed explicitly in office and administrative roles while at least another twenty percent are in professional roles likely situated in offices.[88] Likewise in the U.K. census of 2021, the most common socio-economic classification in England and Wales was "lower managerial, administrative and professional occupations" – office workers – at just under twenty percent of those surveyed.[89] New television shows, films and novels – like Apple TV+'s Orwellian *Severance* (2022), Kazuo Ishiguro's 2022 film *Living* (itself adapted from the Japanese film *Ikiru* of 1952), Netflix's comedy *Unstable* (2023) and Natalie Sue's *I Hope This Finds You Well* (2024) – demonstrate the ongoing interest in office-based cultural representations. While changes during the COVID-19 pandemic meant that many started to question the future of the office, amid predictions that much of the existing infrastructure (office buildings, commuter rails, coffee shops, convenience stores) would be rendered obsolete by home working, those trajectories seem overly alarmist. Many "office workers" indeed have the potential for home or hybrid working rather than being situated in the office space five days a week, but the physical spaces, social interactions and methods of arranging work have largely settled into a new normal of around half of the working week spent on site. As a result, both historical and contemporary depictions of the office, as cultural products that simultaneously mirror and shape our expectations of the users and uses of this working environment, remain significant, relatable to audiences and thus worthy of understanding.

NOTES

[1] The Office, British Broadcasting Corporation (2003).
[2] Christopher J. Olson and CarrieLynn D. Reinhard, The Greatest Cult Television Shows of All Time (London, 2020), 141.
[3] Ingrid Jeacle and Lee Parker, 'The "Problem" of the Office: Scientific Management, Governmentality and the Strategy of Efficiency', in Business History, 55/7 (2013), 1074.
[4] Charles Lamb, 'The Superannuated Man', in idem, The Last Essays of Elia (London, 1833), 85.
[5] Charles Dickens, 'A Christmas Carol', in idem, Christmas Books (London, s.d.), 8.
[6] Scott Banville, '"A Book-Keeper, not an Accountant": Representing the Lower Middle Class from Victorian Novels and Music-hall Songs to Television Sitcoms', in Journal of Popular Culture, 44/1 (2011), 30.
[7] T.W.H. Crosland, The Suburbans (London, 1905), 22.
[8] Banville, A Book-Keeper.
[9] E.M. Forster, Howards End (London, 1961), 44.
[10] The Chartered Insurance Agency mentions a woman who took over her husband's role on his death in 1822 but explains that this was a rare occurrence. Instead, it suggests that the Prudential Insurance Company's employment of women from 1871 is the more accurate marker of a general acceptance of this extension to the workforce for a particular type of repetitive labour. Gregory Anderson's study The White Blouse Revolution also takes 1870 as its starting point. See 'The 19th Century Feminisation of the Insurance Office' (via https://insurancehistory.cii.co.uk); Anderson, The White Blouse Revolution: Female Office Workers Since 1870 (Manchester, 1988).
[11] Michelle Johansen, '"The Supposed Paradise of Pen and Ink": Self-Education and Social Mobility in the London Public Library (1880-1930)', in Cultural and Social History, 16/1 (2019), 56.
[12] Charles Dickens, Sketches by Boz (London, 1995), 7.
[13] Ibid.
[14] See for instance Dan Evans, A Nation of Shopkeepers: The Unstoppable Rise of the Petty Bourgeoisie (London, 2023); Nicola Bishop, Lower-Middle-Class Nation: The White-Collar Worker in British Popular Culture (London, 2021).
[15] Rita Felski, 'Nothing to Declare: Identity, Shame, and the Lower Middle Class', in PMLA, 115/1 (2000), 34.
[16] Stephen Mihm, 'Clerks, Classes, and Conflicts: A Response to Michael Zakim's "The Business Clerk as Social Revolutionary"', in Journal of the Early Republic, 26 (2006), 608.
[17] Evans, A Nation; Michael Heller, London Clerical Workers 1880-1914: Development of the Labour Market (London, 2011); Ross McKibbin, Classes and Cultures: England 1918-1951 (Oxford, 1998); Geoffrey Crossick (ed.), The Lower Middle Class in Britain, 1870-1914 (London, 1977); Gregory Anderson, Victorian Clerks (Manchester, 1976); Michel Crozier, The World of the Office Worker (London, 1971); David Lockwood, The Blackcoated Worker (London, 1958); F.D. Klingender, The Condition of Clerical Labour (London, 1935).
[18] Robertson's work is an interestingly lower-middle-class-centred chapter in a collection otherwise about the working class. See Nicole Robertson, 'Women at Work: Activism, Feminism and the Rise of the Female Office Worker During the First World War and its Immediate Aftermath', in Keith Laybourn and John Shepherd (eds.), Labour and Working-Class Lives: Essays to Celebrate the Life and Work of Chris Wrigley (Manchester, 2017). See also Helen Glew, Gender, Rhetoric and Regulation: Women's Work in the Civil Service and the London County Council, 1900-55 (Manchester, 2016); Anderson, White Blouse Revolution; Julie Berebitsky, Sex and the Office: A History of Gender,

Power and Desire (New Haven, 2012); Graham Lowe, Women in the Administrative Revolution (Cambridge, 1987); Meta Zimmeck, 'Clerical Work for Women, 1850-1914,' in Angela V. John (ed.), Unequal Opportunities: Women's Employment in England, 1800-1918 (Oxford, 1986); Meta Zimmeck, 'Strategies and Stratagems for the Employment of Women in the British Civil Service, 1919-1939', in The Historical Journal, 27/4 (1984).

19 John Carey, The Intellectuals and the Masses (London, 1992).
20 Jonathan Rose, The Intellectual Life of the British Working Classes (London, 2002), 407.
21 Jeremy Lewis, The Chatto Book of Office Life (London, 1992), 114.
22 Jonathan Wild, The Rise of the Office Clerk in Literary Culture, 1880-1939 (Basingstoke, 2006), 7.
23 See for instance Connie Wachter and Christoph Ehland (eds.), Middlebrow and Gender, 1890-1945 (Leiden, 2016) (particularly my chapter 'Middlebrow "Everyman" or Modernist Figurehead? Experiencing Modernity through the Eyes of the Humble Clerk'); Erica Brown and Mary Grover (eds.), Middlebrow Literary Cultures: The Battle of the Brows, 1920-1960 (London, 2012); Nicola Humble, The Feminine Middlebrow Novel, 1920s-1950s: Class, Domesticity and Bohemianism (Oxford, 2001).
24 A. James Hammerton, 'The Perils of Mrs Pooter: Satire, Modernity and Motherhood in the Lower Middle Class in England, 1870-1920', in Women's History Review, 8/2 (1999); A. James Hammerton, 'Pooterism or Partnership? Marriage and Masculine Identity in the Lower Middle Class, 1870-1920', in Journal of British Studies, 38/3 (1999).
25 Richard Higgins, 'Feeling like a Clerk in H.G. Wells', in Victorian Studies, 50/2 (2008).
26 Lena Wånggren, 'Typewriters and Typists: Secretarial Agency at the Fin de Siècle', in idem (ed.), Gender, Technology and the New Woman (Edinburgh, 2017).
27 Erica van Boven, 'The Emergence of the Middlebrow Novel in the Netherlands: The "New Novels" Series of World Library', in Belphégor, 15/2 (2017).
28 Leah Price and Pamela Thurschwell (eds.), Literary Secretaries/Secretarial Culture (Abingdon, 2017), 10.
29 Carl Rhodes and Robert Westwood, Critical Representations of Work and Organization in Popular Culture (London, 2008), 2.
30 Alexia Panayiotou, '"Macho" Managers and Organizational Heroes: Competing Masculinities in Popular Films', in Organization 17/6 (2010), 661.
31 Francis Duffy, 'Office Buildings and Organisational Change', in Anthony D. King (ed.), Buildings and Society: Essays on the Social Development of the Built Environment (London, 1980), 157.
32 He mentions David Copperfield in Charles Dickens's novel and Charley Tudor in Anthony Trollope's The Three Clerks. See Banville, A Book-Keeper, 17.
33 See for instance Michael Homberg, Laura Lükemann and Anja-Kristin Abendroth, 'From "Home Work" to "Home Office Work"? Perpetuating Discourses and Use Patterns of Tele(home)work Since the 1970s: Historical and Comparative Social Perspectives', in Work Organisation, Labour & Globalisation, 17/1 (2023), 75; Eva Lindell, Irina Popova and Anna Uhlin, 'Digitalization of Office Work: An Ideological Dilemma of Structure and Flexibility', in Journal of Organizational Change Management, 35/8 (2022).
34 Sigurd O. Schmidt, 'Great Works of Literature as a Source of Historical Knowledge', in Russian Studies in History, 47/1 (2008), 14.
35 Andrew Crisell, A Study of Modern Television: Thinking Inside the Box (London, 2006).
36 Allan H. Pasco, 'Literature as Historical Archive', in New Literary History, 35/3 (2004), 374.
37 Paul Jordan, The Author in the Office: Narrative Writing in Twentieth-Century Argentina and Uruguay (Woodbridge, 2006), 1.
38 Johansen, The Supposed Paradise, 51.
39 See for instance Geoffrey Spurr, 'The London YMCA: A Haven of Masculine Self-Improvement and Socialization for the Late-Victorian and Edwardian Clerk', in Canadian Journal of History, 37/2 (2002).
40 Timothy Alborn, 'Quill-Driving: British Life Insurance Clerks and Occupational Mobility, 1800-1914', in Business History Review, 82/1 (2008), 51; Jerome Bjelopera, City of Clerks: Office and Sales Workers in Philadelphia, 1870-1920 (Urbana, 2005).
41 Felski, Nothing to Declare, 36.
42 E.g. George Bernard Shaw, Richard Church and Anthony Trollope.
43 Lewis, The Chatto Book, 80.

44 Alborn, Quill-Driving, 40.
45 Ceri Sullivan, Literature in the Public Sphere: Sublime Bureaucracy (London, 2013), 1-2.
46 Ibid.
47 Colin's Sandwich, British Broadcasting Corporation (1988-1990).
48 Ali Haggett, A History of Male Psychological Disorders, 1945-1980 (London, 2015), 7.
49 TV Tropes (https://tvtropes.org).
50 The Office (U.S.), NBC Universal (2005-2015).
51 Gail Honeyman, Eleanor Oliphant is Completely Fine (London, 2017), 3.
52 Charles Dickens, The Pickwick Papers (London, 1900), 276; Charles Dickens, Dombey and Sons (London, 1890), 137.
53 Shan Bullock, Robert Thorne (London, 1907), 37.
54 Shan Bullock, Mr Ruby Jumps the Traces (London, 1917), 8.
55 P.D. James, 'A Very Commonplace Murder', in idem, The Mistletoe Murder and Other Stories (London, 2016), 67.
56 Frank Swinnerton, The Young Idea: A Comedy of Environment (London, 1910), 233. See for instance also Edwin Pugh, The Broken Honeymoon (London, 1908), 119.
57 Elizabeth Jane Howard, 'After Julius', in Lewis, The Chatto Book, 55.
58 David Nobbs, The Fall and Rise of Reginald Perrin (London, 1990), 7.
59 The Fall and Rise of Reginald Perrin, British Broadcasting Corporation (1976-1979).
60 Hugh Leonard, Out After Dark (London, 1989), 76.
61 B.S. Johnson, Christie Malry's Own Double Entry (London, 2001), 4.
62 John Lanchester, 'Foreword', in Johnson, Christie Malry's Own Double Entry, 1.
63 Nigel Williams, The Wimbledon Poisoner (London, 1990), 5.
64 Ibid., 7.
65 Ibid., 299.
66 Ibid., 173. For more on this trope in Christie's work, see Nicola Bishop, 'Mundane or Menacing? "Nobodies" in the Detective Fiction of Agatha Christie', in Clues: A Journal of Detection, 34/1 (2016).
67 The Office, British Broadcasting Corporation (2001-2003); Victor Canning, Mr Finchley Discovers His England (London, 1972), 7; H.G. Wells, The History of Mr. Polly (London, 1969), 20; Dad's Army, British Broadcasting Corporation (1969-1977).
68 George Grossmith and Weedon Grossmith, Diary of a Nobody (Hertfordshire, 2006), 117; T.S. Eliot, 'The Love Song of J. Alfred Prufrock', in idem, The Complete Poems and Plays (ed. by Archie Burnett) (London, 1969), 14.
69 Blackadder Goes Forth, British Broadcasting Corporation (1989); R.F. Delderfield, The Dreaming Suburb (London, 1987), 11.
70 Shan Bullock, Robert Thorne (London, 1907), 37.
71 Ibid., 38.
72 Ibid., 37-38.
73 Ibid., 141.
74 Georg Lukács, History and Class Consciousness: Studies in Marxist Dialectics (London, 1968), 88.
75 Shan Bullock, Robert Thorne, 73.
76 Cited by David Lockwood, The Blackcoated Worker (Oxford, 1969), 90.
77 The Good Life, British Broadcasting Corporation (1975-1978).
78 Keith Waterhouse, Office Life (London, 1986), 59.
79 P.G. Wodehouse, 'A Sea of Troubles', in idem, The Man with Two Left Feet [Kindle edition], 128-129; D.H. Lawrence, Sons and Lovers (London, 1995), 94; Delderfield, The Dreaming Suburb, 15.
80 George Orwell, Keep the Aspidistra Flying (Harmondsworth, 1987), 1; Jerome K. Jerome, Three Men in a Boat (London, 1994), 8.
81 J.B. Priestley, Angel Pavement (Letchworth, 1953), 20.
82 Anderson, Victorian Clerks, 18.
83 Michael Zakim, 'The Business Clerk as Social Revolutionary, or a Labor History of the Nonproducing Classes', in Journal of the Early Republic, 26/4 (2006), 571.

84   Nicola Bishop, 'Ruralism, Masculinity, and National Identity: The Rambling Clerk in Fiction, 1900-1940', in Journal of British Studies, 54/3 (2015); Rose, Intellectual Life, 402.
85   Ricky Gervais and Stephen Merchant, The Office: The Scripts (Series 1) (London, 2004), 267.
86   Abigail Schoneboom, 'The Romance of the Lowly Clerk: Recognizing the Tradition of Office Intellectualism', in Organization, 22/6 (2015), 833.
87   Rose, Intellectual Life, 393.
88   Andrea Hammermann and Oliver Stettes, 'Büroarbeit im Wandel: Analyse der Arbeitsbedingungen von Bürobeschäftigten', IW-Report 62 (2024) (via www.iwkoeln.de); 'May 2023 National Occupational Employment and Wage Estimates' (via www.bls.gov).
89   'Statistical bulletin, Industry and Occupation, England and Wales' (2022) (via www.ons.gov.uk).

BIBLIOGRAPHY

Timothy Alborn, 'Quill-Driving: British Life Insurance Clerks and Occupational Mobility, 1800-1914', in Business History Review, 82/1 (2008), 31-58.
Gregory Anderson, Victorian Clerks (Manchester, 1976).
Gregory Anderson, White Blouse Revolution: Female Office Workers Since 1870 (Manchester, 1988).
Scott Banville, '"A Book-Keeper, not an Accountant": Representing the Lower Middle Class from Victorian Novels and Music-hall Songs to Television Sitcoms', in Journal of Popular Culture, 44/1 (2011), 16-36.
Julie Berebitsky, Sex and the Office: A History of Gender, Power and Desire (New Haven, 2012).
Nicola Bishop, 'Ruralism, Masculinity, and National Identity: The Rambling Clerk in Fiction, 1900-1940', in Journal of British Studies 54/3 (2015), 654-678.
Nicola Bishop, 'Mundane or Menacing? "Nobodies" in the Detective Fiction of Agatha Christie', in Clues: A Journal of Detection, 34/1 (2016), 82-95.
Nicola Bishop, Lower-Middle-Class Nation: The White-Collar Worker in British Popular Culture (London, 2021).
Jerome Bjelopera, City of Clerks: Office and Sales Workers in Philadelphia, 1870-1920 (Champaign, 2005).
Erica van Boven, 'The Emergence of the Middlebrow Novel in the Netherlands: The "New Novels" Series of World Library', in Belphégor, 15/2 (2017).
Erica Bown and Mary Grover (eds.), Middlebrow Literary Cultures: The Battle of the Brows, 1920-1960 (London, 2012).
Shan Bullock, Robert Thorne (London, 1907).
Victor Canning, Mr Finchley Discovers His England (London, 1934).
John Carey, The Intellectuals and the Masses (London, 1992).
Agatha Christie, The ABC Murders (London, 1936).
Andrew Crisell, A Study of Modern Television: Thinking Inside the Box (London, 2006).
Thomas William Hodgson Crosland, The Suburbans (London, 1905).
Gregory Crossick (ed.), The Lower Middle Class in Britain, 1870-1914 (London, 1977).
Michel Crozier, The World of the Office Worker (London, 1971).
Ronald Frederick Delderfield, The Dreaming Suburb (London, 1987).
Charles Dickens, 'A Christmas Carol', in idem, Christmas Books (London, s.d.), 7-87.
Charles Dickens, Dombey and Sons (London, 1890).
Charles Dickens, Pickwick Papers (London, 1900).
Charles Dickens, Sketches by Boz (London, 1995).
Francis Duffy, 'Office Buildings and Organisational Change', in Anthony D. King (ed.), Buildings and Society: Essays on the Social Development of the Built Environment (London, 1980), 140-157.
Thomas Stearns Eliot, The Complete Poems and Plays (London, 1969).
Dan Evans, A Nation of Shopkeepers: The Unstoppable Rise of the Petty Bourgeoisie (London, 2023).
Rita Felski, 'Nothing to Declare: Identity, Shame, and the Lower Middle Class', in PMLA, 115/1 (2000), 33-45.
Edward Morgan Forster, Howards End (London, 1961).
Ricky Gervais and Stephen Merchant, The Office: The Scripts (Series 1) (London, 2004).
George Gissing, The Odd Women (London, 1987).

Helen Glew, Gender, Rhetoric and Regulation: Women's Work in the Civil Service and the London County Council, 1900-55 (Manchester, 2016).
George Grossmith and Weedon Grossmith, Diary of a Nobody (Hertfordshire, 2006).
Ali Haggett, A History of Male Psychological Disorders, 1945-1980 (London, 2015).
A. James Hammerton, 'The Perils of Mrs Pooter: Satire, Modernity and Motherhood in the Lower Middle Class in England, 1870-1920', in Women's History Review, 8/2 (1999), 261-276.
A. James Hammerton, 'Pooterism or Partnership? Marriage and Masculine Identity in the Lower Middle Class, 1870-1920', in Journal of British Studies, 38 (1999), 291-321.
Michael Heller, London Clerical Workers 1880-1914: Development of the Labour Market (London, 2011).
Richard Higgins, 'Feeling like a Clerk in H.G. Wells', in Victorian Studies, 50/2 (2008), 457-475.
Michael Homberg, Laura Lükemann and Anja-Kristin Abendroth, 'From "Home Work" to "Office Work"? Perpetuating Discourses and Use Patterns of Tele(home)work Since the 1970s: Historical and Comparative Social Perspectives', in Work Organisation, Labour & Globalisation, 17/1 (2023), 74-116.
Gail Honeyman, Eleanor Oliphant is Completely Fine (London, 2017).
Thomas Hughes, The Scouring of the White Horse: or, the Long Vacation of a London Clerk (London, 1959).
Nicola Humble, The Feminine Middlebrow Novel, 1920s-1950s: Class, Domesticity and Bohemianism (Oxford, 2001).
Phyllis Dorothy James, The Mistletoe Murder and Other Stories (London, 2016).
Ingrid Jeacle and Lee Parker, 'The "Problem" of the Office: Scientific Management, Governmentality and the Strategy of Efficiency', in Business History, 55/7 (2013), 1074-1099.
Jerome K. Jerome, Three Men in a Boat (London, 1994).
Michelle Johansen, '"The Supposed Paradise of Pen and Ink": Self-Education and Social Mobility in the London Public Library (1880-1930)', in Cultural and Social History, 16/1 (2019), 47-65.
Bryan Stanley Johnson, Christie Malry's Own Double Entry (London, 2001).
Paul Jordan, The Author in the Office: Narrative Writing in Twentieth-Century Argentina and Uruguay (Woodbridge, 2006).
Francis Donald Klingender, The Condition of Clerical Labour (London, 1935).
Charles Lamb, 'The Superannuated Man', in idem, The Last Essays of Elia (London, 1833), 83-94.
David Herbert Lawrence, Sons and Lovers (London, 1995).
Hugh Leonard, Out After Dark (London, 1989).
Jeremy Lewis, The Chatto Book of Office Life (London, 1992).
Eva Lindell, Irina Popova and Anna Uhlin, 'Digitalization of Office Work: An Ideological Dilemma of Structure and Flexibility', in Journal of Organizational Change Management, 35/8 (2022), 103-114.
David Lockwood, The Blackcoated Worker (London, 1958).
Graham Lowe, Women in the Administrative Revolution (Cambridge, 1987).
Georg Lukács, History and Class Consciousness: Studies in Marxist Dialectics (London, 1968).
Ross McKibbin, Classes and Cultures: England 1918-1951 (Oxford, 1998).
Stephen Mihm, 'Clerks, Classes, and Conflicts: A Response to Michael Zakim's "The Business Clerk as Social Revolutionary"', in Journal of the Early Republic, 26 (2006), 605-615.
Christopher J. Olsen and CarrieLynn D. Reinhard, The Greatest Cult Television Shows of All Time (London, 2020).
George Orwell, Keep the Aspidistra Flying (Harmondsworth, 1987).
Alexia Panayiotou, '"Macho" Managers and Organizational Heroes: Competing Masculinities in Popular Films', in Organization 17/6 (2010), 659-683.
Allan H. Pasco, 'Literature as Historical Archive', in New Literary History, 35/3 (2004), 373-394.
Leah Price and Pamela Thurschwell (eds.), Literary Secretaries/Secretarial Culture (Abingdon, 2017).
Edwin Pugh, The Broken Honeymoon (London, 1908).
Carl Rhodes and Robert Westwood, Critical Representations of Work and Organization in Popular Culture (London, 2008).
Nicole Robertson, 'Women at Work: Activism, Feminism and the Rise of the Female Office Worker During the First World War and its Immediate Aftermath', in Keith Laybourn and John Shepherd (eds.), Labour and Working-Class Lives: Essays to Celebrate the Life and Work of Chris Wrigley (Manchester, 2017), 172-193.

Sigurd Ottovich Schmidt, 'Great Works of Literature as a Source of Historical Knowledge', in Russian Studies in History, 47/1 (2008), 14-29.
Abigail Schoneboom, 'The Romance of the Lowly Clerk: Recognizing the Tradition of Office Intellectualism', in Organization, 22/6 (2015), 832-846.
Geoffrey Spurr, 'The London YMCA: A Haven of Masculine Self-Improvement and Socialization for the Late-Victorian and Edwardian Clerk', in Canadian Journal of History, 37/2 (2002), 275-301.
Natalie Sue, I Hope This Finds You Well (New York, 2024).
Ceri Sullivan, Literature in the Public Sphere: Sublime Bureaucracy (London, 2013).
Frank Swinnerton, The Young Idea: A Comedy of Environment (London, 1910).
Cornelia Wächter and Christoph Ehland, Middlebrow and Gender, 1890-1945 (Leiden, 2016).
Lena Wånggren, Gender, Technology and the New Woman (Edinburgh, 2017).
Keith Waterhouse, Office Life (London, 1986).
Herbert George Wells, The Wheels of Chance (London, 1896).
Herbert George Wells, Love and Mr Lewisham (London, 1899).
Jonathan Wild, The Rise of the Office Clerk in Literary Culture, 1880-1939 (Basingstoke, 2006).
Nigel Williams, The Wimbledon Poisoner (London, 1990).
Pelham Grenville Wodehouse, 'A Sea of Troubles', in idem, The Man with Two Left Feet [Kindle edition].
Francis Brett Young, Mr. Lucton's Freedom (London, 1940).
Meta Zimmeck, 'Strategies and Stratagems for the Employment of Women in the British Civil Service, 1919-1939', in The Historical Journal, 27/4 (1984), 901-924.
Meta Zimmeck, 'Clerical Work for Women, 1850-1914', in Angela V. John (ed.), Unequal Opportunities: Women's Employment in England, 1800-1918 (Oxford, 1986), 153-177.

Film and television works

Blackadder Goes Forth, British Broadcasting Corporation (1989).
Bridget Jones's Diary, Miramax (2001).
Colin's Sandwich, British Broadcasting Corporation (1988-1990).
Dad's Army, British Broadcasting Corporation (1969-1977).
Ever Decreasing Circles, British Broadcasting Corporation (1984-1989).
The Fall and Rise of Reginald Perrin, British Broadcasting Corporation (1976-1979).
Girl from Rio, Lolafilms and Casanova Pictures Productions (2001).
The Good Life, British Broadcasting Corporation (1975-1978).
The IT Crowd, Channel 4 (2006-2013).
Keeping Up Appearances, British Broadcasting Corporation (1990-1995).
The Legacy of Reginald Perrin, British Broadcasting Corporation (1996).
Living, Film Four (2022).
Mary Poppins, Walt Disney (1964).
Men Behaving Badly, ITV/British Broadcasting Corporation (1993-1999).
The Office, British Broadcasting Corporation (2001-2003).
The Office (U.S.), NBC Universal (2005-2015).
Paddington, StudioCanal (2014).
Paddington 2, StudioCanal (2017).
The Rebel, Associated British Picture Corporation (1961).
Severance, AppleTV+ (2022-2025).
Unstable, Netflix (2023-24).

PART 2
THE IMPACT OF NORMATIVITY AND STANDARDISATION ON THE OFFICE AS AN "ENVIRONMENT"

Chapter 3
Too Cold? Gendered Conflicts over Mechanical Cooling in Early Post-war Japanese Office Spaces

Tatsuya Mitsuda

INTRODUCTION

A key feature of the modern workplace is the extent to which white-collar employees around the world spend a significant proportion of their working lives "encased" in air-conditioned offices, hermetically sealed off from the outside urban environment.[1] Since the Milam Building in San Antonio, Texas provided the first fully air-conditioned office in 1928 – "to out-of-town firms whose personnel were not used to the local climate" – climate control technology has become a standard feature of curtain wall office towers.[2] It has even been adopted in temperate regions, where external climatic conditions do not necessarily make the installation of air-conditioning a foregone thermal solution. According to architectural historian Carol Willis, who has studied high-rises in New York and Chicago, before the 1950s commercial buildings interacted with the outside environment: office interiors relied on natural light and air to make the workplace habitable.[3] From the 1950s, however, skyscrapers became increasingly disconnected from their surroundings, as office buildings became self-sufficient in manufacturing artificial light and air through electrical and mechanical means. As a result, office buildings have become largely dependent on fossil fuels to maintain optimal indoor climatic conditions, laying the foundations for today's criticism of the impact of air-conditioning on global warning.

Much of the appeal for employers behind the self-manufacture of "perfect weather conditions" – to paraphrase the marketing claim made by the management of the Milam Building – was the technology's potential to extract more labour out of workers' bodies during periods when their performance lagged.[4] Air-conditioning thus dovetailed with the scientific management principles of Frederick Winslow Taylor, whose influential 1911 book inspired managers to apply factory-floor insights to the office to boost productivity and efficiency in clerical work. In the words of one satisfied client, who became one of the first 565 occupants of the Milam Building:

> [The] deciding factor was the prime efficiency of the building provided by the modern air-conditioning system. Being able to work in a constant comfortable temperature undisturbed by noise, drafts and dust, every day sees more work accomplished with less fatigue and more real enjoyment.[5]

As the architectural historian Joseph Siry has recently shown, the investors who underwrote the construction of office buildings in the United States believed that air-conditioning was critical for keeping tenants and securing high rents. During the Great Depression, offices equipped with air-conditioning were calculated to be 50 percent more valuable than those without it. Such financial benefits to developers, real estate agents and employers alike have remained relevant, shaping the character of office buildings as embodiments of capitalism. However, as demand for air-conditioning has grown, the International Energy Agency has warned that increased reliance on mechanical cooling, particularly in hot and developing countries, poses an existential global energy crisis that could have severe environmental consequences.[6]

As "cool" office spaces have become the norm, scholars have shown that mechanical cooling can also have profound social and cultural consequences. Historian Raymond Arsenault argued that the "regional distinctiveness" of the American South was lost when air-conditioning colonised 90 percent of high-rise office buildings, banks, apartments and railway carriages by the mid-1970s.[7] In his damning verdict, the technology served to irreparably alter "the daily and seasonal rhythms that were once an inescapable feature of southern living".[8] In an overview of the global impact of the "homogenising" tendencies of air-conditioning, geographer Stephen Healy similarly pointed out how the "thermal monotony" of mechanical cooling has transformed "climatically influenced and thermally configured practices".[9] In Mexico, for example, the rise of cool offices has led to a decline in the practice of the siesta; the national government went so far as to ban the custom of napping in government offices in 1999, forcing civil servants to conform to the capitalist and Western norm of working without interruption throughout the day and year.[10] Thermal comfort researchers have contended that the imposition of universal thermal standards which ignore "important cultural, climatic, social and contextual dimensions of comfort" has led "to an exaggerated 'need' for refrigerated, cool still air".[11] The social historian Marsha Ackermann has argued, applying a Foucauldian lens, that "air-conditioning can be and has been used to discipline both the individual human body and the social order, forbidding sweat, enforcing uniform and continuous productivity, and muddling traditional connections with time, weather and season".[12] As air-conditioning becomes increasingly embedded in modern societies, some have recently called for policymakers to promote alternative, low-tech or traditional thermal coping strategies before it is too late.[13]

Building on these insights, my chapter asks how and why office spaces in Japan – which is one of the most air-conditioned countries in the world – became "cool". In doing so, it follows the work done on Singapore to provide a much-needed example from outside the United States – on which most past research has focused – to enrich the history behind the rise of "thermal modernity".[14] Focusing on the 1960s as the critical period when a decisive shift towards an air-conditioned society took place, the chapter shows that, as in the United States, which was highly influential in the adoption of mechanical cooling in Japan, economic priorities took precedence in the diffusion of climate control technology. Viewed as a necessary investment in a country that was considered to suffer from the "wrong" climate for economic growth, especially during the hot and humid summer months when commercial activity could be severely affected, I argue that the colonisation of office space by the air-conditioner was by no means inevitable. Initially, traditional thermal norms – which taught people to endure rather than escape summer – did not make mechanical cooling the most obvious solution, especially in vernacular houses that had been designed for the summer. Eventually, as Western-style commercial buildings – which tended to amplify the thermal experience – came to dominate the cityscape, the case for installing air-conditioning in offices to improve productivity became compelling. Equally important to the creation of cool offices, I argue, was the need to maintain stable climatic and hygienic conditions where electronic computers could operate. Finally, skyscrapers cemented the place of cool offices, as the constant exposure of upper floors to high levels of radiation and wind made it essential for these buildings to manufacture their own climates throughout the year.

In exploring the relationship between the office and mechanical cooling, this chapter also takes seriously the call made by historians

Gianenrico Bernasconi and Stefan Nellen to interrogate the spaces where office life unfolded. Bernasconi and Nellen frame the office as a complex space in which "architectural shells, the interior design, the placement of machines and the adaptation to atmospheric conditions" shaped workers' interactions in powerful and disciplinary ways.[15] Because men and women shared the same office space, such interactions were also highly gendered: in the interwar period, male bosses constructed office spaces where an army of female clerks, working as typists and data punchers, were made to collaborate with machines in the production of information.[16] It was into this "gendered economy" that air-conditioners became embedded in the post-war era. In his chapter on the history of the filing cabinet, media historian Craig Robertson writes that there were discussions about appropriate clothing for female workers: he shows how female clerks in the interwar United States were required to wear clothes that were neither too revealing nor obstructive in order to do their jobs as filers properly.[17] Within the Japanese post-war context, a major consequence of the rise of mechanical cooling in buildings was its disproportionate impact on the bodies of so-called "office ladies". As part of their emancipation from a patriarchal society, women had embraced lighter, more revealing clothing for the summer. But as the cool office spread, female workers struggled to acclimatise and were instructed to dress up, nominally to protect their health. In the heated debates about appropriate summer dress, it was thus invariably women, not men, who had to change their clothes. Although they were subjected to withering criticism about their own style of dress, men benefitted from the advent of cool offices: they could cling on to their shirts, jackets and ties in the summer. It was only when the political and economic risks of reliance on imported fossil fuels from the Middle East became apparent in the 1970s that men began to shed some of their clothing, in response to state encouragement. In this way, the chapter demonstrates – echoing arguments from science and technology studies – that air-conditioning was far from a neutral piece of technology: it helped reinforce office hierarchies and discipline female bodies.[18]

THE SWELTERING OFFICE

In the summer of 1955, Tokyo experienced a prolonged heat wave, with highs consistently exceeding 30 degrees Celsius and 75 percent relative humidity.[19] As the long summer dragged on, the *Asahi* newspaper reported on scenes of sweltering workplaces, mocking the ineffective methods used by male office workers to cope with the heat and humidity of the capital's summer, where the urban heat island effect was beginning to exacerbate the thermal experience.[20] At the Ministry of Construction Building, where officials from various ministries worked in cramped conditions, workers from the manager to the catering staff took off their shirts and stripped down to their vests. Trying to work through the heat and humidity, workers took turns buying ice, leaving their seats from time to time to douse themselves with cold water and rearranging their desks to maximise exposure to the outside air. Because of the humidity, this did little to cool their bodies. The indoor climate of the nearby Prime Minister's Residence was no better: the American architect Frank Lloyd Wright had not taken into account the unpleasantness of the Tokyo summer and had designed a poorly ventilated building in which about a hundred mandarins worked in oven-like conditions. The two exceptions to the lack of cool spaces in the government district of Kasumigaseki were the Cabinet Room and the Ministers' Room, to which the Prime Minister Hatoyama Ichirō escaped during Diet sessions.[21] Two kilometres away, in the Daiichi Insurance Building, where General Douglas MacArthur directed the politics of the American occupation, office workers laboured in a pleasantly cool indoor environment, with air-conditioning helping to keep the temperature at 27 degrees throughout the building. Employees were reportedly so happy with their cool office space that they chose to stay at work rather than go home or take summer holidays.

In the 1950s, most office buildings in Japan did not have air-conditioning. A few units had been installed in factories in the 1920s and 1930s, where the primary purpose was not to cool human bodies but to preserve the value of goods – a precedent that later cast shadows on how human bodies interacted with mechanical cooling. As in the United States, manufacturing facilities producing food, medicines, cotton, matches, weapons, prints and photographs needed to fabricate stable climatic conditions to prevent either spoilage or combustion.[22] Mechanical cooling was also introduced in the livestock industry, where the same economic rationale was applied to cool down animal bodies to prevent the loss of meat or dairy. The production of uniform products, achieved by limiting exposure to seasonal variations and the vagaries of the weather, was a must for businesses involved in the mass production of goods at stable prices. Mechanical cooling was then extended to theatres, cinemas, department stores and offices, most of which were concentrated in the two major metropolitan areas of Tokyo and Osaka. However, the uptake of air-conditioning was slow. Between 1926 and 1931, for example, only about ten units were installed in offices nationwide, mostly in banks that could afford them.[23]

Cost was not the only factor holding back the spread of mechanical cooling. Traditional thermal norms that encouraged people to endure heat and humidity also played a part.[24] Exposure to the summer sun was considered healthy for strengthening body and mind; morning exercises designed to warm rather than cool the body were encouraged to prepare workers for the hot and humid day ahead; and cultivating the right frame of mind by visualising cool places was also common practice in the pre-air-conditioning era. Crucially, Japanese vernacular architecture, which was built primarily with the summer in mind, helped to mitigate the effects of the heat and humidity. In Tokyo, houses were typically built on an east-west axis to invite the summer winds to pass through the dwellings; floors were raised to reduce the impact of refracted sunlight; wooden corridors and verandas that formed the perimeter of the houses shielded the living areas from the scorching sun; sliding doors and blinds that would otherwise function as room dividers could be rolled back to expose the dwelling to natural ventilation and coolness. As climate change has sparked an interest in environmental architecture, architects have looked to Japan and Asia for inspiration on how to make buildings more sustainable.[25]

In contrast to domestic housing, less attention was paid to designing office buildings with summer in mind, as public buildings modelled on modern European architectural styles predominated. In the 1930s, the German architect Bruno Taut, living in Japan as an exile from the Nazi regime, criticised how Western-style architecture was exacerbating thermal conditions in places such as schools and offices. On a visit to a governor's office, Taut was alarmed to find that the building completely ignored local climatic conditions because it had "thick massive walls" and was "without any draught":

> The European windows had no eaves and there were stone tiles on the big balcony. [...] The blazing sky dazzled us and the tiles on the balcony heated the air which entered the room. The cloudy sky seemed to burn more than ever. Its diffused rays penetrated everywhere. There were no cool shadows: the heat and light blazed intolerably.[26]

It is important to note that such descriptions did not mean that workers could not stand the heat and humidity. Most rarely complained about

Fig. 3.1. The Marunouchi financial district in the late 1950s before the advent of curtain-wall towers. (Reproduced with permission from Ikuta Makoto.)

their thermal predicament and turned to practices that maintained a cool mindset – a mindset that the state exploited to full effect in wartime propaganda that called on the country to show thermal solidarity with troops fighting in hotter and more humid conditions in the Asia-Pacific.[27]

Office buildings were certainly not climate indifferent. To palliate the heat and humidity (as well as to compensate for the lack of light), office buildings in Tokyo (whose height was limited to 31 metres because of fears of earthquakes, typhoons and fires) were largely built in the shape of a cube or a rectangle, with a central courtyard that served as a pathway through which air and light could enter the buildings to cool and refresh the bodies of their occupants.[28] As Carol Willis has written about New York and Chicago, office interiors – before the advent of artificial light and air – depended on sunlight and breezes for lighting and ventilation.[29] For less temperate climates such as southern Europe and South America, Le Corbusier famously conceived climatically-sensitive buildings with brise-soleils, louvers, screens and blinds to mitigate the effects of the sun and adapt building façades to local conditions.[30] By the 1950s, however, it had become increasingly clear that such buildings were becoming part of the urban heat island problem.[31] As the post-war construction boom transformed the cityscape of the Japanese capital (which had been devastated by aerial bombing), concerns arose about the ability of existing office buildings to generate sufficient levels of natural cooling. Courtyards shrank in size and densely packed office buildings – built with very little space between them – intensified the thermal experience, especially in Tokyo's financial district of Marunouchi, where office buildings were sprouting up (Fig. 3.1.). The sweltering workplaces in the neighbouring government district, reported by *Asahi*, became part of a trend. Despite the existence of climate control technology, a high-tech solution was not a foregone conclusion in the early to mid-1950s. The *Asahi* itself looked to more tropical regions for inspiration, calling for the introduction of siestas: workers should be allowed to go home, take a nap and return to the office.[32]

MECHANICAL COOLING AND "RATIONALISATION"

Before the advent of cool office spaces, traditional (and masculine) thermal norms were seen as an obstacle to rationalising the behaviour of white-collar workers. Male office workers – the so-called "salarymen" – were ridiculed by women for clinging to formal attire. Although there were exceptions during extremely hot weather conditions, the seeming stubborn determination of men to wear jackets and ties – a sartorial style derived from the very different climate of northern Europe – became a bone of contention. In 1954, the women's pages of the *Yomiuri* newspaper took issue with the sight of sweating male workers.[33] Echoing the *Asahi*'s calls for the introduction of siestas, it suggested that office workers could learn a thing or two from the tropical south, which was portrayed as dealing with climate conditions more "rationally". The paper advised men to wear silk Hawaiian aloha shirts instead, praising them as cheap, soft and cool on the skin. To further increase air circulation, the shirts could also be worn with the shirttails hanging out of the trousers. A more radical suggestion made by the *Yomiuri* was to urge young workers to embrace cotton polo shirts, which were presented as a boon to housewives, freeing them from the chore of ironing. Recognising that the suggestion might be too controversial, the paper was quick to reassure the public that it was not referring to the ostentatious kind typically worn by delinquents. It also warned readers that the shirttails should be tucked into trousers when worn in the office. In an editorial a year later, the *Yomiuri* mocked women's suggestions about aloha shirts, which the male writer thought went too far and gave the wrong impression at formal meetings.[34] The most male workers could be expected to accept was to remove their ties, he wrote. In this way, calls for male office workers to dress more casually were slapped down.

Much of the impetus for promoting mechanical cooling came from civil engineers frustrated with traditional thermal norms that made a virtue of enduring the heat and humidity. More needed to be done, they argued from the mid-1930s onwards, for Tokyo to overcome its "inferior" climate and become more like Berlin, Chicago, London or Paris – a reference to the influential ideas of Ellsworth Huntington (1915) who claimed a causal link between climate and levels of civilisation.[35] The civil engineer Tsuji Jirō was one of the first to call for air-conditioning as a means of accelerating the country's post-war growth. He observed that, in advanced cities such as New York, mechanical cooling was becoming standard, not only in commercial buildings but also in homes.[36] As a resident of Tokyo, Tsuji observed that air-conditioning had already made significant inroads into places of consumption such as department stores, theatres, cinemas, exclusive restaurants, hotels and inns, matching the installations already in place in world-famous public places such as Selfridges in London or the Louvre Museum in Paris. However, Tsuji was uncomfortable with the sight of "cool hunters" freeloading on the coolness offered by department stores, and he criticised the absence of cool in places that were the real contributors to economic growth: the factories and offices of exporting companies. He was convinced that were these places as air-conditioned as the cinema, efficiency would increase, and the nation's recovery from war would be boosted.

This push for the installation of air-conditioning benefited from arguments that mechanical cooling contributed to increased efficiency, productivity and cleanliness. By eliminating the need to open windows, air-conditioning made the office a quieter and more hygienic place where workers could concentrate without being distracted by and exposed to the noise and dirt of the outside world.[37] Office workers also no longer had to waste their time and energy turning on electric fans or opening windows because management could relieve them of the task of adjusting the indoor climate. Compared to natural ventilation, which brought in not only fresh air but also pollutants and pests, the air machines manufactured for the office were also purer and cleaner. Guidebooks for management on the organisation and operation of offices pointed to the results that had been achieved in other industries which had first adopted mechanical cooling on a large scale.[38] The productivity of coal miners – previously exposed to excruciating heat and humidity – was said to have increased with the introduction of air-conditioning, while chemical factories also benefited from stable climatic conditions in which they could produce uniform products throughout the year. Reference was made to research conducted by management experts in the United States: George R. Terry's influential book on management – which went through eight editions – was translated in 1959 to show that the productivity of office workers could be increased by 20 percent thanks to air-conditioning.[39] Terry himself recommended that office temperatures not exceed 21 degrees. At the Institute for the Science of Labour, Katsuki Shinji and Miura Toyohiko – both trained as physicians – set out to investigate Japanese as opposed to American bodies to show the business community the optimum climatic conditions that offices should achieve, with Katsuki showing that temperatures between 23 and 29 degrees were ideal for intellectual labour. Studies of typists' efficiency showed that levels dropped when temperatures exceeded 30 degrees and indicated that the best conditions were between five [sic!] and 25 degrees. These varying results showed that indoor climate control needed to take into account not only ethnic differences, but also the type of work people were doing. Offices could not be climatically uniform, and conditions had to be tailored to the needs of each office. Despite Michelle Murphy's suggestion that air-conditioning was tantamount to imposing universal standards everywhere, the Japanese experience shows a degree of customisation.[40]

In the 1960s, as it became increasingly fashionable to install air-conditioning in offices – most new buildings were fitted with it as standard – optimism about its potential grew. In a book on building management, Abe Makoto, an employee of Tokyo Tatemono, a real estate company, waxed lyrical about the "epochal" changes that air-conditioning was bringing to buildings.[41] He reiterated the hygienic benefits of climate control technology, which created the perfect climate by removing polluted air and producing clean air. Abe also believed that air-conditioning would make it possible not only to create the best possible environment for bodies to work in, but also to prevent spoilage and damage to products stored in the same buildings. Since it was now possible to create an artificial and sealed environment that was independent of the outside world, he continued, it was no longer necessary for architects to think about the direction in which buildings should face. It was even possible to construct windowless buildings, which not only further reduced noise and pollution but also saved a lot of money, including cleaning costs. Less optimistic about air-conditioning was Nakabayashi Yoshikatsu, an office management expert who welcomed the introduction of mechanical cooling in the office in principle but stopped short of embracing windowless offices.[42] In his book on office management, Nakabayashi expressed unease about the extent to which climate control technology was severing the office's relationship with nature. He noted how buildings of the past, such as the Marunouchi Building in Tokyo's financial district, had relied on natural ventilation and lighting. Central courtyards in the middle of the buildings had served to bring air and light into the office space. Both air-conditioning and electric lighting made them obsolete. The ducts that had to be installed in the ceilings to mechanically cool offices also meant that the ceiling had to be lowered. Nakabayashi understood that windowless offices were highly rational: they had the advantages of reducing construction costs, were hygienic because they prevented polluted air from entering the building and contributed to increased productivity because workers were less distracted and did not have to constantly adjust the lighting depending on the time of day or the season. For Nakabayashi, however, windowless offices were a step too far: they felt too "pressurised", he explained, and were risky if the air-conditioning broke down.

SHARING COOL OFFICE SPACE

It is important to note that the impetus for the creation of cool offices had much to do not only with creating the necessary climatic and hygienic conditions for the human body, but also with the introduction, operation and maintenance of electronic computers. Before the advent of electronic computers, office work involving the storage and processing of large amounts of information relied largely on manual labour: a pool of female card punchers typed, calculated and stored data on paper.[43] Electronic computers, such as the UNIVAC, which was commercialised and marketed for general use by the Eckert-Mauchly Computer Corporation (EMCC), promised to reduce the amount of menial labour involved in card punching by storing data on magnetic tapes.[44] In response to the competition, IBM, which had built its business empire on punched card machines, invested heavily in computers and achieved a commercial breakthrough with the IBM 650, a mass-produced model that was compared to Ford's Model T for making computers affordable and usable for the broader economy. Thanks in part to the 650, IBM monopolised the American computer market by the mid-1950s, contributing to the demise of EMCC. As a result, male and female workers had to share workspace not only with one another, but also with bulky computers that had different thermal needs to the machines they had previously worked with.

One of the first to import the IBM 650 was the Onoda Cement Company. In its newly built office in Tokyo's Yaesu district, opposite Tokyo Station, a room was created to house the large computer units.[45] In order for the IBM 650 to function properly, it was necessary to create an environment that maintained not only a high level of hygiene but also a perpetual coolness, with temperatures between 20 and 20.5 degrees. This required a brigade of air-conditioning units to cool heat- and dust-sensitive equipment from all sides of the room, all year round. Given the need to process vast amounts of data, the financial sector was the most eager to embrace computers. At Sanwa Bank, which installed the first computer in 1952, IBM and Remington Rand (which had acquired EMCC) computers were used for a total of 190 different statistical tasks, including processing data for foreign exchange transactions, human resources and administration.[46] Compared to the manual labour of punched card data entry and processing, computers could do the same job ten times faster. Although they sped up the process and made female clerks redundant, women remained in the office to operate them and feed them data. Not surprisingly, because of the need to be near computers in air-conditioned rooms, women were exposed to mechanical cooling for long periods of time. In the Onoda Cement Company's so-called IBM room, female workers complained of neuralgia and rheumatism.[47] As a result, these office ladies were encouraged to give up their skirts and wear trousers.

Female office workers in the financial and construction sectors were not the first to notice the impact of mechanical cooling on their physical health. Early evidence came from the department store sector, which was at the forefront of installing air-conditioning.[48] Female customers who frequented the stores noticed changes in their bodies as they tried to cope with the extreme climatic changes they were exposed to. Doctors warned that the alternating shocks of heat and cold from mechanical cooling could harm internal organs. They highlighted risks such as fluctuating blood pressure, hormonal imbalances, disrupted digestion, impaired kidney and liver function and the onset of metabolic disorders.[49] Newspapers also warned female workers in department stores and offices about "air-con cold" (*reibōkaze*) – described in the media as a "modern disease" (*kindai byō*) caused by new technology – which could lead to menstrual disorders, implying that women's reproductive capacities could be compromised.[50]

Constant exposure to mechanical cooling claimed its first victim in 1961. A Tokyo office lady, Noda Fusa, a resident of the Azabu area, had fallen ill in June the year before, coinciding with the installation of air-conditioners in her office.[51] She caught a cold and struggled to recover until the autumn, when they were turned off. However, when the air-conditioners were switched back on in May, she fell ill again and was taken to hospital, where she was pronounced dead the same day. Investigations revealed that the company had installed one air-conditioning unit for each floor and set the room temperature at 18 or 19 degrees, very low by today's standards. Noda had been sitting near the unit and had been disproportionately exposed to the cool air. At the Institute for the Science of Labour, Miura studied the problem and showed that even in warmer air-conditioned rooms, around 44 percent of the female bank employees he surveyed complained of a variety of ailments.[52] Some 24 percent said their lower bodies felt cold, seven percent complained of neuralgia, nearly five percent of back pain, the same proportion said their backs felt heavier, and around 28 percent said they suffered from *reibōkaze*.

Such cases made health experts sceptical about the hype surrounding mechanical cooling. In his introductory book on occupational science, Miura expressed unease about the effects of air-conditioning as it made its way into workplaces.[53] Although Miura understood that air-conditioning was needed to create indoor climate conditions in which workers could compete in a more liberalised, global market, he was critical of the way in which department stores, banks and insurance companies were implementing air-conditioning. While recognising the need for these companies to run computers, he pointed out that employees "felt the pain", intimating that the welfare of the workers was subordinated to that of the machines.[54] Similarly, the doctor Kobayashi Yōtaro challenged the thinking of engineers who equated optimal thermal comfort with satisfying the interests of the majority.[55] He criticised engineers for targeting 70 to 80 percent of users, while leaving the remaining 20 to 30 percent to doctors whose welfare he accused engineers of caring little about. He therefore urged engineers to design cooling technology that would allow the weaker minority to customise the climatic environment in which they had to work, rather than having to conform to the thermal norms of the strong majority. For most workers, offices may be cool, but for a significant minority they may be cold.

Despite Kobayashi's invective, the "chilliness" experienced by female workers in department stores and financial institutions was not entirely due to the technology itself, but to its application in the broader context of retail. In a nationwide survey conducted by Fuji Bank, it found that there were striking differences between head offices and branches in how mechanical coolness was experienced, with head office workers generally happy about the effectiveness of the air-conditioning while branch workers complained about it more.[56] The bank's health department found that most branches reported complaints about mechanical cooling being overly effective, creating an office environment that felt cold rather than comfortably cool. Such findings revealed more than just the technical problem of distributing coolness evenly throughout the building. Units in the basement might have too much power that overcooled the lower floor, while the ducts might be to blame for the uneven distribution of coolness. More significantly, the thermal imbalance showed how commercial enthusiasm to attract customers to the bank's premises – employees at head offices had less contact with customers – could be responsible for the air-conditioning being run to excess. A similar situation was found in department stores and cafes, where the eagerness to attract customers to come in (but not stay too long) sacrificed the well-being of their mostly female employees.

THE TRIUMPH OF THE COOL OFFICE

Trapped in a cold office, a number of stakeholders made recommendations to limit the impact of mechanical cooling on employees' health. As a general measure, management was urged to design the office so that employees were less exposed to the cold air blowing down from the ducts. They were also encouraged to position electric fans in and around office spaces to distribute the coolness more evenly. More prescriptive measures were aimed at the women themselves. Men were conspicuous by their absence from these instructions, as they were already protected by their trousers, jackets and ties. Women who dressed lightly – which had been a symbol of female emancipation – were told to wear trousers, jumpers and cardigans to keep their bodies warm.[57] There seems to have been very little choice for these women but to acclimatise to the air-conditioned working environment. Writing in a book aimed at a female readership, the doctor Ōya Hitomi – fully aware that the air-conditioner symbolised post-war capitalism's relentless drive for efficiency – struggled to come up with alternatives.[58] She was critical of companies that sought to capitalise on the consumer penchant for cool spaces. She accused management of deliberately turning down the temperature in places such as cafés so that customers who felt cold would want to leave, thus increasing turnover. To combat the problem of women having to deal with sudden temperature fluctuations, she could only counsel women to be wary of cold shocks when entering cafés, restaurants and department stores. Ultimately, Ōya thought it best for female workers, once inside an air-conditioned space, to stay there and avoid going outside as much as possible – in other words, to accept being encased in mechanically cooled interiors. Demands for salarymen to dress properly for the summer were muted, as women by and large accepted that it was in their interest to add layers to their bodies – not remove them. While both men and women experienced discomfort, the key difference was that men's attire remained culturally fixed despite the heat, whereas women's clothing was treated as flexible – making them disproportionately responsible for adapting to the office climate.

In the 1960s, mechanical cooling in the workplace was still largely a seasonal event. As Noda's example has shown, air-conditioning was generally limited to the hot and humid months. But the advent of skyscrapers changed all that. Planners responding to the problem of urban sprawl began toying with ideas for high-rise buildings in the early 1960s. Commuters travelling from the suburbs to the centre of Tokyo – dubbed "commuter hell" because of overcrowded trains – could spend up to two hours a day in public transport. With the nation's economic progress expected to continue, experts predicted that the demand for office space would continue to grow, adding to the fear that office workers would have to travel farther. To slow this process, city planners looked to the skies for new spaces to colonise. In his book *The Dawn of the Skyscraper* (*Chōkōsō biru no akebono*), Mutō Kiyoshi, the leading architect and structural engineer behind the Kasumigaseki Building – Tokyo's first skyscraper – touted skyscrapers as the solution to urban sprawl (Fig. 3.2.).[59] Co-authored with the corporate filmmaker and screenwriter Iwasa Hisashi, who was commissioned to make a film about the project, the book was written so that even children could understand the rationale behind skyscraper construction – a reflection of the developer's (Kajima Corporation) determination to win public trust for its high-rise plans. In this spirit, Mutō promoted the construction of skyscrapers as being better for the environment. Low-rise buildings tended to be built with little space between them. Because the restrictions on height tended to crowd out space for sunlight to enter, the "valley between the buildings" (*tanima*) became a dark and dingy place. Likening skyscrapers to rectangular chocolate boxes, Mutō and Iwasa explained that skyscrapers were built with the base (the smallest area) facing upwards, unlike existing buildings, which were built with the side (the largest area) facing upwards. Moreover, compared to European metropolises, where there was more greenery, Tokyo did not meet the common standard of 60 square metres of parkland per resident. Skyscrapers would free up more space for greenery, and as long as there was enough space

Fig. 3.2. 1968 photo of the cool office space of the Kasumigaseki Building, then newly opened and equipped with year-round air-conditioning. (Reproduced with permission from the Mitsui Fudosan Company.)

between the high-rises, the valley between the buildings would not block sunlight from entering the space between them. For a long time, the risk of fires, earthquakes and typhoons had limited the height of buildings to just 31 metres, or eight storeys. Mutō himself, as a professor at the University of Tokyo's School of Engineering, had pioneered research on earthquake-resistant buildings. These efforts, together with legal changes to the building code in 1962, meant that developers – such as his own Kajima Corporation – were now able to build into the sky.

When the Kasumigaseki Building was constructed, engineers were well aware that building above the 31-metre threshold meant that skyscrapers would be more exposed to the elements than ever before.[60] Standard office buildings were huddled together, their walls often touching. Skyscrapers, on the other hand, stood tall and alone, making them more vulnerable to high levels of radiation and wind. The use of lighter steel and the preference for glass in skyscraper construction often resulted in interior temperatures being almost as high in winter as in summer, particularly in south-facing areas during Tokyo's typically mild winter weather. Glass, favoured for its appearance and lightness, was a material that further

Fig. 3.3. Prime Minister Ōhira Masayoshi showing off his "energy-saving look" (shōene rukku), 6 June 1979. (Reproduced with permission from Kyodo News.)

intensified the heat, making the office dependent on air-conditioning to cool and maintain bodies and machinery.[61] As a result, keeping the skyscraper cool and hygienic meant that air-conditioning had to run all year round. Of course, opening the windows would not have been an option in a skyscraper because of the disruption that strong winds could cause to office work. It is thus highly likely that the rise of air-conditioned skyscrapers created internal thermal conditions in which salarymen could continue to wear their jackets, shirts and ties.

In the 1970s, political instability in the oil producing Middle East sent energy prices soaring, exposing the country's dependence on the region for economic growth. Such a change in the international geopolitical context forced the state to intervene to reduce electricity consumption, with strong pleas issued to restrict the use of lifts and neon lights, and to reduce the opening hours of department stores, supermarkets and restaurants. Perhaps the most iconic image of this energy-saving initiative was the figure of the Prime Minister, Ōhira Masayoshi, whose appearance on national television sporting a sleeveless jacket – an inspiration from the tropics – was widely ridiculed (Fig. 3.3.). As part of this campaign, fossil-fuel-dependent air-conditioners were also targeted, with the government encouraging the country to raise the thermostat to 28 degrees and to follow the Prime Minister's example by wearing lighter clothes. Electricity companies and public authorities took the lead in implementing a no-tie policy in their offices. In Ehime, the prefectural government went so far as to issue two short-sleeved shirts to male public servants for the duration of two years, to be worn at work between 16 June and 15 September.[62] For fear of appearing disrespectful, the local government was careful not to enforce the no-jacket and no-tie policy outside the office, which meant that employees were able to dress more formally on business trips and at public events. The banks also got on board. Daiichi Kangyō Bank responded to government requests to raise the thermostat in its 320 branches to 28 degrees.[63] It also strongly encouraged, but did not require, its 13,500 male employees to remove their ties. Bowing to customer sentiment that employees should dress formally, the bank allowed front office staff to dress up. There was some scepticism about the no-tie policy, with one trade union representative complaining that this government campaign smacked of the authoritarian measures the country had taken during war. Despite these reservations, there was some success. Of the 86 companies and public agencies surveyed by the Ministry of Trade and Industry in 1979, 62 percent replied that they would comply with the state's request to raise the thermostat.[64] When asked about their clothing policy, some 83 percent replied that they would allow office workers to wear light clothing (*keisō*). In this way, a modicum of thermal equality was achieved in the office. Renewed public campaigns in recent years for salarymen to shed their ties and jackets, albeit in the very different context of climate change, are a reminder that the struggle for thermal office equality is still an ongoing process.[65]

CONCLUSION

In their investigation into the rise of an air-conditioned society, architectural historians Jiat-Hwee Chang and Tim Winter have shown how and why mechanical cooling conquered tropical Singapore.[66] Like the Japanese experience, the spread of air-conditioning in the pre-war period was limited to the wealthy and to places such as cinemas and hotels, which relied heavily on imported American technology to cool interiors. Equally striking is the extent to which colonial ideas about climate and civilisation formed a powerful undercurrent to the country's drive to free itself from the debilitating economic effects of heat in the post-independence era, which also saw financial institutions embrace the technology. A marked difference from Japan, however, was the extent to which the Southeast Asian city-state adopted "air-conditioned comfort as a central canon of post-independence socio-economic development".[67] Facilitated by legal changes that allowed the government to buy land cheaply on which to build high-rises, Chang and Winter argue that the state was the driving force behind Singapore's addiction to mechanical coolness. In contrast to the Kasumigaseki Building, which was very much a private project, albeit facilitated by legal liberalisation, they see the construction of the 22-storey Ministry of National Development, opened in 1969, as a watershed building project that was part of the state's attempts to "socially engineer and discipline the population to turn them into modern subjects and productive workers".[68] They argue that as a result "a social contract has formed between the state and the Singaporean citizen around the provision of what might best be described as 'comfort security'".[69]

In the Japanese context, there was no such social contract with the citizenry to maintain comfort security. Much of the driving force behind the introduction of air-conditioning in commercial buildings was the capitalist thirst for efficiency, productivity and profit. In this respect, it was similar to the North American experience. Driven by the dual need to maintain optimal indoor climatic conditions in order to increase the productivity of both workers and machines, mechanical cooling increasingly cut office buildings off from their natural surroundings and delivered cool, clean, artificial air to enclosed workers. After an initial period in which traditional thermal norms and practices prevailed, the construction of Western-style office buildings facilitated the colonisation of office space by mechanical cooling, which served as a techno-economic tool for extracting the maximum amount of labour from both humans and machines. As Michelle Murphy observed: "The cool, comfortable air of the office building was not simply a pleasant and passive backdrop, but the material manifestation of a historically specific, gendered, and racialized way of understanding the relationship between office workers' bodies and the spaces that ordered their labor".[70] In the specific context of early post-war Japan, gendered contests characterised the politics of the cool office, which preserved salarymen's insistence on wearing jackets and ties, while women were forced to acclimatise to the chilly office by adding layers to their clothing. And it was not until the 1970s, when the nation's dependence on the Middle East for its energy needs became apparent, that the state intervened, with the unintended consequence of helping to loosen male preoccupation with formal attire and contributing to a more equitable thermal office space.

NOTES

[1] Eziaku Onyeizu Rasheed, Maryam Khoshbakht and George Baird, 'Time Spent in the Office and Workers' Productivity, Comfort and Health: A Perception Study', in Building and Environment, 195 (2021); Russell Hitchings and Shu Jun Lee, 'Air-Conditioning and the Material Culture of Routine Human Encasement: The Case of Young People in Contemporary Singapore', in Journal of Material Culture, 13/3 (2008).

[2] Joseph M. Siry, Air-Conditioning in Modern American Architecture, 1890-1970 (Pennsylvania, 2021), 115.

[3] Carol Willis, Form Follows Finance: Skyscrapers and Skylines in New York and Chicago (New York, 1995), 8.

[4] Siry, Air-Conditioning, 116; Michelle Murphy, Sick Building Syndrome and the Problem of Uncertainty: Environmental Politics, Technoscience, and Women Workers (Durham, 2006), 34.

[5] Cited by Siry, Air-Conditioning, 120.

[6] 'The Future of Cooling: Opportunities for Energy-Efficient Air Conditioning' (via www.iea.org).

[7] Raymond Arsenault, 'The End of the Long Hot Summer: The Air-Conditioner and Southern Culture', in The Journal of Southern History, 50/4 (1984), 616.

[8] Ibid., 628.

[9] Stephen Healy, 'Air-Conditioning and the "Homogenization" of People and Built Environments', in Building Research & Information, 36/4 (2008), 319.

[10] Elizabeth Shove, 'Converging Conventions of Comfort, Cleanliness and Convenience', in Journal of Consumer Policy, 26/4 (2003), 399.

[11] Richard de Dear and Gail Schiller Brager, 'The Adaptive Model of Thermal Comfort and Energy Conservation in the Built Environment', in International Journal of Biometeorology, 45/2 (2001), 100.

[12] Marsha Ackermann, Cool Comfort: America's Romance with Air-Conditioning (Washington D.C., 2002), 184.

[13] Niamh Murtagh et al., 'Living with Air-Conditioning: Experiences in Dubai, Chongqing and London', in Buildings and Cities, 3/1 (2022).

[14] On the U.S., see Siry, Air-Conditioning; Salvatore Basile, Cool: How Air-Conditioning Changed Everything (New York, 2014); Ackermann, Cool Comfort; Gail Cooper, Air-Conditioning America: Engineers and the Controlled Environment, 1900-1960 (Baltimore, 1998). On Singapore, see Jiat-Hwee Chang and Tim Winter, 'Thermal Modernity and Architecture', in The Journal of Architecture, 20/1 (2015).

[15] Gianenrico Bernasconi and Stefan Nellen, 'Einleitung', in idem (eds.), Das Büro: Zur Rationalisierung des Interieurs, 1880-1960 (Bielefeld, 2020), 10-11.

[16] Delphine Gardey, '"Espèces d'espaces", Raumarten: Soziale, technische und politische Aspekte', in Bernasconi and Nellen, Das Büro.

[17] See also Craig Robertson, The Filing Cabinet: A Vertical History of Information (Minneapolis, 2021), 206-207.

[18] See also Murphy, Sick Building Syndrome.

[19] 'Kansoku kaishi kara no maitsuki no atai' (via www.jma.go.jp). This chapter will use the Celsius scale throughout.

[20] Except for 27 June, when the highest temperature dipped to around 21 degrees, the highest temperatures in Tokyo averaged more than 30 degrees between the beginning of June and the end of August. See 'Mōsho-burikaesu: ase daku no shokuba', in Asahi Shimbun, 10 Aug. 1955, 7.

[21] In this chapter, Japanese names will be given with surnames first and first names last, unless they appear in English-language publications.

[22] Arsenault, 'Hot Summer', 602-603; Reibō zadan-kai sokkiroku (Tokyo, 1935), 3.

[23] Inoue Uichi, Reitō kūchōshi (Tokyo, 1993), 297-320.

[24] Tatsuya Mitsuda, 'From Endurance to Escape: The Tokyo Summer as Lived Experience in the Twentieth Century', in Journal of Urban History, 51/1 (2024).

[25] Jose Maria Cabeza Lainez, 'The Japanese Experience of Environmental Architecture through the Works of Bruno Taut and Antonin Raymond', in Journal of Asian Architecture and Building Engineering, 6/1 (2007).

26 Bruno Taut, Houses and People of Japan (Tokyo, 1937), 55.
27 Mitsuda, From Endurance.
28 Wakariyasui kenchiku kōza 6 (Tokyo, 1964), 26.
29 Willis, Form Follows Finance, 8.
30 Daniel A. Barber, Modern Architecture and Climate: Design Before Air Conditioning (Princeton, 2020).
31 'Toshin yori suzushii gunbu: biru-gai wa ōku netsu sutte', in Asahi Shimbun, 8 Aug. 1952, 4.
32 Mōsho-burikaesu.
33 'Ase daku no keishiki shugi wa muimi: otoko mo suzushii keisō o manabu beku aroha sutairu', in Yomiuri Shimbun, 7 Aug. 1954, 5.
34 'Henshū techō', in Yomiuri Shimbun, 11 June 1955, 1.
35 Reibō zadankai sokkiroku (Tokyo, 1935), 3; Ellsworth Huntington, Civilization and Climate (New Haven, 1915).
36 Tsuji Jirō, 'Kinō kyō: reibō', in Asahi Shimbun, 8 July 1955, 3.
37 Asano Sadashi, Kūki chōwa kōgaku: reibō (Tokyo, 1953), 196.
38 Kawaguchi Terutake, Jimu gaido bukku (Tokyo, 1959), 34.
39 G.R. Terry et al., Jimu kanri no kagaku jōka (Tokyo, 1959).
40 Murphy, Sick Building Syndrome, 25.
41 Abe Jun, Biru no kanri to keiei (Tokyo, 1963).
42 Nakabayashi Yoshikatsu, Jimu nōritsu zōkyō no karute: Ofisu reiauto no hanashi (Tokyo, 1963), 231.
43 Delphine Gardey, Écrire, calculer, classer: Comment une révolution de papier a transformé les sociétés contemporaines, 1800-1940 (Paris, 2008).
44 Martin Campbell-Kelly et al., Computer: A History of the Information Machine (Boulder, 2014), 99.
45 Mizuguchi Masakatsu, 'Natsu ofisu no reibō: IBM-shitsu o chūshin ni', in Rōdō no kagaku, 15/7 (1960).
46 Nihon Denshi Keisanki Sentā (ed.), Denshi keisanki benran (Tokyo, 1963), 194-196.
47 Mizuguchi, Natsu, 45.
48 'Fujin: ondo no kyūhen', in Yomiuri Shimbun, 11 Aug. 1956, 5.
49 Ibid.
50 'Ofisu tsutome no kindai-byō', in Yomiuri Shimbun, 27 May 1960, 9.
51 'Tsuyosugiru reibō: byōki o akkasuru?', in Asahi Shimbun, 16 June 1961, 11.
52 'Reibō-byō ni konna chūi o: natsu no fuku-sō de wa dame, kanarazu sētā-rui o yōi', in Yomiuri Shimbun, 19 July 1961, 9.
53 Miura Toyohiko, Rōdō kagaku nyūmon: rōdō jōken to kankyō ni tsuite no atarashii kangaekata (Tokyo, 1963), 205-206.
54 Ibid., 205.
55 Kobayashi Yōtaro, 'Reibō no jintai ni oyobosu eikyō', in Nihon kikai gakkai-shi 69/570 (1966).
56 Ōmi Akira, 'Ginkō no kaki reibō,' in Rōdō no kagaku 15/7 (1960).
57 Mitsuda, From Endurance.
58 Ōya Hitomi, Chie aru seikatsu: kore dake wa shitte okou (Tokyo, 1961), 158-161.
59 Mutō Kiyoshi and Iwasa Hisashi, Chōkōsō biru no akebono (Tokyo, 1968).
60 Ishida Shigenosuke, Chōkōsō biru: saisho no kokoromi no kiroku (Tokyo, 1968), 116.
61 Shimizu Kunio, Jimusho kenchikubutsu no kūki chōwa (Tokyo, 1968), 4.
62 Ōshima Mitsuru, 'Natsu ba no no necktie sei', in Chihō kōmuin geppō, 7/180 (1978), 28-29.
63 'GS kyūjitsu kyūgyō, no necktie aircon boom', in Chūbu zaikai, 22/11 (1979), 72.
64 'Sekiyū setsuyaku shuyō kigyō mazu mazu', in Asahi Shimbun, 27 May 1979, 3.
65 See for example 'Super Cool Biz', in The Japan Times, 12 June 2011; 'Aloha Shirts OK as Japan Seeks to Beat Heat', Reuters Press Report, 2 June 2011.
66 Chang and Winter, Thermal Modernity.
67 Ibid., 102.
68 Ibid., 107.
69 Ibid., 118.
70 Murphy, Sick Building Syndrome, 19.

BIBLIOGRAPHY

Abe Jun, Biru no kanri to keiei (Tokyo, 1963).
Marsha Ackermann, Cool Comfort: America's Romance with Air-Conditioning (Washington D.C., 2002).
Raymond Arsenault, 'The End of the Long Hot Summer: The Air-Conditioner and Southern Culture', in The Journal of Southern History, 50/4 (1984), 597-628.
Daniel A. Barber, Modern Architecture and Climate Design Before Air Conditioning (Princeton, 2020).
Salvatore Basile, Cool: How Air-Conditioning Changed Everything (New York, 2014).
Gianenrico Bernasconi and Stefan Nellen, 'Einleitung', in idem (eds.), Das Büro: Zur Rationalisierung des Interieurs, 1880-1960 (Bielefeld, 2020), 9-26.
Jose Maria Cabeza Lainez, 'The Japanese Experience of Environmental Architecture through the Works of Bruno Taut and Antonin Raymond', in Journal of Asian Architecture and Building Engineering, 6/1 (2007), 33-40.
Martin Campbell-Kelly et al., Computer: A History of the Information Machine (Boulder, 2014).
Jiat-Hwee Chang and Tim Winter, 'Thermal Modernity and Architecture', in The Journal of Architecture, 20/1 (2015), 92-121.
Gail Cooper, Air-Conditioning America: Engineers and the Controlled Environment, 1900-1960 (Baltimore, 1998).
Richard de Dear and Gail Schiller Brager, 'The Adaptive Model of Thermal Comfort and Energy Conservation in the Built Environment', in International Journal of Biometeorology, 45/2 (2001), 100-108.
Delphine Gardey, Écrire, calculer, classer: Comment une révolution de papier a transformé les sociétés contemporaines (1800-1940) (Paris, 2008).
Delphine Gardey, '"Espèces d'espaces", Raumarten: Soziale, technische und politische Aspekte', in Gianenrico Bernasconi and Stefan Nellen (eds.), Das Büro: Zur Rationalisierung des Interieurs, 1880-1960 (Bielefeld, 2020), 277-286.
Stephen Healy, 'Air-Conditioning and the "Homogenization" of People and Built Environments', in Building Research & Information, 36/4 (2008), 312-322.
Russell Hitchings and Shu Jun Lee, 'Air-Conditioning and the Material Culture of Routine Human Encasement: The Case of Young People in Contemporary Singapore', in Journal of Material Culture, 13/3 (2008), 251-265.
Ellsworth Huntington, Civilization and Climate (New Haven, 1915).
Inoue Uichi, Reitō kūchōshi (Tokyo, 1993).
Kawaguchi Terutake, Jimu gaido bukku (Tokyo, 1959).
Kobayashi Yōtaro, 'Reibō no jintai ni oyobosu eikyō', in Nihon kikai gakkai-shi 69/570 (1966), 932-939.
Michelle Murphy, Sick Building Syndrome and the Problem of Uncertainty: Environmental Politics, Technoscience, and Women Workers (Durham, 2006).
Nakabayashi Yoshikatsu, Jimu nōritsu zōkyō no karute: Ofisu reiauto no hanashi (Tokyo, 1963).
Miura Toyohiko, Rōdō kagaku nyūmon: rōdō jōken to kankyō ni tsuite no atarashii kangaekata (Tokyo, 1963).
Mizuguchi Masakatsu, 'Natsu ofisu no reibō: IBM-shitsu o chūshin ni', in Rōdō no kagaku 15/7 (1960), 39-45.
Tatsuya Mitsuda, 'From Endurance to Escape: The Tokyo Summer as Lived Experience in the Twentieth Century', in Journal of Urban History, 51/1 (2024), 61-71.
Mutō Kiyoshi and Iwasa Hisashi, Chōkōsō biru no akebono (Tokyo, 1968).
Niamh Murtagh et al., 'Living with Air-Conditioning: Experiences in Dubai, Chongqing and London', in Buildings and Cities 3/1 (2022), 10-27.
Ōmi Akira, 'Ginkō no kaki reibō', in Rōdō no kagaku 15/7 (1960), 46-54.
Ōshima Mitsuru, 'Natsu ba no no necktie sei', in Chihō kōmuin geppō, 7/180 (1978), 28-29.
Eziaku Onyeizu Rasheed, Maryam Khoshbakht and George Baird, 'Time Spent in the Office and Workers' Productivity, Comfort and Health: A Perception Study', in Building and Environment, 195 (2021).
Craig Robertson, The Filing Cabinet: A Vertical History of Information (Minneapolis, 2021).
Shimizu Kunio, Jimusho kenchikubutsu no kūki chōwa (Tokyo, 1968).

Elizabeth Shove, 'Converging Conventions of Comfort, Cleanliness and Convenience', in Journal of Consumer Policy 26/4 (2003), 395-418.
Joseph M. Siry, Air-Conditioning in Modern American Architecture, 1890-1970 (Pennsylvania, 2021).
Bruno Taut, Houses and People of Japan (Tokyo, 1937).
G.R. Terry et al., Jimu kanri no kagaku jōka (Tokyo, 1959).
Tsuji Jirō, 'Kinō kyō: reibō', in Asahi Shimbun, 8 July 1955, 3.
Carol Willis, Form Follows Finance: Skyscrapers and Skylines in New York and Chicago (New York, 1995).

Chapter 4
Thresholds of Comfort: Managing Light, Sound and Focus in the Post-War Office Environment

Joeri Bruyninckx

INTRODUCTION

When the small Pilkington Research Unit at the University of Liverpool's Department of Building Science published its report *Office Design: A Study of Environment* in 1965, it had set itself an ambitious target. Architect Peter Manning had assembled a multidisciplinary team (consisting of a psychologist, a physicist and a geographer) to establish a comprehensive picture of the modern office "environment".[1] The group found that this term was often applied loosely and imprecisely, but they considered it to mean the "essence of architecture": the sum of all physical sensations that people experience when they use a building, encompassing bodily comfort, aesthetics and even social relationships. To examine what they called the "*total* environment", the authors collected both new and existing data on what they saw as its key dimensions – aural, thermal, social, spatial and visual. An image depicting two office workers at their desks, framed by a cloud of technical terms, illustrated the vast scope of their ambition (Fig. 4.1.).

The report marks an interesting moment in the architectural history of environmental management – a term that I use here in two ways. First, "environmental management" defines a technically codified control over the built interior, an attempt to engineer its performance and comfort for users in measurable ways. While technological control over light, heat and sound in buildings has a long history,[2] in the 20th century, the notion of the architectural *environment* connoted a growing concern with buildings' multi-layered ambience – a "total" experience, defined not just by objective measures but also by how people encounter buildings subjectively. As architectural historians have shown, the post-war rise in environmental

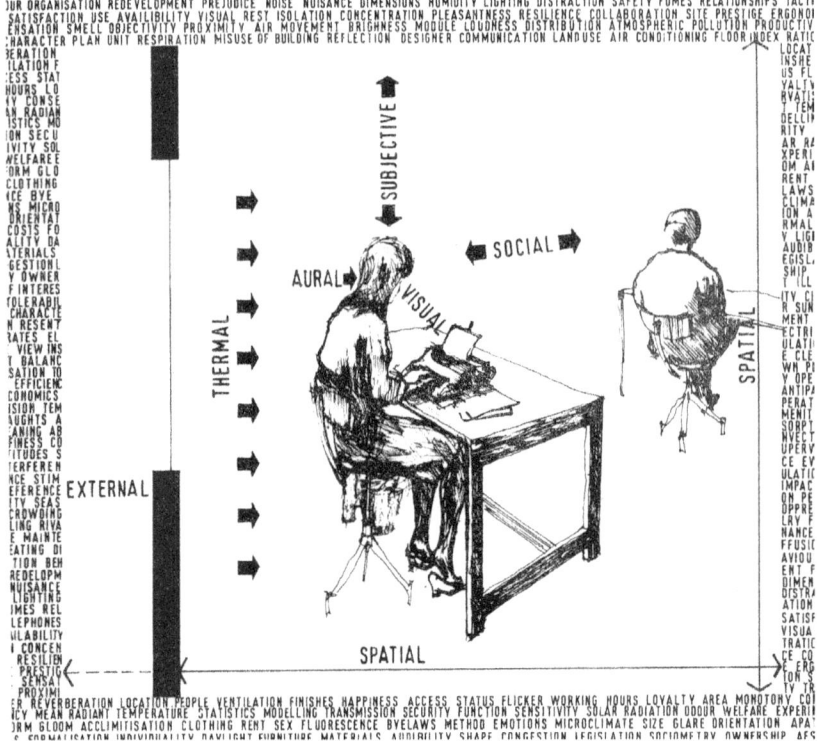

Fig. 4.1. The components of "environment", as seen by Alan G. Swerdlow. (Peter Manning, Office Design: A Study of Environment [Liverpool, 1965], 24. © Pilkington Research Unit)

design as a field led architects to endorse the study of users' physical, psychological and social needs as a basis for design.[3] That users came to be the measure of environments is illustrated by the Pilkington report, which described its approach "to design on the basis of thinking outwards from the office worker to his workplace".[4]

Second, it is perhaps not surprising that Manning and his colleagues turned to the office to showcase the promise of environmental research for architecture and planning. After all, management of work has long gone hand in hand with management of the physical environment.[5] Early-20th-century scientific management handbooks, for instance, highlighted the influence of "atmospheric conditions" in the workplace – a shorthand for proper illumination, ventilation and acoustics – on workers' energy and efficiency.[6] Although 1930s human relations theory shifted attention to *social* environments and their influence on employees' attitudes and morale, post-war ergonomics and environmental psychology refocused on the physical environment as a factor to promote comfort.[7] While the influence of environmental factors on efficiency remained notoriously hard to demonstrate conclusively, the notion persisted that better environments resulted in better work. In that sense, managing white-collar workspaces as environments also doubled as a way of managing the people inhabiting these environments.

In this chapter, I examine how these two aspects of "environmental management" were coupled in the British and American post-war office. I do this by tracing how in the 1950s and 1960s, users' perceptions and subjective experiences found their way into the appraisal of buildings as well as into notions of the ideal workplace. I particularly focus on two professional communities working at the interface of architecture, building science and engineering: light engineering in Britain and architectural acoustics in the United States. In dealing with vision and sound, these fields invoked different sets of problems, research practices and expertise. And yet, they came to understand the workspace in a similar way – namely as a perceptual environment that could be fine-tuned, based on a detailed knowledge of users' preferences. I am interested in how these users and their environmental experiences came to be known – or rather, were *made* to be known – as well as how such knowledge, in turn, came to be inscribed in the imagined and material environment of the office.

I will explore these questions in two case studies, which trace the making of two planning instruments in these fields: the Glare Comfort Index for light and the Articulation Index for sound. These instruments were developed to provide architects with a guideline to ensure the materials and fittings they specified permitted visual and acoustic comfort. To do this, both indices determined what I call a "threshold of comfort". Based on surveys and psychophysical studies of users' subjective experiences, such thresholds defined how much light or sound a user was willing to tolerate; at what point, in other words, did their comfort turn into discomfort? I argue that the development of these indices can highlight how (dis)comfort was codified and operationalised in specific ways. In particular, perceptual comfort came to be defined by a concern for users' ability to remain attentive or become distracted from the task at hand. In both fields, this definition affected environmental management in the office. For decades, office design had focused on blanketing entire rooms or open-plan floors with maximum illumination and minimum reverberation. But these indices would promote a more localised approach, whereby light and sound were used to texture a space such that users would be able to distinguish their tasks more easily in the foreground, while the rest of the workspace turned into a generic background. By calibrating the ambient levels of light and sound in precise ways, engineers sought to define perceptual spaces within large open-plan buildings that seemed to situate each worker within their own inwardly focused but immaterial enclosure.

In other words, the office came to be reimagined as an all-encompassing environment, the subjective experience of which could be engineered by technical means, and this notion was also reflected in the material organisation of the office. Tracing this technical history is relevant because it complicates our understanding of architectural and managerial innovations such as the open office. The preferred design choice in managerial literature since the early 20th century, it regained fashionability in the 1960s and 1970s in the form of the office landscape. As historians of the office have shown, this layout was promoted as a solution for modern-day "knowledge work", encompassing white-collar jobs that involved producing, sorting and organising complex information, from the punched card operator to the engineer.[8] But as I aim to show, making an open office a pleasurable and productive environment for information work also required aligning a far more extensive body of scientific, technical and architectural knowledge about both users and buildings.

OFFICE ILLUMINATION AND THE GLARE DISCOMFORT INDEX

Light engineering was one of the fields in which users' subjective reactions to the office environment began to be studied and quantified. Efforts had long focused on ensuring that (office) workers had access to sufficient light for their tasks: lighting engineers defined minimum criteria and employed building techniques to maximise daylight. This shifted after World War II, however, in part because of the efficiency of new lighting technologies. Fluorescent lighting offered a similar intensity, distribution and colour temperature to natural daylight, but at reduced temperatures and cost.[9] When spaced uniformly across the office, it also ensured a near shadow-less distribution of light, making possible the large open-space plans that characterised much post-war office architecture in the United States.[10] Such technologies drove a significant rise in illumination standards.[11] In the 1950s and 1960s, in response to these developments, lighting engineers began to shift their efforts from providing adequate lighting for the job to ensuring visual comfort for users at work. After all, rising illumination levels also raised concerns about a phenomenon that lighting engineers termed "glare".[12] Concern over glare was not new; already in 1913, American efficiency experts such as John William Schulze had warned office planners about the serious and frequent error of "over-lighting", which was expensive and subjected workers unnecessarily to eyestrain, severe headaches and loss of efficiency.[13] Research on glare had hitherto focused on its disabling effects, such as when street lights or sunlight directly impeded one's ability to see. Yet in the 1950s, British researchers began to insist that even minimal amounts of glare could cause subtle forms of discomfort which would result in irritation, distraction and inefficiency in the workplace.[14] This shift is best illustrated by work at the British government-funded Building Research Station (BRS). The station became a focal point for post-war investigations and building recommendations on so-called "glare discomfort", which were explicitly derived from subjective appraisals of user experience.

The BRS had been established by the Department of Scientific and Industrial Research after World War I as an institute for the scientific investigation of building materials and construction methods, in response to housing shortages.[15] While the institute had initially focused on building physics and fire safety, after World War II, new research programmes on illumination and acoustics set the tone for a new approach to building research.[16] Since 1948, the department had worked on an experimental programme that the station's director characterised as a highly "unorthodox" yet "powerful weapon for attack on many lighting problems".[17] BRS lighting engineer Ralph G. Hopkinson summarised this approach in a handbook in 1963, stating that "we are, in fact, concerned with the scientific study of the needs of people who work in buildings, and of the means of satisfying those needs".[18] In Hopkinson's view, such needs required a new type of building science because it shifted the appraisal of efficiency and performance of a building from physics and engineering to the human user and their experience of comfort. Hopkinson and his colleagues relied on "people as *meters* to register for us their experiences in the environment, to tell us how warm or how cold they are, whether a place is noisy or not".[19]

Their approach, which drew on insights from psychology, physiology, physics and engineering, was coined "architectural psychophysics", with a nod to pioneering 19th-century psychophysicist Gustav Fechner. Lighting was a key domain for psychophysics, Hopkinson proposed, because in spite of a body of knowledge on the physics and physiology of light, little was actually known about the ways in which factors such as its position, brightness, intensity and the size and shape of its source affected the experience of human comfort. The application of this approach is illustrated by the work that Hopkinson and his colleagues did on "glare discomfort", where they studied both the conditions in which light was produced and its effects on the user.[20] For instance, trained observers were presented with a model room in which different light sources generated various degrees of brightness and glare. Observers were then asked to adjust its parameters to match what they considered "just intolerable", "just uncomfortable" or "just acceptable" light. Tracing these physical settings, while controlling observers' consistency over time, allowed the experimenters to establish a series of "criteria" or "threshold values" at which the users expressed discomfort.[21] The experiments suggested that glare discomfort was produced not just by bright illumination, as had long been assumed; rather, the BRS researchers concluded that discomfort occurred when surroundings appeared too bright for the task or when there were too many bright light sources in an observer's line of sight. These conditions described most general ceiling lighting at the time; regular patterns of bright incandescent or fluorescent light sources ensured uniform distribution of light, but the fittings were typically also found to be too bright and hung too low in their field of vision for users' comfort (Fig. 4.2.).

Another series of experiments suggested that such lighting conditions affected not only users' comfort but also their attention and distraction.[22] Observers were asked to perform a visual task while lights of variable brightness appeared in their peripheral vision. By filming the observers and plotting their behaviour and eye movements, Hopkinson and his collaborators sought to establish the conditions under which observers became distracted. Conclusions were not easy to draw; under experimental conditions, some observers displayed nervous behaviour, which disturbed the measurements. But the findings did seem to confirm that attention remained on the working area more effectively if it was locally lit than if it was seen only in general illumination, and that bright light sources in the field of view tended to distract attention from the task at hand. Such findings suggested direct implications for lighting engineering in the workplace. Summarising this line of experiments for an audience of ergonomists a few years later, Hopkinson and J.B. Collins concluded that the ratio in brightness between a task and its surroundings had to be carefully fine-tuned. Otherwise, "the worker will be under continual strain in trying to maintain attention on the work [...] and will become prone to feelings of tiredness and fatigue".[23]

Figure 2. Modern drawing office with general lighting alone. The ceiling acts as a strong distraction to the eyes to look up from the work.

Fig. 4.2. Image and caption of a drawing office, meant to illustrate the distracting effect that general ceiling lighting can have on an observer. (R.G. Hopkinson and J. Longmore, 'Attention and Distraction in the Lighting of Work-Places', in Ergonomics, 2/4 [1959].)

Based on these experiments, Hopkinson and his collaborators proposed a set of empirical formulae that could be used to describe the subjective experience of glare discomfort. One formula determined a so-called "Glare Constant", which expressed the complex relationship between the luminance, size, surroundings, angle and viewing direction of one or more light sources with a single numerical value, indicating the degree of glare that was to be expected from a given installation. Based on their experiments, Hopkinson and his colleagues also produced a diagram that plotted how their samples of trained observers and about 50 random observers had on average judged these glare constants (Fig. 4.3.).[24] The researchers proposed that by combining the formula and the diagram, lighting engineers could easily determine whether the lighting installation they had specified would produce a discomfort that was "just perceptible" or "just intolerable". By adjusting the parameters of their lighting plan accordingly, engineers could expect, at least in theory, that 85 percent

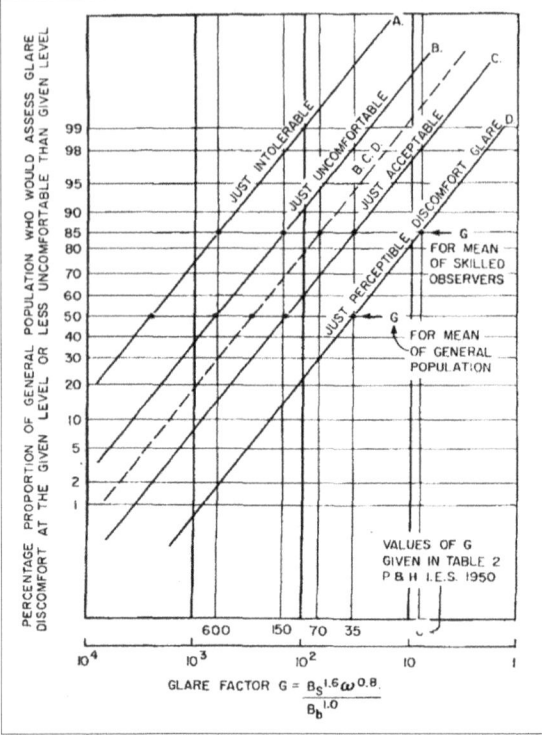

Fig. 4.3. Mean probability diagram, which plots assessment of a glare constant by the general population and trained observers. As a general rule, untrained observers were found to be one constant less sensitive than trained observers. (R.G. Hopkinson, 'Evaluation of Glare', in Illuminating Engineering Society Transactions 20 [1957], 315. Courtesy of the Illumination Engineering Society.)

of the general population would experience the light safely under the so-called borderline of comfort/discomfort ("B.C.D.").

For most of the decade, these formulae remained largely within the academic realm. But by 1959, Hopkinson had managed to convince the British Illumination Engineering Society to form a committee that would test and develop a more robust method for practising lighting engineers to calculate and prevent glare discomfort. The panel revised the formulae and came up with a simplified "Glare Index" to interpret the results on a numerical scale. It also checked the computer-calculated indices of a number of installations with the subjective appraisals of trained and untrained observers to determine a level of accordance between the theoretical model and experience in the field.[25] Since the formulae themselves were laborious to calculate by hand, the panel issued tables with which the Glare Index could easily be calculated for various spaces, light fittings and setups. This allowed the panel to position its theoretical model as an appropriate representation of the sensation of glare and discomfort that could be expected among the general population. In 1961, the Illumination Engineering Society recommended a first version of the Glare Index in its revised code for lighting building interiors. This code had long been based exclusively on the minimum level of illumination that was needed for a given visual task. Yet by including the Glare Index, it now supported a lighting practice in which environmental and task lighting were adjusted to one another and tuned to capture and hold the user's attention.[26] In 1967, the Illumination Engineering Society also issued a technical report, complete with worksheets, conversion graphs and tabulated data, to aid practising lighting engineers in evaluating glare discomfort.[27]

But while the Glare Index provided a metric with which glare discomfort could be evaluated, any influence on the practice of lighting engineers and architects was indirect and far from immediate, for several reasons. First, as a survey conducted by the Building Research Station of almost 3,000 office spaces of all kinds and their appraisal by 9,309 office users of all ranks showed, users seemed rather unconcerned about lighting. Two-thirds of the offices built after 1949 were found to be illuminated with fluorescent lighting.[28] Yet while users spontaneously expressed complaints about internal and external (traffic) noise and ventilation, very few had remarks about over-brightness and glare as a problem in their experience. This may be because the surveyors found more small-size rooms (for single or double occupancy), where comfortable lighting was easier to achieve. Second, technical innovations in lighting design had already begun to address the problem of glare. The lighting installations that Hopkinson's group had studied frequently made use of exposed fluorescent tubes that were too bright for office tasks.[29] However, manufacturers responded quickly to such issues with a variety of lighting designs that sought to prevent direct glare.[30] New types of fixtures, for instance, encapsulated the tubes or integrated them in ceilings to cut off the viewing angles that caused excessive brightness levels. Other elements such as louvres and reflectors served to diffuse and redistribute the light in predictable ways. By the early 1960s, manufacturers had already begun to implement theoretical recommendations on preventing glare discomfort in their products. This is confirmed by visual documentation of office environments in the late 1950s and 1960s, for instance in the Pilkington report on office design.[31] A third reason for the slow uptake of this and other lighting standards was the relative neglect of lighting practice in 1950s architectural education, and conversely the lack of attention to building design in the training of lighting engineers.[32] By the beginning of the 1960s, however, some architectural and engineering programmes placed greater emphasis on the importance of "environmental conditions", both practically and theoretically. Lighting experts such as Hopkinson took an active role in ensuring that architecture students were taught lighting practice.[33]

The influence of engineering research on glare discomfort can be seen more clearly in the 1970s, when office planners and lighting engineers began to advocate the use of localised task lighting as a more effective alternative to general ceiling illumination. This may relate to two major factors: the proliferation of office landscape concepts and the 1970s oil crisis, which prompted efforts to reduce superfluous energy use. In the United States, for instance, in 1978 the office interior designer John Pile advised a lighting scheme that balanced "ambient lighting" with "task lighting":

> Ambient lighting fills the total space, circulation and other non-task areas with sufficient light to make it easy to move about and prevent extreme brightness contrast between task areas and surroundings. [...] It generates a far pleasanter ambience than the blasting glare of the usual ceiling fluorescents and is at least as pleasant as the best installations of low-brightness ceiling fixtures.[34]

By that time, manufacturers of panel and storage-wall furniture for the open-plan office had begun to incorporate task lighting equipment in their standard product lines. In Britain in 1979, office planner and designer Geoffrey Salmon likewise advocated a variety of lighting types to avoid uncomfortable degrees of contrast and glare.[35] One visual, for instance, illustrates the various sources of illumination that needed to be balanced in a typical office environment. A functionally lit but comfortable visual environment required general lighting, task lighting and daylight.

We can draw some preliminary conclusions from this case study. First, it illustrates how by mid-century, building research at the BRS had begun to focus on user experiences as part of its efforts to evaluate and improve building performance. Second, it shows how user preferences were measured, aggregated into a threshold of comfort and turned into an index for general use in office design. Finally, it calls attention to an emerging insight among lighting engineers and architects that light is not just a functional requirement for work; rather, it is a constitutive element of a particular working environment. Instead of exposing the entire office to the same uniform level of brightness, Hopkinson and his colleagues established experimentally that bright lights distracted workers' attention. They recommended that thought should be given to illumination for the entire visual field, through a careful balancing of background and local lighting, to distinguish a visual task from its surroundings and focus workers' attention. What Hopkinson and his colleagues suggested, and what designers came to realise and implement in the mid- to late 1970s, is that light could serve as an instrument for situating workers in a smaller perceptual field by guiding their attention and limiting distraction in an open-space environment. In the next section, I will develop these points further with reference to a second case study.

OFFICE ACOUSTICS AND THE ARTICULATION INDEX

Room acoustics is a second field in which post-war engineers and planners began to integrate models of user perception in office architecture. Sound management has long been a key concern for office architects, planners and managers, who have sought to balance public visibility and managerial surveillance with productivity.[36] In the modern office building, such needs were often seen as contradictory. In the 1920s, the open-plan layout of "bullpen" offices was found to be particularly noisy because of the reverberation of typewriter noise, telephones, conversation and street noise. Equated with physiological or psychological stress, such sounds were presented as disturbances that affected workers' efficiency and ultimately their productivity.[37] As historian of technology Emily Thompson has shown, this association between a quiet environment and efficiency was exploited by an emerging industry centred around sound absorptive building technologies. As one 1920 sales brochure noted, for instance, "an unbearable increase in unnecessary noise, confusion and nervous excitement [...] had a marked effect on the normal efficiency of both executives and office workers".[38] By tackling reverberations with increasingly absorptive materials, technologies such as floor carpeting, acoustic tile ceilings and isolating wall panelling promised office managers a clean, comfortable and more efficient atmosphere that Thompson described as a "soundscape of modernity".[39] But as I will argue below, this approach changed between 1950 and the mid-1970s. Drawing on their experience with wartime psychoacoustic research, post-war acoustic consultants turned their focus from the effects of noise on users to users' *tolerance* for noise. Combining noise control technologies with models of user perception shifted the definition of noise in the office.

This shift is best illustrated by zooming in on the influential work by the American consultancy firm Bolt Beranek and Newman (henceforth BBN) on improvements in office acoustics. The firm was formed in 1948 in Cambridge, MA by Leo Beranek and his colleague Richard Bolt (they were later joined by Bob Newman) to repurpose the expertise in acoustical engineering they had gained over the preceding wartime years. During the war, Beranek had directed the Harvard acoustics laboratory that undertook acoustical research for defence purposes. Tasked with engineering improved communication acoustics in vehicle cockpits under conditions of combat, the Harvard laboratory had developed extensive programmes for researching and testing noise reduction materials and improving the acoustic performance of speech communication systems.[40] After the war, Beranek partnered with his Massachusetts Institute of Technology colleagues to consult on a variety of problems in acoustical engineering: from redesigning a privacy-enhancing telephone receiver called Hush-a-Phone or predicting the noise levels emitted by ventilation systems, to the acoustic design of auditoria (such as, famously, the United Nations Assembly Hall) and office spaces. Acquiring recognition for the latter, Beranek and his colleagues drew on wartime (psycho)acoustics to reconceptualise the problem of office acoustics in at least two significant ways.

The first was by quantifying workers' *tolerance* for particular noise levels. To determine how quiet the ideal office should be, Beranek surveyed ambient sound and office users' responses to it in different kinds of offices at MIT, General Radio and a metal production company. As the consultants took their noise measurements, they asked executives, clerical workers and business machine operators in each space to rate the noise level on a scale from "very quiet" to "intolerably noisy", while also rating the maximum noise levels at which they could converse with colleagues, telephone and "accomplish their duties without loss of performance".[41] BBN further developed this approach when it was contracted to study persistent noise complaints at U.S. Air Force base offices. In a more traditional approach to noise control, surveyors measured the absolute noise levels that workers were exposed to in their office, which included aircraft flyovers and business machine operations. Since the behavioural impact of such noise on work efficiency was difficult to determine, Beranek and his collaborators used questionnaires to solicit workers' own *subjective* rating of the noise levels and the extent to which they interfered with their duties: were they able to converse on the phone, could they type up a report or concentrate on reading when necessary?[42] By plotting the noise ratings together with the sound level measurements that they had collected while the questionnaires were completed, Beranek and his colleagues calculated a set of "Noise Criterion Curves".[43] Such curves and a set of accompanying tables charted a range of sound levels that most users found acceptable for particular applications (Fig. 4.4.).[44]

Table II. Recommended Noise Criteria for Offices

Noise measurements made for the purpose of judging the satisfactoriness of the noise in an office by comparison with these criteria should be performed with the office in normal operation, but with no one talking at the particular desk or conference table where speech communication is desired (i.e., where the measurement is being made). Background noise with the office unoccupied should be lower, say by 5 to 10 units.

NC Curve of Fig. 3	Communication Environment	Typical Applications
NC-20 to NC-30	Very quiet office—telephone use satisfactory—suitable for large conferences.	Executive offices and conference rooms for 50 people.
NC-30 to NC-35	"Quiet" office; satisfactory for conferences at a 15-ft table; normal voice 10 to 30 ft; telephone use satisfactory.	Private or semi-private offices, reception rooms, and small conference rooms for 20 people.
NC-35 to NC-40	Satisfactory for conferences at a 6- to 8-ft table; telephone use satisfactory; normal voice 6 to 12 ft.	Medium-sized offices and industrial business offices.
NC-40 to NC-50	Satisfactory for conferences at a 4- to 5-ft table; telephone use occasionally slightly difficult; normal voice 3 to 6 ft; raised voice 6 to 12 ft.	Large engineering and drafting rooms, etc.
NC-50 to NC-55	Unsatisfactory for conferences of more than two or three people; telephone use slightly difficult; normal voice 1 to 2 ft; raised voice 3 to 6 ft.	Secretarial areas (typing), accounting areas (business machines), blueprint rooms, etc.
Above NC-55	"Very noisy"; office environment unsatisfactory; telephone use difficult.	Not recommended for any type of office.

Fig. 4.4. Table for recommended Noise Criteria. (Leo L. Beranek, 'Revised Criteria for Noise in Buildings', in Noise Control, 3/1 [1957], 25.)

As a projection of comfort, these median curves outlined a threshold that architects and consultants could make use of when planning acoustic treatment of offices in accordance with specific job needs. Since individual tolerances were likely to be affected by local customs, expectations and experiences, Beranek also proposed an alternative curve that could be used if extreme economy was needed or if a "calculated risk of complaint" could be taken. Importantly, however, the values for noise tolerance that they conveyed were defined on the basis of the workplace rather than the employee; curves tracked the point at which an employee claimed to be able to perform their tasks, rather than the employee's own subjective sense of well-being or comfort in the workplace.[45] In other words, just like the Glare Comfort Index would do for light, this Noise Criterion quantified a threshold at which employees' discomfort just turned to comfort. The objective implied by this metric, then, was not so much to *eliminate* noise as to *reduce* it to just tolerable levels.

Secondly, Beranek and his colleagues redefined the problem of office noise from one of *absolute* noise levels to levels that were *relative* to their background. Two years after Beranek, MIT alumni and BBN employees William R. Farrell and B.G. Watters convinced acoustic isolation manufacturer Owens-Corning to commission them to come up with a simplified method for modelling noise reduction and planning for acceptable office acoustics. In the 1950s, architects increasingly specified lightweight partitions to separate private offices. Yet these typically came at the cost of acoustic isolation, which resulted in complaints about noise and a lack of privacy in adjacent offices. While testing building materials for noise transmission, the group recognised that speech privacy constituted a particular problem in offices. Their observations suggested that noise was less easily tolerated when it was *intelligible*. Just as hushed whispers in a silent library could be more disturbing than a raised voice in a noisy bar, they argued, it was not the loudness of a noise but the ambient sound levels that determined its intrusiveness. To study the conditions underpinning intelligibility, the acoustical consultants conducted a series of psychophysical experiments which simulated a private office setup in the laboratory. While varying parameters of speech and noise, they asked office workers to indicate when speech from a nearby office would become "bothersome" or insufficiently private to them.[46] Reporting on their studies in 1962, the consultants concluded that "an increase in the background level has the same effect on intelligibility as an increase in noise reduction between spaces".[47] Testing the relationship between background noise and users' assessments of privacy in 37 of the offices they were called in to consult on, they determined and refined an acoustic threshold that promised tolerable levels of privacy and noise in a wide range of circumstances. Such data suggested that the relationship between intelligible speech and background levels correlated with an existing instrument known as the Articulation Index.

    The Articulation Index had evolved out of a series of pre-war articulation tests by Bell Telephone Laboratories, which had served to determine the acoustic structure of the conversational human voice to improve the performance of their microphones, telephones and receivers. Bell researchers discovered that speech intelligibility varied greatly with frequency and loudness, and that high frequency sounds were most important to speech comprehension.[48] During the war, this approach had found its way into the Harvard sound control laboratories that were tasked with improving communication under the intensely noisy conditions of combat.[49] The Harvard researchers found that noise on aircrafts had a peculiar structure, with all frequencies added together, "producing a noise that is to sound what white light is to light".[50] Such "white noise" was not so much disabling because it was disagreeable to listeners, but rather because its overlap with critical frequency bands reduced the intelligibility of human speech in the cabin to about 50 percent. Because aeronautical design did not tolerate acoustic isolation that was heavy enough to be effective, the researchers had focused their efforts on improving the ratio of speech signal to surrounding noise by improving earphones and microphones instead. Conducting articulation tests with human users, however, was laborious and time-consuming. That is why, after World War II, the Bell Labs and Harvard researchers plotted their measurement of the average intelligibility of normal male speech – to hundreds of listeners – into a standardised and highly idealised spectrum: the Articulation Index. This index was based on 200 standard values with which the relative contribution of each individual frequency band to an intelligible speech signal could be weighed. Comparing this profile of a standard signal against any acoustic measurements of a noisy ambience produced a ratio that was indicative of the intelligibility of the human voice in these surroundings.[51]

Although the index had been developed to study *intelligibility* in speech communication, the BBN acoustical consultants now working on the problem of office noise repurposed a simplified version of the Articulation Index as an inverted measure of *privacy*. An Articulation Index score of 0.20 meant, for instance, that people who were not part of the conversation could understand just 20 percent of the words spoken, which ensured a good level of privacy. The consultants proposed combining the index with spectra of background noise in actual offices to determine the bandwidth of speech levels that remained intelligible to nearby bystanders, as well as the level of background noise required to mask the speech. Paired with the Noise Criterion Curves, it was possible to predict – at least in theory – when such background noise became so unacceptably loud that it affected workers' performance. Both the Noise Criteria and the Articulation Index, in other words, turned aggregated user perceptions into a standard for the ideal relationship between background noise and intelligibility in the office.

This new approach to office acoustics began to gain traction among office planners and acousticians in around 1970, when problematic acoustics threatened the success of new open-plan office concepts. In the preceding decades, American offices had typically been divided between private offices for higher-level staff and open spaces for lower-level clerical workers. Yet by the late 1960s, management consultants, architects and furniture designers had begun to promote layouts such as Herman Miller's Action Office II and Quickborner Team's *Bürolandschaft* as a radically new way of organising office work. As Jennifer Kaufmann-Buhler has argued, seating executives and clerical workers next to each other promised a horizontal, flexible and efficient culture of communication.[52] But although these promises were initially widely embraced by managers, by 1970, the office landscape concept had also led to criticism from ergonomists and users. The first reports had failed to reveal any inherent advantages in workers' effectiveness or productivity. Instead, experts had reverted to measuring users' *experiences* based on so-called post-occupancy evaluations – questionnaires which sampled occupants' attitudes and appreciation of their new environment.[53] Such evaluations in turn highlighted a particular concern among users with acoustics and privacy. One book-length study, for instance, had surveyed employees in a new open office over a five-year period and concluded that workers generally felt distracted by intrusions of animated conversations, typewriters, ringing telephones, machine handling and the ambient noises generated by HVAC. Meanwhile, employees on the executive floors had become concerned over their own lack of acoustical privacy, with sound travelling freely across the office floor.[54] Although concerns over noise in the office were not new, both as a general problem and to advocates of the open-plan office concept, they were initially dismissed as temporary adjustment issues or resistance to progressive ideals.[55] Nevertheless, the fact that these concerns were shared by both clerical and executive employees gave them more traction than before, forcing manufacturers to come up with solutions that maintained the original concept.

To do so, manufacturers and designers worked closely with acousticians, who adapted the Noise Criteria and the Articulation Index to model users' experience of privacy in open-plan offices. Ranger Farrell, who had been instrumental in BBN's private office studies, for instance, established his own consultancy firm specialised in improving office acoustics. Robert Propst, who headed the Herman Miller Research Corporation that was responsible for the successful Action Office furniture line, collaborated closely with acoustic consultant Richard Hamme to come up with solutions for sound conditioning in the office.[56] However, limiting speaker intelligibility (and thus achieving enhanced privacy) in open offices proved complex. Without physical walls, speech intelligibility could vary immensely, depending on speaker orientation, effort and distance. Achieving privacy therefore involved careful use of available materials such as screens, partitions, ceilings and carpets to attenuate and absorb sounds and reduce reflections.[57] To that end, Herman Miller developed a consulting service to assist with the review and acoustic fine-tuning

Fig. 4.5. "Circles of influence" in open office planning: "intelligible" (I), "almost fully intelligible" (AFI), "partly intelligible" (PI), "audible" (A), "inaudible" (IA). (Ranger Farrell, 'Sounds of the Open Plan', in Environment Magazine: Planning and Design [July/Aug. 1970], 8.)

of Action Office installations. In the mid-1970s, moreover, it published a handbook on acoustics in open-plan spaces, which outlined the state of the art in acoustic research for the office planner.[58]

In keeping with this state of the art, acousticians and office planners not only advocated conventional means of noise reduction to control how sound travelled; they also proposed the strategic placement of masking sources to ensure that sounds that did travel were rendered unintelligible. Initially, their efforts walked a fine line between solving and amplifying noise complaints, for instance when they recycled the sonic exhaust of ventilation terminals or traffic noise, or seated frantically typing secretaries adjacent to conference rooms.[59] By the mid-1970s, however, many had

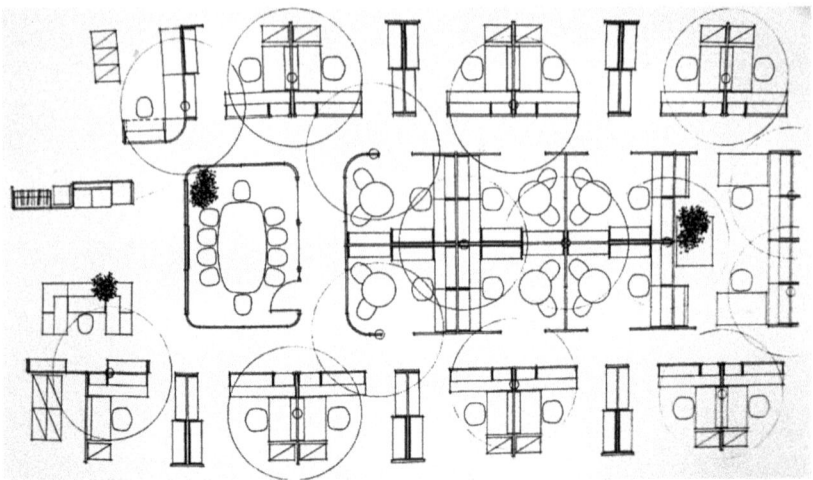

Fig. 4.6. Ideal typical open office floor plan with circles indicating the positioning of sound masking devices and the acoustic privacy zones they generate. (Robert L. Propst and Michael Wodka, The Action Office Acoustic Area Conditioner: An Examination of the Masking Sound Requirements of Action Office Installations [Ann Arbor, 1974], 25. Courtesy of the Herman Miller Archives.)

resorted to electronic sound masking systems that subtly sprayed noise spectra that were calibrated to mask human speech. As part of a range of acoustical products (such as improved acoustical screens and physical enclosures), for instance, Herman Miller developed and marketed a product known as the "Action Office Acoustic Area Conditioner", a device that generated a noise whose profile was calibrated to mask intelligible speech at relatively close distances in the office.[60]

By introducing rather than reducing noise in the office, acousticians used instruments such as the Articulation Index, Noise Curves and calibrated sources of natural or artificial masking sound to engineer what acoustic consultant Ranger Farrell called "circles of influence".[61] These represented a set of concentric zones that could be projected around individuals or groups of coworkers with similar requirements (Fig. 4.5.). Such circles were defined by the levels of intelligibility of the individuals or groups in the middle, ranging from inaudible to intelligible, depending on an auditor's distance from the source. By acoustically adjusting the office environment or raising background sounds, the circles served to engineer what Robert Propst and the environmental consultant Michael Wodka called "acoustic privacy zones" (Fig. 4.6).[62] These perceptual zones resulted when acoustic and visual environments were consistent with one another, and adjoining work areas did not "leak" or "interfere" with others in terms of speech intelligibility.

As this case shows, then, acoustical consultants such as those at BBN aggregated the results of acoustic measurements and user surveys to develop a set of instruments that turned office workers' experiences into a standard for keeping speech from interfering with productive work. By turning descriptions of users' current expectations of comfort into a prescription for the acoustically sound workplace, this process tended to reproduce an organisational hierarchy: Noise Curves for executive suites, for instance, initially specified less tolerance for noise than those for stenographic groups. Moreover, such curves represented a threshold of discomfort (rather than comfort) at which workers indicated that they were unable to perform their tasks. As such, acoustics was introduced to facilitate the ideal of the open-plan office environment, in which all employees were equally accessible and visible to one another but their speech did not interrupt each other's focus on work. The principles of acoustics were used to balance too much and too little noise at any point within the open space, in order to delineate enclosures – zones of intelligibility – against a generally unintelligible background.

CONCLUSION

My two case studies help trace the contours of an approach to environmental management of the post-war office, as seen in different professional domains in the United States and Britain. Office environments were conceived as integrated, engineered spaces whose lighting, acoustic, thermal, ventilation, spatial and social dimensions were expected to have an influence on users' mental state, physical comfort and health. By reconstructing the development of two such instruments, I have sought to show how the built interior was imagined as a protective "environment" that could be controlled and managed with precision.[63] Such precision was expressed through a set of curves that represented users' subjective experiences and perceptions as a guideline for designing physical environments. In the technical papers, reports and building codes that constituted such guidelines, users rarely emerged as articulate, individual voices. While surveys often took pains to ensure a representative sample of office workers in different clerical and executive roles, their perspectives were typically invoked as aggregated expressions of (dis)comfort. In this way, user experiences were quantified into a single threshold value or curve that, once part of a building code or redesign practice, permitted designers, planners and engineers to claim a calculated, comparable and predictable level of acceptance and comfort among actual users.

As a guideline or planning tool, they were not enforceable in actual design practice, nor were they easily implemented on the work floor. These instruments do, however, provide an insight into the kinds of environments that offices were imagined to be. As I have sought to show by reconstructing how the curves were developed, they were calculated with particular working conditions in mind. Criteria for office environments were defined by workers' ability to perform their tasks, rather than a general sense of comfort or well-being. The perceptual research underlying these guidelines envisaged a precise technique for managing not just the office space itself, but workers' experience in that space, by attuning the former to the limits of the latter. Environmental management turned knowledge of users' perceptions into a design principle that sought to structure their attention. In the fields of both light and sound engineering, after all, knowledge of threshold values was linked to attempts to limit the distracting sensory effects that large rooms or open office environments were found to have on their inhabitants. Whether by limiting the subtle distractions of glare due to overhead lighting or by masking intelligible speech, perceptual comfort was defined by workers' ability to focus on their tasks at hand. It is here that the two meanings of environmental management merge.

In the open office of the 1960s and 1970s, such perceptual engineering was expected to function as a "technique of enclosure" – a term I borrow from historian of architecture Alexandra Quantrill.[64] Quantrill uses this term to describe a post-war approach to environmental management that was brought about by modern architecture's fascination with glass wall panelling exteriors for office buildings. These glass enclosures posed problems of heating, ventilation and light control that necessitated a precise conditioning of the interior atmosphere to make it suitably stable for work. As Quantrill shows, this invoked an elaborate set of techniques of enclosure, such as air-conditioning systems, weathering protection and sealants, that helped to constitute the office floor as a set of "inwardly focused spaces quite separate from the outside world".[65] I propose that the techniques of perceptual engineering that are condensed in the Glare Comfort and Articulation indices may also be read as an effort at environmental containment, albeit at a smaller scale. These instruments aimed to create a stable and comfortable ambience, focusing not on the inside-outside divide of glazing but on ways of carving up the large open office environment into an array of perceptual (and often immaterial) spaces. The aim of situating the worker in the middle of an envelope of task-focused light or a limited zone of intelligibility was to renegotiate the purported advantages of the large room or open-plan office floor to architects and management based on users' apparent preferences – maintaining the suggestion of comfort, privacy and focus in a visually open, transparent and flexible architecture. Even though such negotiations were far from stable, difficult to implement and at times resisted by users, they did become part of the material infrastructure of the post-war office.

Examining a history of techniques of enclosure and how they configured the "office environment" highlights the processes of co-production between users (or at least their proxy representations) and the material organisation of the office over time. The open-plan office layout that has helped configure contemporary notions of the workspace to this day has been long in the making – and just as the open-plan layout itself has a long history, so too have the perceptual techniques that were envisaged to enable it. Tracing these techniques offers a condensed insight into the extensive networks of disciplinary communities, research institutes employers and users, as well as the surveys, laboratories, curves, standards, buildings, materials, interior designs and user requirements that had to be aligned so that the open-plan layout and the managerial beliefs it materialised could be stabilised into a promised solution to the demands of late-20th-century knowledge work.

NOTES

[1] Peter Manning, Office Design: A Study of Environment (Liverpool, 1965), 17.
[2] Dean Hawkes, The Environmental Imagination: Technics and Poetics of the Architectural Environment (London, 2008); John E. Crowley, The Invention of Comfort: Sensibilities and Design in Early Modern Britain and Early America (Baltimore, 2003); Reyner Banham, The Architecture of the Well-Tempered Environment (London, 1969).
[3] Larry Busbea, The Responsive Environment: Design, Aesthetics, and the Human in the 1970s (Minneapolis, 2020); Joy Knoblauch, The Architecture of Good Behavior: Psychology and Modern Institutional Design in Postwar America (Pittsburgh, 2020); Avigail Sachs, Environmental Design: Architecture, Politics, and Science in Postwar America (Charlottesville, 2018).
[4] Manning, Office Design, 7.
[5] P.J. Carlino, 'Tied to the Desk: The Somatic Experience of Office Work, 1870-1920', in Journal of Interior Design, 46/1 (2021); Gianenrico Bernasconi and Stefan Nellen (eds.), Das Büro. Zur Rationalisierung des Interieurs, 1880-1960 (Bielefeld, 2019); Anson Rabinbach, The Human Motor: Energy, Fatigue, and the Origins of Modernity (Berkeley, 1990).

6. William H. Leffingwell, Making the Office Pay: Tested Office Plans, Methods, and Systems that Make for Better Results (Chicago, 1918), 95-109.
7. Franklin Becker, 'Workplace Planning, Design, and Management', in Ervin H. Zube and Gary T. Moore (eds.), Advances in Environment, Behavior, and Design (New York, 1991); Francis Duffy, 'Office Design and Organizations: 1 – Theoretical Basis', in Environment and Planning B, 1/1 (1974).
8. See for instance Jennifer Kaufmann-Buhler, Open Plan: A Design History of the American Office (London, 2021); Renyi Hong, 'Office Interiors and the Fantasy of Information Work', in tripleC, 15/2 (2017).
9. Thomas W. Leslie, 'Fluorescent Lamps', in Construction History, 35/2 (2020); Margaret Maile Petty, 'Fluorescent Fields: Electric Lighting and the Rationalization of the Modern Corporate Workplace', in Pietro Zennaro (ed.), Colour and Light in Architecture (Verona, 2010).
10. Maile Petty, Fluorescent Fields. The American trend for deep open-plan offices was not embraced as enthusiastically in Europe, where office spaces tended to be narrower. See Juriaan van Meel, The European Office: Office Design and National Context (Rotterdam, 2000), 29.
11. Thomas W. Leslie et al., 'Deep Space, Thin Walls: Environmental and Material Precursors to the Postwar Skyscraper', in Journal of the Society of Architectural Historians, 77/1 (2018). Between 1918 and 1952, lighting standards for clerical work rose up to twenty-fold in Britain, and more in the U.S. See F.J. Langdon, Modern Offices: A User Survey (London, 1966), 4; P.V. Burnett, 'Office Lighting', in Illuminating Engineering Society Transactions [hereafter Trans. Illum. Eng. Soc.], 18/6 (1953); The Lighting of Office Buildings (London, 1952).
12. M. Luckiesh and L.L. Holladay, 'Glare and Visibility: A Resumé of the Results Obtained in Investigations of Visual and Lighting Conditions Involving These Factors', in Trans. Illum. Eng. Soc., 20 (1925).
13. Leffingwell, Making the Office Pay, 100-102; John William Schulze, The American Office: Its Organization, Management and Records (New York, 1913), 78-79.
14. P. Petherbridge and R.G. Hopkinson, 'Discomfort Glare and the Lighting of Buildings', in Trans. Illum. Eng. Soc., 15/2 (1950).
15. F.M. Lea, Science and Building: A History of the Building Research Station (London 1971), 123; I.G. Evans, 'Building Research in Great Britain', in Nature, 157 (1946).
16. Roger Courtney, 'Building Research Establishment: Past, Present and Future', in Building Research & Information, 25/5 (1997); Evans, Building Research.
17. For context on post-war reconstruction, see Nicholas Bullock, Building the Post-war World: Modern Architecture and Reconstruction in Britain (London, 2002); Lea, Science and Building, 123.
18. Ralph Galbraith Hopkinson, Architectural Physics: Lighting (London, 1963), 4.
19. Ibid., 3 (emphasis in the original).
20. For readability, I refer to R.G. Hopkinson and "his colleagues" or "collaborators". While Ralph Galbraith Hopkinson was a frequent lead author on the BRS's publications on glare in (office) buildings, he collaborated closely with several others, including P. Petherbridge, J.B. Collins, W.A. Allen and James Longmore, as well as Frederick J. Langdon, as specified in the citations listed.
21. Petherbridge and Hopkinson, Discomfort Glare.
22. R.G. Hopkinson and J. Longmore, 'Attention and Distraction in the Lighting of Work-Places', in Ergonomics, 2/4 (1959).
23. R.G. Hopkinson and J.B. Collins, 'The Prediction and Avoidance of Glare in Interior Lighting', in Ergonomics, 6/4 (1963).
24. R.G. Hopkinson, 'Evaluation of Glare', in Trans. Illum. Eng. Soc., 52 (1957).
25. W. Robinson et al., 'The Development of the IES Glare Index System', in Trans. Illum. Eng. Soc., 27/1 (1962).
26. R.G. Hopkinson, 'A Proposed Luminance Basis for a Lighting Code', in Trans. Illum. Eng. Soc., 30/3 (1965).
27. I.E.S. Technical Report No 10 – Evaluation of Discomfort Glare: The I.E.S. Glare Index System for Artificial Lighting Installations (London, 1967).
28. Langdon, Modern Offices, 4 and 15.

29 Strikingly, the installations were primarily found at headquarters of firms with a history in conducting advanced lighting research such as Atlas Lighting, Associated Electrical Industries and General Electric Company.
30 Thomas W. Leslie, '"Partners in Light": How Plastics Enabled Fluorescent Lighting and the Modern Office', in Building Technology Educator's Society, 30/1 (2019).
31 Manning, Office Design, 24.
32 Alan Lewis, 'The Mathematisation of Daylighting: A History of British Architects' Use of the Daylight Factor', in The Journal of Architecture, 22/7 (2017); Derek Phillips, 'Lighting in Buildings: Training and Practice', in Lighting Research & Technology, 21/3 (1956).
33 Lyall Addleson and James Bell, 'Lighting in Architectural Education', in Trans. Illum. Eng. Soc., 33/4 (1968).
34 John Pile, Open Office Planning: A Handbook for Interior Designers and Architects (New York, 1978), 125; John Pile, Interiors: 3rd Book of Offices (New York, 1976), 182-184.
35 Geoffrey Salmon, The Working Office (London, 1979), 40-41.
36 Emily Thompson, The Soundscape of Modernity: Architectural Acoustics and the Culture of Listening in America, 1900-1933 (Cambridge, MA, 2002); Jens van de Maele, 'From Bentham to Guadet: "Auditory Visibility" in Nineteenth-Century Theories on Government Offices', in International Journal for History, Culture and Modernity, 7/1 (2019); Reinhold Martin, 'Acoustic Tile', in Timon Beyes, Robin Holt and Claus Pias (eds.), The Oxford Handbook of Media, Technology, and Organization Studies (Oxford, 2019).
37 Thompson, The Soundscape, 196-199; James G. Mansell, The Age of Noise in Britain: Hearing Modernity (Chicago, 2017).
38 Cited by Thompson, The Soundscape, 196.
39 Thompson, The Soundscape.
40 Leo L. Beranek, Riding the Waves: A Life in Sound, Science, and Industry (Cambridge, MA, 2008).
41 Leo L. Beranek and Robert B. Newman, 'Speech Interference Levels as Criteria for Rating Background Noise in Offices', in The Journal of the Acoustical Society of America, 22/5 (1950), 671.
42 Leo L. Beranek, 'Criteria for Office Quieting Based on Questionnaire Rating Studies', in The Journal of the Acoustical Society of America, 28/5 (1956).
43 Noise rating surveys were collected from about 300 employees in total, in offices at a university, an aluminium company, an electronic equipment company, and the U.S. Air Force operating base at Wright-Patterson.
44 Leo L. Beranek, 'Revised Criteria for Noise in Buildings', in Noise Control, 3/1 (1957).
45 Kathleen Casey, 'Noise Making Subjects', PhD thesis (University of California), 2005.
46 W.R. Farrell and B.G. Watters, 'Study of Speech Privacy', in The Journal of the Acoustical Society of America, 31/11 (1959), 475; W.J. Cavanaugh et al., 'Speech Privacy in Buildings', in The Journal of the Acoustical Society of America, 34/4 (1962).
47 Cavanaugh et al., Speech Privacy, 487.
48 N.R. French and J.C. Steinberg, 'Factors Governing the Intelligibility of Speech Sounds', in The Journal of the Acoustical Society of America, 19/90 (1947).
49 Olga Touloumi, 'Architectures of Global Communication: Psychoacoustics, Acoustic Space, and the Total Environment, 1941-1970', PhD thesis (Harvard University), 2014.
50 L.D. Carson, W.R. Miles and S.S. Stevens, 'Vision, Hearing, and Aeronautical Design', in Journal of the Aeronautical Sciences, 10/4 (1943), 129.
51 Karl D. Kryter, 'Methods for the Calculation and Use of the Articulation Index', in The Journal of the Acoustical Society of America, 34/11 (1962).
52 Kaufmann-Buhler, Open Plan.
53 Malcolm J. Brookes, 'Office Landscape: Does It Work?', in Applied Ergonomics, 3/4 (1972), 226; Malcolm J. Brookes, 'A Maze of Contradictions', in Progressive Architecture (Nov. 1969), 130.
54 Mildred R. Hall and Edward T. Hall, The Fourth Dimension in Architecture: The Impact of Building on Behavior: Eero Saarinen's Administrative Center for Deere & Company, Moline, Illinois (Santa Fe, 1975).

55 Robert L. Propst and Michael Wodka, The Action Office Acoustic Handbook: A Guide For The Open Plan Facility Manager, Planner and Designer (Ann Arbor, 1975).
56 Benson Ford Research Center (Dearborn, MI), Robert L. Propst Papers, Acc. 2010.83, Drawer D6, Folder 'Environmental review – Cummins', Letter from Geiger and Hamme Inc. to Robert Propst (12 Oct. 1967).
57 Rein Pirn, 'Acoustical Variables in Open Planning', in The Journal of the Acoustical Society of America, 49/5A (1971).
58 Propst and Wodka, The Action Office Acoustic Handbook.
59 R.A. Waller, 'Office Acoustics: Effect of Background Noise', in Applied Acoustics, 2/2 (1969); William R. Farrell, 'Evaluation of the Effectiveness and Acceptability of Masking Noise for Providing Speech Privacy in Buildings', in The Journal of the Acoustical Society of America, 32/11 (1960), 1523.
60 Kaufmann-Buhler, Open Plan; Joeri Bruyninckx, 'Tuning the Office: Sound Masking and the Architectonics of Office Work', in Sound Studies, 9/1 (2023).
61 Ranger Farrell, 'Sounds of the Open Plan', in Environment Magazine: Planning and Design, July 1970.
62 Propst and Wodka, The Action Office Acoustic Handbook, 18.
63 On this matter, see also Michelle Murphy, Sick Building Syndrome and the Problem of Uncertainty: Environmental Politics, Technoscience, and Women Workers (Durham, 2006).
64 Alexandra Quantrill, 'The Aesthetics of Precision: Environmental Management and Technique in the Architecture of Enclosure', PhD thesis (Columbia University), 2017, 8.
65 Ibid., 262.

BIBLIOGRAPHY

Lyall Addleson and James Bell, 'Lighting in Architectural Education', in Illuminating Engineering Society Transactions, 33/4 (1968), 119-135.
Reyner Banham, The Architecture of the Well-Tempered Environment (London, 1969).
Franklin Becker, 'Workplace Planning, Design and Management', in Ervin H. Zube and Gary T. Moore (eds.), Advances in Environment, Behavior, and Design (New York, 1991), 115-151.
Leo Leroy Beranek, 'Criteria for Office Quieting Based on Questionnaire Rating Studies', in The Journal of the Acoustical Society of America, 28/5 (1956), 833-852.
Leo Leroy Beranek, 'Revised Criteria for Noise in Buildings', in Noise Control, 3/1 (1957), 19-27.
Leo Leroy Beranek, Riding the Waves: A Life in Sound, Science, and Industry (Cambridge MA, 2008).
Leo Leroy Beranek and Robert B. Newman, 'Speech Interference Levels as Criteria for Rating Background Noise in Offices', in The Journal of the Acoustical Society of America, 22/5 (1950), 671.
Gianenrico Bernasconi and Stefan Nellen (eds.), Das Büro: Zur Rationalisierung des Interieurs, 1880-1960 (Bielefeld, 2019).
Malcolm J. Brookes, 'A Maze of Contradictions', in Progressive Architecture (Nov. 1969), 130-131.
Malcolm J. Brookes, 'Office Landscape: Does It Work?', in Applied Ergonomics, 3/4 (1972), 224-236.
Joeri Bruyninckx, 'Tuning the Office: Sound Masking and the Architectonics of Office Work', in Sound Studies, 9/1 (2023), 64-84.
Nicholas Bullock, Building the Post-War World: Modern Architecture and Reconstruction in Britain (London, 2002).
P.V. Burnett, 'Office Lighting', in Illuminating Engineering Society Transactions, 18/6 (1953), 166-176.
Larry Busbea, The Responsive Environment: Design, Aesthetics, and the Human in the 1970s (Minneapolis, 2020).
P.J. Carlino, 'Tied to the Desk: The Somatic Experience of Office Work, 1870-1920', in Journal of Interior Design, 46/1 (2021), 27-43.
Leon D. Carson, Walter R. Miles and S. S. Stevens, 'Vision, Hearing, and Aeronautical Design', in Journal of the Aeronautical Sciences, 10/4 (1943), 129-149.
Kathleen Casey, 'Noise Making Subjects', PhD thesis (University of California), 2005.

W.J. Cavanaugh et al., 'Speech Privacy in Buildings', in The Journal of the Acoustical Society of America, 34/4 (1962), 475-492.
J.B. Collins and R.G. Hopkinson, 'The Prediction and Avoidance of Glare in Interior Lighting', in Ergonomics, 6/4 (1963), 379-383.
Roger Courtney, 'Building Research Establishment: Past, Present and Future', in Building Research & Information, 25/5 (1997), 285-291.
John E. Crowley, The Invention of Comfort: Sensibilities and Design in Early Modern Britain and Early America (Baltimore, 2003).
Francis Duffy, 'Office Design and Organizations: 1. Theoretical Basis', in Environment and Planning B, 1/1 (1974), 105-118.
I.G. Evans, 'Building Research in Great Britain', in Nature, 157 (1946), 282-285.
William R. Farrell, 'Evaluation of the Effectiveness and Acceptability of Masking Noise for Providing Speech Privacy in Buildings', in The Journal of the Acoustical Society of America, 32 (1960), 1523.
W.R. Farrell and B.G. Watters, 'Study of Speech Privacy', in The Journal of the Acoustical Society of America, 31/11 (1959), 475.
Ranger Farrell, 'Sounds of the Open Plan', in Environment Magazine: Planning and Design (July/Aug. 1970), 1-8.
N.R. French and J.C. Steinberg, 'Factors Governing the Intelligibility of Speech Sounds', in The Journal of the Acoustical Society of America, 19/90 (1947), 90-119.
Mildred R. Hall and Edward T. Hall, The Fourth Dimension in Architecture: The Impact of Building on Behavior – Eero Saarinen's Administrative Center for Deere & Company, Moline, Illinois (Santa Fe, 1975).
Dean Hawkes, The Environmental Imagination: Technics and Poetics of the Architectural Environment (London, 2008).
Renyi Hong, 'Office Interiors and the Fantasy of Information Work', in tripleC, 15/2 (2017), 540-562.
Ralph G. Hopkinson, 'Evaluation of Glare', in Illuminating Engineering Society Transactions, 52 (1957), 305-316.
Ralph G. Hopkinson, Architectural Physics: Lighting (London, 1963).
Ralph G. Hopkinson, 'A Proposed Luminance Basis for a Lighting Code', in Illuminating Engineering Society Transactions, 30/3 (1965), 63-76.
Ralph G. Hopkinson and J. Longmore, 'Attention and Distraction in the Lighting of Work-Places', in Ergonomics, 2/4 (1959), 321-334.
Jennifer Kaufmann-Buhler, Open Plan: A Design History of the American Office (London, 2021).
Joy Knoblauch, The Architecture of Good Behavior: Psychology and Modern Institutional Design in Postwar America (Pittsburgh, 2020).
Karl D. Kryter, 'Methods for the Calculation and Use of the Articulation Index', in The Journal of the Acoustical Society of America, 34/11 (1962), 1689-1697.
Frederick John Langdon, Modern Offices: A User Survey (London, 1966).
Jens van de Maele, 'From Bentham to Guadet: "Auditory Visibility" in Nineteenth-Century Theories on Government Offices', in International Journal for History, Culture and Modernity, 7/1 (2019), 673-685.
Juriaan van Meel, The European Office: Office Design and National Context (Rotterdam, 2000).
Frederick Measham Lea, Science and Building: A History of the Building Research Station (London, 1971).
William Henry Leffingwell, Making the Office Pay: Tested Office Plans, Methods, and Systems that Make for Better Results (Chicago, 1918).
Thomas W. Leslie, '"Partners in Light": How Plastics Enabled Fluorescent Lighting and the Modern Office', in Building Technology Educator's Society, 30/1 (2019), 1-11.
Thomas W. Leslie, 'Fluorescent Lamps', in Construction History, 35/2 (2020), 89-112.
Thomas W. Leslie et al., 'Deep Space, Thin Walls: Environmental and Material Precursors to the Postwar Skyscraper', in Journal of the Society of Architectural Historians, 77/1 (2018), 77-96.
Alan Lewis, 'The Mathematisation of Daylighting: A History of British Architects' Use of the Daylight Factor', in The Journal of Architecture, 22/7 (2017), 1155-1177.

M. Luckiesh and L.L. Holladay, 'Glare and Visibility: A Resumé of the Results Obtained in Investigations of Visual and Lighting Conditions Involving These Factors', in Illuminating Engineering Society Transactions, 20 (1925), 221-247.
Peter Manning, Office Design: A Study of Environment (Liverpool, 1965).
James G. Mansell, The Age of Noise in Britain: Hearing Modernity (Chicago, 2017).
Reinhold Martin, 'Acoustic Tile', in Timon Beyes, Robin Holt and Claus Pias (eds.), The Oxford Handbook of Media, Technology, and Organization Studies (Oxford, 2019), 15-25.
Michelle Murphy, Sick Building Syndrome and the Problem of Uncertainty: Environmental Politics, Technoscience, and Women Workers (Durham, 2006).
P. Petherbridge and Ralph Galbraith Hopkinson, 'Discomfort Glare and the Lighting of Buildings', in Illuminating Engineering Society Transactions, 15/2 (1950), 38-71.
Margaret Maile Petty, 'Fluorescent Fields: Electric Lighting and the Rationalization of the Modern Corporate Workplace', in Pietro Zennaro (ed.), Colour and Light in Architecture (Verona, 2010), 218-225.
Derek Phillips, 'Lighting in Buildings: Training and Practice', in Lighting Research & Technology, 21/3 (1956), 49-73.
John Pile, Interiors: 3rd Book of Offices (New York, 1976).
John Pile, Open Office Planning: A Handbook for Interior Designers and Architects (New York, 1978).
Rein Pirn, 'Acoustical Variables in Open Planning', in The Journal of the Acoustical Society of America, 49/5A (1971), 1339-1345.
Robert L. Propst and Michael Wodka, The Action Office Acoustic Handbook: A Guide for the Open Plan Office (Michigan, 1968).
Robert L. Propst and Michael Wodka, The Action Office Acoustic Area Conditioner: An Examination of the Masking Sound Requirements of Action Office Installations (Ann Arbor, 1974).
Alexandra Quantrill, 'The Aesthetics of Precision: Environmental Management and Technique in the Architecture of Enclosure', PhD thesis (Columbia University), 2017.
Anson Rabinbach, The Human Motor: Energy, Fatigue, and the Origins of Modernity (Berkeley, 1990).
W. Robinson et al., 'The Development of the IES Glare Index System', in Illuminating Engineering Society Transactions, 27/1 (1962), 9-26.
Avigail Sachs, Environmental Design: Architecture, Politics, and Science in Postwar America (Charlottesville, 2018).
Geoffrey Salmon, The Working Office (London, 1979).
John William Schulze, The American Office: Its Organization, Management and Records (New York, 1913).
Sharon Sutton, Calling Up: How Women Architects Transformed the Practice of Architecture in the United States (Seattle, 2003).
V. Tandy, 'The Modern Office: Some Design Principles', in British Journal of Industrial Medicine, 6/3 (1949), 126-136.
Emily Thompson, The Soundscape of Modernity: Architectural Acoustics and the Culture of Listening in America, 1900-1933 (Cambridge MA, 2002).
J. Toon et al., Ambient Noise and Hearing (London, 1965).
Olga Touloumi, 'Architectures of Global Communication: Psychoacoustics, Acoustic Space, and the Total Environment, 1941-1970', PhD thesis (Harvard University), 2014.
R.A. Waller, 'Office Acoustics: Effect of Background Noise', in Applied Acoustics, 2/2 (1969), 121-130.

Chapter 5
Surviving the Office: Workplace Design, Activism and the Health of Women Workers in 20th-Century Britain

Amy Thomas

INTRODUCTION

Look around your office. Do people look well? Or do you all feel tired at the end of the day, exhausted at the end of the week? Do you get headaches, sore throats, upset stomachs, rashes, back-ache? It's probably your job that's doing it [...]. If you work in an office you know it's not the easy life of tea breaks and chats that many people believe. Offices are often tiring and stressful places to work, and have their health hazards – physical, chemical and emotional.[1]

In this opening paragraph to *Office Workers' Survival Handbook: A Guide to Fighting Health Hazards in the Office* (1981), feminist and activist Marianne Craig sought to awaken white-collar workers to an overlooked aspect of their work: it could be dangerous for their health. "Offices on the whole may be cleaner and safer than factories, and occupational accidents and disease perhaps less dramatic", explains Craig, *"but that does not mean they should be taken less seriously*; while the hazards of office work may not kill you on the spot, they do cause serious problems if you have to face them day after day".[2] The guide was written to help office workers identify these hazards in order to have the knowledge to fight for their rights to a safer workplace environment. More specifically, it was addressed to women office workers who occupied the vast majority of lower-paid clerical positions. In an act of political resistance, the book emphasised "how your social class and your sex affect your state of health as much as what job you do... which is itself determined by our social class and sex".[3]

Craig was a member of the Women and Work Hazards Group (WWHG), an affiliate of the British Society for Social Responsibility in

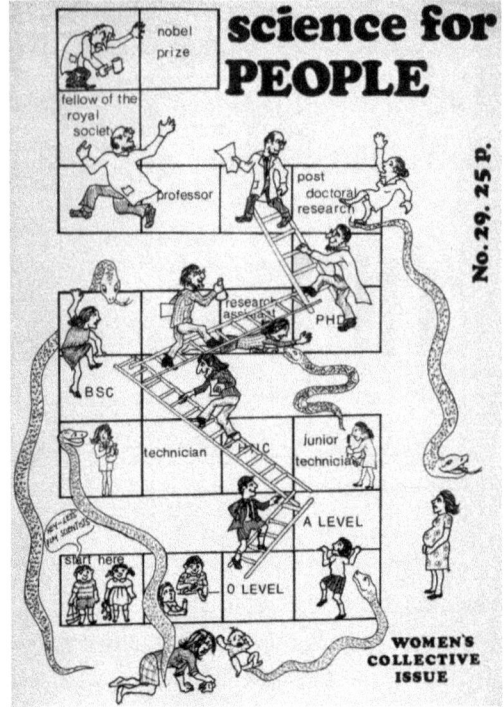

Fig. 5.1. Front cover of *Science for People – Women's collective issue*, published by the British Society for Social Responsibility in Science, 1975. (Wellcome Collection, London, SA/BSR.)

Science (BSSRS). Established in 1977, the WWHG set out to re-centre women's health in the intertwined women's liberation and labour movements, and to show how occupational health was influenced by wider social contexts.[4] In line with a growing awareness of occupational health and safety in Europe, the British Health and Safety at Work Act of 1974 had for the first time enshrined the employer's responsibility for the general welfare of employees in law.[5] With this the work hazards reform movement emerged – comprising grassroots organisations like BSSRS, alongside trade unions and other labour activists – seeking to improve conditions and decrease occupational mortality rates.[6] Yet despite success in implementing regulatory changes to workplace health and safety, women's work and health were largely overlooked in the legislation, primarily because of the devaluation of the work women did in those places.[7] The group argued that very little effort had been made to look at the occupational health risks faced by women, including in domains where they formed the majority of the workforce, such as offices, hospitals and domestic labour (Fig. 5.1.).

The office was uncharted territory in the field of occupational health and safety at the time Craig and her colleagues were working on these issues. While in the post-war decades, health and safety in other industrialised workplaces had been politicised through unions, the comparatively benign character of clerical and managerial work had ensured that office buildings were largely omitted from the discussion. This was despite the fact that clerical work, in its routine and repetitive nature, was posited by some critics, like political economist Harry Braverman in the U.S., as little better than factory work in terms of worker alienation.[8] The WWHG claimed that women were most exposed to the office's health hazards because of their lower positioning within the organisation. By end of the 1970s, women's position within the labour market had shifted dramatically in Britain due to the erosion of the "marriage bar" convention (the requirement for women to leave their jobs on getting married), the implementation of the Equal Pay Act in 1970, the Sexual Discrimination Act of 1975, and the Employment Protection Act of 1975 (the latter rendering maternity pay and job retention obligatory). Census data reveals that by 1981, 57.7 percent of women were engaged in paid work, compared to 36.3 percent three decades earlier.[9] This in turn reconfigured the demographic landscape of the office, with the same census showing that over a third of working women were in secretarial and administrative positions – substantially more than any other sector.[10] Although the number of women in work had risen dramatically, they continued to occupy the lowest paid positions because of the legacy of their historical absence from the labour market and the ongoing discrimination against women in organisations.

Following in the tradition of feminist workplace reformers of the 19th century, the WWHG sought to reframe the office as a site of women's oppression – and, thus, as a site for their emancipation. Yet unlike previous generations of reformers, achieving health equity was not an end in itself: the 19th-century focus on women's factory working conditions was driven more by a broader biopolitical concern with the neglect and malnourishment of children than by a genuine commitment to women's liberation.[11] The WWHG, on the other hand, were seeking to mobilise office workers to claim agency in the workplace and take part in a wider feminist-socialist campaign. As Craig reflects, "we were trying to radicalise [...]; it was our way of trying to raise awareness and bring about a revolution".[12] Comprising women with backgrounds in trade unions, health and safety law, social and medical sciences and the women's liberation movement, the group saw the office as another representation of the patriarchy in an unjust capitalist society. These highly conditioned and designed environments both symbolised and actualised women's lower status in society; women could only thrive if they could take control over these spaces. The WWHG offer an alternative lens through which to view the history of British office design: first, through their emphasis on user knowledge and (particularly female) experience, and second, through their specific emphasis on an expanded definition of the workplace "environment".

Fig. 5.2. Front cover of the pamphlet *Danger – Women at Work: An Introduction to Health and Safety for Women at Work*, published by the Women and Work Hazards Group, 1980s. (Wellcome Collection, London, SA/BSR/B/14/3.)

For the WWHG, women working in the office were not only subjected to discrimination through the design, organisation and culture of the workplace itself; their experiences were also influenced by their personal and collective experiences beyond the workplace, at home, in the city and in society in general (Fig. 5.2.).

This chapter explores this more generous understanding of the workplace environment as a physical, psychosocial and political space by examining one specific notion that garnered much attention from the WWHG: stress. Despite the fact that ideas about stress had been popularised by key publications emanating from the U.S., in the post-war years, the concept was not commonly used in British workplace settings of the 1970s.[13] Feminist worker movements like the WWHG began to use stress as a term to describe the combined effects of the systemic and personal discrimination faced by women and the tangible and perceived threats posed by the office. They argued that the combination of ongoing care- and house-work responsibilities, the repetitive and unstimulating nature of the work, the exposure to potentially harmful toxins and the unrelenting sexual harassment and discrimination created a hostile environment, which in turn had very real physiological effects. Women's health and status in society was a product of this environment. Consequently, the office became the object of scrutiny in pamphlets and articles (Fig. 5.3.). As Michelle Murphy has written in her compelling study of Sick Building Syndrome in America, the women workers' movements of the 1970s came to view the office as being "composed of an oppressive tide of small

Fig. 5.3. *Women's Health, Work and Stress* pamphlet, published by the Women and Work Hazards Group, 1979. (Wellcome Collection, London, SA/BSR/B/14/5.)

details, what one could call the microphysics of office work", which was not simply holding women back but harming them, both physically and psychologically. Through their activism, as Murphy notes, "the office was rematerialized as a site of oppression and pathology".[14]

From an architectural historian's perspective, the WWHG highlighted a fundamental discord between the ideals underpinning the design and conception of the office and the real lived experiences of those working in it. This would seem an obvious point to make, but such observations remain scant in the literature on the history of the British office. Of the architectural histories that we have (far fewer than in the American context), most emphasise the significant impact of developments in technology, architectural style and real estate processes, as well as the shift from cellular, highly domestic offices to hybrid layouts fusing elements of European office landscaping and American open plans.[15] But very few pay attention to the inherent tensions between design intent and user experience.[16] Even fewer have explored the extent to which changing discourses on occupational health and psychology have influenced discourses on design. Through the work of the feminist WWHG, this chapter explores the changing conceptualisation of health and well-being in office design in the closing decades of the 20th century. Focusing on the United Kingdom, it reinterprets specific historical ideas about British office design; terms like "hierarchy", "open plan" and "flexibility" are interrogated and rearticulated through the experiences of women workers. In doing so, it is users and grassroots organisations supporting users, rather than designers and architects, who become the protagonists.

RADICALISING THE FEMINISED WORKPLACE

The office was not an obvious place to start a radical occupational health movement in the 1970s. Clean, non-life-threatening and full of middle-class employees, British offices were not high on the priority list of trade unions or the newly formed Health and Safety Executive regulatory body, which continued to emphasise industrial health and safety.[17] Office work had a cultural reputation for being safe and unexciting, with male clerks earning the stereotype of being meek and weak because of the sector's highly feminised character.[18] Marianne Craig herself was all too aware of the seeming incompatibility of the office with the radical hazards movement. She recalls:

> My dad was an engine driver [...], a Glaswegian working class man. [...] And when I said I was going to write a book about women and work hazards in offices, he looked at me with contempt and he said, "What? Don't chew your lead pencil?"[19]

But while the office may not have been the clearest example of a hazardous workplace, it was an ideal sector from which to recruit women to the feminist cause. The combined impact of growth in the service sector and the legacy of women's employment during the Second World War meant that there were more women working in offices than ever before. By 1951, 60 percent of all clerical workers in Britain were female, in comparison to 0.1 percent a century earlier.[20] It was not only the number of female office workers that rendered them ideal targets for the WWHG, but also their profile. Since their entry into the white-collar workforce in the 19th century, women in the office had been, for the most part, young and unmarried. This was not accidental. Marriage bars had been implemented by organisations since women first joined the labour force in the late 19th century, in order to avoid competition with their male counterparts. The lack of prospects for long-term career progression and the idea that women were well-suited to repetitive menial work meant wages could be kept low, with no entitlement to pension provision or other benefits.[21] But the new office workers of the 1970s were quite different. Many were married, with families and other commitments outside work.[22] This group was unlike their single predecessors, since they were dealing with the double burden of paid and unpaid work, the lack of childcare provision from the state and the litany of other pressures experienced by women in two-earner households. The new legislation of the 1970s may have entitled women to equitable employment, but many aspects, like maternity provision and the right to reinstatement, were minimal and partial, catering to only a tiny subset of the female workforce.[23] These grievances, in tandem with ongoing cultural discrimination against working women, rendered these women ideal candidates for mobilisation by the WWHG. Their activities were part of a broader belief within the Women's Liberation Movement that getting women into paid labour was a way to develop women's collective political consciousness, helping them to build confidence, learn collectively and share problems.[24]

Although a far cry from the hazardous environments faced by miners or chemical plant workers, most British offices in the 1970s were not particularly pleasant spaces. Building controls on commercial buildings emphasised structure and fire protection, neglecting aesthetic and environmental concerns and leading to a fairly conservative office stock.[25] One study by the Building Research Station in the 1960s revealed that many British offices' building services – ventilation, heating and electrical systems – originated from the 1900s, with some government offices still being heated by open coal fires in the 1950s.[26] The rapidity of rebuilding after the Second World War had also catalysed the production of swathes of poor calibre, developer-led office buildings. Here commercial architects were hired to maximise floor space within the given regulations, to the minimum specifications.[27] As one developer of the period noted, they did this by

> limiting floor to ceiling heights to the minimum permitted by building bylaws. Hardly a single building incorporated air-conditioning. Central heating boilers were oil-fired rather than gas-fuelled, and there were generally insufficient electric power outlets.[28]

The implementation of a new Offices, Shops and Railway Premises Act in 1963 somewhat protected workers with safety provisions that included restrictions on workplace density, maintenance and daylighting in offices. Yet these regulations were rather vague, with terms such as "sufficient and suitable lighting", "adequate supplies of fresh or artificially purified air" and, on the matter of seating, the provision of "a seat of a design, construction and dimensions suitable for him".[29] Indeed, whereas the welfare-state-led housing projects of the post-war decades involved sociologists and extensive surveys of use patterns, office buildings were hardly considered in terms of the user experience. The limited number of studies that were carried out focused on the impact of sound, heat, light and air on worker productivity and efficiency, rather than workers' feelings or perceptions about their work spaces.[30] One early ground-breaking study of boredom and fatigue in female clerical workers (1937) explored personal perceptions of status, identity and physical exhaustion in the workplace, but did not link these issues to the design of the space.[31] In Britain, the precedent for such a study was in factories, rather than offices.[32] In the 19th and early 20th centuries, feminist organisations scrutinised the working conditions of women factory workers in numerous studies, surveys and observations.[33] Vicky Long has shown how this sometimes led to the provision of better facilities for the workers, including women-only rest rooms, better canteens and women's club houses.[34] Yet similar adjustments were very rarely made for female clerical workers. The WWHG in the 1970s were the first to bring the daily activities and struggles of these women into popular debate, in turn catalysing a wider conversation about women's health and well-being in the white-collar workplace.

The WWHG's reframing of health and safety in the office as a political conversation occurred at a moment when the relationships between individuals and their environment were being recast in popular debate. In particular, the idea that the manmade environment was a source of potential danger coincided with the rise of the environmental movement in the 1960s and 1970s. At the core of this conversation was a criticism of the problematic co-dependency of the technologies and materials that drove societal progress and the humanitarian-ecological disasters that occurred because of them, such as the nuclear meltdown at Three Mile Island.[35] Environmental activism during this period sought not only to raise awareness of the damaging effects of chemicals, oil spills and other such contaminants, but also challenge the ways in which the scientific establishment was interconnected with political economic power structures. It is within this context that the WWHG emerged as a subset of a larger radical science group, the British Society for Social Responsibility in Science. Formed in 1969 by scientist-activists, BSSRS promoted community science and grassroots research, working with residents and citizens with the aim of equalising the power to collect evidence. Their aim was to expose the public to the political machinations of science, creating public debate within the scientific community and encouraging public participation in setting the agenda for research and development.[36] They claimed that

> science and technology serve the interests of those who fund them. And in serving these interests, they help perpetuate them. To a considerable extent, therefore, science and technology have become instruments of state and industrial power.[37]

BSSRS aspired to operate as a legal-aid equivalent for the public, and became involved in supplying accessible information and support for environmental issues like pollution and occupational health. Here, the notion of the environment found expression on multiple scales, from the neighbourhood (like the grassroots investigation of the so-called "Battersea Smell" caused by a glucose factory and gin distillery) to the office desk or the body of the worker. Following the introduction of the Health and Safety at Work Act 1974, members of BSSRS became more involved with the labour and work hazards reform movement. They campaigned for Safety Representative Regulations, and publicised a number of industrial hazards such as noise, asbestos and vinyl chloride, partially through their influential and long-standing magazine *Hazards*.[38]

Believing that the trade union movement had failed women, particularly those in non-unionised workplaces (like offices) and those engaged in part-time or casual labour who could not be protected, the WWHG formed to open up the male-dominated work hazards conversation to women.[39] They worked across three spheres: providing free advice to individuals and organisations through letters and calls in the U.K. as well as internationally (as far away as New Zealand and Fiji); making accessible literature such as pamphlets with information about a wide range of hazards women might face at work; and disseminating this information in workshops, meetings, conferences, print media and even a documentary film broadcast on national television, funded by the Greater London Council's Women's Committee. Collaborating with trade unions, women's health centres and many other grassroots organisations, the aim was to inform those responsible for workplace health and safety of the challenges experienced by women at work, but also to implore the women's health community to see working conditions as an important factor. In this context, the group thus saw themselves as "part of the new politics of preventative healthcare" that emerged in the 1970s, which emphasised the social and environmental causes of poor health rather than the symptoms and treatment of individuals, popularised within the feminist movement via magazines like *Spare Rib* and women's centres across the country.[40]

WOMEN AND WORK STRESS

As a consciousness-raising tool, the concept of stress was a prominent and powerful topic for the feminist group, featuring highly in publications and pamphlets. Its power resided in concision: stress drew attention to the multiplicity of injustices experienced by women at work and legitimised those experiences by grouping them into a single nameable phenomenon. Stress was not the "bosses' disease", as it was understood by lay people, but was prevalent if not more common among lower paid workers – and particularly women.[41] The group argued that women were not more vulnerable than men to stress, but that they were more likely to be exposed to stressful situations because of their position in society. Women were not only doing the double shift of paid labour at work and unpaid labour at home; they also experienced job role segregation because of the long-standing inequalities in the labour market. They were predominantly in lower-paid and often less fulfilling jobs like clerical work and cleaning, or occupying extremely physically demanding jobs in nursing or the service and care sectors.[42] "Stressors" were thus both social and physical, ranging from lower earnings, restricted opportunities for promotion, job precariousness, low sense of job satisfaction, inflexible hours and sexual harassment, to exposure to chemicals, poor ventilation, temperature, repetitive strain injury and bad lighting. In the office, clerical workers could be exposed to unrealistic deadlines, repetitive and boring work, new technologies such as visual display units (VDUs) which might damage eyesight, and poor physical conditions such as unergonomic furniture and exposure to chemicals from photocopiers and carpets. Office cleaners on the other hand had to deal with unsocial hours, shift work, noise, chemicals and the general "frustration of cleaning up other people's mess". Furthermore, given the higher number of migrant women working as cleaners, they might be more exposed to racist discrimination.[43] Through stress, the conceptualisation of the workplace environment was thus expanded from simply a place of physical hazards to a container of socio-political hazards.

Although the causes of stress were environmental, the effects were bodily: the hormonal responses to these stressors could cause a large range of symptoms from colds, indigestion and muscle pain to fatigue, insomnia, anxiety, depression and even heart disease. "Stress has *social* causes and can therefore be prevented", explained Marianne Craig in her *Office Workers' Survival Handbook*:

> All too frequently the early symptoms of stress – nervousness, headaches, irritability and so on – are written off as "female problems", "menopause" or "your imagination". [...] [Stress] is the result of pressure on your mind, which can end in health breakdown. Such pressures are numerous and complex.[44]

Rather than simply being "women's problems", stress was an occupational health issue that began in the workplace. As Michelle Murphy argues in reference to the women workers' movement in the U.S., feminist groups refused to accept the "analysis that stress was rooted in gendered psychology", instead explaining stress as a physiological issue: "Stress was a *biological* reaction to *social* conditions."[45]

The WWHG's consciousness-raising campaigns were an extension and continuation of the self-help activities promoted by women's groups like the National Housewives Register and the Pre-school Playgroups Association in the 1960s for housewives suffering with depression and anxiety.[46] While the normal treatment of doctors had been to prescribe tranquillisers or anti-depressants, by the 1960s women were becoming more vocal about the social and environmental causes of their stress, and in turn about the possibility for collective solutions. Railing against popular but under-researched notions like "suburban neurosis" (which claimed that "young suburban housewives were prone to a new type of neurosis that resulted from modern civilization frustrating instinctive desires and from the failure to achieve emotional balance"), feminists instead began to locate the problem in the tension between societal expectations of womanhood, the physical and social isolation this brought, and women's desires for greater independence.[47] Pioneering writers like Hannah Gavron, in her devastating critique *The Captive Wife* (1966), linked stress to the purposelessness felt by women at home, which was agitated by a growing societal impulse towards emancipation; more women wanted to go out to work, but were unable to do so because of cultural beliefs and societal structures (e.g. very limited state provision of childcare facilities). Increasingly, as more women entered into part-time work roles, sociologists like Alva Myrdal and Viola Klein located women's stress in the conflict of the two spheres of work and home.[48] Yet they also noted that women who worked experienced less depression and anxiety that those who did not.[49]

The WWHG were looking at the spatial corollary to women's domestic stress in the wake of women's rapid entry into the workplace in the 1970s. They sought to empower women to take control of their work environment, identifying stress as a syndrome brought about by the patriarchy at work and, in particular, the lack of control women had over their work environment and activities. The group were influenced by new studies that correlated higher levels of stress with lower status and agency within the organisation.[50] A highly significant longitudinal study of over 18,000 British civil servants across 38 departments investigated the social determinants of health, especially the prevalence of cardiovascular disease and higher mortality numbers. Known as the Whitehall Study, the research began in 1967 and ran over a period of ten years. It revealed that lower grade employees were roughly 30 percent more likely to die than those at higher grades, instigating a large discussion about work stress as a major contributor to cardiological diseases.[51] It also showed that women had higher levels of sickness absences in the workplace compared to their male counterparts, taking 70 percent more time off for predominantly minor complaints. Married women's absences were higher than those of single women, implying that much of the stress was linked to women's "divided loyalties".[52]

The 1970s represented a shift in the British discourse on work stress. Based on the writing of American stress theorists, early post-war understandings linked stress to the character (or weakness) of the individual. In the U.S., "role stress theorists" emphasised individual perceptions, expectations and the ability to adapt, rather than social structure and other external factors. As Wainwright and Calnan note, "the highly individualized conception of role stress effectively depoliticized the work stress discourse, facilitating its easy passage into corporate human resources management".[53] But by the next decade, financial and energy crises, high unemployment, the uncertainties of new technologies like automation, and the increased feminisation and precariousness of the job market brought about both more heavy-handed approaches to management and increased anxiety in the workplace. Within this context, job stress was reframed as a product of the wider socio-political environment in Britain, becoming grounded in the arena of labour movements, class consciousness and public-sector investigations.[54]

Stress research in Britain had always been tied to the labour movement, with early research starting with the founding of the Industrial Fatigue Research Board after World War I.[55] Much of this early work investigated the causes of sick leave in industrial workplaces, focusing on individual rather than structural causes. Yet by the post-World War II period, the rise of social epidemiological studies under the welfare state placed a greater emphasis on the relationship between social class and health. This research was further influenced by Scandinavian work stress discourses, which argued that stress was a product of one's working environment. Emerging with industrial workers' organisations, the aim of the Scandinavian movement was to improve both the social work environment and the physical workplace instead of mainly promoting productivity.[56] In the mid-1970s, the work of key researchers in this field had a direct impact on legislation, reformulating the power balance between employee and employer and making clear prescriptions about the physical workplace as a safe space.[57] This research rippled into the British academic discourse on work stress in the fields of applied sociology and occupational health, as researchers emphasised the quality of work life and industrial democracy. They claimed that stress arose as a product of employees' alienation from society and lack of power and resources to manage their situation.[58]

The emphasis on public health, status and welfare was reflected in the writing of the WWHG, which drew attention to both societal causes and collective solutions to the work stress problem. Work stress was politicised as a product of a misogynistic and deeply unjust capitalist society, which was only getting worse with the heady conservativism of the Thatcher years. The group argued that "further public expenditure cuts affect the provision of services which might alleviate some of the stress, [such as] nurseries [and] public transport".[59] The solution, they argued, was to organise internally and to join a trade union. Under the 1974 Health and Safety at Work Act, trade unionists were granted the right to elect safety representatives. These representatives were given a number of rights, including the ability to investigate health complaints, accidents and workplace health issues, conduct regular inspections, and access information on chemicals, machinery and environmental hazards. They also had the authority to call in an external inspector if necessary. Furthermore, stress was recognised as an occupational health issue, making it closely linked to the careful scrutiny of the workplace environment.

The WWHG charged female clerical workers with reclaiming their workplace environment through collective action: "History has shown that we cannot rely on the law or our employers to provide us with a safe, stress-free working environment, so it's down to us – and we are much stronger if we are in a trade union and fighting together."[60] However, the unions, which had grown dramatically in size and influence under the auspices of the welfare state, were contentious within the feminist movement.[61] In addition to almost entirely neglecting women-related occupational health and safety issues and failing to actively recruit women, these male-dominated organisations had refused to support feminist issues like the ban of the marriage bar or equal pay.[62] To overcome this bias, the group also advised women to organise themselves internally, first via the distribution of a survey (Fig. 5.4.). This method aimed to get (presumably non-activist) women to wake up to day-to-day injustices and to think about the way their work environment was affecting them.[63] This

SURVEY OF JOB RELATED STRESS

1. Knowing what you know now, if you had to decide all over again whether to take the job you now have, what would you decide?
   (a) Decide definitely not to take the job
   (b) Have some second thoughts
   (c) Decide without hesitation to take the same job

2. During the past 6 months, how many sick leave days have you taken? _____ days

3. During the past 6 months, did you visit a doctor or take prescription medicine for any illness?

4. During the past 6 months, how often did you experience the following symptoms?

	Never or hardly ever	Sometimes	Often
a Colds/flu/sore throat	1	2	3
b Tightness or pressure in the chest	1	2	3
c Shortness of breath	1	2	3
d Indigestion or heartburn	1	2	3
e Stomach ache	1	2	3
f Pain/stiffness in back, shoulder, neck	1	2	3
g Pain/stiffness in hands or wrists	1	2	3
h Pain/stiffness in legs or feet	1	2	3
i Skin irritation or rash	1	2	3
j Mouth ulcers	1	2	3
k Eye strain or irritation	1	2	3
l Fatigue or exhaustion	1	2	3
m Trouble sleeping	1	2	3
n Headaches	1	2	3
o Feeling tense, anxious	1	2	3
p Feeling depressed	1	2	3
q Feeling irritated/frustrated		2	3
r Feeling burned out	1	2	3
s Painful/abnormal periods	1	2	3

Fig. 5.4. Fragment of a survey from the *Women's Health, Work and Stress* pamphlet, 1979. (Wellcome Collection, London, SA/BSR/B/14/5.)

might then lead to larger-scale organising, they claimed, like the 1976 protests by the Department of Health and Social Security workers in Brighton about high temperatures in their office. In this case, their initial attempts to go through the unions failed. In response, they decided to self-organise: 50 office workers walked out, and they were heard. Fans were installed and a winter walk-out in the cold succeeded in getting supplementary heating. "A quick effective communal action can succeed where long negotiations often fail", the WWHG concluded.[64]

THE FEMALE OFFICE WORKER AS THE NON-STANDARD USER

On the surface, the physical changes to the office suggested by the WWHG were not too different from those that women's health and safety organisations had argued for at the beginning of the 20th century.[65] "You may be able to organise proper lunch rooms, or put pressure on management to provide a rest room to relax in", suggested one WWHG pamphlet. Other possibilities included better canteens, more comfortable furniture, and adjustments to temperature, noise levels and ventilation.[66] But the critical difference was the agency that women were given in the process. While the domestic setting – women's so-called "natural place" – had long been the target of design solutions to enable women to manage their environment efficiently and with mastery, in the office women had no such agency because of their low position within the organisation. Historically, design interventions to help female clerks had been top-down; women were considered as manual workers and were the subject of experiments in furniture and lighting to facilitate productivity rather than improve well-being. As Adrian Forty and Katherine Schonfield have shown, this was in contrast to higher-paid male workers, whose private offices – or "thinking" spaces – were furnished with all the psychological comforts of home.[67] If male managers were offered *furniture*, female clerical workers were given *equipment*, suited to their repetitive, manual labour.

The WWHG drew on literature highlighting how the assumption that women were inherently suited to domestic roles put them at risk in the workplace. This belief led to the failure to collect baseline occupational health data for women and their intentional exclusion from related biomedical research.[68] The group argued that "women's occupational ill-health continues to be an invisible problem", not simply because of their devaluation in the labour market but also because "official government statistics on occupational mortality still classify married women by their husband's and not their own occupation". Similarly, accident records in Britain had only recently begun to cover employment areas where women were more likely to work, such as offices, administration and services.[69] Where women's occupational health was taken into account, it was only in relation to their reproductive capacities: protective legislation in industrial workplaces existed to protect the ability to bear children, removing women (rather than the hazards) from environments where they might be exposed to lead or radiation. This emphasis meant that other serious health problems were overlooked. Consequently, it was male bodies that were used as the standard for testing the effects of shift work, stress and exposure to hazardous substances, overlooking women's lower body weight and hormonal changes.[70] In conclusion, they argued that

> it is important not to wait for "scientific" or other expert evidence before taking action. Not only is such evidence frequently derived from studies of male workers, […] but it gives rise to limits and standards based on averages which can still leave workers at risk.[71]

Though the group members were not actively thinking about design, they were channelling wider concerns about norms and standards in the construction of everyday environments. Within the architectural discipline, there was a growing scepticism of the supposed universality that modernist architecture had propagated, both in the mainstream shift towards postmodernism and on the fringes among activist architects demanding more inclusive environments. In the U.K., feminist architecture practices like the Matrix collective and the Women's Design Service were the most outspoken on this issue. As Matrix wrote in their manifesto *Making Space: Women and the Man-Made Environment* (1984), "[modern] architects' grandiose theories did not fit the way of life people wanted to follow", pandering to economic forces rather than social needs and resulting in "characterless office blocks and disastrous 'streets in the sky'".[72] They went on: "We believe that the question of what has 'gone wrong' with modern architecture cannot be discussed adequately without an awareness of the invisibility of women's lives to the professionals who plan buildings and cities."[73] Matrix worked actively with women to develop places from their perspective, from childcare facilities and women's centres to housing and professional workshops to get them into male-dominated craft and construction jobs. Like the WWHG, the goal of Matrix was to expose man-made environments as places that "contain ideas about women, about our 'proper place', about what is private and what is public activity, about which things should be kept separate and which put together".[74] Although the WWHG were not thinking explicitly about architecture, they were concerned with the same central paradox that women represented the non-standard user in a largely female-dominated work environment.

SICK BUILDING SYNDROME: THE ARCHITECTURAL MANIFESTATION OF WORK STRESS

By the 1980s, many of the grievances expressed by women about their offices had entered into the mainstream health and architectural discourse through the so-called Sick Building Syndrome (SBS) epidemic. What is remarkable is the similarity with which SBS and work stress were discussed in terms of symptoms and effects. Like stress, SBS was a described as a nebulous syndrome with myriad causes and a wide range of symptoms. Difficult to define, "a sick building is simply one where people who work in it have a higher level of illness than expected".[75] How could one tell if a building was sick? Tiredness, lethargy, stuffy nose, dry throat, itching eyes, chest tightness, difficulty breathing and headache were just some of the immediate indicators. But like stress, SBS might not be immediately obvious and could take time to manifest in more serious ways; longer-term effects could be mental health disorders like depression and absenteeism.[76] While the causes of work stress orbited around the individual and the organisation, SBS initially located the problem in the physical environment. Causes were thought to be poor ventilation and water-based air-conditioning systems, cheaply built (often public-sector) offices, tinted glass windows, high temperatures, low humidity, high noise levels, carpets, open-plan settings, and the general build-up of air-borne particles in hermetically sealed buildings (including carbon dioxide, water vapour, body odour and a build-up of human-shed micro-organisms in airtight buildings).

Quite quickly, it became clear that women appeared to be worse affected than men. Self-reporting showed that clerical workers experienced symptoms more frequently than managers and that women occupied the majority of clerical positions. It was perhaps unsurprising that the initial response to these self-reported symptoms was to consider SBS a form of mass hysteria (a historically problematic term for women that was often used in discussions about women's stress or "madness", locating women's physical or mental health problems around menstruation and the uterus).[77] While most early studies attributed the symptoms to the kinds of spaces in which clerical workers spent their time, research began to reveal that a key factor was a feeling of lack of control over one's environment. In hermetically sealed buildings, this was largely interpreted as a lack of control of air flow and lighting. The technical interpretation was tackled through "personal environmental systems" that enabled employees to have more control of these immediate environmental factors at their desks.[78] Yet some more progressive SBS publications argued instead that it was the perception of loss of control of one's *wider* environment (i.e. managing to balance home, job design, colleagues and travel, as well as the light and air flow in one's workplace) that was the fundamental stressor causing the physiological reactions associated with SBS. The latter reflected developments in social epidemiological thinking on work stress, a discipline that emphasised the influence of social conditions on the health of populations.[79] Whitehall II, the successor to the first Whitehall study, was particularly significant here. Led by Sir Michael Marmot, the longitudinal study investigated the relationships between work, stress and health among a cohort of 10,308 civil servant office workers.[80] It identified that the cause of the inverse social gradient – why office workers lower down in the organisation were at higher risk of death – was linked to the stress of managing the "work/home interface" and a lack of control in the work environment. The latter was explained using the "demands-control-support" model, which predicted how job strain would be most potent in workplaces where job demands were high, employees had little control and social support was low.[81]

The WWHG had long argued that a prominent source of stress for women was a lack of agency over their working environment and their job, but through SBS this was conceptualised in spatial and architectural terms. A woman's spatial positioning within an office building was indicative of her position within the organisation. As the sociologist Daphne Spain indicated in her 1992 study of gender, space and power relations in the workplace, the large open-plan spaces in which women worked contributed to a sense of powerlessness and purposelessness in the organisation.[82] Such ideas were supported by the research done into gender and SBS. One study revealed that women who were isolated in single-person secretarial offices or in large open offices (with over 50 workers) were significantly more likely to report symptoms of SBS, implying that factors such as social isolation, extreme surveillance and lack of mobility were at play.[83]

SBS emerged as a topic of interest at a moment when the general quality and composition of British office buildings was changing because of economic and technological developments. There was a general improving of office standards with the internationalisation of businesses, which accelerated the Americanisation of office culture and office architecture, not to mention developments in building technology.[84] The rise of the service economy also shifted the symbolic function of buildings from being simply advertisements of the firm to being attractors of talent, placing the "health" of the building higher on the priority list. Simultaneously the rapid and dramatic uptake of personal computers within office buildings in the 1980s was thought by some researchers to decrease the quality of the workplace environment in many offices: dropped ceilings and raised plenum flooring for wiring and cooling reduced floor-to-ceiling heights, providing employees with less air space per person; the lengthening of the working day for many increased the number of hours employees were spending inside the building; and the use of computer terminals – then called visual display units – introduced screen work to the office for the first time, which had negative health effects.[85]

The mass adoption of IT in offices gained a significant amount of attention among the WWHG and its associates. Letters from concerned women about the possible negative impact of VDU work on pregnancies, fertility and health amounted to the largest amount of correspondence ever received by the group, causing them to write a number of pamphlets and articles on the subject and advice for outsider publications.[86] At the core of their concern was the notion that the VDU had somehow re-industrialised the office; the increased pace of work, its repetitive nature, the sterile mechanical aesthetic, and the fear of unknown levels of electromagnetic radiation were causing significantly higher levels of stress among clerical workers.[87] The WWHG's emphasis on the risks of using VDUs may have been tactical, since unions had historically had much success pushing through health and safety legislation in industrial environments. Unlike in Norway and Sweden, stress was not recognised as an official danger to work in the 1974 Health and Safety Act, but injury through the use of machinery was.[88] One could argue that this concern was ultimately founded, as in 1987 offices were re-classified in British planning law under the "B1" use class and categorised as light industrial spaces.[89]

In the mid-1990s, the discourse around SBS began to change as more epidemiological research began to challenge the emphasis on architectural and infrastructural causes. A key piece of research came out of the Whitehall II study, which sought to determine "the role and significance of the physical and psychosocial work environment in explaining SBS".[90] The investigation, conducted by architects Alexi Marmot and Joanna Eley in collaboration with the Whitehall II scientists, was notable for revealing that the elevated symptoms linked to SBS were "due less to poor physical conditions than to a working environment characterised by poor psychosocial conditions".[91] Assessing over 4,000 participants across 44 government buildings, the study argued that "control over work, job demands and work overload, job category, social stressors, mental stress at work, and personality traits have all been related to a similar set of symptoms" and that the "physical attributes of buildings have a small influence on symptoms". All of which suggested that "'sick building syndrome' may be wrongly named".[92]

The appointment, in 1996, of psychology professor Gary Raw as the head of the Building Research Establishment's "Healthy Building Centre", dedicated to investigating SBS, might have given the illusion of a general acceptance of this view within the architectural discipline.[93] In reality, SBS discourse became even more focused on technical aspects and was gradually reduced to a focus on indoor air quality. In Britain, unlike in Scandinavia, the psychosocial needs of users only narrowly entered the architectural discourse via workplace strategy firms like DEGW, founded by Francis Duffy and John Worthington.[94] Here, however, the interest in socially healthy buildings was skewed more towards flexibility and productivity rather than employee welfare. Well-being in the office became divided into two disciplinary-distinct conversations: the "hard" science of comfort, involving the technicalities of light, heat, sound and air, which was the domain of architecture and building technology; and the "soft" factors of employees' mental health, which fell to an imprecise and unstable coalition between psychology, self-help and management theory.[95]

CONCLUSION

Paradoxically, as stress in organisations began to be looked at more empirically through social epidemiology, treatment became more focused on the individual. These studies gave stress legitimacy as an occupational disease, but in the process, it was depoliticised; discourse no longer emphasised the Nordic model of social equality and responsibility. In Britain, the decline in trade unions (beginning under Thatcher) caused unions to shift their focus from structural labour relations to individual workers.[96] In turn, employers were encouraged to protect the health of their workers through human resource management, encouraging coping mechanisms like therapy, exercise and relaxation.[97] This was echoed through new human-oriented approaches to management and mirrored through real estate programmes that incorporated more "leisure" spaces, such as bars and gyms, into office complexes.[98] Today the provision of spaces like cry rooms and yoga centres in the office can be seen as the architectural equipment of this self-help approach, but they are no more revelatory than the nicer lunch rooms and rest spaces women campaigned for in the last century.

As women's position in the labour market changed and the flexibilisation of labour in the new global landscape became the norm, the geographies of work and home became blurred. There was a growing awareness that the basis of women's stress might not be located in the office itself, but in the messy and often painful relationship between work and home. "Spillover", "juggling" and "balancing" became key words to describe the experiences of working mothers in the 1990s, implying a hostile encroachment of one sphere into the other. As Dana Becker has written, the proliferation of gender-targeted self-help techniques implied that "women own the work-family conflict", reinstating the spatialised male/female binaries of work and home.[99] Yet, as this chapter has shown, the geographical and architectural separation of the so-called "two spheres" has been at the root of all conversations around women's work stress since the removal of marriage bars after World War II. Women's inability to "do both" in a society that assigned women to the domestic realm only, despite their continued work outside the home, rendered the office a space beyond women's control. The WWHG saw this as the problem but also the route to emancipation: through the language of occupational health and safety, they gave women the consciousness and ability to take control of their work environments.

Like SBS, the vagueness and plurality of the idea of stress rendered it a useful concept for discussing a wide range of grievances related to the white-collar workplace. The rise of social epidemiological studies of work stress, as well as the Scandinavian labour movement, contributed to a rethinking of the office as a hazardous environment. In parallel, the women's movement focused in on work stress as the bodily manifestation of women's inequality in society. For the WWHG it was a term that encapsulated and legitimised the effects of ongoing sexual discrimination, but also reflected the complete absence of the female body and its attendant societal responsibilities in the conception of the physical workplace. Today, in the wake of the Covid-19 pandemic, the health of office workers has come to the fore with workplace strategy firms, architects and governments paying greater attention to the impact of the office environment on physical and mental well-being.[100] Despite women's professional gains in the workplace since the 1970s, they continue to self-report lower levels of mental and physical well-being than their male counterparts, a fact that was seemingly exacerbated with the increase in care responsibilities during the pandemic.[101] Yet even in this context, gender differences are almost never considered in the design of workplaces.

Unlike housing in the 20th century, office design has rarely (if ever) been used as an infrastructure for social change; it has simply moved with the mode of production because of the continued necessity for productivity under capitalism. If the office is arguably the modernist building par excellence, with its emphasis on modularity, standardisation and mass-production of prefabricated elements, it is quite striking that there was no great challenge to its predominance during a period where the universalising tenets of modernism were being questioned and overhauled. While exceptional outliers like Herman Hertzberger's Centraal Beheer offices in Apeldoorn in the Netherlands (1972) attempted something user-focused and reformist, most offices remained a product of the economic logic of standardisation. Within this context, labour groups like the WWHG were design's closest allies. Their legacy was not to change the course of office design, but rather to give women users agency over their workplace and to remove the cultural distinction between the domestic and work spheres. Through the conversation about work stress, the group reintroduced the "user" as a non-standard entity into the discourse of office design, and this was later picked up by SBS. With this activism, the workplace environment was transformed from a contained immediate space of work to a permeable and slippery domain that shifted between the societal and the personal.

ACKNOWLEDGEMENT

The research for this chapter was funded by the Dutch Research Council (NWO) under the VENI Talent Programme.

NOTES

1. Marianne Craig, Office Workers' Survival Handbook: A Guide to Fighting Health Hazards in the Office (London, 1981), 6.
2. Ibid., 7 (emphasis in the original).
3. Ibid., 8.
4. 'British Society for Social Responsibility in Science (BSSRS) Online Archive' (https://sites.google.com/site/bssrsarchive/home).
5. Diana Gagliardi et al., 'Occupational Safety and Health in Europe: Lessons from the Past, Challenges and Opportunities for the Future', in Industrial Health, 50/1 (2012). On this matter, see also Bernd Holtwick's chapter in the present volume.
6. Wellcome Collection (London), British Society for Social Responsibility in Science Archives, SA/BSR/A/2, BSSRS Constitution (c. 1970).
7. Barbara Harrison, Not Only the Dangerous Trades: Women's Work and Health in Britain, 1880-1914 (London, 2005), 1.
8. Harry Braverman, Labor and Monopoly Capital: The Degradation of Work in the Twentieth Century (New York, 1974).
9. Heather E. Joshi, Richard Layard and Susan J. Owen, 'Why Are More Women Working in Britain?', in Journal of Labor Economics, 3/1 (1985), table 4.
10. Shirley Dex, Kelly Ward and Heather Joshi, 'Changes in Women's Occupations and Occupational Mobility Over 25 Years', in Jacqueline Scott, Shirley Dex and Heather Joshi (eds.), Women and Employment (Cheltenham, 2008).
11. Helen McCarthy, Double Lives: A History of Working Motherhood (London, 2020), 25-26.
12. Interview with Marianne Craig (Women and Work Hazards Group) by the author, Zoom, 28 July 2023.
13. For the American publications, see Richard S. Lazarus, Psychological Stress and the Coping Process (New York, 1966); Hans Selye, The Stress of Life (New York, 1956). For more on the common understandings of stress in post-war Britain, see Jill Kirby, 'Working Too Hard: Experiences of Worry and Stress in Post-War Britain', in Mark Jackson (ed.), Stress in Post-War Britain, 1945-85 (London, 2015).
14. Michelle Murphy, Sick Building Syndrome and the Problem of Uncertainty: Environmental Politics, Technoscience, and Women Workers (Durham, 2006), 58.
15. Rob Harris, London's Global Office Economy: From Clerical Factory to Digital Hub (Oxfordshire, 2021); Murray Fraser, Architecture and the "Special Relationship": The American Influence on Post-War British Architecture (Oxfordshire, 2007); Alan Powers, Britain: Modern Architectures in History (London, 2007); Susan S. Fainstein, The City Builders: Property Development in New York and London, 1980-2000 (Lawrence, 2001); Juriaan van Meel, The European Office: Office Design and National Context (Rotterdam, 2000); Francis Duffy, The Changing Workplace (London, 1992); Francis Duffy, 'Office Buildings and Organisational Change', in Anthony D. King (ed.), Buildings and Society: Essays on the Social Development of the Built Environment (London, 1980).
16. There are three notable exceptions to this: Katherine Shonfield, Walls Have Feelings: Architecture, Film and the City (London, 2000), 75-107; Daphne Spain, Gendered Spaces (London, 1992); Adrian Forty, 'Design in the Office', in idem, Objects of Desire: Design and Society, 1750-1980 (London, 1986). I have also touched on this issue in previous publications, including Amy Thomas, 'Risk in "the Room": Negotiating New Economic Paradigms in the Architecture of Lloyd's of London Insurance Market', in Architectural Theory Review, 26/1 (2022); Amy Thomas, 'The Political Economy of

Flexibility: Deregulation and the Transformation of Corporate Space in the Post-War City of London', in Kenny Cupers, Helena Mattsson and Catharina Gabrielsson (eds.), Neoliberalism: An Architectural Project (Pittsburgh, 2019); Amy Thomas, 'Prejudice and Pragmatism: The Commercial Architect in the Development of Postwar London', in Grey Room, 71 (2018).
17 Arthur McIvor, 'Guardians of Workers' Bodies?: Trade Unions and the History of Occupational Health and Safety', in Labour History, 119/1 (2020). The Health and Safety Executive was formed alongside the new 1974 health and safety legislation.
18 Arthur McIvor, Working Lives: Work in Britain since 1945 (Basingstoke, 2013), 77-90. On this matter, see also Nicola Bishop's chapter in the present volume.
19 Interview with Marianne Craig (Women and Work Hazards Group) by the author, Zoom, 28 July 2023.
20 Anne Bridger, 'A Century of Women's Employment in Clerical Occupations: 1850-1950, with Particular Reference to the Role of the Society for Promoting the Employment of Women', PhD thesis (University of Gloucestershire, 2003), 98.
21 The General Post Office, for example, implemented a marriage bar just six years after female clerks were first appointed in 1870. See McCarthy, Double Lives, 82.
22 Ibid., 324.
23 Ibid., 331-32.
24 Ibid., 351.
25 Francis Duffy, Andrew Laing and Vic Crisp, The Responsible Workplace: The Redesign of Work and Offices (Oxford, 1993), 133.
26 A Qualitative Study of Some Buildings in the London Area (London, 1964).
27 Thomas, Prejudice.
28 Jack Rose, The Dynamics of Urban Property Development (London, 1985), 146.
29 'Offices, Shops and Railway Premises Act 1963' (www.legislation.gov.uk/ukpga/1963/41).
30 See for instance 'A Re-Examination of the Home Office Experimental Office Building, Kew, London; Architects: Ministry of Public Buildings & Works', in Architects' Journal, 151 (1970); Frederick John Langdon et al., Modern Offices: A User Survey (London, 1966); A.W.W. Robinson, 'Working in The City', in Occupational Medicine, 15/1 (1965). On this matter, see also Joeri Bruyninckx' chapter in the present volume.
31 S. Wyatt and J.N. Langdon, Fatigue and Boredom in Repetitive Work (London, 1937).
32 More investigations into women's clerical labour were carried out in the U.S. and Canada. See Kate Boyer, '"Neither Forget nor Remember Your Sex": Sexual Politics in the Early Twentieth-Century Canadian Office', in Journal of Historical Geography, 29/2 (2003); Ellen Lupton, Mechanical Brides: Women and Machines from Home to Office (New York, 1997).
33 In the 19th century, female industrial labour became a key area of study, with numerous studies and observations by women reformers, including the 1891 Royal Commission to inquire into workplace conditions, the Women's Industrial Council, the Fabian Women's Group, the Women's Labour League, the Women's Co-operative Guild, and the National Federation of Women Workers. See McCarthy, Double Lives, 24-25.
34 Vicky Long, 'Industrial Homes, Domestic Factories: The Convergence of Public and Private Space in Interwar Britain', in Journal of British Studies, 50/2 (2011).
35 Anthony Giddens, 'Risk and Responsibility', in The Modern Law Review, 62/1 (1999); Ulrich Beck, Scott Lash and Brian Wynne, Risk Society: Towards a New Modernity (London, 1992).
36 Despite their radicalism, the group had institutional renown in Britain: their inaugural meeting at the Royal Society (RS) was addressed by Nobel Prize-winning scientist Maurice Wilkins (the then RS president) and acquired the support of a long list of prominent names, including Francis Crick, Julian Huxley, Bertrand Russell, J.D. Bernal and many more. See Alice Bell, 'Beneath the White Coat: The Radical Science Movement', in The Guardian (18 July 2013).
37 BSSRS Constitution.
38 'British Society for Social Responsibility in Science (BSSRS) Online Archive'.
39 Harrison, Not Only the Dangerous Trades, 1.

40 Ibid.; Zoe Strimpel, 'Spare Rib, The British Women's Health Movement and the Empowerment of Misery', in Social History of Medicine, 35/1 (2022); Sarah Crook, 'The Women's Liberation Movement, Activism and Therapy at the Grassroots, 1968-1985', in Women's History Review, 27/7 (2018); Mathew Thomson, Psychological Subjects: Identity, Culture, and Health in Twentieth-Century Britain (Oxford, 2006).
41 Stress and VDU Work (London, 1989), 5. The pamphlet refers to a 1977 study by the American National Institute of Safety and Health, which found secretarial work to be the second most stressful job out of the 130 most common occupations for women. See Michael J. Colligan, Michael J. Smith and Joseph J. Hurrell, 'Occupational Incidence Rates of Mental Health Disorders', in Journal of Human Stress, 3/3 (1977).
42 I draw on the plethora of pamphlets and publications in the Women and Work Hazards archive at the Wellcome Collection in which such issues were repeatedly mentioned and discussed. These include Craig, Office; Women's Health in History (London, 1982); Danger – Women at Work: An Introduction to Health and Safety for Women at Work (London, s.d.); Barbara Harrison and Jennie Popay, 'Women Workers and Health Hazards (Draft)', in Health Struggles and Community Action (unpublished, s.d.); Women's Health, Work & Stress (London, 1979); 'Work Can Be Dangerous to Your Health', in Women's Report (Dec. 1978); 'Photocopier Hazards', in Hazards Bulletin (s.d.).
43 Bitter Wages: A Film Made for and with the Women and Work Hazards Group (London, 1984); Women's Health, Work & Stress.
44 Craig, Office, 10.
45 Murphy, Sick Building Syndrome, 75 (emphasis in the original).
46 '10-Minute Talks: Women and Mental Health – Talking about Feelings (podcast)' (via www.thebritishacademy.ac.uk).
47 Debbie Palmer, 'Cultural Change, Stress and Civil Servants' Occupational Health, c. 1967-85', in Mark Jackson (ed.), Stress in Post-War Britain, 1945-85 (London, 2015), 98; Stephen Taylor, 'The Suburban Neurosis', in The Lancet, 231 (1938).
48 Alva Reimer Myrdal and Viola Klein, Women's Two Roles: Home and Work (London, 1968).
49 Palmer, Cultural Change, 98.
50 Craig, Women and Work Hazards Group.
51 'Life and Death in 1960's Civil Service: Whitehall Study I Collection Now Available' (via https://blogs.lshtm.ac.uk); M.G. Marmot et al., 'Health Inequalities among British Civil Servants: The Whitehall II Study', in The Lancet, 337 (1991).
52 Palmer, Cultural Change, 103-104.
53 David Wainwright and Michael Calnan, Work Stress: The Making of a Modern Epidemic (Buckingham, 2002), 42.
54 Joseph Melling, 'Labouring Stress: Scientific Research, Trade Unions and Perceptions of Workplace Stress in Mid-Twentieth-Century Britain', in Mark Jackson (ed.), Stress in Post-War Britain, 1945-85 (London, 2015).
55 Palmer, Cultural Change, 96.
56 Ari Väänänen et al., 'Formulation of Work Stress in 1960-2000: Analysis of Scientific Works from the Perspective of Historical Sociology', in Social Science & Medicine, 75/5 (2012), 788.
57 Examples include the Norwegian Work Environment Act (1977) and the Swedish Act of Co-determination (1976).
58 Influential studies conducted at the Social and Applied Psychology Unit at the University of Sheffield, the Institute of Work, Health and Organizations at the University of Nottingham, and through a significant occupational stress research programme at the Manchester School of Management, sparked a strong interest in the experiences and welfare of workers. See Väänänen et al., Formulation, 790-791.
59 Women's Health, Work & Stress.
60 Women and Work Hazards Group.
61 As McIvor notes: "In the U.K., union membership and density rose from a nadir of less than five million members and a quarter of the workforce in 1930 to a peak of 13 million members and over 50 per cent in the late 1970s." See McIvor, Guardians, 9.

62 Ibid., 5.
63 Harrison and Popay, Women Workers.
64 Ibid., 26.
65 McCarthy, Double Lives; Long, Industrial Homes; Vicky Long and Hilary Marland, 'From Danger and Motherhood to Health and Beauty: Health Advice for the Factory Girl in Early Twentieth-Century Britain', in 20th Century British History, 20/4 (2009).
66 Women's Health, Work & Stress.
67 Forty, Design; Shonfield, Wives.
68 The group were most deeply influenced by the groundbreaking American occupational health scientist Jeanne Stellman, who opened the first "Women's Resource Centre" for Occupational Health in New York in 1979. See Jeanne Mager Stellman, Women's Work, Women's Health (New York, 1988).
69 Harrison and Popay, Women Workers, 8.
70 Ibid., 7-9.
71 Ibid., 22.
72 Making Space: Women and the Man-Made Environment (London, 2022), 5.
73 Ibid., 6.
74 Ibid., 10.
75 Helen Donoghue, 'Is Your Workplace Sick?', in Everywoman (May 1990).
76 As the Women and Work Hazards Group wrote of stress: "While the hazards of office work may not kill you on the spot, they do cause serious problems if you have to face them day after day." See Craig, Office, 7.
77 Cecilia Tasca et al., 'Women and Hysteria in the History of Mental Health', in Clinical Practice and Epidemiology in Mental Health, 8/1 (2012); Dana Becker, 'Women's Work and the Societal Discourse of Stress', in Feminism & Psychology, 20/1 (2010); L. Soine, 'Sick Building Syndrome and Gender Bias: Imperilling Women's Health', in Social Work in Health Care, 20/3 (1995).
78 Jack Rostron, Sick Building Syndrome: Concepts, Issues, and Practice (London, 1997), 20-21.
79 Sick Building Syndrome: Causes, Effects and Control (London, s.d.), 64.
80 Marmot et al., Health Inequalities.
81 Palmer, Cultural Change, 108.
82 Spain, Gendered Spaces.
83 S. Brasche et al., 'Why Do Women Suffer from Sick Building Syndrome More Often than Men? Subjective Higher Sensitivity versus Objective Causes', in Indoor Air, 11/4 (2001), 219.
84 Amy Thomas, The City in the City: Architecture and Change in London's Financial District (Cambridge, MA, 2023); Fraser, Architecture.
85 'Interview with Pat O'Sullivan', Building (28 April 1989). On VDUs, see also Bernd Holtwick's chapter in the present volume.
86 Wellcome Collection (London), British Society for Social Responsibility in Science Archives, SA/BSR/B/14/1, Women and Work Hazards Group, Correspondence 1979-1989 and 'Stress and VDU Work'. 'Stress and VDU Work' was published by City Centre, an information, advice and resource centre for London's office workers, set up in September 1984 and funded by the (soon defunct) Greater London Council and later by the London Borough Grants Scheme. They provided information to trade unionists, women's groups, black worker groups and individual office workers regarding employment rights, technology, harassment, etc. The group launched a major study and campaign on the stressful effects of VDU work, showing how women as well as black and ethnic minority groups were worse affected.
87 This fed into longer-standing anxieties about the effects of automation on women workers, which had triggered developments in stress research in Britain on issues such as job loss, deskilling, increased monotony and psycho-physical strain, as well as physical isolation in suburban back-office environments. See Sarah Hayes, 'Industrial Automation and Stress, c. 1945-79', in Mark Jackson (ed.), Stress in Post-War Britain, 1945-85 (London, 2015), 75-80.
88 Stress and VDU Work, 1.
89 Duffy, Laing and Crisp, The Responsible Workplace, 129; Robert Home, 'The Evolution of the Use Classes Order', in The Town Planning Review, 63/2 (1992).

90 A.F. Marmot et al., 'Building Health: An Epidemiological Study of Sick Building Syndrome in the Whitehall II Study', in Occupational and Environmental Medicine, 63/4 (2006), 283.
91 Marmot et al., Building Health, 287.
92 Ibid.
93 Ruth Slavin, 'Building for Health', in Architects' Journal, 10 Oct. 1996, 46.
94 For a more detailed appraisal of the impact of DEGW on British office design and theory, see Amy Thomas, 'Architectural Consulting in the Knowledge Economy: DEGW and the ORBIT Report', in The Journal of Architecture, 24/7 (2019); Thomas, The Political.
95 For an example of this technical approach, see Sabah A. Abdul-Wahab, Sick Building Syndrome in Public Buildings and Workplaces (Berlin, 2011).
96 Wainwright and Calnan, Work Stress, 44.
97 Ibid., 43.
98 Väänänen et al., Formulation, 792.
99 Becker, Women's Work, 45 and 48.
100 See for instance Jeremy Myerson and Philip Ross, Unworking: The Reinvention of the Modern Office (London, 2022); Is Hybrid Working Here to Stay? Office for National Statistics' (23 May 2022) (via https://www.ons.gov.uk); Charlie Warzel and Anne Helen Petersen, Out of Office: The Big Problem and Bigger Promise of Working from Home (Knopf, 2021); Monica Sharma, 'Female Staff Report Lower Happiness and Motivation than Men When Remote Working', HR Review (16 Nov. 2020) (via https://www.hrreview.co.uk).
101 See for instance Jessica Wilson, Evangelia Demou and Theocharis Kromydas, 'Covid-19 Lockdowns and Working Women's Mental Health: Does Motherhood and Size of Workplace Matter? A Comparative Analysis Using Understanding Society', in Social Science & Medicine, 340 (2023); Abbi Hobbs, 'The Impact of Remote and Flexible Working Arrangements' (29 April 2021) (via https://post.parliament.uk); 'Working from Home: From Invisibility to Decent Work' (ILO report, 13 Jan. 2021) (via www.ilo.org); Sarah Marsh, 'Women Bear Brunt of Covid-Related Work Stress, UK Study Finds', in The Guardian, 9 Oct. 2020; Sharma, Female Staff.

BIBLIOGRAPHY

Sabah A. Abdul-Wahab, Sick Building Syndrome in Public Buildings and Workplaces (Berlin, 2011).
Ulrich Beck, Scott Lash and Brian Wynne, Risk Society: Towards a New Modernity (London, 1992).
Dana Becker, 'Women's Work and the Societal Discourse of Stress', in Feminism & Psychology, 20/1 (2010), 36-52.
Kate Boyer, '"Neither Forget nor Remember Your Sex": Sexual Politics in the Early Twentieth-Century Canadian Office', in Journal of Historical Geography, 29/2 (2003), 212-229.
Nicola Bishop, Lower-Middle-Class Nation: The White-Collar Worker in British Popular Culture (London, 2021).
S. Brasche et al., 'Why Do Women Suffer from Sick Building Syndrome More Often than Men? Subjective Higher Sensitivity Versus Objective Causes', in Indoor Air, 11/4 (2001), 217-222.
Harry Braverman, Labor and Monopoly Capital: The Degradation of Work in the Twentieth Century (New York, 1974).
Anne Bridger, 'A Century of Women's Employment in Clerical Occupations: 1850-1950, with Particular Reference to the Role of the Society for Promoting the Employment of Women', PhD thesis (University of Gloucestershire), 2003.
Michael J. Colligan, Michael J. Smith and Joseph J. Hurrell, 'Occupational Incidence Rates of Mental Health Disorders', in Journal of Human Stress, 3/3 (1977), 34-39.
Marianne Craig, Office Workers' Survival Handbook: A Guide to Fighting Health Hazards in the Office (London, 1981).
Sarah Crook, 'The Women's Liberation Movement, Activism and Therapy at the Grassroots, 1968-1985', in Women's History Review, 27/7 (2018), 1152-1168.

Shirley Dex, Kelly Ward and Heather Joshi, 'Changes in Women's Occupations and Occupational Mobility Over 25 Years', in Jacqueline Scott, Shirley Dex and Heather Joshi (eds.), Women and Employment (Cheltenham, 2008), 54-80.
Helen Donoghue, 'Is Your Workplace Sick?', in Everywoman (May 1990).
Francis Duffy, 'Office Buildings and Organisational Change', in Anthony D. King (ed.), Buildings and Society: Essays on the Social Development of the Built Environment (London, 1980), 140-157.
Francis Duffy, The Changing Workplace (London, 1992).
Francis Duffy, Andrew Laing and Vic Crisp, The Responsible Workplace: The Redesign of Work and Offices (Oxford, 1993).
Susan S. Fainstein, The City Builders: Property Development in New York and London, 1980-2000 (Lawrence, 2001).
Adrian Forty, 'Design in the Office', in idem, Objects of Desire: Design and Society, 1750-1980 (London, 1986), 120-155.
Murray Fraser, Architecture and the "Special Relationship": The American Influence on Post-War British Architecture (Oxfordshire, 2007).
Diana Gagliardi et al., 'Occupational Safety and Health in Europe: Lessons from the Past, Challenges and Opportunities for the Future', in Industrial Health, 50/1 (2012), 7-11.
Anthony Giddens, 'Risk and Responsibility', in The Modern Law Review, 62/1 (1999), 1-10.
Rob Harris, London's Global Office Economy: From Clerical Factory to Digital Hub (Oxfordshire, 2021).
Barbara Harrison, Not Only The Dangerous Trades: Women's Work And Health In Britain 1880-1914 (London, 2005).
Sarah Hayes, 'Industrial Automation and Stress, c. 1945–79', in Mark Jackson (ed.), Stress in Post-War Britain, 1945-85 (London, 2015).
Robert Home, 'The Evolution of the Use Classes Order', in The Town Planning Review, 63/2 (1992), 187-201.
Heather E. Joshi, Richard Layard and Susan J. Owen, 'Why Are More Women Working in Britain?', in Journal of Labor Economics, 3/1 (1985), 147-176.
Jill Kirby, 'Working Too Hard: Experiences of Worry and Stress in Post-War Britain', in Mark Jackson (ed.), Stress in Post-War Britain, 1945-85 (London, 2015), 59-74.
Frederick John Langdon et al., Modern Offices. A User Survey (London, 1966).
Vicky Long and Hilary Marland, 'From Danger and Motherhood to Health and Beauty: Health Advice for the Factory Girl in Early Twentieth-Century Britain', in 20th Century British History, 20/4 (2009), 454-481.
Vicky Long, 'Industrial Homes, Domestic Factories: The Convergence of Public and Private Space in Interwar Britain', in Journal of British Studies, 50/2 (2011), 434-464.
Ellen Lupton, Mechanical Brides: Women and Machines from Home to Office (New York, 1997).
A.F. Marmot et al., 'Building Health: An Epidemiological Study of Sick Building Syndrome in the Whitehall II Study', in Occupational and Environmental Medicine, 63/4 (2006), 283-289.
M.G. Marmot et al., 'Health Inequalities among British Civil Servants: The Whitehall II Study', in The Lancet, 337 (1991), 1387-1393.
Helen McCarthy, Double Lives: A History of Working Motherhood (London, 2020).
Arthur McIvor, 'Guardians of Workers' Bodies? Trade Unions and the History of Occupational Health and Safety', in Labour History, 119/1 (2020), 1-30.
Arthur McIvor, Working Lives: Work in Britain since 1945 (Basingstoke, 2013).
Juriaan van Meel, The European Office: Office Design and National Context (Rotterdam, 2000).
Joseph Melling, 'Labouring Stress: Scientific Research, Trade Unions and Perceptions of Workplace Stress in Mid-Twentieth-Century Britain', in Mark Jackson (ed.), Stress in Post-War Britain 1945-85 (London, 2015), 161-176.
Michelle Murphy, Sick Building Syndrome and the Problem of Uncertainty: Environmental Politics, Technoscience, and Women Workers (Durham, 2006).
Jeremy Myerson and Philip Ross, Unworking: The Reinvention of the Modern Office (London, 2022).
Alva Reimer Myrdal and Viola Klein, Women's Two Roles: Home and Work (London, 1968).

Debbie Palmer, 'Cultural Change, Stress and Civil Servants' Occupational Health, c. 1967-85', in Mark Jackson (ed.), Stress in Post-War Britain, 1945-85 (London, 2015), 95-109.
Alan Powers, Britain: Modern Architectures in History (London, 2007).
A.W.W. Robinson, 'Working in The City', in Occupational Medicine, 15/1 (1965), 42-56.
Jack Rose, The Dynamics of Urban Property Development (London, 1985).
Jack Rostron, Sick Building Syndrome: Concepts, Issues, and Practice (London, 1997).
Katherine Shonfield, Walls Have Feelings: Architecture, Film and the City (London, 2000).
Ruth Slavin, 'Building for Health', in Architects' Journal, 10 Oct. 1996.
L. Soine, 'Sick Building Syndrome and Gender Bias: Imperiling Women's Health', in Social Work in Health Care, 20/3 (1995), 51-65.
Daphne Spain, Gendered Spaces (London, 1992).
Jeanne Mager Stellman, Women's Work, Women's Health (New York, 1988).
Zoe Strimpel, 'Spare Rib, The British Women's Health Movement and the Empowerment of Misery', in Social History of Medicine, 35/1 (2022), 217-236.
Cecilia Tasca et al., 'Women and Hysteria in the History Of Mental Health', in Clinical Practice and Epidemiology in Mental Health, 8/1 (2012), 110-119.
Stephen Taylor, 'The Suburban Neurosis', in The Lancet, 231 (1938), 759-762.
Amy Thomas, 'Prejudice and Pragmatism: The Commercial Architect in the Development of Postwar London', in Grey Room, 71 (2018), 88-115.
Amy Thomas, 'Architectural Consulting in the Knowledge Economy: DEGW and the ORBIT Report', in The Journal of Architecture, 24/7 (2019), 1020-1044.
Amy Thomas, 'The Political Economy of Flexibility: Deregulation and the Transformation of Corporate Space in the Post-War City of London', in Kenny Cupers, Helena Mattsson and Catharina Gabrielsson (eds.), Neoliberalism: An Architectural Project (Pittsburgh, 2019), 127-150.
Amy Thomas, 'Risk in "The Room": Negotiating New Economic Paradigms in the Architecture of Lloyd's of London Insurance Market', in Architectural Theory Review, 26/1 (2022), 7-34.
Amy Thomas, The City in the City: Architecture and Change in London's Financial District (Cambridge, MA, 2023).
Mathew Thomson, Psychological Subjects: Identity, Culture, and Health in Twentieth-Century Britain (Oxford , 2006).
Ari Väänänen et al., 'Formulation of Work Stress in 1960-2000: Analysis of Scientific Works from the Perspective of Historical Sociology', in Social Science & Medicine, 75/5 (2012), 784-794.
David Wainwright and Michael Calnan, Work Stress: The Making of a Modern Epidemic (Buckingham, 2002).
Charlie Warzel and Anne Helen Petersen, Out of Office: The Big Problem and Bigger Promise of Working from Home (Knopf, 2021).
Jessica Wilson, Evangelia Demou and Theocharis Kromydas, 'COVID-19 Lockdowns and Working Women's Mental Health: Does Motherhood and Size of Workplace Matter? A Comparative Analysis Using Understanding Society', in Social Science & Medicine, 340 (2023).
S. Wyatt and J.N. Langdon, Fatigue and Boredom in Repetitive Work (London, 1937).

Chapter 6
Measuring, Evaluating and Configuring: The German Debate about Safe and Healthy Screen Work

Bernd Holtwick

INTRODUCTION

Architectural concepts materialise in offices, as do ideas related to the organisation of work. The tangible, physical elements of the office environment – encompassing everything from ordinary objects like chairs and desks to indoor climate, lighting and noise levels – play a crucial role in shaping workers' experiences. Aesthetic judgments, managerial concepts and especially regulatory requirements all influence office environments, even at seemingly minute levels. This chapter focuses on regulatory aspects, particularly occupational safety and health in relation to screen-based, "digitised" office work in (West) Germany. The debate over preventive measures, sparked by the 1974 "Humanisation of Working Life" government programme, eventually culminated in the 1996 Screen Work Regulation (*Bildschirmarbeitsverordnung*), marking a key period of transformation in office work.[1] Analysing regulatory norms requires a political-historical approach that considers state action alongside mediating actors and organisations that influenced, or were influenced by, such action. In this context, I will examine the discourses surrounding rule-making processes, focusing on how the relevance and value of screen work were contested and debated. The premise is that these discourses, in turn, shaped perceptions of office work and influenced how offices were perceived, designed and used. To explore this idea, the debate on the Screen Work Regulation must be viewed as the culmination of a longstanding process of "technologisation" of administrative tasks that began in the early 20th century.

The library of the German Federal Institute for Occupational Safety and Health (*Bundesanstalt für Arbeitsschutz und Arbeitsmedizin*) in

Dortmund offers a wealth of materials on this subject. Although many of its items are available elsewhere, the library has uniquely catalogued and keyworded journal articles and chapters from edited volumes, providing a level of accessibility that surpasses other collections. The institute collected these publications not only for the purposes of research, but also to advise the Federal Ministry of Labour and Social Affairs during the rule-making process. As a result, the debate can be analysed in breadth and depth. However, the preserved literature mainly reflects the perspectives of "experts" rather than those of the general public or office workers. Consequently, this chapter is a first step that requires further expansion and refinement for a more comprehensive analysis of the discourse on screen work. The 1996 legal framework serves as a starting point, marking a decisive intervention by the German federal government that ended a protracted debate, but ironically did little to prepare office workers for 21st-century developments.

EXPERTS AND THE OFFICE

In theory, the December 1996 regulation addressed "work with display screen equipment (DSE)" (*Arbeit an Bildschirmgeräten*), encompassing not only the physical workspace – "workstations with DSE" (*Bildschirmarbeitsplätze*) – but also the broader work process. However, the bulk of the regulation comprised provisions about the physical conditions required for working with display screens, with half of the text dedicated to a list of "requirements for workstations".[2] The optical dimension was particularly emphasised: employers were required to provide eye tests for workers and cover the cost of glasses if needed. Additionally, the regulation mandated that screens must display characters clearly and without flickering, with a sharp contrast and no reflections. Overall office lighting had to be adapted to minimise glare on display screens, and the importance of an ergonomic keyboard that could be adjusted by the individual worker was also highlighted. The regulation then addressed desks and office chairs, as well as requirements to reduce noise, thermal discomfort and radiation. In contrast, work processes themselves were largely neglected. In the section entitled "Interactions between humans and equipment" (*Zusammenwirken Mensch – Arbeitsmittel*), the text did discuss software involved in DSE work, introducing the term "user-friendliness". Yet the concept remained vague and lacked clear criteria for assessment. Only four lines of the three-page regulation addressed the issue of workflow, simply recommending that screen work be interrupted at regular intervals for other activities or breaks.[3]

The frequent use of the terms "ergonomic" and "ergonomics" – which appear six times in the regulation – is notable, even though the text does not offer a definition. A contemporary German manual considered the task of ergonomics to be the analysis of "physical and chemical environmental factors, the anatomy of humans, the [...] science of human body measurements and body shapes [...], with the aim of designing facilities, workplaces, workstations, machines and devices in technically optimal ways". Ergonomic know-how was to provide precise information about how equipment and environments were to be conceived and put into practice technically.[4] Connections to psychology or the social sciences did not appear in the 1996 regulation, with the emphasis being primarily on the physical aspects of work. This was also reflected in the perspective of German ergonomic experts regarding DSE workstations, which focused on the "user-friendliness of software programs", primarily understood as character legibility on screens.[5] When experts did discuss "work organisation", the topic was usually narrowed down to measurements of the duration of DSE work per day and "contact with colleagues".[6] For the lawmakers behind the 1996 regulation, reliance on the scientific authority of ergonomists reduced the need to provide specific design criteria for work environments; they merely suggested that these should be updated regularly in line with advancements in research. While this may have seemed like a flexible adaptation to scientific progress, it effectively positioned a single discipline as the primary authority on healthy working conditions, diminishing the importance of workers' experiences and assessments. In this context, the contribution of ergonomic experts, despite their purported neutrality and objectivity, can be seen as an instrument of power that disciplined workers "for their own good", replacing negotiations with top-down assessments. Two key aspects in the regulation therefore warrant further exploration: the reliance on scientific arguments and the commitment to a biological-medical interpretation of scientific authority. Both aspects have their roots in the early days of modern office work, when new forms of office-related expertise emerged in response to the social, economic, managerial and technological shifts brought about by industrialisation.

The advent of the typewriter in the late 19th century symbolises this transformation of the administrative workplace. Until that point, male secretaries had a wide array of responsibilities, ranging from bookkeeping to crafting meticulously phrased business letters, which necessitated extensive qualifications. Yet as companies grew, they implemented increasingly complex administrative processes, resulting in a greater volume of written material. This surge in administrative tasks led to higher costs, prompting a quest for more efficient procedures and a shift to cheaper labour – an approach commonly referred to as rationalisation. The rationalisation of production (whether industrial or administrative) involved breaking processes down into individual steps, thereby reducing costs by replacing human labour with machines or minimising the range of tasks performed by workers. This approach required less training, justifying lower wages. Typewriters mechanised the process of preparing documents, while writing from dictation – first using shorthand and later Dictaphones – separated the act of writing from the drafting of text. This process reduced writing to mere "typing", which no longer demanded a deep understanding of content.[7] Previously, office work required clean, precise handwriting, but this became less significant with the rise of "machine-writing". Calculating machines, although they received less public attention, also mechanised procedures, particularly in bookkeeping.[8] While more sophisticated and better-paid office roles remained reserved for male employees, typing work was predominantly assigned to women, which allowed them to earn an income immediately after leaving school without the need for costly formal vocational training.[9] Furthermore, administrative work was often viewed as more prestigious than industrial production or agriculture.[10] However, this advancement came with a downside: women were largely confined to subordinate roles, with limited opportunities for career progression.

In quantitative terms, female office work was not yet well established in Germany around 1900. Over half of the 5.25 million economically active women were employed in agriculture (2.75 million), while just under a third worked in industry, commerce and mining (1.52 million), primarily in production rather than administration.[11] Statistics from 1895 show that only 0.8 percent of economically active women worked in administration, a figure that had risen to 2.1 percent by 1907. That same year, women made up just under 16 percent of office assistants and 28 percent of commercial clerks.[12] After the First World War, the figure of the female office worker was frequently depicted in films and literature, indicating their increasing presence in the workforce.[13] By 1925, women accounted for 40 percent of commercial clerks in Germany, a figure that continued to rise after the Second World War.[14] By 1973, statistics for West Germany showed that 2.9 million women were employed in administration, offices and services,

Fig. 6.1. "Poor posture impairs breathing and circulation, and constricts the digestive organs." Poster for health education, 1920s. (Deutsches Hygiene-Museum, Dresden.)

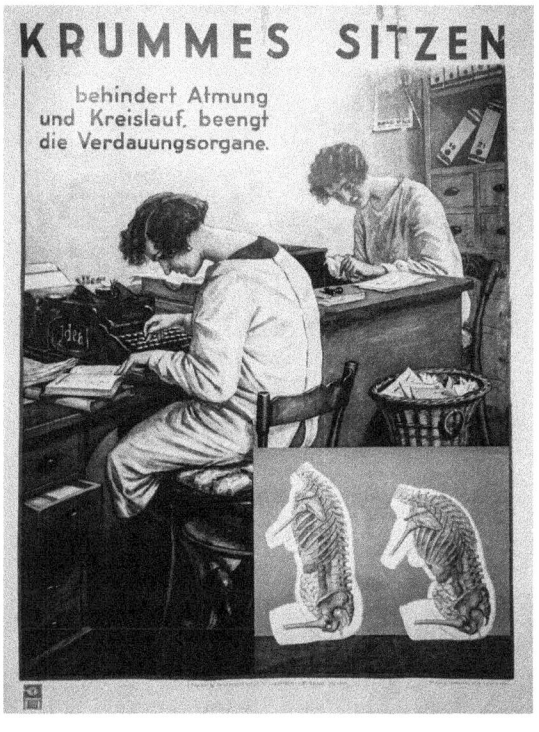

compared to 2.7 million men. Women made up at least two-thirds of workers in fields such as accounting, budgeting, electronic data processing and filing.[15]

As was the case elsewhere, the early-20th-century "rationalisation" of office work in Germany was heavily influenced by the work of Frederick Winslow Taylor, whose writings were translated into German even before the First World War.[16] Taylor's approach, particularly as further developed by Frank B. Gilbreth, had a lasting impact on academic debates in Germany.[17] Specifically with regard to typing, increasing efficiency by speeding up the writing process and reducing errors became a natural goal (Fig. 6.1.). The new discipline of "psychotechnics" integrated both physical and psychological factors in this pursuit. The Institute for Industrial Psychotechnics (*Institut für industrielle Psychotechnik*) was founded in Berlin in 1918 and initiated several research projects, one of which was Erich Alexander Klockenberg's doctoral thesis on the conditions for rapid and accurate typing.[18] Klockenberg sought to measure typists' strain and fatigue, collecting data on their posture at the desk and typing speeds in various seated positions. Other experiments examined finger fatigue, while Klockenberg also tested different positions for the copyholder and documented typists' lines of sight to identify the most efficient desk arrangements. The final part of his research focused on "aptitude" tests for typists, a common aspect of psychotechnics. While the primary goal was clearly performance enhancement, occupational safety and health were not entirely neglected: preventing overstraining also helped maintain productivity and thus achieve better results.

Besides psychotechnics, the academic discipline of industrial hygiene (which was established in the 1870s) also examined office work from the 1920s onwards. Both disciplines developed at international level, with industrial hygiene being significantly influenced by French trends.[19] Aimed at identifying and preventing adverse health effects caused by work, its scope extended beyond medical concerns to include legislation and potentially even the broader "social question of workers", with the limitation of the working day to eight hours seen by some as part of its mission.[20] Before the First World War, industrial hygienists also focused on reducing the risk of accidents or infections and the danger of hazardous substances in workplaces in the primary and secondary economic sectors.[21] It was only in the 1920s that German industrial hygienists turned their attention to offices, particularly the physical strain of typing, which could lead to back and neck pain and notably tendinitis, also termed "typewriter's cramp".[22] The design of desks and office chairs, the use of footrests, and bright, glare-free lighting were all promoted to keep typists healthy.[23] Good ventilation, fresh air and exercise were also recommended; as early as 1930, the idea of task variation was proposed. However, questions regarding the organisation of work or the task profiles of workers were largely neglected. The focus was on elements that could be measured "objectively", such as the recommended height of the desktop (68 cm), the distance between the typist's eyes and the copyholder (28 cm) or the space between the upper body and the space bar (13 cm).[24] There was no mention of "job enrichment" – a term not coined until 1968 by the American psychologist Frederick Herzberg.[25] In contrast to psychotechnics, which was clearly committed to increasing efficiency, industrial hygiene did maintain a critical distance from discourses on rationalisation, especially when it involved solely reducing costs and boosting productivity without considering "human beings in their physiological and psychological uniqueness".[26] Nevertheless, while the discipline acknowledged the importance of variety, respect and appropriate pay as key factors in motivating workers,[27] it remained focused on establishing clear, quantifiable criteria and rules to improve office work, which was mostly performed by women. It was widely believed that problems could be addressed by gathering scientific data and analysing it through professional expertise, an approach that minimised the importance of non-physical aspects of work design and reduced office workers to mere subjects of scientific observation and measurement. Despite their differing objectives, industrial hygiene and psychotechnics shared significant parallels with Taylorism in this regard (Fig. 6.2.).

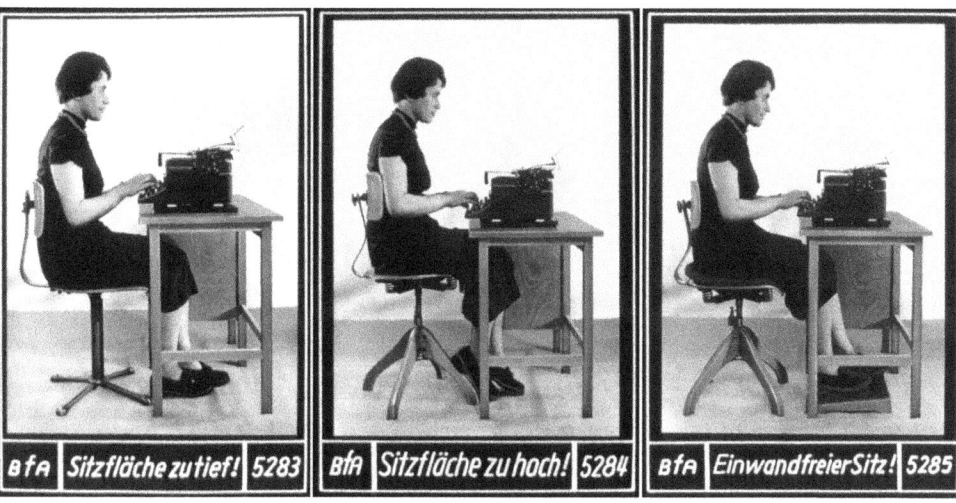

Fig. 6.2. "Seat surface too low!"; "Seat surface too high!"; "Perfect posture!". Slides for vocational training, 1950s. (DASA, Dortmund.)

These parallels extended to ergonomics, which took on a new international prominence in the 1960s as an academic field rooted in psychotechnics and industrial hygiene.[28] The Ergonomics Research Society, established in the United Kingdom in 1949, successfully promoted ergonomics as a new guiding concept that quickly gained traction with the support of the European Productivity Society.[29] According to a 1961 definition, "ergonomics [is] the application of the human biological sciences in conjunction with the engineering sciences to achieve the optimum mutual adjustment of man and his work, the benefits being measured in terms of human efficiency and well-being".[30] This definition left open questions about the focus of research – whether it should prioritise increasing efficiency, improving occupational safety and health, or fostering more humane working conditions. The relationship between ergonomics and industrial engineering also remained unclear. Swiss researcher Etienne Grandjean (1967) wrote that "ergonomics brings together the biological disciplines of occupational science (*Arbeitswissenschaften*); it places physiology, psychology and anatomy at the service of occupational science".[31] This positioned ergonomics as a subdiscipline of occupational science, which also encompassed psychotechnics.[32]

Office work received relatively little attention in the broader debate on ergonomics, particularly regarding health and safety.[33] A 1959 survey conducted by the Advisory Board of the German Business Community for

Rationalisation (*Rationalisierungskuratorium der Deutschen Wirtschaft*, RKW) included responses from office workers, but its findings revealed that women in office jobs reported far fewer health issues than their counterparts in industrial production.³⁴ Around the same time, the German Salaried Employees' Union (*Deutsche Angestelltengewerkschaft*) did seek to highlight the challenges of office work. In 1957, referring to women as being caught in the "mill of office technology", the union presented anonymised testimonies from women and medical experts that emphasised the physical and mental strain of office work.³⁵ However, these efforts appeared to be less about addressing these issues directly and more about encouraging women – traditionally hard to recruit – to join the union. The campaign nonetheless gave women a platform to voice their concerns and offered a means to advocate for long-term improvements through union membership. The union's demands largely reflected earlier research from the 1920s calling for noise reduction and the adoption of office furniture and equipment designed to accommodate the "structure of the female body".³⁶ Once again, it was the voices of experts, rather than the women themselves, that ultimately shaped the discourse, with a focus on quantifiable, physical data over subjective experiences.

TECHNICAL DEVELOPMENTS AND POLITICAL PROGRAMMES

A new impetus to examine office work emerged in the early 1970s. The Socialist-Liberal coalition under Willy Brandt prioritised improving working conditions in all economic sectors, as outlined in the government's 1969 policy statement: "Regarding the humanisation of working life, legislators and collective bargaining parties must guarantee the protection of employees in the workplace. Occupational safety and health care in the workplace shall be expanded".³⁷ Over the following years, key institutions and a legislative framework were established. In 1971, the Federal Institute for Occupational Health and Accident Research (*Bundesanstalt für Arbeitsschutz und Unfallforschung*, now the Federal Institute for Occupational Safety and Health) began its work in Dortmund. That same year, a regulation on hazardous substances in the workplace was introduced, followed in 1972 by the Act on Occupational Physicians, Safety Engineers and Other Occupational Safety Specialists. In 1974, the "Humanisation of Working Life" (*Humanisierung des Arbeitslebens*) programme was launched, focusing on research and knowledge dissemination. Its budget grew from 15 million marks in 1974 to 100 million annually by 1979. The programme adopted a comprehensive approach, involving employers, trade unions, scientists from multiple disciplines, policymakers, public authorities and the general public. It aimed to address the effects of labour on workers' health and well-being and contributed to a broader societal debate about "quality of life".[38] Participants often disagreed on priorities: while trade unions emphasised humanisation, employers focused on rationalisation, leading to ongoing tensions over the programme's objectives.

Aside from political, administrative and legal developments, technological advancements also prompted a renewed examination of office work.[39] Businesses increasingly invested in electronic data processing, leading to the wider adoption of input terminals and a gradual rise in the number of employees working with screens. By the early 1980s, approximately 15 percent of all office workers in West Germany regularly used screens.[40] This shift brought new challenges, which unions identified as a source of strain for users. Academic ergonomics also began to address the issue, though early discussions were often unstructured.[41] The lack of consistent terminology reflected the fluidity of the debate, with various terms in circulation, including "data display workstation" (*Datensichtarbeitsplatz*), "visual display device" (*Sichtanzeigegerät*), "screen terminal" (*Bildschirmterminal*) and "data terminal workstation" (*Datenterminalarbeitsplatz*).[42] A 1976 dictionary listed additional terms such as "data display panel", "screen device", "optical display system" and "cathode ray tube display unit".[43] By the early 1980s, however, *Bildschirmgeräten* (display screen equipment) and *Bildschirmarbeitsplatz* (DSE workstation) had emerged as standard terms, with other expressions gradually falling out of use.

When compared to industrial work, interest initially remained limited: of the more than 1,000 projects funded under the Humanisation of Working Life programme up to 1983, only 42 focused on office work.[44] Engagement with the topic grew steadily over time, however. In 1977, specific funding opportunities for office-related topics were introduced, while in 1981, office work was established as a priority funding area.[45] In 1978, a project group based in Munich completed its research on "work in word processing, taking particular account of the impact on women", producing a report of nearly 800 pages. Exploring opportunities for human-centred design in both technology and work organisation, it foreshadowed two future scenarios: either the typing pool "would be mostly disbanded [and] degenerate into a data entry department", or it would develop into a "qualified service centre".[46] While the study received little attention, in 1980, the Federal Institute for Occupational Health and Accident Research did organise a major conference on DSE work in Dortmund, which attracted 2,000 attendees.[47] By 1985, a bibliography of international publications on working with display screens had documented over 3,000 titles. This surge in research mirrored the rapid increase in DSE workstations in West Germany, which rose from an estimated 50,000 in 1975 to about one million by 1985.[48]

THE ROLE OF INTEREST GROUPS

As outlined above, both technological developments and political signals throughout the 1970s made it increasingly logical to examine office work and its transformation more closely. This applied not only to policymakers but also to key interest groups such as trade unions, employers' associations and employers' liability insurance associations. Each contributed its own perspectives and objectives, playing decisive roles in the debate. Among these actors, trade unions were particularly significant. Re-established in post-war West Germany as unified unions, they were structured to represent all workers in a given sector without internal competition. In 1949, most of these unions joined to form the German Trade Union Federation (*Deutscher Gewerkschaftsbund*, DGB), with the exception of the German Salaried Employees' Union (*Deutsche Angestelltengewerkschaft*), which remained independent.[49] Several DGB member unions, such as the Industrial Union for Printing and Paper, the Union for Retail, Banking and Insurance, the Trade Union for Public Services and Transport, and the German Postal Workers' Union, had significant numbers of office workers among their members. Nonetheless, the issue of office work extended across all sectors. Remarkably, it was the Industrial Union of Metalworkers (*Industriegewerkschaft Metall*, IG Metall) that emerged as one of the most active participants in the debates. IG Metall also played a prominent role in the Humanisation of Working Life programme.[50] The union viewed DSE work as a defining trend and believed that West German society stood at a critical juncture: either effective regulations could be implemented to humanise work and mitigate its challenges, or the principles of assembly line labour – long associated with manufacturing – would extend into office environments in new forms. This shift, they warned, could lead to increased psychological and physical strain, the loss of many jobs and the reduction of others to mere data-entry tasks.[51]

This concern raised urgent questions: How could such far-reaching negative consequences of screen work be avoided? What measures were needed to guide developments in a positive direction, and what tools would be effective in achieving these goals? From IG Metall's perspective, the decisive tool for shaping screen work in offices was co-determination (*betriebliche Mitbestimmung*), grounded in the Works Constitution Act (*Betriebsverfassungsgesetz*).[52] This law allowed workers to elect works councils or staff councils, with varying competences depending on the company's nature and size. Unions were strongly represented in these councils and were thus able to influence management decisions.[53] In 1983, drawing on the earlier report on the humanisation of word processing, IG Metall for instance called for greater focus on work organisation, advocating for "qualified mixed work". This approach emphasised task variety, communication among colleagues, increased qualifications and improved career prospects.[54] While such proposals appeared innocuous, they did hold considerable potential for conflict. For example, allowing typists to take on more intellectually demanding tasks could have led to higher pay and better advancement opportunities.[55] To avoid disputes over increased labour costs, the unions refrained from pushing their demands too vigorously.[56] The unions' specific demands therefore centred on reducing the physical risks of screen work, particularly eye strain and musculoskeletal issues affecting the neck and back.[57] These concerns echoed the industrial hygiene discourse of the 1920s, highlighting continuity in the debate over workplace health and safety.

Employers' organisations rejected most of the unions' demands, viewing DSE work as a powerful means of increasing productivity. They depicted employees' representatives as hostile to progress, focusing solely on the negative potential of new technologies and even framing the future as a dystopian scenario.[58] Employers thus argued that regulations and employee co-determination concerning screen work should be minimal, dismissing claims of physical and mental stress as exaggerated. While this created an apparent impasse between employers and trade unions, a potential resolution emerged through calls for further ergonomic research. Employers' organisations indeed expressed concern about the overly emotional nature of the debate and welcomed efforts to address the issue through scientific inquiry.[59] In this context, employers' liability insurance associations played a crucial role as third-party intermediaries.

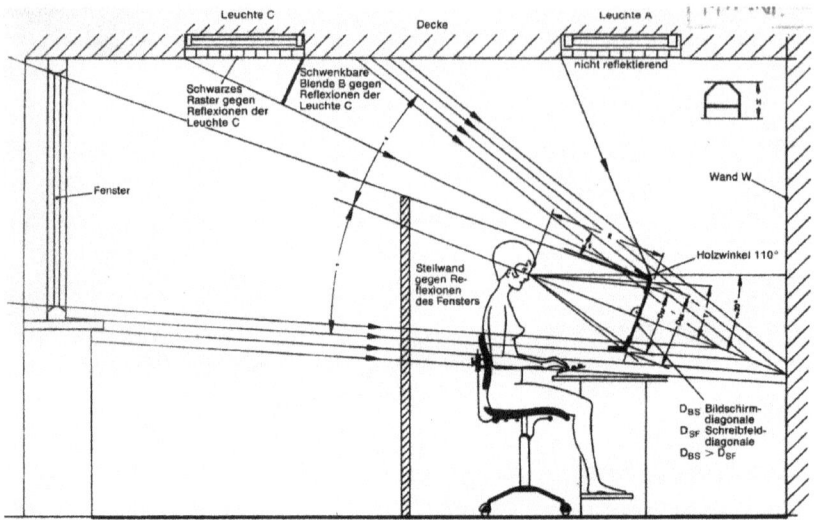

Fig. 6.3. Drawing of light reflections at a computer terminal. ('Bildschirmarbeitsplätze, wie sie sein müssen: Die heutigen gesicherten arbeitswissenschaftlichen Erkenntnisse', in Form und Technik [1978], 6.)

Established under public law and funded by mandatory employer contributions, their management was overseen by representatives from both employers and employees, elected every six years. These institutions, which trace their origins to the 1880s, functioned as neo-corporatist bodies within a tripartite framework, bringing together management and labour under state regulation. Despite often being underappreciated, they wielded significant power, as they possessed de facto legislative authority to set health and safety regulations for all enterprises within their scope.[60] From the perspective of insurance institutions, the proliferation of display screen equipment was not a novel development but rather a new element within the realm of traditional office work: screen work was regarded with the same low status as typewriting, characterised by repetitive and mechanistic tasks.[61] This perspective left little room for considering the potential for enhancing the status of screen work; at most, efforts were directed at ensuring that people working with DSE did not become relegated to the role of mere "assistants" to the computer system.[62] As a result, insurance institutions focused primarily on the physical specifics of workstation design, the organisation of regular breaks and the provision of eye tests.[63] These measures were to be laid down in health and safety regulations, as well as in a standard of the *Deutsches Institut für Normung* (DIN).[64]

In summary, employers and employers' liability insurance associations sought clear, actionable guidelines underpinned by ergonomic research. The unions, while likely preferring a more comprehensive approach, accepted the framework established by industrial hygiene in the 1920s. The federal government, meanwhile, did not push for a change in direction, which allowed ergonomic research on screen work to remain dominant. Throughout the 1980s, the volume of publications grew significantly, with research becoming increasingly detailed. Yet the focus remained primarily on the physical aspects of DSE workstations and office environments, while software ergonomics received little attention.[65] This objectification of workers in ergonomics research, which involved establishing standardised physical measures, was aligned with global practices.[66] Much like the early days of classic Taylorism, office workers were frequently depicted in diagrams featuring stylised human figures at workstations. In these representations, workers were reduced to their physical dimensions, and their tasks were quantified in terms of height, distance and angle (Fig. 6.3.).[67]

FROM RESEARCH TO REGULATION

As ergonomic knowledge advanced, questions arose about how this knowledge should be applied practically in companies and public authorities. The DIN addressed screen work in the 1980s with various standards, although the application of its guidelines remained voluntary.[68] At the beginning of the decade, employers' liability insurance associations and other accident insurance institutions introduced the "Safety Rules for Screen Work in Offices" (*Sicherheitsregeln für Bildschirm-Arbeit im Bürobereich*), which had a more direct impact than the DIN norms and outlined ergonomic requirements for hardware. Employers who disregarded these rules risked liability if an employee suffered an injury due to office work, as such negligence could be legally actionable. However, in the absence of binding legislation, even these guidelines had limited effectiveness. Consequently, it is unsurprising that, by the early 1990s, fewer than half of all DSE workstations in Germany were compliant with these safety rules.[69] Up until that time, the federal government had indeed made no significant efforts to legally regulate screen work. Decisive action ultimately did arise from the transnational European level: when Germany was still focused on research and debate, the European Community began addressing the social dimension of the Common Market. In 1987, the Council of the European Communities adopted a resolution highlighting the importance of occupational safety and health, calling for vigorous efforts to promote these issues, including the European Year of Safety and Health at Work in 1992.[70] In 1989, it issued a directive establishing the framework for regulating occupational safety and health at both European and national levels.[71] This directive shaped the way in which screen work was regulated in two key ways: by taking a broad approach to workplace safety and health, and by assigning responsibility for its implementation to employers, with Member States ensuring compliance.[72] Less than two years later, the Council introduced a further directive setting out "minimum requirements" for work with display screen equipment. Employers were required to analyse workstation safety and health conditions, provide workers with comprehensive information and take measures to mitigate risks. The rules also mandated regular breaks, eye and eyesight tests and access to glasses or other optical aids where necessary. Detailed specifications on the physical and organisational conditions for screen work were included in an appendix. Member States were to enact these rules by the end of 1992, with existing workstations given until the end of 1996 to comply.[73]

The federal government took over six years to issue the Screen Work Regulation. A comparison of the 1990 European directive with the 1996 German regulation reveals significant similarities: much of the content was directly taken from the European directive, although the right of workers and their representatives to a hearing was omitted, likely due to Germany's co-determination system. The primary distinction is that the German regulation placed far greater emphasis on ergonomics. While the European directive mentioned ergonomics in the preamble and an appendix, the German regulation made it a central focus. This shift reflects the German discourse, in which conflicts between interest groups were often addressed through the scientific lens of ergonomics. Once again, this focus narrowed the debate to scientifically analysable, "objective" factors, largely omitting broader concerns about the organisation of screen work and the psychological well-being of workers.[74] Objectification also extended to how workers, particularly women, were perceived. Although the focus was indeed on *people*, they were primarily treated as objects of measurement, evaluation and configuration. Screen work thus followed the tradition of typing: screen terminals were viewed as mere data-entry machines – essentially typewriters with a screen. Efforts to improve office work – especially for women, potentially offering new career opportunities – failed to progress: screen work was seen as mechanical and repetitive, requiring dexterity and accuracy but not expertise or creativity. Consequently, workers' skills were neither assessed nor developed. It is unsurprising, therefore, that the prevailing ergonomic view offered little inspiration for innovations in office architecture and interior design. The few examples in ergonomics literature were very elementary and typically aimed at demonstrating the practical application of standardised quantitative requirements.[75]

CONCLUDING REMARKS

Although the proliferation of work with display screen equipment became a prominent topic in debates from the late 1970s onwards, its transformative impact on the world of work only became clear in the 1990s. The German Screen Work Regulation, issued during this period of profound change driven by digitalisation, reflected an approach rooted in the 1980s, which, in its focus on screen work as an extension of traditional typing, remained closer to early-20th-century concepts than to the emerging realities of the digital era. International scientific debates were increasingly recognising these broader shifts, focusing on both humanisation and a holistic approach to work – with ergonomics playing only a minor role, primarily concerning software and scarcely addressing hardware or office equipment.[76] The German regulation failed to capture ongoing changes: marking the end of 20th-century office work, it offered little relevance for the evolving office work practices of the 21st century. In the new century, typing as a distinct job vanished as screens became ubiquitous in offices and almost all workplaces. No longer viewed as a subordinate task associated with female labour, the role of typing diminished further as software grew more complex, and computers took control of an increasing range of tasks. The graphical user interface played a key part in this transformation, while the advent of email rendered Dictaphones obsolete, making typing an essential skill for *all* office workers. The division between intellectual authorship and the physical act of typing, which had existed since the early 20th century, thus disappeared nearly a century later. Today, even the office desk of a global CEO features a computer screen as standard equipment, reflecting a shift in status and meaning that deserves further exploration, particularly through its portrayal in popular culture and advertising.[77] Regardless of the mechanisms behind it, screen work increasingly became associated with higher qualifications and more diverse tasks. The changes also eased the physical strain of fixed postures, as the standard office environment began to embrace greater flexibility with adjustable furniture, including height-adjustable desks.[78] This shift echoed a finding from the late 1970s: "There appears to be a reciprocal relationship between the level of qualification and the degree of discomfort and fatigue; in other words, highly qualified workers performing tasks suited to their skills report lower levels of stress".[79]

Translated from the German by Sandra Lustig.

NOTES

1. Bundesgesetzblatt 1996 (part 1, number 63), 1843-1845.
2. Ibid., 1844.
3. Ibid., 1843.
4. Siegfried Marquardt, Handbuch der Ergonomie (Weiden 1997), 9.
5. Gert Zülch, Rainer von Kiparski and Klaus Grießer, Messen, Beurteilen und Gestalten von Arbeitsbedingungen: Handbuch für die betriebliche Praxis zur Umsetzung ergonomischer Erkenntnisse (Heidelberg, 1997), 157-178; Rolf-Dieter Jenner und Günter Berger, Arbeitsplatzgestaltung und Körpermaße: Gestaltungsmethoden, Konstruktionshinweise, Beispiele (Cologne, 1986), 74.
6. Zülch, Von Kiparski and Grießer, Messen, 177.
7. Hans-Joachim Fritz, 'Der Weg zum modernen Büro: Vom Sekretär zur Sekretärin', in Rolf Stümpel (ed.), Vom Sekretär zur Sekretärin: Eine Ausstellung zur Geschichte der Schreibmaschine und ihrer Bedeutung für den Beruf der Frau im Büro (Mainz, 1985), 48-49.
8. Ellen Lorentz, Büro 1880-1930: Frauenarbeit und Rationalisierung (Frankfurt/M., 1984), 64-67.
9. Friedrich Weltz et al., Menschengerechte Arbeitsgestaltung in der Textverarbeitung, vol. 3 (Eggenstein-Leopoldshafen, 1978), 511-521.
10. Ibid., 565.
11. Ibid., 522.
12. Sabine Segelken, Stenographie und Schreibmaschine: Wirtschaftliche und gesellschaftliche Bestimmungsmomente traditioneller Arbeitstechniken unter besonderer Berücksichtigung ihres Einflusses auf die Arbeit der weiblichen Angestellten (Bad Salzdetfurth, 1991), 215-216; Ute Frevert, 'Traditionale Weiblichkeit und moderne Interessenorganisation: Frauen im Angestelltenberuf 1918-1933', in Geschichte und Gesellschaft, 7/3-4 (1981), 511. In the United States, the proportion of women working in offices around the turn of the century was somewhat higher, though still less than one-quarter. See Weltz et al., Menschengerechte Arbeitsgestaltung, 528.
13. Julia Freytag and Alexandra Tacke, 'Einleitung', in idem (eds.), City Girls: Bubiköpfe & Blaustrümpfe in den 1920er Jahren (Cologne, 2011).
14. Frevert, Traditionale Weiblichkeit, 511.
15. Weltz et al., Menschengerechte Arbeitsgestaltung, 541. In the United States, clerical, filing and secretarial work was almost exclusively performed by women as early as the mid-1920s. See Nikil Saval, Cubed: A Secret History of the Workplace (New York, 2014), 76.
16. Frederick Winslow Taylor, Die Grundsätze wissenschaftlicher Betriebsführung (Munich, 1913); Frederick Winslow Taylor, Die Betriebsleitung insbesondere der Werkstätten (Berlin, 1909).
17. Günter Spur, Sabine Voglrieder and Thorsten Klooster, 'Von der Psychotechnik zur Arbeitswissenschaft: Gründung und Entwicklung des Instituts für Industrielle Psychotechnik

an der TH Berlin-Charlottenburg 1918 bis 1933', in Sonja Ginnow (ed.), Berlin-Brandenburgische Akademie der Wissenschaft: Berichte und Abhandlungen, vol. 8 (Berlin, 2000), 374; Günter Spur et al., Von der Psychotechnik zur Arbeitswissenschaft: 75 Jahre arbeitswissenschaftliche Forschung in Berlin – Projektbericht (Berlin, 1994), 20-24.

[18] Erich A. Klockenberg, Beiträge zur Psychotechnik der Schreibmaschine und ihrer Bedienung (Berlin, 1924). On the institute, see Spur, Voglrieder and Klooster, 'Von der Psychotechnik', 371; Spur et al., Von der Psychotechnik, 101 and 158.

[19] Alexandre Elzéar Layet, Hygiène des professions et des industries: Précédée d'une étude générale des moyens de prévenir et de combattre les effets nuisibles de tout travail professionnel (Paris, 1875). This title was translated as Allgemeine und specielle Gewerbe-Pathologie und Gewerbe-Hygiene (Erlangen, 1877).

[20] On the social question and legislation, see Hermann Eulenberg, Handbuch der Gewerbe-Hygiene (Berlin, 1876), v and vi (citation). On limiting the length of the working day, see specifically Ignaz Zadek, Der Achtstundentag, eine gesundheitliche Forderung: Eine Einführung in die Gewerbehygiene (Berlin, 1906).

[21] H. Albrecht (ed.), Handbuch der Praktischen Gewerbehygiene mit besonderer Berücksichtigung der Unfallverhütung (Berlin, 1896); 'Sammlung von Gegenständen zur Krankheits- und Unfallverhütung', in Das Institut für Gewerbehygiene zu Frankfurt am Main, Börsenstraße 19 (Frankfurt/M., 1910).

[22] Dyonis Kremer and Ernst Holstein, Hygiene im Büro und im kaufmännischen Betriebe (Berlin, 1931), 12.

[23] Ibid., 37.

[24] Ibid., 19, 23, 29 and 43.

[25] Frederick Herzberg, 'One More Time: How do you Motivate Employees?', in Harvard Business Review, 46/1 (1968).

[26] Walter G. Waffenschmidt, Hermann F. Gerbis and Hermann Eibel, Arbeiterschutz and Rationalisierung (Berlin, 1929), 11.

[27] Ibid., 24-26.

[28] Etienne Grandjean added the subtitle *Leitfaden der Ergonomie* to the second edition of his book Physiologische Arbeitsgestaltung (Thun, 1967).

[29] Kenneth Frank Hywel Murrell, Ergonomics: Man in His Working Environment (London, 1965), viii; 'Ergonomics: The Scientific Approach to Making Work Human', in International Labour Review 83/1 (1961), 9.

[30] Ergonomics: The Scientific Approach, 1.

[31] Grandjean, Physiologische Arbeitsgestaltung, 9.

[32] Spur et al., Von der Psychotechnik, 239.

[33] Murrell, Ergonomics; Richard Selwyn and Francis Schilling, Modern Trends in Occupational Health (London, 1960).

[34] Frauenarbeit: Ergebnisse einer Befragung (Berlin, 1959), 29. In 1969, nearly 4,300 *industrial* workplace accidents involving women were registered. See Bundesminister für Arbeit und Sozialordnung: Unfallverhütungsbericht – 1968/69 (Bonn, 1971), 11.

[35] Frauen im Mahlwerk der Bürotechnik (Hamburg, 1957).

[36] Ibid., 3.

[37] 'Regierungserklärung Willy Brandt', 1969 (via www.willy-brandt-biografie.de), 24.

[38] Stefan Müller, 'Das Forschungs- und Aktionsprogramm "Humanisierung des Arbeitslebens" (1974-1989)', in Nina Kleinöder, Stefan Müller and Karsten Uhl (eds.), "Humanisierung der Arbeit": Aufbrüche und Konflikte in der rationalisierten Arbeitswelt des 20. Jahrhunderts (Bielefeld, 2019), 81.

[39] Edmund Callis Berkeley, Die Computer-Revolution: Elektronengehirne, Automation und Gesellschaft (Frankfurt/M., 1966).

[40] Bernd Meier, Büroarbeit im Wandel: Daten, Trends und Argumente zur Diskussion um die Folgen moderner Bürotechnik (Cologne, 1985).

[41] Gustav Kocherscheid, 'Bildschirmarbeitsplätze: Der Gesundheit muß Rechnung getragen werden', in Die Quelle: Funktionärszeitschrift des Deutschen Gewerkschaftsbundes, 27/3 (1976); Theodor

Peters, Arbeitswissenschaft für die Büropraxis: Ein Handbuch der Büro-Medizin und -Ergonomie (Ludwigshafen, 1976); Fred Margulies, 'Schlechte Sicht am Bildschirm', in Der Gewerkschafter: Monatsschrift für die Funktionäre der IG Metall, 23/9 (1975).

42 Ahmet Cakir, H.-J. Reuter and L. von Schmude, 'Gestaltung von Datensichtarbeitsplätzen', in Sicher ist sicher, 29 (1978); G.K. Busch, 'Probleme der Ergonomie bei der Anwendung von Sichtanzeigegeräten im Bank- und Versicherungswesen', in Afa-Informationen, 28 (1978); Gerald W. Radl, 'Ergonomische Gesichtspunkte bei Bildschirmterminals', in Orgadata, 6 (1978); Theodor Peters, 'Datenterminalarbeitsplätze aus arbeitsmedizinisch-ergonomischer Sicht', in Arbeitsmedizin, Sozialmedizin, Präventivmedizin, 10/10 (1975).

43 Erich Bürger, Wörterbuch Datenerfassung, Programmierung: Englisch, Deutsch, Französisch, Russisch (Thun, 1976), 70, 74, 170 and 213.

44 Christoph Kasten, Christoph Skarpelis and Heinz Thunecke, 'Die Förderung der Anwendung neuer Technologien in Büro und Verwaltung im Rahmen des Programms "Forschung zur Humanisierung des Arbeitslebens"', in Office-Management, 32 (1984), 586.

45 Ibid., 587.

46 Weltz et al., Menschengerechte Arbeitsgestaltung, 593-705 (quotation on 649). See also Friedrich Weltz and Veronika Lullies, Innovation im Büro: Das Beispiel Textverarbeitung (Frankfurt/M., 1983); Ursula Jacobi, Veronika Lullies and Friedrich Weltz, Textverarbeitung im Büro: Alternativen der Arbeitsgestaltung (Frankfurt/M., 1980).

47 On this conference, see Manfred Hagenkötter, 'Eröffnung der Tagung', in Bildschirmarbeitsplätze: Vorträge der Informationstagung (Bremerhaven, 1980).

48 Siegfried Grune, Bildschirmarbeitsplätze: Eine Bibliographie (Munich, 1985), v.

49 Michael Schneider, Kleine Geschichte der Gewerkschaften: Ihre Entwicklung in Deutschland von den Anfängen bis heute (Bonn, 1989).

50 Moritz Müller, 'Die IG Metall im Diskurs um die Humanisierung des Arbeitslebens', in Nina Kleinöder, Stefan Müller and Karsten Uhl (eds.), "Humanisierung der Arbeit": Aufbrüche und Konflikte in der rationalisierten Arbeitswelt des 20. Jahrhunderts (Bielefeld, 2019), 257.

51 Andreas Drinkuth, 'Thesen aus gewerkschaftlicher Sicht zum Bildschirm am Arbeitsplatz', in Angewandte Arbeitswissenschaft: Zeitschrift für die Unternehmenspraxis, 84 (1980), 30-31; Caspar von Stosch, 'Der Einsatz von Bildschirmarbeit aus der Sicht der Gewerkschaften', in Bildschirmarbeitsplätze: Vorträge der Informationstagung, 26.

52 Von Stosch, Der Einsatz, 33. See also Müller, Die IG Metall, 262.

53 Drinkuth, Thesen, 30.

54 Angelika Bahl-Benker, Bessere Arbeitsbedingungen für die Frauen in der Textverarbeitung: Beispiel zur Humanisierung der Büroarbeit (Frankfurt/M., 1983), 38. See also Von Stosch, Der Einsatz, 28.

55 On this debate, see Margot Schmidt, 'Im Vorzimmer: Arbeitsverhältnisse von Sekretärinnen und Sachbearbeiterinnen bei Thyssen nach dem Krieg', in Lutz Niethammer (ed.), Lebensgeschichte und Sozialkultur im Ruhrgebiet, 1930-1960 (Berlin, 1983), 226-228; Monika Held, Beruf Sekretärin: Reportagen, Protokolle, Analysen (Munich, 1982), 188-197; Ruth Höh, Was ist los in den Büros? Ergebnisse einer Fragebogenaktion für Sekretärinnen, Schreibkräfte, Typistinnen, Chefassistentinnen, Schreibdienstleiterinnen (Hamburg, 1981), 21; Cakir, Reuter and Von Schmude, Gestaltung, 620.

56 Von Stosch, Der Einsatz, 28 and 33.

57 Schlieter, 'Arbeit an Datensichtgeräten: Fragen der Ergonomie, Arbeitsorganisation, Strahlenproblematik, Fehlbeanspruchung bei Büroarbeit', in Heinz Partikel (ed.), Arbeit und Gesundheit: Zentrale Arbeitstagung der IG Metall, 21/22 (1985), 236-267; 'Arbeit am Bildschirm: Führt zu Sehstörungen und Schwindelanfällen', in Druck und Papier, 2 (1978); 'Bildschirmarbeitsplätze, wie sie sein müssen: Die heutigen gesicherten arbeitswissenschaftlichen Erkenntnisse', in Form und Technik, 9 (1978); Margulies, Schlechte Sicht.

58 Peter Knevels, 'Der Einsatz von Bildschirmgeräten aus der Sicht der Arbeitgeberverbände', in Bildschirmarbeitsplätze: Vorträge der Informationstagung, 16.

59 Ibid., 21; Heribert Pflügler, 'Ist die Gestaltung von Bildschirmarbeitsplätzen wissenschaftlich abgesichert? Stellungnahme zu einem Forschungsbericht', in Bürotechnik: Datenverarbeitung, Organisation, Bürogestaltung, 26/9 (1978), 101.

60 Klaus Buhmann, 'Der Einsatz von Bildschirmgeräten aus der Sicht der Berufsgenossenschaften', in Bildschirmarbeitsplätze: Vorträge der Informationstagung, 39.
61 Ibid., 37.
62 Ibid., 43
63 Ibid., 39-42.
64 Ibid., 36; Harald Koch and Lutz Groenke, 'Deutsche Normungsarbeit zur Gestaltung von Bildschirmarbeitsplätzen führend in der Welt', in DIN-Mitteilungen und Elektronorm, 5 (1978).
65 For examples of the growing volume, see Sehen und Bildschirmarbeit: Podiumsdiskussion "Experten für die Praxis" vom 25. März 1995 in der Bundesanstalt für Arbeitsmedizin (Bremerhaven, 1995); Im Mittelpunkt der Mensch: Für mehr Gesundheit und Sicherheit am Bildschirm-Arbeitsplatz (Karben, 1995). On software, see for instance Mechtild Allerbeck, 'Neue Geräte und Arbeitstechniken im Büro: Gestaltung nach Vorgabe der Ergonomie', in Humane Produktion, humane Arbeitsplätze, 10/6 (1988), 36-39.
66 Elise Pechter Morse, Virginia M. Summers and Leonard D. Pagnotto, A Study of the Health Effects of Video Display Terminals in the Workplace: Commissioned by the Massachusetts Legislature, July 1984 (West Newton, 1986); Etienne Grandjean (ed.), Ergonomics and Health in Modern Offices: Proceedings of the International Scientific Conference on Ergonomic and Health Aspects in Modern Offices, Held in Turin, Italy on 7-9 November 1983 (London, 1984).
67 Im Mittelpunkt der Mensch, 71; The American National Standard for Human Factors Engineering of Visual Display Terminal Workstations (Santa Monica, 1988), 48 and 54; 'Bildschirmarbeitsplätze, wie sie sein müssen: Die heutigen gesicherten arbeitswissenschaftlichen Erkenntnisse', in Form und Technik, 9 (1978), 6; Erwin Panitz, 'Physische und psychische Beanspruchungen bei Tätigkeiten am Bildschirmarbeitsplatz', in GMD-Spiegel, 4 (1978), 99.
68 'DIN-Entwurf 66 234: Bildschirmarbeit nimmt Norm an', in Computerwoche (18 May 1979). See also Helmut Strasser, 'Bildschirmarbeitsplätze', in T. Hettinger and G. Wobbe (eds.), Kompendium der Arbeitswissenschaft (Ludwigshafen/Rhein, 1993) 22.
69 Ulrich Riese and Anette Rückert, 'Bildschirmarbeit: Umsetzung der EG-Richtlinie', in Bundesarbeitsblatt: Arbeitsmarkt und Arbeitsrecht, 9 (1992), 21; H. Achatz, 'Ergonomie trifft auf taube Ohren', in PC-Woche, 2 (1991); Klaus Buhmann, 'Sicherheitsregeln für Bildschirm-Arbeitsplätze im Bürobereich: Hintergründe und rechtliche Verbindlichkeit', in Messen & Prüfen: Fachmagazin für angewandte Meß- u. Prüftechnik, 19/3 (1983).
70 Council Resolution of 21 Dec. 1987 on Safety, Hygiene and Health at Work.
71 Council Directive of 12 June 1989 on the Introduction of Measures to Encourage Improvements in the Safety and Health of Workers at Work (89/391/EEC).
72 Ulrich Riese, 'Umsetzung der EG-Richtlinien in deutsche Regelungen', in Ahmet Cakir and Gisela Cakir (eds.), Europa 1992: Was bringen die Europäischen Regelwerke für Bildschirm-Arbeitsplätze? (Berlin, 1991), 8.
73 Ibid., 10.
74 Council Directive of 29 May 1990 on the Minimum Safety and Health Requirements for Work with Display Screen Equipment (90/270/EEC). See also Karl-Josef Keller, 'Wie stehen die Arbeitgeber zur EG-Richtlinie "Bildschirmarbeitsplätze" und ihrer beabsichtigten Umsetzung', in Cakir and Cakir, Europa, 104.
75 For an example, see Schlieter, Arbeit, 254.
76 On the role of ergonomics, see for instance Holger Luczak (ed.), World Wide Work: Proceedings of the 6th International Scientific Conference on Work with Display Units (Berlin, 2002).
77 Maxim Pouska, Computer – Werbung 1935-2010: Grafik-Design und Kunst (Norderstedt, 2011).
78 Dieter Messner, 'Das Büromöbelkonzept "Arbeitshaltung 2000"', in Sichere Arbeit: Internationales Fachmagazin für Prävention in der Arbeitswelt, 4 (1996).
79 Cakir, Reuter and Von Schmude, Gestaltung, 619. See also Georg Arnold, 'Bildschirmarbeit', in Die Berufsgenossenschaft 12 (1978).

BIBLIOGRAPHY

H. Achatz, 'Ergonomie trifft auf taube Ohren', in PC-Woche, 2 (1991), 17-18.
H. Albrecht (ed.), Handbuch der Praktischen Gewerbehygiene mit besonderer Berücksichtigung der Unfallverhütung (Berlin, 1896).
Mechtild Allerbeck, 'Neue Geräte und Arbeitstechniken im Büro: Gestaltung nach Vorgabe der Ergonomie', in Humane Produktion, humane Arbeitsplätze, 10/6 (1988), 36-39.
Georg Arnold, 'Bildschirmarbeit', in Die Berufsgenossenschaft, 12 (1978), 684-685.
Angelika Bahl-Benker, Bessere Arbeitsbedingungen für die Frauen in der Textverarbeitung: Beispiel zur Humanisierung der Büroarbeit (Frankfurt/M., 1983).
Edmund Callis Berkeley, Die Computer-Revolution: Elektronengehirne, Automation und Gesellschaft (Frankfurt/M., 1966).
Klaus Buhmann, 'Der Einsatz von Bildschirmgeräten aus der Sicht der Berufsgenossenschaften', in Bildschirmarbeitsplätze: Vorträge der Informationstagung (Bremerhaven, 1980), 36-43.
Klaus Buhmann, 'Sicherheitsregeln für Bildschirm-Arbeitsplätze im Bürobereich: Hintergründe und rechtliche Verbindlichkeit', in Messen & Prüfen: Fachmagazin für angewandte Meß- u. Prüftechnik, 19/3 (1983), 125-127.
Erich Bürger, Wörterbuch Datenerfassung, Programmierung: Englisch, Deutsch, Französisch, Russisch (Thun, 1976).
G.K. Busch, 'Probleme der Ergonomie bei der Anwendung von Sichtanzeigegeräten im Bank- und Versicherungswesen', in Afa-Informationen, 28 (1978), 3-18.
Ahmet Cakir, H.-J. Reuter and L. von Schmude, 'Gestaltung von Datensichtarbeitsplätzen', in Sicher ist sicher, 29 (1978), 614-620.
Andreas Drinkuth, 'Thesen aus gewerkschaftlicher Sicht zum Bildschirm am Arbeitsplatz', in Angewandte Arbeitswissenschaft: Zeitschrift für die Unternehmenspraxis, 84 (1980), 30-31.
Hermann Eulenberg, Handbuch der Gewerbe-Hygiene (Berlin, 1876).
Ute Frevert, 'Traditionale Weiblichkeit und moderne Interessenorganisation: Frauen im Angestelltenberuf 1918-1933', in Geschichte und Gesellschaft, 7/3-4 (1981), 507-533.
Julia Freytag and Alexandra Tacke, 'Einleitung', in idem (eds.), City Girls: Bubiköpfe & Blaustrümpfe in den 1920er Jahren (Cologne, 2011), 9-20.
Hans-Joachim Fritz, 'Der Weg zum modernen Büro: Vom Sekretär zur Sekretärin', in Rolf Stümpel (ed.), Vom Sekretär zur Sekretärin: Eine Ausstellung zur Geschichte der Schreibmaschine und ihrer Bedeutung für den Beruf der Frau im Büro (Mainz, 1985), 48-60.
Etienne Grandjean, Physiologische Arbeitsgestaltung: Leitfaden der Ergonomie (Thun, 1967).
Etienne Grandjean (ed.), Ergonomics and Health in Modern Offices: Proceedings of the International Scientific Conference on Ergonomic and Health Aspects in Modern Offices, Held in Turin, Italy on 7-9 November 1983 (London, 1984).
Siegfried Grune, Bildschirmarbeitsplätze: Eine Bibliographie (Munich, 1985).
Manfred Hagenkötter, 'Eröffnung der Tagung', in Bildschirmarbeitsplätze: Vorträge der Informationstagung (Bremerhaven, 1980), 5-6.
Monika Held, Beruf Sekretärin: Reportagen, Protokolle, Analysen (Munich, 1982).
Frederick Herzberg, 'One More Time: How do you Motivate Employees?', in Harvard Business Review, 46/1 (1968), 53-62.
Ruth Höh, Was ist los in den Büros? Ergebnisse einer Fragebogenaktion für Sekretärinnen, Schreibkräfte, Typistinnen, Chefassistentinnen, Schreibdienstleiterinnen (Hamburg, 1981).
Ursula Jacobi, Veronika Lullies and Friedrich Weltz, Textverarbeitung im Büro: Alternativen der Arbeitsgestaltung (Frankfurt/M., 1980).
Rolf-Dieter Jenner and Günter Berger, Arbeitsplatzgestaltung und Körpermaße: Gestaltungsmethoden, Konstruktionshinweise, Beispiele (Cologne, 1986).
Christoph Kasten, Christoph Skarpelis and Heinz Thunecke, 'Die Förderung der Anwendung neuer Technologien in Büro und Verwaltung im Rahmen des Programms "Forschung zur Humanisierung des Arbeitslebens"', in Office-Management, 32 (1984), 586-592.

Karl-Josef Keller, 'Wie stehen die Arbeitgeber zur EG-Richtlinie "Bildschirmarbeitsplätze" und ihrer beabsichtigten Umsetzung', in Ahmet Cakir and Gisela Cakir (eds.), Europa 1992: Was bringen die Europäischen Regelwerke für Bildschirm-Arbeitsplätze? (Berlin, 1991), 95-108.

Erich A. Klockenberg, Beiträge zur Psychotechnik der Schreibmaschine und ihrer Bedienung (Berlin, 1924).

Peter Knevels, 'Der Einsatz von Bildschirmgeräten aus der Sicht der Arbeitgeberverbände', in Bildschirmarbeitsplätze: Vorträge der Informationstagung (Bremerhaven, 1980), 15-24.

Harald Koch and Lutz Groenke, 'Deutsche Normungsarbeit zur Gestaltung von Bildschirmarbeitsplätzen führend in der Welt', in DIN-Mitteilungen und Elektronorm, 5 (1978), 275-277.

Gustav Kocherscheid, 'Bildschirmarbeitsplätze: Der Gesundheit muß Rechnung getragen werden', in Die Quelle: Funktionärszeitschrift des Deutschen Gewerkschaftsbundes, 27/3 (1976), 126-127.

Dyonis Kremer and Ernst Holstein, Hygiene im Büro und im kaufmännischen Betriebe (Berlin, 1931).

Alexandre Elzéar Layet, Hygiène des professions et des industries: Précédée d'une étude générale des moyens de prévenir et de combattre les effets nuisibles de tout travail professionnel (Paris, 1875).

Alexandre Elzéar Layet, Allgemeine und specielle Gewerbe-Pathologie und Gewerbe-Hygiene (Erlangen, 1877).

Ellen Lorentz, Büro 1880-1930: Frauenarbeit und Rationalisierung (Frankfurt/M., 1984).

Holger Luczak (ed.), Work with Display Units: World Wide Work: Proceedings of the 6th International Scientific Conference on Work with Display Units (Berlin, 2002).

Fred Margulies, 'Schlechte Sicht am Bildschirm', in Der Gewerkschafter: Monatsschrift für die Funktionäre der IG Metall, 23/9 (1975), 18-19.

Siegfried Marquardt, Handbuch der Ergonomie (Weiden 1997).

Bernd Meier, Büroarbeit im Wandel: Daten, Trends und Argumente zur Diskussion um die Folgen moderner Bürotechnik (Cologne, 1985).

Dieter Messner, 'Das Büromöbelkonzept "Arbeitshaltung 2000"', in Sichere Arbeit: Internationales Fachmagazin für Prävention in der Arbeitswelt, 4 (1996), 39-44.

Elise Pechter Morse, Virginia M. Summers and Leonard D. Pagnotto, A Study of the Health Effects of Video Display Terminals in the Workplace: Commissioned by the Massachusetts Legislature, July 1984 (West Newton, 1986).

Moritz Müller, 'Die IG Metall im Diskurs um die Humanisierung des Arbeitslebens', in Nina Kleinöder, Stefan Müller and Karsten Uhl (eds.), "Humanisierung der Arbeit": Aufbrüche und Konflikte in der rationalisierten Arbeitswelt des 20. Jahrhunderts (Bielefeld, 2019), 255-275.

Stefan Müller, 'Das Forschungs- und Aktionsprogramm "Humanisierung des Arbeitslebens" (1974-1989)', in Nina Kleinöder, Stefan Müller and Karsten Uhl (eds.), "Humanisierung der Arbeit": Aufbrüche und Konflikte in der rationalisierten Arbeitswelt des 20. Jahrhunderts (Bielefeld, 2019), 59-88.

Kenneth Frank Hywel Murrell, Ergonomics: Man in His Working Environment (London, 1965).

Erwin Panitz, 'Physische und psychische Beanspruchungen bei Tätigkeiten am Bildschirmarbeitsplatz', in GMD-Spiegel, 4 (1978), 94-101.

Theodor Peters, 'Datenterminalarbeitsplätze aus arbeitsmedizinisch-ergonomischer Sicht', in Arbeitsmedizin, Sozialmedizin, Präventivmedizin, 10/10 (1975), 193-196.

Theodor Peters, Arbeitswissenschaft für die Büropraxis: Ein Handbuch der Büro-Medizin und -Ergonomie (Ludwigshafen, 1976).

Heribert Pflügler, 'Ist die Gestaltung von Bildschirmarbeitsplätzen wissenschaftlich abgesichert? Stellungnahme zu einem Forschungsbericht', in Bürotechnik: Datenverarbeitung, Organisation, Bürogestaltung, 26/9 (1978), 99-101.

Maxim Pouska, Computer – Werbung 1935-2010: Grafik-Design und Kunst (Norderstedt, 2011).

Gerald W. Radl, 'Ergonomische Gesichtspunkte bei Bildschirmterminals', in Orgadata, 6 (1978), 4-12.

Ulrich Riese, 'Umsetzung der EG-Richtlinien in deutsche Regelungen', in Ahmet Cakir and Gisela Cakir (eds.), Europa 1992: Was bringen die Europäischen Regelwerke für Bildschirm-Arbeitsplätze? (Berlin, 1991), 5-14.

Ulrich Riese and Anette Rückert, 'Bildschirmarbeit: Umsetzung der EG-Richtlinie', in Bundesarbeitsblatt: Arbeitsmarkt und Arbeitsrecht, 9 (1992), 20-23.

Nikil Saval, Cubed: A Secret History of the Workplace (New York, 2014).

B. Schlieter, 'Arbeit an Datensichtgeräten: Fragen der Ergonomie, Arbeitsorganisation, Strahlenproblematik, Fehlbeanspruchung bei Büroarbeit', in Heinz Partikel (ed.), Arbeit und Gesundheit: Zentrale Arbeitstagung der IG Metall, 21/22 (1985), 236-267.

Margot Schmidt, 'Im Vorzimmer: Arbeitsverhältnisse von Sekretärinnen und Sachbearbeiterinnen bei Thyssen nach dem Krieg', in Lutz Niethammer (ed.), Lebensgeschichte und Sozialkultur im Ruhrgebiet, 1930-1960 (Berlin, 1983), 191-232.

Michael Schneider, Kleine Geschichte der Gewerkschaften: Ihre Entwicklung in Deutschland von den Anfängen bis heute (Bonn, 1989).

Richard S.W. Schilling, Modern Trends in Occupational Health (London, 1960).

Sabine Segelken, Stenographie und Schreibmaschine: Wirtschaftliche und gesellschaftliche Bestimmungsmomente traditioneller Arbeitstechniken unter besonderer Berücksichtigung ihres Einflusses auf die Arbeit der weiblichen Angestellten (Bad Salzdetfurth, 1991).

Günter Spur, Sabine Voglrieder and Thorsten Klooster, 'Von der Psychotechnik zur Arbeitswissenschaft: Gründung und Entwicklung des Instituts für Industrielle Psychotechnik an der TH Berlin-Charlottenburg 1918 bis 1933', in Sonja Ginnow (ed.), Berlin-Brandenburgische Akademie der Wissenschaft: Berichte und Abhandlungen, vol. 8 (Berlin, 2000), 371-401.

Günter Spur et al., Von der Psychotechnik zur Arbeitswissenschaft: 75 Jahre arbeitswissenschaftliche Forschung in Berlin – Projektbericht (Berlin, 1994).

Caspar von Stosch, 'Der Einsatz von Bildschirmarbeit aus der Sicht der Gewerkschaften', in Bildschirmarbeitsplätze: Vorträge der Informationstagung (Bremerhaven, 1980), 25-35.

Helmut Strasser, 'Bildschirmarbeitsplätze', in T. Hettinger and G. Wobbe (eds.), Kompendium der Arbeitswissenschaft (Ludwigshafen/Rhein, 1993) 217-227.

Frederick Winslow Taylor, Die Grundsätze wissenschaftlicher Betriebsführung (Munich, 1913).

Frederick Winslow Taylor, Die Betriebsleitung insbesondere der Werkstätten (Berlin, 1909).

Walter G. Waffenschmidt, Hermann F. Gerbis and Hermann Eibel, Arbeiterschutz and Rationalisierung (Berlin, 1929).

Friedrich Weltz and Veronika Lullies, Innovation im Büro: Das Beispiel Textverarbeitung (Frankfurt/M., 1983).

Friedrich Weltz et al., Menschengerechte Arbeitsgestaltung in der Textverarbeitung, vol. 3 (Eggenstein-Leopoldshafen, 1978).

Ignaz Zadek, Der Achtstundentag, eine gesundheitliche Forderung: Eine Einführung in die Gewerbehygiene (Berlin, 1906).

Gert Zülch, Rainer von Kiparski and Klaus Grießer, Messen, Beurteilen und Gestalten von Arbeitsbedingungen: Handbuch für die betriebliche Praxis zur Umsetzung ergonomischer Erkenntnisse (Heidelberg, 1997).

PART 3
OFFICE USES CONCEPTUALISED BY AND FOR THE MANAGERIAL ELITE

Chapter 7
A "Facility Based on Change" (for the Worse): Leveraging Labour Process Theory to Understand the Evolution of Herman Miller's Action Office

Petra Seitz

INTRODUCTION

Many histories of the commercial office would have us believe that contemporary office workers are the fortunate beneficiaries of a century-long evolution of office spaces from the dank and oppressive cave-like offices of the early 20th century, via the rationalised, streamlined and flexible spaces of the mid-century, to the technology- and amenity-laden campuses of contemporary Silicon Valley.[1] This narrative of perpetual progress pinpoints the mid-20th-century office as a crucial turning point in office architecture. Steeped in the era's optimism for the future and constructed using new technologies and materials, the mid-century office, with its characteristic light, colour, flexibility and humanity, is frequently presented as a positive departure from previous spaces.[2]

The basic contours of this era of office architecture and design are well covered by the literature. After the end of the Second World War, amid a significant economic shift in the (over)developed world from industrial manufacturing and production to more sedentary professions based on information and paperwork, commercial office workplaces proliferated across major metropolises and their suburbs. This newly reinvigorated subsection of the built environment soon attracted some of the leading architectural names of the time, including Walter Gropius (PanAm Building, 1952), Gordon Bunshaft (Lever House, 1952), Ludwig Mies van der Rohe (Seagram Building, 1958) and Eero Saarinen (GM Technical Center, 1956; Bell Labs, 1962; John Deere Headquarters, 1964). Characterised by the implementation of newly available or affordable materials, the mid-century office promised a spatial revolution, making white-collar workstations more comfortable, more efficient and more beautiful for both those working within them and those passing by. Bolstered by additional interest and research into efficiency and the growing field of ergonomics, the mid-century office claimed to make scientific strides towards an empirically better workplace.[3]

Despite positive critical and scholarly reception, problems emerge from the mid-century office and its historical legacies.[4] While the progenitors of mid-century office spaces set out to inspire creativity, engender cooperation and communication and allow for continual change within office spaces, as their products became more widely available on the office furniture market, these designs evolved, ending, as numerous scholars and pundits have suggested, in perhaps the most disliked office design of all time: the cubicle.[5] The mid-century era thus presents a contradiction: if the open office was "a progressive solution that promised to provide a comfortable and attractive work space" and "an expression of progressive organizational change", how were these designs so easily co-opted into the conservative and inflexible cubicle?[6]

This chapter uses the case study of Herman Miller's Action Office system to unpack these contradictions, delving into the relationships between the design of office spaces and conceptions of work, the worker and the labour process held by many designers, researchers and manufacturers of the mid-century (Fig. 7.1.). Introduced to the market in 1967, Herman Miller's Action Office II system promised to revolutionise the office furniture and office architecture industries. The system was designed to improve the work environment by adding humanity and flexibility into the space and place of the commercial office. Despite such positive intentions, 25 years after the system's launch, Action Office became widely understood as the primary precursor of the dreaded cubicle. What had started out as a utopian attempt to humanise the office had become the opposite: a space described by Action Office I designer George Nelson as having a "dehumanizing effect as a working environment".[7]

Existing literature on Action Office generally follows patterns set by analysis of the mid-century office more broadly. It is often claimed that unintended negative impacts and effects of the system resulted from individuals who failed to implement it properly.[8] Such approaches, however, have the effect of deflecting responsibility for the negative historical legacy of Action Office away from its designers and manufacturer, and toward clients and users of the furniture system. This chapter argues that explanations for the devolution of the open office rooted in individual

Fig. 7.1. Action Office depicted in the 1979 Herman Miller brochure *Managing the Work Environment*. (Courtesy of Herman Miller Archive.)

or personal failings lead to incomplete analysis and understanding of Action Office both as a discrete furniture system and as a precursor to subsequent office designs. To fully understand Action Office, this chapter suggests that attention must be turned to the ideologies and assumptions underlying the system and motivating its design specifics; particularly those related to work, the labour process and labour relations.

Such motivations, understandings and assumptions are largely absent within the prevailing literature. It is striking, for instance, that none of the many architectural and design historians writing about Action Office has enquired about the management philosophies and systems in place at Herman Miller when the system was being developed.[9] When probed, management practices at Herman Miller reveal themselves to be highly relevant to and interrelated with the development of products for the white-collar workplace. For many years, including the timeframe within which Action Office I and II were developed, Herman Miller used a bespoke Scanlon gainsharing plan, soliciting input and suggestions from employees to improve productivity in exchange for a percentage of additional profits gained or costs saved as a result of implemented suggestions.

Through an examination of Herman Miller's Scanlon plan, this chapter outlines the attitudes taken towards labour at the company, mapping these attitudes and understandings onto the physical reality of the office furniture systems the company designed. Beginning with an introduction to Herman

Miller and the Action Office system, the chapter details the development, design and implementation of Herman Miller's Scanlon plan before turning to the labour process implications of this gainsharing system. Through an exploration of Herman Miller's conception of the worker and office user, the chapter argues that the company's abstracted and idealistic understanding of white-collar work opened the door for the "cubicleisation" of the Action Office system. The chapter concludes by exploring how such changes may have impacted the end users of office spaces.

THE HERMAN MILLER COMPANY

Herman Miller's Action Office is an ideal case study through which to reevaluate the experience and legacy of the mid-century commercial office because of the system's large geographical reach and its central position in histories of the office. Action Office was, and has remained, a popular furniture system across the United States and throughout the world. While contemporary client lists are not publicly available, a 1973 "User List", held within the company archives, shows that Action Office II users included the U.S. Federal Reserve, Pan American Airways, Metropolitan Life Insurance, Hallmark Cards, Alcoa, Procter & Gamble, General Electric, IBM, Xerox, Ford, Chevrolet, Chrysler and Pitney Bowes, alongside 21 medical centres, 46 educational organisations and 19 government offices.[10] Spread across the U.S. from the East to West coasts and encompassing a wide variety of industries and companies of different sizes, Action Office's client base, and through this the reach of its design, was (and remains) significant. In addition to its physical presence across the world, the system is also conceptually ever-present in dialogue and conversations regarding office spaces through its frequent use as a case study or practical example of the mid-century office interior.[11]

Action Office was designed and manufactured by furniture manufacturer Herman Miller. Located in Zeeland, Michigan and founded in 1905 as the Star Furniture Company, the company produced generic wooden, Victorian-styled furniture for its first two decades of operation.[12] Amid a competitive furniture market and global economic depression, the company pivoted to the creation and dissemination of modernist furniture in 1933 under the guidance of CEO D.J. De Pree and creative director and designer Gilbert Rohde.[13] The De Pree/Rohde era gave rise to creative partnerships with notable modernist designers (Charles and Ray Eames,

George Nelson, and Isamu Noguchi), who crafted now iconic designs such as the Noguchi Table (1947), Eames Lounge Chair (1956) and Marshmallow Sofa (1956, 1961).[14] Following the success of Action Office II in the late 1960s, the company shifted its focus away from the domestic sphere and towards the commercial office, breaking new ground in the design of ergonomic office furniture. This pivot began with Bill Stumpf's 1976 Ergon chair, followed by Stumpf and Don Chadwick's 1994 Aeron chair, Studio 7.5's Mirra chair in 2003, and several successive office systems in line with the overarching principles of Action Office.[15] Herman Miller was led by a succession of De Pree family members until 1987, when the rapidly growing company was entrusted to outside leadership for the first time. In the 21st century, Herman Miller has continued to expand, acquiring several other notable modernist furniture sellers (and former competitors) including Design Within Reach and Knoll. As of 2023, the company trades as MillerKnoll and has retained its historic Michigan headquarters.[16]

Action Office is indisputably the brainchild of inventor Robert Propst, originally hired by Herman Miller as a part-time freelance researcher and product developer in 1958.[17] After dropping out of a chemical engineering programme in college and pivoting to fine arts studies at the University of Colorado Denver, Propst served as a Line Officer in the U.S. Navy during the Second World War before beginning his professional career as a graphic artist, teacher and sculptor, subsequently switching careers again to establish his own product development company.[18] Propst initially joined Herman Miller via a retainer employing him for two-fifths of his time to conduct research into a variety of topics including "human factors in workstations, the development of a litter for burn victims and a mechanical and automatic bed-chair for quadriplegics".[19] After three years of collaboration, Propst was contracted by CEO Hugh De Pree to become the head of the newly formed Herman Miller Research Division and tasked to explore "problems for which 'a product not necessarily furniture' might be the solution".[20]

Located outside Herman Miller's Zeeland headquarters, the Research Division was based in the small Ann Arbor Research Park, in close proximity to the University of Michigan. From this facility, Propst and his team began research and work on "a staggering range of projects, all of them afield from traditional Herman Miller activities". These projects spanned the spectrum of products and ideas, from designs for hospital storage and organisation (what would become the Co/Struc system) to machinery for processing lumber more effectively.[21] The Research Division styled and promoted itself as the focal point for information and knowledge gathering at Herman Miller, positioning its work as grounded in scientific and empirical processes.[22] However, despite the division's self-styling and frequent mentions of its research in publicity and promotional materials, few records of its work appear to be available within the company's otherwise extensive archives.

ACTION OFFICE I AND II

Propst's first large-scale project as head of the Research Division was to investigate and accommodate his own ways and methods of working.[23] Noticing that "tasks were migrating to the drafting table and all the walls were becoming areas for display",[24] Propst went to work searching for solutions, monitoring his own working habits, and crafting and disseminating surveys for other Research Division employees.[25] While Propst accumulated information on office tasks and on work more abstractly, his background and skill set lay within product development, not aesthetics. To create a market-ready product, designer George Nelson was brought into the Action Office project with the aim of creating "a union of Propst's ideas and Nelson's design details".[26] The result of this union was Action Office I: a sleek steel and wood-panelled suite of office furniture, carrying a price tag to match its sophisticated design and high-end materials and manufacturing techniques (Fig. 7.2.).

Action Office I products featured curved wooden and metal surfaces supported by elegantly shaped metallic legs resting upon delicate feet. Many desks included wooden roll-top covers hovering inches above the writing surface, able to be slid over any unfinished work at the end of a business day to maintain the privacy and confidentiality of ongoing work as well as the illusion of tidiness within the workplace. Desks and shelving units were edged with rounded square panels in neutral and unobtrusive blue, black, green and grey tones. The system attempted to address every storage need, from books and papers to new office technologies, offering specialised compartments within desks for pens, pencils, erasers and other stationery products. The needs of the modern office worker were further accommodated through the system's modular approach to office interiors: as work tasks changed, elements of Action Office could be rearranged and reassembled to create new combinations of work surfaces and storage at various heights.

Fig. 7.2. Drawing by Robert Propst of a potential Action Office I implementation including standing desk, chalkboard, Eames office chair, bookshelves and side table. ('Writer Reasoner Action Office', April 1964. Courtesy of Herman Miller Archive.)

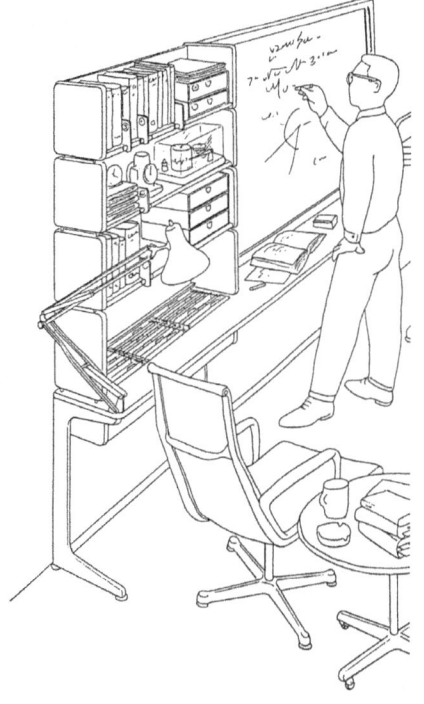

As such, Action Office I sought to accommodate the changing nature of white-collar work, which was increasingly being influenced and shaped by ever-evolving technologies and a more interconnected and inter-networked world. The system debuted to significant critical acclaim in popular and trade publications, which lauded its aesthetic characteristics and the efficiency it enabled.[27] Attention and praise from press and industry insiders, however, were not sufficient to inspire sales. Post mortems of Action Office I, both within and outside Herman Miller, suggested that the system had failed to catch on within the wider American and global workplace because of its high production and retail price and potentially "cumbersome" design.[28]

Following the commercial failure of Action Office I, Propst returned to his research and set about developing a second iteration of the system. During the window between the release of Action Office I and the planning for Action Office II, Nelson and Propst ended their creative partnership, with the former leaving the project but remaining involved in broader design activities at Herman Miller.[29] The precise date of Nelson's departure and the specific reasons for the rupture with Propst remain unclear. Regardless of rationale, Nelson's departure is visible in the system's final aesthetics and design. Chrome and wood features prominent in the first iteration were replaced with more contemporary upholstered fabric and plastic elements. Bookshelves, included by Nelson to provide personal privacy and simultaneously allow for storage of necessary objects, gave way to fabric-covered partition walls, designed to create sufficient privacy while simultaneously enabling frequent reorganisation of both individual workstations and entire office floor plans. This new signature

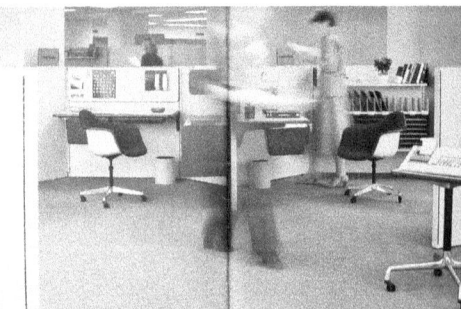

Figs. 7.3.–7.6. Photos from an undated Herman Miller brochure (*Action Office: Principles, Concept, Application*) depicting potential uses of Action Office II for "secretaries" (top left), "clerks" (top right), "supervisors" (bottom left) and "directors" (bottom right). (Courtesy of Herman Miller Archive.)

design element would create what Propst described as "a facility based on change".[30]

The Herman Miller archives provide a selection of evocative full-colour photographs from the 1960s and 70s of these varying combinations and their intended audience and usage (Figs. 7.3.–7.6.). Secretarial spaces could be formed by opening up the partition panels, providing only a backing and side surface, with minimal storage. Clerical workers could be provided with slightly more storage, technological machinery and more work surfaces. Supervisors could be outfitted with standalone desks, a larger work surface area, additional storage furniture and a more defined and enclosed space. Even company directors and executives could use Action Office II components, albeit within private, enclosed rooms.

Following its commercial release, Action Office II was installed throughout Herman Miller headquarters in "all office areas, including two administration buildings, both converted manufacturing buildings, its data processing, technical center, sales offices and manufacturing offices".³¹ As the system spread across the company campus, it also spread throughout the world: brochures and marketing training documents reflect its global adoption, with yearly folders of promotional materials in an increasingly large variety of languages, emanating from an expanding network of local showrooms and sales offices.

As understood by its creators, Action Office was designed to revolutionise the design and use of office spaces for the better, simultaneously humanising and streamlining them. The Action Office II system was promoted by Herman Miller as "more than just another group of modern furniture".³² It was, in the words of Hugh De Pree, "a true innovation, perhaps the first innovation in the office field in quite a number of years".³³ According to promotional materials, the system facilitated "the renewed rise of individuality" in the workplace, preventing "a continuation of sterile uniformity with status as the only definition" by introducing easily interchangeable and alterable components.³⁴ Propst described Action Office II as rooted in several years of research and development which would re-emphasise the human performer in the workplace, facilitating a "break with convention" geared toward the increase of worker "vitality, fluency and productivity".³⁵

While Action Office II *would* turn out to be "more than just another group of modern furniture", it would not fulfil this prediction and aspiration in the ways Propst and Herman Miller leadership envisioned. Shortly after its launch, derivative products appeared on the marketplace, with taller, greyer partitions not designed with employee reconfiguration as a core feature.³⁶ Instead of being used as Propst envisioned to facilitate increased collaboration and communication, partition walls were used to permanently divide, further depriving workers of any vestiges of natural air and sunlight which might have previously existed.³⁷ Something, somewhere, had gone quite wrong.

Although Propst acknowledged negative changes to Action Office II's implementation and use, throughout the rest of his career the designer attributed the grey and inflexible trajectory of the system not to faults in the design but to user error. In a 1998 retrospective interview with *Metropolis* magazine, Propst suggested that "the dark side […] is that not all organizations are intelligent and progressive; lots are run by crass people who can take the same kind of equipment and create hellholes".³⁸ By referring to facilities managers of cubicleised offices as "crass", Propst implied that responsibility for the cubicleisation of Action Office II lay not with him as the product's creator, nor with Herman Miller, nor even with the product itself or the research behind it. Instead, according to Propst, the fault lay with clients, implementors and users of the system – and particularly the personal flaws and motivations of these individuals. While character flaws on the part of managers implementing and adapting Action Office II is one explanation for the system's negative changes and reception, it is far from the most convincing. It is more likely that the worldwide rise of the cubicle had a more structural cause, that there was an underlying motivator drawing corporate and facilities managers across industries and across the world to the architecture and design of a cubicleised office.

Application of labour process theory to the case of Herman Miller's Action Office system provides insights into the changes the system underwent on the open market. This analysis suggests that the self-fashioned and perhaps ungeneralisable understandings of labour and the white-collar labourer held by Propst and Herman Miller resulted in the creation of a furniture system which could easily be overtaken by capitalist logic and lead to less-than-ideal results.

UNDERSTANDINGS OF LABOUR AT HERMAN MILLER: THE SCANLON PLAN

Attitudes towards and understandings of labour at Herman Miller during the time period of Action Office's design can be reconstructed through an exploration and analysis of the company's Scanlon gainsharing plan. Scanlon plans attempt to simultaneously increase the financial well-being of company management and employees by implementing employee-led modifications to the way work is conducted and redistributing resulting profits to employees.[39] In the words of CEO Hugh De Pree:

> The Scanlon Plan is an innovative strategy for managing an organization. It is innovative in philosophy – participative. It is innovative in structure – formal committees to involve all employees in the decision-making process. It is innovative in compensation – a productivity sharing bonus. It combines the leverage of capital, the skill of managers, the creativity and competence of all employees and the opportunities of technology into a system supported by participation and an equitable sharing of productivity to meet the needs of customer, owner and employee.[40]

The plan's concept was developed by Joseph Scanlon, a cost accountant and local leader of the United Steelworkers union during the Great Depression.[41] In his role as a union representative, Scanlon brokered an arrangement between steelworkers and management at the Empire Steel and Tin Plate Company.[42] This deal offered increased employee contribution to workflows and work processes in exchange for a proportion of the additional profits generated by the suggested changes.[43] Through this arrangement, Empire Steel was able to stay fiscally viable during a contracting economic climate, and employees were compensated for their labour – both intellectual and physical.[44]

Scanlon's eponymous plan philosophically and intellectually emerged from a core set of understandings regarding the capitalist labour process. In developing his plan, Scanlon adopted a Marxist conception of labour relations characterised by a consistent and "underlying" conflict of interest between management and labourers.[45] Marxist economics and political thought operate under the understanding that capitalism's continued success revolves around the generation of ever-increasing profits extracted from labourers.[46] Capitalism depends on the exploitation of one group (labourers) to increase the wealth of another (capitalists). Because of this, relationships between workers and management are fundamentally characterised by conflict. As summarised by political economist Harry Braverman:

> Labor and capital are the opposite poles of capitalist society [...]. Whatever its form, whether as money or commodities or means of production, capital is labor: it is labor that has been performed in the past, the objectified product of preceding phases of the cycle of production which becomes capital only through appropriation by the capitalist and its use in the accumulation of more capital. As such, the working class is first of all raw material for exploitation.[47]

Despite, or perhaps because of, such underlying tensions, Scanlon positioned conversation and cooperation between employees and management, in so far as it was possible, as a core element of any successful gainsharing plan. Conversation and cooperation were necessary, according to Scanlon, because line employees executing work tasks, and *only* these employees, held essential and irreplaceable knowledge of work process; of how work was, and could be, done.[48] It follows, then, that Scanlon believed plans such as his own were only feasible through an earnest exchange between labour and management. Success required a genuine attempt by labour to share their knowledge of the labour process with management and a simultaneously genuine commitment by management to respect suggestions made by employees and provide proportional wage increases based on implemented ideas.[49] As a union representative, Scanlon conceptualised the position of the worker in his systems as being represented by organised labour – by unions functioning as the mouthpiece and conduit of the employees' interests.[50] Through union bargaining and representation, the voices of individual workers could be greatly magnified, and collective understandings of workers' experiences and needs could be developed.

Scanlon plans have been studied extensively in labour, economics and management texts.[51] The literature concludes that Scanlon plans, particularly when implemented fully, are successful in making "significant cost savings" and resulting in "significant health and safety improvements".[52] Scanlon plans have been linked with a rise in employee satisfaction, a decrease in employee grievances and an increase in perceived employee voice in decision-making. Further, when implemented robustly, research suggests a Scanlon plan can make employees feel that their jobs are easier to perform.[53] Herman Miller's Scanlon plan, while largely absent from literature exploring the company's designs, is frequently covered in management literature.[54] The company's plan has been featured in *Training* magazine (1987), *Sloan Management Review* (1982) and *Human Resource Management* (1999). These articles praise its success and the company's overall approach to labour relations and employee treatment: "[Herman Miller] has always been a values-driven company, with a historical reputation for innovation in its relationships with employees as well as in its products".[55] This literature outlines in broad strokes the operation of the plan ("it consisted of three basic elements: a participation structure, a bonus system [...] and a communications process")[56] and makes the case that the plan was instrumental to Herman Miller's continued corporate and financial successes.[57]

Herman Miller's Scanlon plan was developed and implemented following Hugh De Pree's attendance at a lecture given by psychologist Carl Frost at the 1950 Grand Rapids Furniture Manufacturers Association.[58] Impressed with his outlook and approach to business relations, De Pree commissioned Frost to develop and implement a bespoke Scanlon-style system.[59] Details of Herman Miller's Scanlon plan can be reconstructed following study of archival materials. These illustrate that despite significant company rhetoric around cooperation and equality, in practice the company's plan followed a rigid and complicated hierarchy and process.

According to an undated overview of Herman Miller's Scanlon Plan, suggestions for alterations to production or corporate processes began with the identification of a problem or generation of an idea by a "suggester". This suggester would complete a "PSA form" and submit the completed form to the "work team leader", alongside "drawings, research, or other documentation". After submission, the work team leader would review the suggestion "for relevance and importance" and to see whether "additional research" was needed. If the suggestion was deemed viable and appropriate, and was small-scale, inexpensive and feasible enough to implement on a local level, the work team leader was empowered to authorise the suggestion. If deemed inappropriate or unnecessary, a suggestion could be rejected at this stage. If the proposed alteration was on a larger scale, more complicated, involved multiple teams or departments or was more costly, the work team leader was instructed to forward the suggestion to their superior, "work team leader 2". This individual could either accept or reject the suggestion or escalate it to "work team leader 3", who in turn could accept, reject or forward it to the "suggestion council". From the suggestion council, proposed alterations could be further escalated to the "cost reduction department". Responses to employees regarding their suggestions seem to have taken a similarly circuitous route – through the "responding council" and a "responding work team" – before arriving back in the hands of the initial suggester (Fig. 7.7.).

While Herman Miller's employee suggestion and profit-sharing programme has become known as a "Scanlon plan" as it comprises similar elements to the titular programme, the company's plan diverges from Scanlon's original approach in several key areas: the degree of communication built into the system, the absence of unions or organised labour, and an operational understanding of labour relations as fundamentally peaceful instead of characterised by strife. While Scanlon set out to build a system and plan based around robust, open and continual communication between employees and management, the Herman Miller profit-sharing system functionally eliminated back-and-forth dialogue, replacing face-to-face interaction and exchange with a highly bureaucratised process. It used forms and paperwork to communicate suggestions, rationales and responses, eliminating face-to-face interaction between management and employees. Through its bureaucratised structure and absence of human interaction and conversation, the plan seems to have prioritised the *system* of soliciting and approving ideas over the ideas and workers themselves. In so doing, the company excluded elements of communication and collaboration so highly valued by Scanlon – the melding of minds between management and workers, and the exploration and negotiation of labour processes and corporate futures.

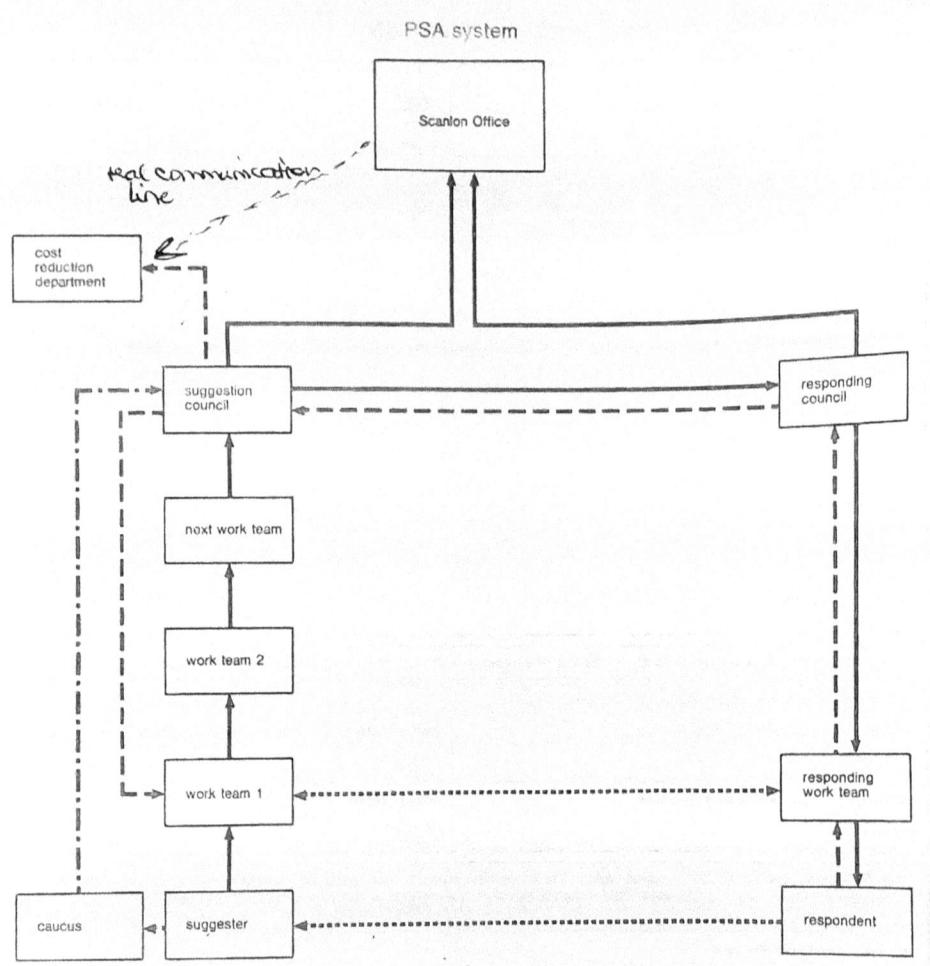

Fig. 7.7. Diagram illustrating the suggestion review process at Herman Miller. ('Scanlon employee suggestion' form, s.d. Courtesy of Herman Miller Archive.)

Joseph Scanlon's plans started from an "underlying assumption that workplace relations should be defined as a conflict of interest between management and nonmanagement employees".[60] Herman Miller's plan, however, appears to have been based on an assumption of harmonious relations between workers and management. While Scanlon designed his plan to bridge the mutually exclusive interests of management and labour, *bringing about* a détente to initiate productive dialogue towards streamlining operations, Herman Miller conceptualised and implemented its plan assuming such a détente *already existed*, aiming to leverage this positive worker-management relationship to improve an already adequate production process. *The Scanlon Plan at Herman Miller*, a company-commissioned report detailing the plan's history, explicitly lays out the firm's belief in their own agreeable labour relations. Unlike a typical non-Scanlon organisation, where "productivity and payroll are [...] viewed as diametrically opposed phenomena" and "the individual worker seeks to maximize the payroll at the expense of production, while the organization seeks to maximize production at the expense of payroll", at Herman Miller it was understood that "all members of the organization seek to optimize the ratio of payroll to production" and that the "objectives of the individual and the organization are [...] integrated". Within this framework of thought, the Scanlon plan was established not to reinvent or alter the company's relationships and power dynamics, but to allow the existing "human system" to become more productive – to amplify already extant practices and behaviours.[61]

Herman Miller's Scanlon plan is also notable for the absence of union participation in the process of soliciting, evaluating and implementing employee suggestions, as well as in the calculation and dispersal of profits. Herman Miller was, and remains, a non-unionised company. In his exploration of the company, Ralph Caplan cites varying degrees of anti-union sentiment, from the statement of an employee that "Herman Miller Employees would never stand for a union" to the assertion of CEO D.J. De Pree that "we can get along without a union".[62] Within Herman Miller it has historically been understood not only that the company did not desire or need organised labour, but that the company's existing policies and Scanlon plan were "actually the equivalent of a union" and were "far superior to any union in benefits".[63]

The absence of organised labour in the conception and implementation of the Herman Miller plan runs counter to the spirit and substance of Scanlon's ideas, and his belief and understanding that unions were necessary to represent the interests of non-management employees.[64] Not only did Scanlon assign a leading role to unions in the practical application of his plans; the entire philosophy underpinning his approach emerged from his own role within union leadership, illustrating how organised labour was central to both the execution of a Scanlon plan and the intellectual conception of the factors behind the plan's potential success.[65]

IDEALISTIC AND ABSTRACT CONCEPTIONS OF THE USER

Together, the research and development process for Action Office II and Herman Miller's approach to the construction and maintenance of its Scanlonesque plan indicate and illustrate the company's wider conception of the office worker and user as an abstract, idealised figure. This conception of the office worker shared numerous characteristics with Robert Propst, Carl Frost, and Herman Miller research staff and management more broadly – of a white, college-educated man working in a relatively self-directed position. While there appear to be few surviving materials regarding the research undertaken for the Action Office system, available documents such as division statements and notes suggest that this research consisted primarily of questionnaires distributed to Herman Miller employees, alongside analyses of working patterns and preferences *within* the Research Division team, particularly those of Propst himself.[66] By focusing workplace research on division staff members, the overwhelmingly white, college-educated, Midwestern men comprising the Research Division staff thus became Herman Miller's de facto definition of the "user" of office spaces. Using this definition, the company would go on to create office furniture products which, while nominally addressing the evolving needs and work patterns of the general category of white-collar worker, were instead tailored to a particular subsection of this group – the researchers themselves.

The company's idealised characterisation of the office user is well encapsulated in the methodology and conclusions of a 1966 report conducted by the company Dunlap and Associates. Undertaken at the request of Herman Miller to "provide information and data which could be used in the promotion of the Action Office", the study reflected the broader research methods used in the design of the Action Office series itself. Only three male test subjects were studied (all employees of Dunlap and Associates), efficiency and productivity were measured by questionnaires, and the study was conducted over a brief period.[67] All three test users were situated within private, enclosed office spaces which were outfitted with Action Office furniture items. The commissioned evaluation of Action Office I encompasses many of the assumptions, values and processes ingrained in the system's design and creation: a narrow conception of the user as a white, college-educated man conducting semi-autonomous work and an assumption that user-led questionnaires are a suitable means to observe work processes and efficiency. Thus, both the Scanlon plan and the research and ideation process leading to the design of Action Office I and II relied on idealised notions of white-collar work and white-collar workers, supported not by meticulous or scientific empirical research but by nebulous assumptions and broader worldviews.

Conceptions and understandings of the nature, behaviour and needs of work and workers at Herman Miller illuminate why and how the Action Office system was so quickly transformed from an idealistic workspace intended to liberate into the limiting and confining cubicle. These understandings are important as they formed the intellectual and ideological basis and starting point for the company's interventions within white-collar workplaces, most notably the Action Office system. While these conceptions may have been accurate to the corporate workplace and process at Herman Miller, they were almost certainly not a universal standard for all white-collar work and workspaces. Although Herman Miller employees may have been able to self-direct their work patterns and tasks, many other white-collar employees were expected to conform to and follow specific working patterns established by management. While Herman Miller employees may have been able to achieve peaceful labour relations without a union, this was not the case within the broader spectrum of white-collar workplaces. And while management and Research Division staff at Herman Miller may have been relatively homogeneous, the wider scope of white-collar workers and workplaces was significantly more diverse in terms of age, race, gender, religion and educational level. An understanding of the ideological framework behind Action Office explains why the possibility of its misuse went completely unseen and unpredicted by Propst and the wider design team: the product was rooted in conceptions and assumptions of labour, labourers and labour relations which simply did and do not match the reality of labour within modern capitalism.

This incongruity between the ideological underpinnings of Action Office and the reality of work within capitalism is clarified by the application of labour process theory and the works of authors such as Braverman. Labour process theory is a Marxist strain of socio-political thought which argues that capitalist control over the circumstances and practices of labour is a necessary part of the capitalist system. The theory posits that when companies began paying employees by the hour, day or week instead of per piece of work completed, a crisis was created within capitalism: companies could no longer be assured that they were getting more value out of their workers than what they were paying each individual labourer.⁶⁸ Under wage labour conditions, workers are paid regardless of how much work is achieved; consequently, company management needed a mechanism which would ensure that workers were completing at least enough work to cover the cost of their wages, and ideally enough work to generate profit for the company.⁶⁹ Labour process theorists suggest that such a mechanism represents control by capitalists and company management over the way work itself is done – over the process of doing labour. By controlling how work is done, companies could be assured that a base line of productivity, and therefore profit, was achieved.⁷⁰ This need, according to many labour process theorists, exists across the spectrum of workplaces and work types – in both the factory and the office, wherever workers are paid salaries and pay is divorced from specific productive tasks.⁷¹ In short, labour process scholars have theorised that much of the experience of modern work is characterised by a fundamental need for capital to control the way individual tasks are accomplished.⁷²

When seen through the lens of capital's need for control, Action Office could never have functioned the way Propst had hoped. Workers could not be allowed to shape, mould and rearrange their own spaces with a variety of interchangeable parts; this was a power which could *only* be assigned to management. What to Propst was misuse, a twisting of the principles and possibilities of Action Office by individually flawed managers, can alternatively be viewed as the natural implementation of modular office furniture systems within capitalism: they were used and modified to extract maximum labour value out of employees. Further, in his assumption of peaceful labour relations within the white-collar workspace, Propst assumed that management would treat employees fairly, with dignity and respect, implementing his designs in ways which were in line with the wishes of workers and with their best interests at heart. But, as has been well studied by the fields of sociology and labour studies (among other disciplines), workers and management within capitalism have intrinsically and fundamentally opposing interests.⁷³ Capital and capitalists are locked into a never-ending quest for ever-increasing profit, which, according to Marx, can only be generated by syphoning more and more value from the labour of workers. While capitalists seek to further their own interests by forcing their employees to work harder, faster or more "efficiently", workers seek to protect themselves and their labour, producing only the work for which they are being fairly paid.⁷⁴ Within this understanding, management is not only unlikely to implement designs or strategies which align with the needs and wants of workers; it *cannot* do so.

Once Action Office hit the commercial market, the system underwent a process of transformation in which concepts and features compatible with capitalist labour processes, like the system's panel walls, were adopted and repeated. Elements which challenged or threatened normal operations of the capitalist workplace were summarily excised from prominent and popular replicas of the system. While modularity was perhaps appropriate for Propst's personal working style and relatively autonomous situation, it appears to have been unacceptable or even inconceivable for many corporate facilities and personnel managers, as well as incompatible with the operating needs of the capitalist labour process. Giving employees the ability, and indeed the suggestion, to reconfigure their working spaces according to personal preferences or perceived requirements, as the modular components and installation guides of Action Office II encouraged, meant giving these workers the freedom and power to control their own labour processes. The fixed panels of the cubicle design, in contrast, nominally provided similar benefits in terms of acoustic and visual privacy, while ensuring that control of office space and work processes remained in the hands of management.

Simultaneously, the potential within Action Office for employees to "hide" themselves away amid panel configurations of their own choosing may have limited managerial observation, thereby obstructing compliance with managerial labour dictates. In contrast, the degree of visual privacy afforded by the cubicle was a known and limited quantity. Cubicular office workers were given restricted privacy from coworkers on either side, but not to their rear. This meant, and continues to mean, that managerial staff could patrol cubicle walkways and observe the work of all their employees from behind their backs. Such changes meant the Action Office system *would* function as a "facility based on change", albeit for the worse; change which removed worker agency and subjected office employees to the surveillance and control of management.

CONCLUSION

This chapter has investigated the evolution of Herman Miller's Action Office system from its origins as an idealistic and humanistic intervention in commercial office interiors to its ultimate reincarnation as the cubicle. Mobilising labour process theory, the chapter has argued that roots of the system's cubicleisation can be found in designer Robert Propst and

Herman Miller's idealistic and non-representational understandings of labour and the white-collar worker, exemplified through the orientation and details of the company's Scanlon plan. Labour process theory strongly suggests that Herman Miller's resulting rose-tinted approach to labour relations blinded it to the realities of labour and the ways the Action Office system might be used, and distorted, on the open market. In view of their need to extract labour, preserve hierarchical labour relations within the workplace and maintain control over the labour process, corporate leaders in a wide range of enterprises saw in Action Office possibilities which Propst, limited by his more humane, idealistic business principles, could not imagine.

Such disconnects between idealistic understandings of labour and the harsh reality of work under capitalism have continued into the 21st century, with successive generations of architects and designers professing an ability to reform and improve the spatial experience of white-collar work. Akin to the history presented in this chapter, such interventions appear largely to have failed. The reality of the office for most workers remains uncomfortable and noisy, providing limited, if any, control over environmental or design factors.[75] When white-collar workers are uncomfortable, physically surveilled and lack environmental autonomy, this is not primarily because of the individual approaches of "crass" managers, or faulty approaches by designers or architects, but because of the operational necessities of capitalism itself. Analysis presented in this chapter therefore suggests that in order to fully understand and potentially alter worker experiences of office spaces, we must first understand and confront capitalism.

ACKNOWLEDGEMENTS

The author would like to thank the staff at the Herman Miller archives for their generosity of time and spirit in allowing and facilitating access to their materials, and the Society for the Study of Labour History for funding this research.

NOTES

[1] In her brief overview of the office, Sheila Liming summarises the trajectory of office spaces as follows: "The open space of the office [...] transitioned from being one built for control [...] to one built for ease and accessibility." See Sheila Liming, Office (New York, 2020), 29. Similar trajectories are outlined in some volumes on (recent) office history, including Aurora Fernández (ed.), The Office on the Grass: The Evolution of the Workplace (Vitoria-Gasteiz, 2017); Gideon Haigh, The Office: A Hardworking History (Melbourne, 2012); Francis Duffy, The New Office (London, 1997).

[2] Adrian Forty, Objects of Desire: Design and Society, 1750-1980 (London, 1989), 140-152. This positive reputation is also discussed in John Harwood, The Interface: IBM and the Transformation of Corporate Design, 1945-1976 (Minneapolis, 2011); Alexandra Lange, 'Tower Typewriter and Trademark: Architects, Designers and the Corporate Utopia, 1956-64', PhD thesis (New York University), 2005; Scott G. Knowles and Stuart W. Leslie, '"Industrial Versailles": Eero Saarinen's Corporate Campuses for GM, IBM, and AT&T', in Isis, 92/1 (2001); Nancy Miller, 'Eero Saarinen on the Frontier of the Future: Building Corporate Image in the American Suburban Landscape, 1939-1961', PhD thesis (University of Pennsylvania), 1999.

[3] Action Office inventor Robert Propst embodies such an approach in his reflection on the Action Office system; see Robert Propst, The Office: A Facility Based on Change (Zeeland, 1968). The scientisation of architecture more broadly and the rise of ergonomics are discussed in detail in Joy Knoblauch, The Architecture of Good Behavior (Pittsburgh, 2020); Avigail Sachs, Environmental Design: Architecture, Politics, and Science in Postwar America (Charlottesville, 2018).

[4] This positive reception can be contrasted with the *popular* portrayal, as discussed in the introduction and Nicola Bishop's chapter, both in this volume.

[5] Gideon Haigh neatly summarises the bad reputation of the cubicle, stating: "In every respect but economic [...] cubicles have disappointed expectation. They were meant to be flexible. In practice, partitions seldom move. They were meant to be roomy. In practice, the office workers often feel like the victim in Poe's *The Pit and the Pendulum*, their walls closing in." See Haigh, The Office, 236. The cubicle has solidified a reputation in popular culture for workplace drudgery, boredom and sameness, well summarised in the comic strip Dilbert, including a volume entitled *Cubicles that Make You Envy the Dead* (2018), suggesting death as a preferable alternative to cubicle habitation. To Dilbert creator Scott Adams, the cubicle is "a constant reminder of the employee's marginal value to the company". See Scott Adams, Cubicles that Make You Envy the Dead (Kansas City, 2018), 71.

[6] Jennifer Kaufmann-Buhler, Open Plan: A Design History of the American Office (London, 2021), 6-9.

[7] Ibid.

[8] Jennifer Kaufmann-Buhler identifies issues with the implementation of open-plan designs as stemming from "mislaid plans, conflicting goals, (and) misguided intentions" rather than problems with the open-plan designs themselves. Gideon Haigh identifies the turning point at which the Action Office concept transitioned into the cubicle as being almost exclusively linked to changes to the U.S. tax code. Nikil Saval, while identifying the devolution of the open-office design into the cubicle, stops short of investigating or naming potential socio-political or economic rationales for such changes. See Kaufmann-Buhler, Open Plan, 9; Haigh, The Office, 267-270; Saval, Cubed (New York, 2014), 5, 6, 206-210 and 211-218.

[9] While the Scanlon plan is mentioned in coffee-table-style books on Herman Miller, it is not discussed in relation to Action Office, and instead is presented as independent information regarding the company's operations and financial success. See for instance John Berry, Herman Miller: The Purpose of Design (New York, 2004), 110-117.

[10] Herman Miller Archives, Zeeland (Michigan), 2.P.2.5.10, 'Action Office II User List' (April 1973). All the listed examples are contained in this one-year client summary, suggesting a more expansive historical and future client list.

[11] See for instance Kaufmann-Buhler, Open Plan, 26-29; Liming, Office, 42-45; Fernández, The Office, 20-21; Saval, Cubed, 5, 6, 206-210 and 211-218; Haigh, The Office, 267-270; Forty, Objects, 148-150.

[12] John R. Berry, Herman Miller (New York, 2004), 13-24.

[13] 'Herman Miller Company Timeline' (via www.hermanmiller.com).

14 Berry, Herman Miller, 69.
15 Ibid., 222-229.
16 'Herman Miller Company Timeline'.
17 Ibid.
18 Leon Ransmeier, 'Live Action: Inventor Robert Propst and the History of the Modern Cubicle', in Pin-Up (via https://archive.pinupmagazine.org); Herman Miller Archives, Accession 3 – Misc Propst Docs – Folder 19, Personnel file for Robert Propst (s.d.).
19 Ralph Caplan, The Design of Herman Miller: Pioneered by Eames, Girard, Nelson, Propst, Rohde (New York, 1976), 76.
20 Stanley Abercrombie, George Nelson: The Design of Modern Design (Cambridge MA, 2000), 210.
21 Caplan, The Design, 73.
22 Herman Miller Archives, HMI Promo VH1501–60, 'An Introduction to Your Action Office Environment' brochure (s.d.).
23 Abercrombie, George Nelson, 210.
24 Cited in Abercrombie, George Nelson, 210.
25 Berry, Herman Miller, 117-125; Caplan, The Design, 76.
26 Caplan, The Design, 76.
27 Nikil Saval, 'The Cubicle You Call Hell was Designed to Set You Free', in Wired (23 April 2014).
28 Caplan quotes then CEO De Pree as having stated that "Action Office I was poorly made, it wasn't really a system, and it was extremely high priced to boot". See Caplan, The Design of Herman Miller, 76.
29 Abercrombie, George Nelson, 219.
30 Evident in the full title of Propst, The Office: A Facility Based on Change.
31 Herman Miller Archives, Accession 3 – Folder 20, 'Propst Planning Team' (s.d.), 2.
32 Herman Miller Archives, Accession 3 – Folder 35, Talk for Action Office press party by Hugh De Pree (16 Nov. 1964).
33 Ibid.
34 Propst, The Office, 17.
35 Henry Ford Museum Archives, Dearborn (Michigan), Accession 2010.83 – Box 42 – Action Office addendum, 'The Influence of Behavioural Sciences on Office Design by Robert Propst' (s.d.).
36 The birth and spread of the cubicle are well-covered topics within office historiography; see Kaufmann-Buhler, Open Plan, 163-169; Liming, Office, 40-44; Saval, The Cubicle; Haigh, The Office, 270-274.
37 Saval, Cubed, 218; Haigh, The Office, 267-274; Jennifer Kaufmann-Buhler, 'From the Open Plan to the Cubicle: The Real and Imagined Transformation of American Office Design and Office Work, 1945-1999', PhD thesis (University of Wisconsin-Madison), 2013, 3. Michelle Murphy's study on Sick Building Syndrome goes in depth into the negative environmental changes within white-collar workspaces brought about, at least in part, by the wholesale adoption of divisive partition furniture systems such as Action Office II. See Michelle Murphy, Sick Building Syndrome and the Problem of Uncertainty: Environmental Politics, Technoscience, and Women Workers (Durham, 2006), 65.
38 Cited in Saval, Cubed, 220.
39 Denis Collins, Gainsharing and Power? Lessons from Six Scanlon Plans (Ithaca, 1998), 10.
40 Herman Miller Archives, Accession 3 – Hugh De Pree Talks – Folder 35 – Part 2, 'Productivity: A National Problem', speech by Hugh De Pree (24 April 1975).
41 Collins, Gainsharing, 9-10.
42 Daniel Wren, 'Joseph N. Scanlon: The Man and the Plan', in Journal of Management History, 15/1 (2009).
43 Collins, Gainsharing, 9-10.
44 Frederick G. Lesieur (ed.), The Scanlon Plan: A Frontier in Labor-Management Cooperation (Cambridge, MA, 1959).
45 Collins, Gainsharing, 25.
46 Harry Braverman, Labor and Monopoly Capital: The Degradation of Work in the Twentieth Century (London, 1974), 52 and 206.

47 Ibid., 377.
48 This in and of itself is also an application of a Marxist principle: the location of labour knowledge with the worker. See Collins, Gainsharing, 33-35.
49 Ibid., 24-25.
50 Ibid., 25.
51 Dow Scott and Paul Davis summarise: "Any student of gain sharing will eventually read about the Scanlon plan. It is one of the longest lasting and most researched approaches to gain sharing [...]." See Dow Scott and Paul Davis, 'Revolutionizing Workplace Culture through Scanlon Gain Sharing', in Lance Berger and Dorothy Berger (eds.), The Compensation Handbook: A State-of-the-Art Guide to Compensation Strategy and Design (New York, 2015), 213. Articles and volumes outlining and studying the efficacy of Scanlon plans appeared as early as 1955. Further works on the Scanlon plan span the subsequent decades and many disciplines, and include: Kenneth W. Thornicroft, 'Promises Kept, Promises Broken: Reciprocity and the Scanlon Plan', in Employee Relations, 13/5 (1991); Michael Schuster, 'The Scanlon Plan: A Longitudinal Analysis', in The Journal of Applied Behavioral Science, 20/1 (1984); J. Kenneth White, 'The Scanlon Plan: Causes and Correlates of Success', in Academy of Management Journal, 22/2 (1979); James W. Driscoll, 'Working Creatively with a Union: Lessons from the Scanlon Plan', in Organizational Dynamics, 8/1 (1979); Robert Ruh, Roger Wallace and Carl Frost, 'Management Attitudes and the Scanlon Plan', in Industrial Relations: A Journal of Economy and Society, 12/3 (1973); Gilbert Krulee, 'The Scanlon Plan: Co-Operation Through Participation', in The Journal of Business, 28/2 (1955).
52 Collins, Gainsharing, 219-221.
53 Ibid., 221.
54 Ibid., 15.
55 Rodney McCowan et al., 'Strategic Human Resource Management at Herman Miller', in Human Resource Management, 38/4 (1999), 303.
56 Judith Ramquist, 'Labor-Management Cooperation: The Scanlon Plan at Work', in Sloan Management Review, 3/23 (1982), 51.
57 Wren, Joseph N. Scanlon, 31.
58 Herman Miller Archives, PUBS4010 – Folder 76, 'The Scanlon Plan at Herman Miller: A General Information Report on its Development, Description, and Impact' by Richard S. Ruch (Sept. 1975).
59 Ibid. Frost remained a fixture at Herman Miller for the rest of his more than 40-year career, becoming so much a part of the firm that an award was eventually created in his name, given every year to the employee who had made the most robust or impactful productivity suggestions.
60 Collins, Gainsharing, 25.
61 Herman Miller Archives, PUBS4010 – Folder 76, 49, 'The Scanlon Plan at Herman Miller: A General Information Report on its Development, Description, and Impact' by Richard S. Ruch (Sept. 1975).
62 Caplan, The Design, 116-117.
63 Ibid.
64 Collins, Gainsharing, 25.
65 While Scanlon was willing for his plans to be implemented in non-unionised companies, he did not picture his plans as replacements for unions. Scanlon refused to work with companies he suspected of trying to subvert or prevent unionisation. See Collins, Gainsharing, 22-25; Wren, Joseph N. Scanlon, 30.
66 Herman Miller Archives, Accession 3 – Misc Propst Docs – Folder 3, 'Herman Miller Inc. Research Division Statement' (1 June 1962).
67 Herman Miller Archives, 'Effectiveness Evaluation of the Herman Miller Action Office' by Dunlap and Associates (Feb. 1966).
68 Braverman, Labor, 57-58.
69 Ibid., 58-67.
70 Ibid., 68.
71 Ibid., 325-326.
72 Ibid., 54-57 and 206.

73 This line of thought begins in Marx's *Capital* and runs through more recent volumes, including Paul Baran and Paul Sweezy, Monopoly Capital (New York, 1989); Michael Burawoy, Manufacturing Consent (Chicago, 1979); Andrew L. Friedman, Industry and Labour: Class Struggle at Work and Monopoly Capitalism (New York, 1977).

74 Karl Marx, 'Wage Labour and Capital' (lecture delivered in Dec. 1847) (via www.marxists.org).

75 Open-plan office designs have continued to proliferate despite a growing body of evidence suggesting that they may not be the most efficacious. Bernstein and Turban have found that open offices may decrease face-to-face communication. Works by Hedge and by Brennan, Chugh and Kline suggest that open offices may lower both perceived and actual job performance. Research by Kaarlela-Tuomaala, Helenius, Keskinen and Hongisto indicates that such spaces may disrupt the execution of work tasks. See Ethan S. Bernstein and Stephen Turban, 'The Impact of the "Open" Workspace on Human Collaboration', in Philosophical Transactions of the Royal Society B, 373 (2018); A. Kaarlela-Tuomaala et al., 'Effects of Acoustic Environment on Work in Private Office Rooms and Open-Plan Offices: Longitudinal Study During Relocation', in Ergonomics, 52/11 (2009); Aoife Brennan, Jasdeep S. Chugh and Theresa Kline, 'Traditional Versus Open Office Design: A Longitudinal Field Study', in Environment and Behavior, 34/3 (2002); Alan Hedge, 'The Open-Plan Office', in Environment and Behavior, 14/5 (1982).

BIBLIOGRAPHY

Stanley Abercrombie, George Nelson: The Design of Modern Design (Cambridge MA, 2000).
Scott Adams, Cubicles That Make You Envy the Dead (Kansas City, 2018).
Paul Baran and Paul Sweezy, Monopoly Capital (New York, 1989).
Ethan Bernstein and Stephen Turban, 'The Impact of the "Open" Workspace on Human Collaboration', in Philosophical Transactions of the Royal Society B, 373 (2018).
John R. Berry, Herman Miller: The Purpose of Design (New York, 2004).
Harry Braverman, Labor and Monopoly Capital: The Degradation of Work in the Twentieth Century (London, 1974).
Aoife Brennan, Jasdeep S. Chugh and Theresa Kline, 'Traditional versus Open Office Design: A Longitudinal Field Study', in Environment and Behavior, 34/3 (2002), 279-299.
Michael Burawoy, Manufacturing Consent (Chicago, 1979).
Ralph Caplan, The Design of Herman Miller: Pioneered by Eames, Girard, Nelson, Propst, Rohde (New York, 1976).
Denis Collins, Gainsharing and Power? Lessons from Six Scanlon Plans (Ithaca, 1998).
James W. Driscoll, 'Working Creatively with a Union: Lessons from the Scanlon Plan', in Organizational Dynamics, 8/1 (1979), 61-80.
Francis Duffy, The New Office (London, 1997).
Aurora Fernández (ed.), The Office on the Grass: The Evolution of the Workplace (Vitoria-Gasteiz, 2017).
Adrian Forty, Objects of Desire: Design and Society, 1750-1980 (London, 1989).
Andrew L. Friedman, Industry and Labour: Class Struggle at Work and Monopoly Capitalism (New York, 1977).
Gideon Haigh, The Office: A Hardworking History (Melbourne, 2012).
John Harwood, The Interface: IBM and the Transformation of Corporate Design, 1945-1976 (Minneapolis, 2011).
Alan Hedge, 'The Open-Plan Office', in Environment and Behavior, 14/5 (1982), 519-542.
A. Kaarlela-Tuomaala et al., 'Effects of Acoustic Environment on Work in Private Office Rooms and Open-Plan Offices – Longitudinal Study during Relocation', in Ergonomics, 52/11 (2009), 1423-1444.
Jennifer Kaufmann-Buhler, 'From the Open Plan to the Cubicle: The Real and Imagined Transformation of American Office Design and Office Work, 1945-1999', PhD thesis (University of Wisconsin-Madison), 2013.
Jennifer Kaufmann-Buhler, 'Progressive Partitions: The Promises and Problems of the American Open Plan Office', in Design and Culture, 8/2 (2016), 205-233.

Jennifer Kaufmann-Buhler, Open Plan: A Design History of the American Office (London, 2021).
Joy Knoblauch, The Architecture of Good Behavior (Pittsburgh, 2020).
Scott Knowles and Stuart W. Leslie, 'Industrial Versailles: Eero Saarinen's Corporate Campuses for GM, IBM, and AT&T', in Isis, 92/1 (2001), 1-33.
Alexandra Lange, 'Tower Typewriter and Trademark: Architects, Designers and the Corporate Utopia, 1956-64', PhD thesis (New York University), 2005.
Frederick G. Lesieur (ed.), The Scanlon Plan: A Frontier in Labor-Management Cooperation (Cambridge, MA, 1959).
Sheila Liming, Office (New York, 2020).
Rodney McCowan et al., 'Strategic Human Resource Management at Herman Miller', in Human Resource Management, 38/4 (1999), 303-308.
Nancy Miller, 'Eero Saarinen on the Frontier of the Future: Building Corporate Image in the American Suburban Landscape, 1939-1961', PhD thesis (University of Pennsylvania), 1999.
Michelle Murphy, Sick Building Syndrome and the Problem of Uncertainty: Environmental Politics, Technoscience, and Women Workers (Durham, 2006).
Robert Propst, The Office: A Facility Based on Change (Zeeland, 1968).
Judith Ramquist, 'Labor-Management Cooperation: The Scanlon Plan at Work', in Sloan Management Review, 3/23 (1982), 49-55.
Robert A. Ruh, Roger L. Wallace and Carl F. Frost, 'Management Attitudes and the Scanlon Plan', in Industrial Relations: A Journal of Economy and Society, 12/3 (1973), 282-288.
Avigail Sachs, Environmental Design: Architecture, Politics, and Science in Postwar America (Charlottesville, 2018).
Nikil Saval, Cubed (New York, 2014).
Michael Schuster, 'The Scanlon Plan: A Longitudinal Analysis', in The Journal of Applied Behavioral Science, 20/1 (1984), 23-38.
Dow Scott and Paul Davis, 'Revolutionizing Workplace Culture through Scanlon Gain Sharing', in Lance Berger and Dorothy Berger (eds.), The Compensation Handbook: A State-of-the-Art Guide to Compensation Strategy and Design (New York, 2015), 211-220.
Kenneth W. Thornicroft, 'Promises Kept, Promises Broken: Reciprocity and the Scanlon Plan', in Employee Relations, 13/5 (1991), 12-21.
Kenneth White, 'The Scanlon Plan: Causes and Correlates of Success', in Academy of Management Journal, 22/2 (1979), 292-312.
Daniel Wren, 'Joseph N. Scanlon: The Man and the Plan', in Journal of Management History, 15/1 (2009), 20-37.

Chapter 8

The European Commission's Office Spaces in the 1950s and 1960s: Constructing a Materialised Imaginary

Marco Ninno

INTRODUCTION

You recognise them immediately on a Friday evening when, arriving on the *Trans Europ Express* from Brussels, they get off at the railway stations in The Hague, Luxembourg, Dortmund, Milan or Paris, their black shoes caked in mud. They carry with them the yellow dirt from the enormous building site that has taken over what was once the *Rond-point de la Loi*, now renamed the Robert Schuman Roundabout. Behind the fences there are nothing but dizzying abysses and imposing metal frameworks of buildings designed to house European officials, who are currently scattered around the Belgian capital. In nearby buildings, hundreds of other "yellow feet" are at their place of work.[1]

Captured in this vivid portrait by *Le Monde* in 1969, Brussels during the 1950s and 1960s emerged as a bustling centre undergoing major transformation, appropriately labelled a "capital under construction" (*capitale en chantier*).[2] Amid this busy setting, the main driver of urban renewal was the construction of administrative buildings, in large part destined to house the European officials referred to in the newspaper article. Seeking to offer a fresh perspective on the everyday experience of European integration, this chapter follows the muddy footprints of the officials as they navigated the corridors of the new buildings. Much has been written about the administration of the European institutions, particularly the Commission, which is usually portrayed in the field of European Union (EU) studies as an "efficient" organisation ruled through capable technocratic management.[3] Other authors have highlighted the popular criticisms towards the technocratic nature of European integration, with the institutions being branded as a dysfunctional bureaucratic behemoth.[4] In both cases, the material aspects of this extensive administrative machinery, specifically the offices, have been largely overlooked. Moreover, when such scrutiny has occurred, it has predominantly focused on exterior symbolism and urban planning.[5]

This chapter seeks to "move beyond the façades" by exploring the spatial and "embodied" aspects of interior organisation. Office interiors were sites where "Europe" was not just a theoretical concept but also took on a physical reality through design, which in turn influenced workplace activities. Indeed, office spaces not only conveyed symbolic ideals and values; they also served as tangible embodiments of the European project and identity. Moreover, by functioning as points of social interaction, the spaces facilitated the practical enactment and lived experience of these ideas among individuals.[6] Carolyn Ban has noted that the European Commission during the 1950s and 1960s represents "an interesting place in which to observe organisational efforts to create a common culture". As the largest European institution, it played a central role in bringing together officials from diverse national backgrounds under a common umbrella, producing a unique blend between supranational institutional unity and the coexistence of various national values.[7] This also shaped office culture and materiality, which I will explore through the lens of what David Adler conceptualised as the "materialized imaginary".[8] I argue that the Commission's self-image was that of a unique and elitist institution, which materialised through small private offices as the preferred mode of interior organisation – even though this went against the preferences of the Belgian government, which initially sought to provide the Commission with open-space offices. The Commission's approach did not stem from an adherence to specific theoretical frameworks, but rather emerged as a construct that mirrored the self-understanding of a highly hierarchical institution.[9] To back up its preference for private office spaces, the Commission produced a report on the matter (1969), which will function as a narrative thread for my chapter and will allow us to follow the "yellow-footed" administrators into their offices. The report explored the links between efficiency and office layout, drawing upon layout manuals, consultations with research institutions and investigations of office use patterns within Western European government administrations. Although the report did not find scientific evidence that could link high productivity to individual offices, it concluded by emphasising the significance attached by top officials to having private workspaces, thus underscoring the influence of psychological factors. I will counterbalance the notable absence of lower-ranking Commission workers in the report by exploring the *Courrier du personnel*, an employee magazine which offered very different views on the office spaces and challenged the top officials' elitist imaginary.

THE APPEAL OF PRIVATE OFFICES

When examining the development of the administrative buildings for the European institutions, it is important to note that the decision on a permanent location remained unresolved for an extended period. While the European Coal and Steel Community (ECSC) had been based in Luxembourg since it was founded in 1952, Brussels gained prominence when the Communities expanded in 1958, with the establishment of the European Economic Community (EEC) and the European Atomic Energy Community (Euratom). The city had seen intensive infrastructure development and rapid modernisation in view of the 1958 World's Fair and had emerged as a convenient temporary location for the two new institutions, which were set to grow considerably.[10] Furthermore, at the end of the 1960s, the three institutions underwent a process of unification, resulting in the merger of the executive bodies of Euratom, the ECSC and the EEC into the Commission of the European Communities. The temporary seat of the new single Commission was once again the city of Brussels. This new institutional arrangement, together with a continuous increase in workforce numbers, meant that more space was needed to house the new staff. In 1969, the newly established Commission thus asked the Council of the European Communities – the ultimate handler of the Communities' budget – for funds to expand its office spaces. In line with the suggestion of the Directorate-General for Personnel and Administration ("DG IX"), this new layout would have extended the use of private offices to all senior officials. These had a so-called "A" grade and were referred to as "*agents de conception*".[11] Hans Michelmann has pointed out that this term applied to "the administrative elite entrusted with what is referred to in French as 'conception', a concept [...] perhaps best translated as 'creative thinking', [which] is contrasted with more routine, administrative tasks".[12] Specifically, these "agents" were responsible for drafting regulations and decisions related to economic, technological and scientific research.

As pointed out by the Commission itself, the "essential function" of the institution was to "contribute to a 'transmutation'", understood as the process of "making Europe". The Commission was primarily responsible for coming up with ideas, facilitating consensus among member states, providing stimulus and offering guidance, especially when persuasion was needed more than legislation.[13] As such, senior officials not only fulfilled administrative roles but also acted as advocates for solutions in areas where regulations were yet to be established.[14] This duality was indeed well encapsulated in the term *"agents de conception"*: they were individuals tasked with conceptualising new ideas and approaches.

Regardless of the nature of the Commission's tasks, the Council refused to grant more funds and asked the Commission to keep on using the old allocation which conferred a private office only to officials with a rank of grade "A3" or above (with "A1" being the most senior grade). The College of Commissioners expressed dissatisfaction with this resolution, citing the negative impact on the working conditions and performance of its officials. While the exact nature of this impact was not clarified, it seemed to touch on various dimensions ranging from efficiency to status. Consequently, commissioners Victor Bodson and Albert Coppé were tasked with preparing a detailed report on the issue of space management, in order to improve the proposal to the Council.[15] The matter was quickly handed over to DG IX, which gave the job to adviser Max Lacroix.[16] Interestingly, Lacroix had personal experience of the disputed matter of office layout: he had been an A3 grade official in the Euratom Commission, but after the Merger Treaty he was demoted to grade A4 in the new European Commission, which theoretically meant that he had to share an office.[17] Not being an expert on the subject himself, Lacroix started by researching literature on office interior planning, mainly Kenneth H. Ripnen's *Office Building and Office Layout Planning* (1960). This American manual provided guidelines for architects and professionals involved in the design of office spaces, delving into classic issues such as workflows, flexibility and adaptability. Moreover, Ripen focused on the critical role of office layout in recognising and embracing employees' individual identities and providing them with an environment that preserved a human dimension. This way, they would not become "submerged in the mass of their colleagues", which was believed to improve efficiency.[18] Lacroix additionally contacted various institutions dealing with office management, who were "very clear about the absence, to their knowledge, of any study on the relationship between 'productivity' and 'cohabitation in the same office'".

Some institutions had attempted similar research, although their results were inconclusive. Office management studies typically focused on quantifiable metrics related to production, while evaluating the productivity of civil servants engaged in intellectual work required more complex and qualitative assessments.[19]

To address this gap, Lacroix provided an overview of office space typologies within government administrations, focusing on the European Communities' member states. Despite the diversity of office buildings and layouts, he identified a clear preference among senior officials for private offices. Lacroix notably approved of the Federal Republic of Germany's formalised rules for its national administration, which mandated that civil servants from the level "A13" onward receive individual offices – roughly equivalent to levels "A6" and "B1" in European terms.[20] Although it is widely recognised that the Commission's organisational structure was largely modelled on the French national administration, the German diplomat Walter Hallstein also played a crucial role in shaping the institution's administrative framework as the first President of the EEC Commission. His vision of a robust, hierarchical administration was reportedly inspired by the West German Foreign Ministry, which he had helped create as State Secretary and which he viewed as a prototype for the European institutions.[21] It is therefore unsurprising that Lacroix saw Germany as a benchmark for office space allocation rules. Additionally, following the widespread destruction of older buildings during the war, German administrative buildings were predominantly modern constructions – a characteristic shared by the offices of the European Commission.

THE EARLY ADMINISTRATIVE BUILDINGS OF THE EUROPEAN COMMISSION IN BRUSSELS

Regarding the Commission, Lacroix pointed out that the current distribution of office space varied depending on the specific building.[22] The first that had been occupied was a rented complex at 51-55, rue Belliard, where almost 200 office rooms were used by the Euratom Commission from 1958 onward. Construction had begun in 1955 under the initiative of the insurance company La Royale Belge; the office floors were designed with an open plan that could be adapted as needed, thanks to standardised removable partitions. Interestingly, the quality of these partitions, including their acoustic insulation, varied based on the rank of the office workers.[23] In his report, Lacroix noted that it was possible to allocate what

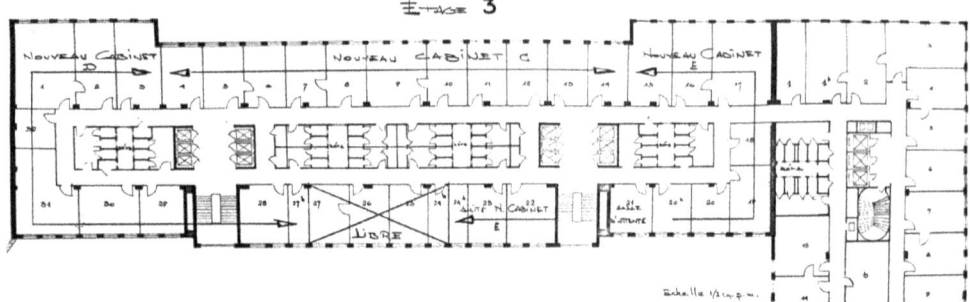

Fig. 8.1. Typical floor plan (1972), Joyeuse Entrée building, Brussels. (HAEC, Commission of the European Communities, BAC 17/1972, 1.)

he described as a "normal" individual office – one with two windows and an area of about 20 square metres – to *agents de conception* at Rue Belliard.[24] Similar considerations applied to another rented building, located at 23-27, avenue de la Joyeuse Entrée, which was again owned by La Royale Belge. Accommodating around 300 office rooms, it was completed in the summer of 1958 and served as the Commission's headquarters from the outset (Fig. 8.1.). In a clear demonstration of hierarchy, President Hallstein and members of his cabinet occupied most of the top floor of this eight-storey building,[25] which was expanded until it occupied an entire urban block by 1963.[26] Both the exterior and interior closely resembled that of the rue Belliard complex: the Commission partitioned the open-plan spaces to create small individual offices, typically featuring two or three windows, and up to four for senior officials.[27] The emphasis on a hierarchical allocation of space is underscored by a 1963 internal report criticising the inappropriate assignment of a three-window office to a top official, who was entitled to a four-window office.[28]

The Berlaymont building – still the Commission's most iconic structure to date – is notable for its origins in an early attempt at collaboration between the Belgian authorities and the Commission to create a dedicated administrative building. In 1959, the Belgian Minister for Public Works established an advisory committee comprising representatives from Belgian ministries, European institutions, and the architects and contractors involved in the project.[29] Coordinated planning was crucial to ensure that the building would meet the needs of both the European Commission *and* the Belgian government, which planned to use the building in the event of a relocation of the Communities.[30] While "certain senior Belgian officials had endeavored to convince the representatives

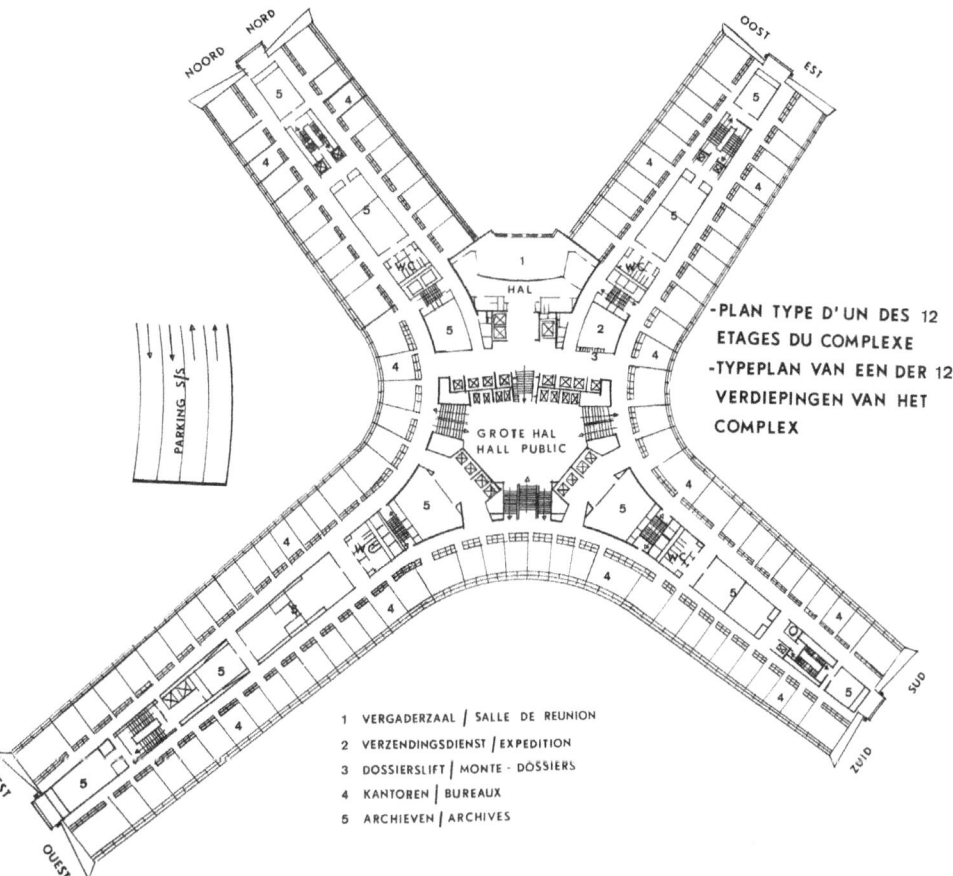

Fig. 8.2. Typical floor plan (1960s), Berlaymont building, Brussels. (Berlaymont: Centre administratif des communatés européennes [Brussels, s.d.].)

of the [Commission] of the advantages of collective office spaces",[31] Daniel Strasser, the Director of Internal Affairs and representative of DG IX on the Berlaymont Advisory Committee, explained that his departments had rejected this proposal. In 1965, Strasser stated that "the tradition of European administrative departments calls for a number of small, comfortable offices – principally one per [senior-ranking] official, rather than large working spaces".[32] To tailor the Berlaymont to the Commission's needs, the open floors were partitioned using modular walls, resulting in offices measuring 5 × 4 metres (Fig. 8.2.).[33] As Lacroix pointed out in his 1969 report, these modules and dimensions were too large to allow for the

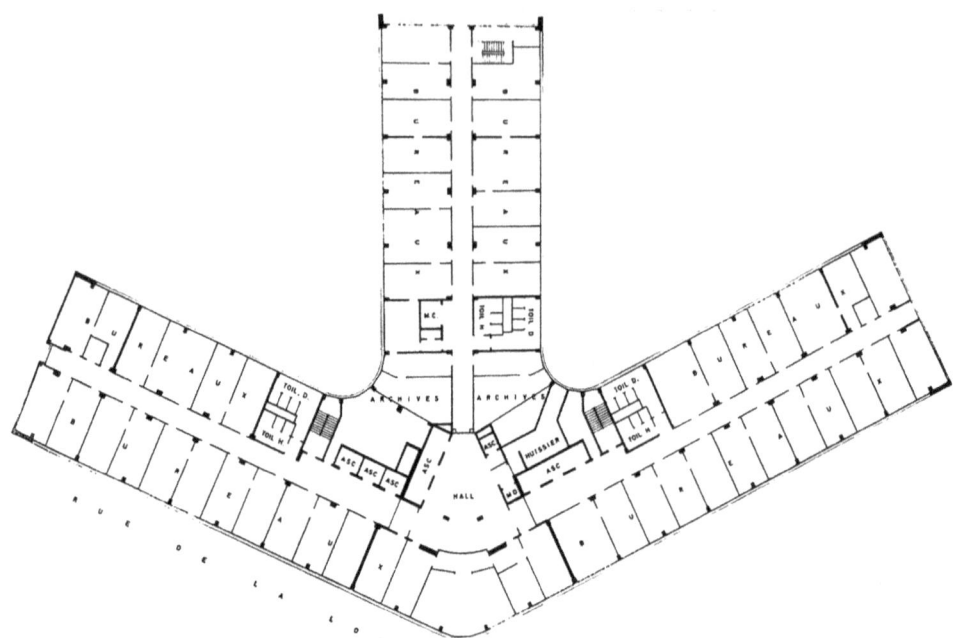

Fig. 8.3. Typical floor plan (c. 1968), Charlemagne building, Brussels. ('Immeuble pour bureaux "Charlemagne" à Bruxelles', in La technique des travaux, Sept.-Oct. 1968.)

construction of individual offices without sacrificing space and incurring significant rental costs, as fees were based on the occupied area. In contrast to the previously mentioned buildings, the area identified by Lacroix as "the smallest 'normal' office" with two windows was approximately 28 square metres. For Lacroix, private offices that were 10 square metres smaller would have sufficed.[34] In 1964, DG IX had also complained that, given the size and number of conference rooms, large entrances, restaurants and additional services, "the Berlaymont complex [was] designed more to accommodate a General Secretariat than an Administration, even a supranational one".[35]

A more satisfactory result was obtained with the Charlemagne building, which was offered to the Commission in October 1964 by the developer *Études et investissements immobiliers*, a subsidiary of the Blaton construction company that was also involved in the Berlaymont project located just opposite it. In this case, the architect, Jacques Cuisinier, engaged directly with the Commission to accommodate its needs. While the Berlaymont was described as "extremely modern and somewhat inadequate", the Commission saw the Charlemagne as more of a "traditional" office building. Each open floor was typically partitioned into three single-window offices, 49 double-window offices, seven three-window offices, and a large corner office (Fig. 8.3.). This arrangement facilitated the allocation of offices in line with the Commission's administrative hierarchy, based on the officials' grades. Moreover, unlike the Berlaymont – where only the top floor, housing the Commission's Presidency, featured opening windows and adjustable radiators in private offices – the Charlemagne building provided these amenities to all users.[36]

Based on the cases examined, the predominant trend in the occupation of the Commission's buildings leaned towards the division of space into private offices, evidence that seemed to support the findings of the Lacroix report. However, given the significant differences among the buildings offered as rental properties, it is impossible to identify a uniform rule. According to Lacroix, this was because they had been designed "taking into account the use of these buildings from the point at which they will no longer be used by the Commission's departments".[37] So as well as the challenge of establishing a clear relationship between efficiency and private offices in his report, Lacroix faced another complication, namely the non-uniform modes of occupation across the Commission's various buildings.

SHIFTING THE FOCUS TO USERS

Drawing a parallel with Ripnen's ideas about the centrality of employee satisfaction, Lacroix eventually moved his focus to the users of these spaces. He linked the demand for private offices to psychological factors specific to the Commission's officials and the nature of their activities. He noted how the *agents de conception* "insisted on receiving an individual office", which "demonstrated the importance the personnel attaches to this aspect of their working conditions". He observed how this desire for individual offices was often seen with officials of a similar senior rank in their respective countries. While the question may not have been officially regulated in all member states, it was, at the very least, customary to provide high-ranking individuals with an individual office. Lacroix argued that Commission officials would likely not accept working conditions that were perceived as inferior to the standards of their respective home countries.[38] This conclusion mirrored concepts already discussed in contemporary literature. Specifically, the notion of "status markers" in relation to office environments had been explored, reinforcing the link between high-ranking officials and private offices. These status markers served various functions such as reward, incentive and communication, contributing to individuals' satisfaction with their workspace. A different scenario might have led to what the American psychologist J.S. Adams (1965) termed "status incongruency": the dissatisfaction that may result when the workspace does not adequately mirror the individual's hierarchical level.[39]

In his report, Lacroix emphasised that the European Communities had a duty to recruit civil servants with the "highest levels of skill, efficiency and integrity". Losing these valuable individuals because of inadequate office space, he argued, would have been unacceptable.[40] He further explained that it would have been discriminatory towards colleagues of other nationalities if special provision had been made for German officials; the only desirable solution was indeed to provide private offices for *all* high-level officials.[41] In his concluding remarks, Lacroix revisited the existing literature, particularly the work of German economist and business organisation expert Hermann Böhrs (1962). Although Böhrs favoured an "open office" solution, he also acknowledged that "the individual office is an absolute necessity for those who have to and can work independently of others, who have to receive visitors, [...] who engage in creative work, and whose tasks have a confidential or even discreet character".[42] In the case of the Commission's *agents de conception*, all these conditions were applicable, justifying the allocation of individual offices. Lacroix noted that the officials considered in his report were "frequently called upon to examine and discuss the questions for which they [were] responsible with colleagues from other directorates-general and directorates and with national officials or experts, either by telephone or during visits required at their workspace". Moreover, Lacroix emphasised that the privacy offered by an individual space would be more conducive to maintaining the confidentiality of the economic and technical matters often discussed within the Commission.[43]

With these reflections on the Commission's organisational dynamics and working environment, Lacroix brought his report to a close before submitting it to DG IX, where it was warmly received by Commissioners Bodson and Coppé, and subsequently presented to the rest of the Commission in August 1969. Based on its findings, the Commissioners concluded that "for a multinational and specialised administration such as ours, the deliberate ignorance by the Council of the practices or even national laws in this area is posing real problems in the operation of our services and for the morale of our staff". They therefore requested a budget increase for 1970, aiming to allocate additional individual office spaces for all *agents de conception*.[44] It is worth noting that these were the remarks of an administration with an increasingly self-confident attitude and high regard for its own mission. This image is in line with accounts of the early history of the Commission, which has been described as an embodiment of "Jean Monnet's model of an administration pursuing a mission and [...] Walter Hallstein's model of a charismatic administration".[45]

If, as the British architect Francis Duffy has pointed out, an office building can be the mirror of the society – or institution – it serves, the Commission's preference for private office spaces aligned well with its administrative culture.[46] This culture blended a "Franco-British tradition of hierarchical interministerial arbitration and a key role for the Secretariat-General" with a "Germanic culture of ministerial independence or autonomy and strong directorates-general".[47] Yet, while on paper the individual office was seen as the quintessential physical emanation of the Commission's essence, this assumption was contested at various levels. Lacroix approached his task by immediately separating the top officials (A category) from the middle- and lower-ranking officials (B and C level), who, as a consequence, are virtually absent from his report. The perspective of the latter categories of office users can be partially reconstructed, however, through the *Courrier du personnel*. Created in 1967 after the merger of the three executive bodies, this employee periodical provided administrative information on promotions, public holidays and job vacancies. Interestingly, the *Courrier* included letters from readers who were granted total freedom of expression (as had been requested by the Staff Committee).[48] The letters section was intended to "open a dialogue, a fascinating conversation [...] between staff, their representatives, the administration and the Commission".[49] In April 1970, a few months after Lacroix' report had been published and disseminated among Commission employees, the *Courrier* featured a cartoon by Roger Faut showing two contrasting scenes (Fig. 8.4.). The top one presents a chaotic office illuminated by strong artificial light and "inhabited" by four civil servants who seem to be fighting each other in the contained space, while a caption states: "Machines neither breathe nor see, so they can be stacked with a minimum of space, air and light." In contrast, the bottom cartoon presents a beautiful spacious office with a large window that illuminates the tastefully furnished space. The only occupant is reclining restfully on his chair with his feet over the large desk, with three dark

Fig. 8.4. Cartoon in the *Courrier du personnel* (107, April 1970).

clouds flying over his head and a pensive expression on his face. The cartoon is accompanied by the text "I THINK, THEREFORE I AM... entitled to demand, all for myself, a spacious office with several windows to be able to 'think' better". To intensify the sarcasm, the cartoon presented a concluding statement: "'TO BE OR NOT TO BE' a 'thinking' official, that is really the question".[50]

The cartoon was undoubtedly a criticism of Lacroix' report. When browsing through various early issues of the *Courrier du personnel*, it becomes clear that the theme of a highly hierarchical administration is a recurring one in the editorials and readers' letters. In particular, following the merger of the executive bodies, many lamented "the partitioning of

Fig. 8.5. Cartoon in the *Courrier du personnel* (113, May 1970).

services, the absence of communications, the depersonalisation of work, the cult of hierarchies, the absence of human relationships". An official reflecting on the topic rhetorically questioned his colleagues: "Should we find it normal or surprising that our organisation has no real human relations department, and that these relations are too often merely hierarchical?"[51] Two more cartoons from the *Courrier du Personnel* (published in 1970 and 1967 respectively) contemplated this theme. One depicted two officials wearing a disproportionately large badge that lists their last name, first name, rank and office (Fig. 8.5.). What the image ironically suggested is that this would make it easier for staff to know how to approach the people they cross paths with as they would know which rank they occupy in the organisational structure. Another cartoon depicted a gathering of European officials waiting to be informed about their new assignment

Fig. 8.6. Cartoon in the *Courrier du personnel* (5, Nov. 1967).

after the merger of the three executive bodies (Fig. 8.6.). To underline the hierarchical differences, we see how individuals belonging to the various "A" grades are depicted as pompous men, occupying the first rows and drawn with clearly recognisable facial features, whereas the rest – the vast mass of "B", "C" and "D" – disappear in a multitude of featureless faces deprived of agency, reflecting their perceived absence from the Commission's reflections on office space.

This feeling of frustration was made explicit in various readers' letters. One from 1970, tellingly entitled "Official or Slave?", targeted a new telephone directory that had just been distributed. The letter noted how Commission officials' names were now accompanied by their roles. This applied only to those in categories A and B, however, whereas the names of those in categories C and D were accompanied only by the DG to which they belonged. This discrepancy raised questions about the treatment of lower-grade civil servants, who were "entirely at their superior's mercy" (*taillable et corvéable à merci*) within their DG's, while being confined to offices that offered only minimum space, light and air, as the letter argued.[52] Three photos published in 1972 offered the reader a rare visual depiction of the working conditions of these lower-ranking officials (Figs. 8.7.–8.9.). The photos of the Commission's Secretariat-General indicate that the above-mentioned concerns were not completely unfounded: some of the offices appear to have been rather crowded. Given the predominance of women in the photographs, it is reasonable to infer that the personnel depicted primarily comprised grade C or B officials, since female personnel was mostly recruited for subaltern tasks. As stressed by Michel Dumoulin, this was in line with prevailing practices within member states where "women were still far from equal to men, particularly from the legal point of view". Although less important than in the past, Dumoulin argued, "the golden rule for women was still the three Cs: children, church and cooking".[53] The photos and letters in the *Courrier du personnel* seem to resonate as an example of the discrepancy between what Henri Lefebvre would define as "lived space" and "conceived space". Lived space refers to the everyday experiences and practices of individuals within a given space, whereas conceived space encompasses the abstract conception of that space by those in authority. In the *Courrier*, accounts of the lived space contrast sharply with the conceived space envisioned by higher authorities within the Commission, as exemplified by Lacroix' defence of comfortable private offices.[54]

Nevertheless, private offices were not without problems either. In a 1969 letter, one A-grade official complained that such offices isolated people: for their occupants, the only opportunity to meet colleagues was in the corridors, "just as it used to be in prison".[55] In particular the Berlaymont building, with its long corridors that resulted from the partitioning of open floors into smaller offices, seemed to be a direct target of these complaints. Even an official report from May 1970, which focused on the "problems of the personnel of the European Commission", highlighted that it was important not to overlook the psychological impact of the conditions under which the services had been moved to the Berlaymont building, as well as the concept of the building itself.[56] Just considering the first issues of the *Courrier*, it is noticeable how as many as one letter per issue addresses the problems of the Berlaymont, describing symptoms of what in the late 1970s would be referred to as Sick Building Syndrome. Prompting protests and even strikes, complaints mainly focused on poor air quality, windows that could not be opened and a fear of being trapped in malfunctioning elevators.[57] By the early 1990s, these concerns took on an existential dimension when the presence of asbestos was recognised as a major health issue for all occupants, resulting in the evacuation of the building and a renovation that lasted until 2004.[58]

On a final note, it is no surprise that, in the bustling office landscape of Brussels in the 1960s and 1970s, the Commission's workers were taking notice of alternative setups. Once again, the *Courrier* served as a platform for such reflections. A letter from 1971 stands out, commenting favourably on the newly inaugurated headquarters of the Royale Belge insurance

Figs. 8.7.–8.9. Photos in the *Courrier du personnel* (231, Nov. 1972).

Fig. 8.10. Office landscape in the Royale Belge office building, Brussels, c. 1970 (*L'Œil*, Nov. 1970.)

company in the Brussels suburb of Boitsfort. This state-of-the-art office building, located in a landscaped park, offered a very different layout to its residents, as it was built around the idea of the *Bürolandschaft*. Most of the company's employees were located in open offices featuring movable partitions, allowing for flexibility in reorganising workplace configurations (Fig. 8.10.). This adaptability aimed to balance the competing demands of privacy and collaboration, theoretically accommodating the dynamic needs of both management and workers. Beyond their functional role, the partitions, alongside a notable abundance of plants, served an aesthetic purpose, creating a rhythmic interplay of private and open areas.[59] While the "cubicalisation" typically associated with open office layouts has, in time, become the object of intense complaints (as is demonstrated in Petra Seitz' contribution to this volume), the aesthetic and functional qualities of the Royale Belge building did sharply contrast with those that could typically be found in the offices of lower-ranking European Commission employees. Indeed, according to the author of the 1971 letter, the Commission's offices were "very backward" and "barrack-like" (*des bureaux-casernes très arriérés*).[60]

CONCLUDING REMARKS

This chapter has demonstrated that examining the materiality of office architecture offers a counterbalance to the abstract and often impersonal nature of large bureaucratic organisations – particularly in the case of the EU, where the complexity of administrative settings is further intensified by the supranational nature of the institutions. A key question arising from this investigation is what features distinguished the office spaces of European officials as uniquely "European". The sources reveal a pronounced emphasis on a highly hierarchical spatial organisation, which manifested most notably in the allocation of private offices to senior officials of the European Commission. This preference was considered so integral to the organisations' functioning that it prompted the creation of a report aimed at justifying its rationale. However, the 1969 Lacroix report ultimately failed to provide any compelling "objective" evidence to support the efficiency of such arrangements, suggesting instead that these offices operated as a "materialised imaginary", embodying and reinforcing the Commission's self-perception as an elite organisation.

This approach to office design was closely aligned with the administrative ethos established under the Commission's first President, Walter Hallstein, whose leadership prioritised the creation of a "strong and hierarchical" organisational structure. The Commission's internal procedures were furthermore heavily shaped by its long-serving Secretary-General, Émile Noël, whose influence contributed to the development of a highly centralised and self-consciously distinct administrative system.[61] This system, while effective in consolidating authority, was characterised by its resistance to external management ideas and an enduring reluctance to undergo significant structural reform over time.[62] Nevertheless, testimonies from lower-ranking officials, which were notably absent from the Lacroix report, present a contrasting perspective that complicates the Commission's self-representation. While these accounts confirm the hierarchical nature of the Commission, they challenge the assumption that its office layouts were "efficient", instead drawing attention to the practical limitations inherent in such designs. This divergence in perspectives highlights the complexity of office dynamics, and underscores the importance of engaging with diverse office users to fully understand the relationship between spatial design, institutional practices and administrative identity.

ACKNOWLEDGEMENT

Funding for the study presented in this chapter was provided by the National Research Fund Luxembourg (FNR) and the Research Foundation – Flanders (FWO), as part of the BUREU research project.

NOTES

1. A.M., 'Les Communautés européennes à l'heure de la fusion', in Le Monde (17 Feb. 1968).
2. Thierry Demey, Bruxelles, chronique d'une capitale en chantier – 2: De l'Expo '58 au siège de la C.E.E. (Brussels, 1992).
3. Neill Nugent, At the Heart of the Union: Studies of the European Commission (London, 2016); Carolyn Ban, Management and Culture in an Enlarged European Commission: From Diversity to Unity? (Basingstoke, 2013); Carolyn Ban, 'Reforming the Staffing Process in the European Union Institutions: Moving the Sacred Cow out of the Road', in International Review of Administrative Sciences, 76/1 (2010); Morten Rasmussen, 'Supranational Governance in the Making: Towards a European Political System', in Wolfram Kaiser, Brigitte Leucht and Morten Rasmussen (eds.), The History of the European Union: Origins of a Trans- and Supranational Polity, 1950-72 (New York, 2009); Peter Nedergaard, European Union Administration: Legitimacy and Efficiency (Leiden, 2007).
4. Les Metcalfe, 'Reforming the Commission: Will Organizational Efficiency Produce Effective Governance?', in Journal of Common Market Studies, 3/5 (2000); Anne Stevens, 'Bureaucrats in Brussels and Beyond', in International Relations, 14/4 (1999).
5. Denis Pohl and Sven Sterken, 'No Europe without Brussels: The Berlaymont Building and the Development of the Léopold Area', in Mauro Casalboni (ed.), Contrast and Harmony: A Photographic Exploration of the European District of Brussels (Rome, 2023); Sebastiano Fabbrini, 'Whatever Happened to Supranational Architecture?', in Ardeth, 7/2 (2020); Thierry Demey, Brussels, Capital of Europe (Brussels, 2007); Carola Hein, The Capital of Europe: Architecture and Urban Planning for the European Union (Westport, 2004); Demey, Bruxelles.
6. For a similar approach in the context of international law, see Miriam Bak McKenna, 'Designing for International Law: The Architecture of International Organizations 1922–1952', in Leiden Journal of International Law, 34/1 (2021).
7. Ban, Management, 2. In this chapter, the term "European Commission" refers to a plurality of institutions over time, including the High Authority of the European Coal and Steel Community (1952-1967), the Commission of the European Economic Community (1958-1967), and the Commission of the European Atomic Energy Community (1958-1967), which merged into the Commission of the European Communities in 1967 following the Merger Treaty.
8. David Adler, 'Solid Futures: Office Architecture and the Labour Imaginary', in Hannes Krämer and Matthias Wenzel (eds.), How Organizations Manage the Future: Theoretical Perspectives and Empirical Insights (Cham, 2018), 302.
9. On elitist leadership ideas within the Commission, see also Didier Georgakakis, European Civil Service in (Times of) Crisis: A Political Sociology of the Changing Power of Eurocrats (Cham, 2017); Didier Georgakakis, Bringing Elites Sociology Back in European Integration Theories: A Case Study

Based on Commissioners and Directors General (Los Angeles, 2009); Marine Lassalle and Didier Georgakakis, 'Genèse et structure d'un capital institutionnel européen: Les très hauts fonctionnaires de la Commission européenne', in Actes de la Recherche en Sciences Sociales, 166-167 (2007); Marine Lassalle and Didier Georgakakis, 'Les Directeurs Généraux de la Commission européenne: Premiers éléments d'une enquête prosopographique', in Regards sociologiques, 24 (2004).

[10] Hein, The Capital, 67–72.
[11] Historical Archives of the European Commission [hereafter HAEC], Commission of the European Communities [hereafter CEC], BAC 259/1980, 114, Meeting 74 (16 April 1969), 35.
[12] Cited by Peter Nedergaard, European Union Administration: Legitimacy and Efficiency (Leiden, 2007), 77.
[13] 'Report of the Round Table on the Problems of the Personnel of the European Commission', in Courrier du personnel (1 May 1970), 4.
[14] Janne Haaland Matláry, 'The Role of the Commission: A Theoretical Discussion', in Neill Nugent (ed.), At the Heart of the Union: Studies of the European Commission (Basingstoke, 2002); Émile Noël, Working Together: The Institutions of the European Community (Brussels, 1979).
[15] HAEC, CEC, BAC 259/1980, 114, Meeting 74 (16 April 1969), 36-38.
[16] HAEC, CEC, BAC 51/1986, 746, 'Note à l'attention de Monsieur Lambert' (16 April 1969) and 'Note à l'attention de Monsieur M. Lacroix' (17 April 1969).
[17] Lacroix had entered the Commission of Euratom as an official of grade A3 but was demoted at the moment of the merger of the institutions, leading to an appeal to the European Court of Justice. See Archives of the European Court of Justice, 'Max Lacroix contre Commission des Communautés européennes: Affaire 30-68' (28 May 1970).
[18] Kenneth H. Ripnen, Office Building and Office Layout Planning (New York, 1960), 2-4.
[19] HAEC, CEC, BAC 51/1986, 746, 'Note d'étude sur l'attribution d'un bureau individuel aux agents de conception dans les services de la Commission' (31 July 1969), 5. Lacroix contacted the International Institute of Administrative Sciences (Brussels), the Technical Institute of Public Administrations (Paris), the Central Service for Organisation and Methods of the French Government (Paris), the General Commission for Scientific Organisation (Paris), the Institute of Sociology (Université libre de Bruxelles), the Centre for Administrative Studies (Université catholique de Louvain), and the Belgian Ministry of Public Service.
[20] Ibid.
[21] On the French influence, see Gérard Bossuat, Émile Noël: Premier secrétaire général de la Commission européenne (Brussels, 2011); Nedergaard, European Union Administration, 179-181; Cris Shore, Building Europe: The Cultural Politics of European Integration (London, 2000), 131; Stephen Martin, The Construction of Europe: Essays in Honour of Émile Noël (Dordrecht, 1994). On the German influence, see Michel Dumoulin, 'The Administration', in idem (ed.), The European Commission 1958-72: History and Memories of an Institution (Brussels, 2014), 221.
[22] HAEC, CEC, BAC 51/1986, 746, 'Note d'étude sur l'attribution d'un bureau individuel aux agents de conception dans les services de la Commission' (31 July 1969), 8.
[23] 'L'Unilever House à Bruxelles', in La technique des travaux, 5-6 (1960).
[24] HAEC, CEC, BAC 51/1986, 746, 'Note d'étude sur l'attribution d'un bureau individuel aux agents de conception dans les services de la Commission' (31 July 1969), 9.
[25] HAEC, CEC, BAC 17/1972, 1, 'Communication de Monsieur Levi-Sandri à MM. les membres de la Commission' (Oct. 1966).
[26] Pohl and Sterken, No Europe, 72. See also 'Joyeuse Exit from Commission's First HQ', in Politico (3 May 2006).
[27] HAEC, CEC, BAC 17/1972, 1, 'Communication de Monsieur Levi-Sandri à MM. les membres de la Commission' (Oct. 1966).
[28] HAEC, CEC, BAC 51/1986, 746, 'Note pour le Cabinet de Monsieur le Président' (9 Jan. 1963).
[29] HAEC, CEC, BAC 51/1986, 649, 'Note sur l'état d'avancement des travaux rélatif au Projet Berlaymont' (7 Jan. 1960).
[30] Sven Sterken, 'Bruxelles, ville de bureaux: Le Berlaymont et la transformation du quartier Léopold', in Bruxelles patrimoines, 15 (2015), 109; Demey, Bruxelles, 190.

31 HAEC, CEC, BAC 51/1986, 649, 'Note sur l'état d'avancement des travaux rélatif au Projet Berlaymont' (7 Jan. 1960).
32 HAEC, CEC, BAC 17/1972, 22, 'Réunion du Groupe de travail Berlaymont' (27 Jan. 1965).
33 HAEC, CEC, BAC 51/1986, 649, 'Note à l'attention de Levi Sandri, Vice-Président de la Commission' (8 Dec. 1964).
34 HAEC, CEC, BAC 51/1986, 746, 'Note d'étude sur l'attribution d'un bureau individuel aux agents de conception dans les services de la Commission' (31 July 1969), 9.
35 HAEC, CEC, BAC 51/1986, 649, 'Note à l'attention de Levi Sandri, Vice-Président de la Commission' (8 Dec. 1964).
36 Ibid.; HAEC, CEC, BAC 47/1985-75, Meeting Joint Committee (22 June 1965).
37 HAEC, CEC, BAC 51/1986, 746, 'Note d'étude sur l'attribution d'un bureau individuel aux agents de conception dans les services de la Commission' (31 July 1969), 10.
38 Ibid., 11.
39 Cited by Ellen Konar, 'Status Demarcation in the Office', in Environment and Behavior, 14/5 (1982), 566.
40 HAEC, CEC, BAC 51/1986, 746, 'Note d'étude sur l'attribution d'un bureau individuel aux agents de conception dans les services de la Commission' (31 July 1969), 11.
41 Ibid., 13.
42 Hermann Böhrs, La rationalisation des services administratifs de l'entreprise (Paris, 1962), 151.
43 HAEC, CEC, BAC 51/1986, 746, 'Note d'étude sur l'attribution d'un bureau individuel aux agents de conception dans les services de la Commission' (31 July 1969), 15.
44 HAEC, CEC, BAC 51/1986, 746, 'Note à nos collègues' (19 Aug. 1969).
45 Michel Mangenot, 'An Administrative Culture in Transition', in Éric Bussière et al. (eds.), The European Commission 1973-86: History and Memories of an Institution (Luxembourg, 2014), 170.
46 Francis Duffy, 'Office Buildings and Organisational Change', in Anthony D. King (ed.), Buildings and Society: Essays on the Social Development of the Built Environment (London, 1980), 140.
47 Michel Mangenot, 'Coordination and Decision-Making Process in the Commission', in Bussière et al., The European Commission, 125.
48 'Letter from the Staff Committee', in Courrier du personnel (5 Nov. 1967).
49 'History of the Courrier du personnel', in Courrier du personnel, 300 (Oct. 1988).
50 'Je pense donc je suis...', in Courrier du personnel, 107 (April 1970).
51 'Les inconnus dans la maison', in Courrier du personnel (23 Jan. 1969).
52 'Fonctionnaire ou serf?', in Courrier du personnel, 145 (Dec. 1970).
53 Michel Dumoulin, 'Like Strangers in the City? European Officials in Brussels', in idem, The European Commission 1958-72, 247. See also Ban, Management.
54 Henri Lefebvre, The Production of Space (Oxford, 1991).
55 J.F. Petitbon, 'Les inconnus dans la maison', in Courrier du personnel (23 Jan. 1969).
56 'Report of the Round Table on the Problems of the Personnel of the European Commission', in Courrier du personnel (1 May 1970).
57 J.F. Petitbon, 'Une préoccupation à l'égard du bâtiment Berlaymont', in Courrier du personnel (17 April 1970); HAEC, CEC, BAC 331/1991, 64, 'Note très urgent à l'attention de Levi Sandri, Vice-Président de la Commission' (22 Jan. 1970).
58 Hein, The Capital, 143-156.
59 On the Royale Belge building, see Jean-Marc Basyn (ed.), La Royale Belge (Brussels, 2023).
60 'Et teneat culti judgera multa solis', in Courrier du personnel (2 Dec. 1971).
61 On Noël, see Janet Coull and Charlie Lewis, 'The Impact Reform of the Staff Regulations in Making the Commission a More Modern and Efficient Organisation: An Insider's Perspective', in EPIAScope 3 (2003); Deirdre Curtin, 'The Commission as Sorcerer's Apprentice? Reflections on EU Public Administration and the Role of Information Technology in Holding Bureaucracy Accountable', in Jean Monnet Working Paper, 6/1 (2001); Metcalfe, Reforming the Commission.
62 Christopher Pollitt and Geert Bouckaert, Public Management Reform: A Comparative Analysis – Into the Age of Austerity (Oxford, 2017), 269.

BIBLIOGRAPHY

David Adler, 'Solid Futures: Office Architecture and the Labour Imaginary', in Hannes Krämer and Matthias Wenzel (eds.), How Organizations Manage the Future: Theoretical Perspectives and Empirical Insights (Cham, 2018), 299-319.
Carolyn Ban, 'Reforming the Staffing Process in the European Union Institutions: Moving the Sacred Cow out of the Road', in International Review of Administrative Sciences, 76/1 (2010), 5-24.
Carolyn Ban, Management and Culture in an Enlarged European Commission: From Diversity to Unity? (Basingstoke, 2013).
Jean-Marc Basyn (ed.), La Royale Belge (Brussels, 2023).
Hermann Böhrs, La rationalisation des services administratifs de l'entreprise (Paris, 1962).
Gérard Bossuat, Émile Noël: Premier secrétaire général de la Commission européenne (Brussels, 2011).
Janet Coull and Charlie Lewis, 'The Impact Reform of the Staff Regulations in Making the Commission a More Modern and Efficient Organisation: An Insider's Perspective', in EPIAScope 3 (2003), 2-9.
Deirdre Curtin, 'The Commission as Sorcerer's Apprentice? Reflections on EU Public Administration and the Role of Information Technology in Holding Bureaucracy Accountable', in Jean Monnet Working Paper, 6/1 (2001).
Thierry Demey, Bruxelles, chronique d'une capitale en chantier – 2: De l'Expo '58 au siège de la C.E.E. (Brussels, 1992).
Thierry Demey, Brussels, Capital of Europe (Brussels, 2007).
Francis Duffy, 'Office Buildings and Organisational Change', in Anthony D. King (ed.), Buildings and Society: Essays on the Social Development of the Built Environment (London, 1980), 140-156.
Michel Dumoulin, 'The Administration', in idem (ed.), The European Commission 1958-72: History and Memories of an Institution (Brussels, 2014), 219-239.
Michel Dumoulin, 'Like Strangers in the City? European Officials in Brussels', in idem (ed.), The European Commission 1958-72: History and Memories of an Institution (Brussels, 2014), 241-272.
Sebastiano Fabbrini, 'Whatever Happened to Supranational Architecture?', in Ardeth, 7/2 (2020), 85-105.
Didier Georgakakis, Bringing Elites Sociology Back in European Integration Theories: A Case Study Based on Commissioners and Directors General (Los Angeles, 2009).
Didier Georgakakis, European Civil Service in (Times of) Crisis: A Political Sociology of the Changing Power of Eurocrats (Cham, 2017).
Carola Hein, The Capital of Europe: Architecture and Urban Planning for the European Union (Westport, 2004).
Ellen Konar, 'Status Demarcation in the Office', in Environment and Behavior, 14/5 (1982), 561-580.
Henri Lefebvre, The Production of Space (Oxford, 1991).
Marine Lassalle and Didier Georgakakis, 'Les Directeurs Généraux de la Commission européenne: Premiers éléments d'une enquête prosopographique', in Regards sociologiques, 24 (2004), 6-33.
Marine Lassalle and Didier Georgakakis, 'Genèse et structure d'un capital institutionnel européen: Les très hauts fonctionnaires de la Commission européenne', in Actes de la recherche en sciences sociales, 166-167 (2007), 38-53.
Michel Mangenot, 'An Administrative Culture in Transition', in Éric Bussière et al. (eds.), The European Commission 1973-86: History and Memories of an Institution (Luxembourg, 2014), 181-192.
Michel Mangenot, 'Coordination and Decision-Making Process in the Commission', in Éric Bussière et al. (eds.), The European Commission, 1973-86: History and Memories of an Institution (Luxembourg, 2014), 125-130.
Stephen Martin, The Construction of Europe: Essays in Honour of Émile Noël (Dordrecht, 1994).
Janne Haaland Matlári, 'The Role of the Commission: A Theoretical Discussion', in Neill Nugent (ed.), At the Heart of the Union: Studies of the European Commission (Basingstoke, 2002), 265-282.
Miriam Bak McKenna, 'Designing for International Law: The Architecture of International Organizations, 1922-1952', in Leiden Journal of International Law, 34/1 (2021), 1-22.
Les Metcalfe, 'Reforming the Commission: Will Organizational Efficiency Produce Effective Governance?', in Journal of Common Market Studies, 3/5 (2000), 817-841.
Peter Nedergaard, European Union Administration: Legitimacy and Efficiency (Leiden, 2007).

Émile Noël, Working Together: The Institutions of the European Community (Brussels, 1979).
Neill Nugent, At the Heart of the Union: Studies of the European Commission (London, 2016).
J.F. Petitbon, 'Les inconnus dans la maison', in Courrier du personnel (23 Jan. 1969).
J.F. Petitbon, 'Une préoccupation à l'égard du bâtiment Berlaymont', in Courrier du personnel (17 April 1970).
Denis Pohl and Sven Sterken, 'No Europe without Brussels: The Berlaymont Building and the Development of the Léopold Area', in Mauro Casalboni (ed.), Contrast and Harmony: A Photographic Exploration of the European District of Brussels (Rome, 2023), 64-73.
Christopher Pollitt and Geert Bouckaert, Public Management Reform: A Comparative Analysis – Into the Age of Austerity (Oxford, 2017).
Morten Rasmussen, 'Supranational Governance in the Making: Towards a European Political System', in Wolfram Kaiser, Brigitte Leucht and Morten Rasmussen (eds.), The History of the European Union: Origins of a Trans- and Supranational Polity, 1950-72 (New York, 2009), 34-55.
Kenneth H. Ripnen, Office Building and Office Layout Planning (New York, 1960).
Cris Shore, Building Europe: The Cultural Politics of European Integration (London, 2000).
Sven Sterken, 'Bruxelles, ville de bureaux: Le Berlaymont et la transformation du quartier Léopold', in Bruxelles patrimoines, 15 (2015), 102-117.
Anne Stevens, 'Bureaucrats in Brussels and Beyond', in International Relations, 14/4 (1999), 33-45.

PART 4
VISUAL ESSAYS

Chapter 9
"Mimic Men" in the Office Spaces of a "Nervous State": The Materiality of Bureaucracy in Late Colonial Congo

Johan Lagae and Jens van de Maele

INTRODUCTION

In the early 20th century, Max Weber famously defined bureaucracy by its ideal-typical capacity to "dominate" through a combination of "knowledge" and "discipline". While government bureaucracies have played an important role in disciplining their populations, the German sociologist emphasised that *self-discipline* among bureaucrats is an essential precondition for any form of "rational administration". Accordingly, bureaucrats operate within a mechanistic logic that requires them to eliminate "subjective or irrational elements of will and mood".[1] This promise of rationality – typical synonyms might include modernity or efficiency – has formed the bedrock of all government administrations, but was especially central to the self-representation of their colonial variants. The postulated irrationality, emotionality, violence and backwardness of local populations in colonised territories, placed in contrast to the presumed rationality and civilised nature of the colonisers, were foundational axioms upon which 19th- and 20th-century projects of colonial occupation were built. Whenever such projects needed to be legitimised, the ideal-typical characteristics from Weberian theory were mobilised in propagandistic discourses. This legitimisation process was not confined to isolated moments, as colonial rule constantly required justification in the face of evolving challenges and criticism. However, within this broader process, certain moments stand out when discourses were recalibrated. The Belgian Congo provides a particularly illustrative example of such recalibrations: first, in 1908, when the Belgian state took over rule from Leopold II and henceforth presented itself as a "responsible" coloniser;

and again after the Second World War, when the colonial government sought to pursue a "developmentalist" path aimed at accelerating improvements in infrastructure and welfare.[2] On both occasions, renewed faith was placed in the role of the colonial bureaucracies, encompassing the metropolitan administration (the Ministry of Colonies in Brussels) and the administrative apparatus in Africa (headed by the *Gouvernement Général* in Kinshasa/Léopoldville).[3] Both were responsible for developing and implementing policies, while also ensuring their justification before a variety of audiences – from global to local levels, and from colonisers to colonised.

In practice, however, colonial bureaucracies were often far from the ideal envisioned by Weberian theory. The realities of colonial rule exposed a stark tension between lofty aspirations – captured by Benoît Henriet as visions of "tropical utopias" – and the inherent tumult and cynicism of occupation (which were only deepened by the vast scale and remoteness of the territories involved).[4] Colonial administrators frequently lacked sufficient knowledge, skills, authority, resources or – indeed – self-discipline, which generated a pervasive sense of "nervousness" (Nancy Rose Hunt) among colonisers themselves in the face of both real and perceived threats.[5] This fundamental insecurity became manifest in the production of ever-growing amounts of paperwork, as colonial authorities in Congo, but also elsewhere, leaned heavily on documentation and correspondence to sustain control (or the illusion thereof). The development of "paper regimes" was further driven by the exploitative dimension of colonialism, which was closely linked to its "developmentalist" counterpart – with both dimensions relying on shared bureaucratic systems to function.[6] Rooted in material infrastructures, these systems depended on offices as the physical sites where governance unfolded. During the early years, colonial administrative setups were often improvised, sometimes consisting of nothing more than a table and chair set up outdoors (Fig. 9.1.). Over time, and especially in the waning years of colonisation, when several imperial powers implemented ten-year plans, such improvisation gradually gave way to "modern" office buildings, some of which had not progressed beyond the planning stage at the time of independence.[7]

Interestingly, the qualitative state of the offices did not necessarily dictate the success of colonial rule: as Michael Harry Port observed, the unhealthy and impractical colonial office buildings in London did not hinder the United Kingdom's emergence as the dominant imperial power during the mid-19th century. The materiality of offices nonetheless

Fig. 9.1. An office setting in colonial Congo partially open to the elements, 1925-26. The original caption describes the scene as "V. Smeekens and his clerk during tax collection among the Ba-Shilele". (Royal Museum for Central Africa, Tervuren [hereafter RMCA], HP.1956.56.216. Unidentified photographer; all rights reserved.)

represents an often-overlooked aspect of colonial history, the analysis of which can deepen our understanding of how administrations shaped society on a day-to-day basis.[8] Above all, offices embodied the colonial ideal of bureaucratic rationalisation, serving as symbols of progress and reason. For many, working in these spaces – as colonisers or as "indigenous" clerks – represented both personal and collective advancement, aligning bureaucracy with the promise of "civilisation" that lay at the heart of colonial aspirations. For Africans in particular, becoming a clerk offered opportunities for empowerment, potentially placing them in a position of authority that "blurred the colonial dichotomies of European and African, white and black, 'civilized' and 'uncivilized'".[9] Through a process of assimilation, emulating the European clerk as a role model, they could become intermediaries – even "cultural commuters" – straddling the divide between tradition and modernity.[10] As a result, they were often viewed with suspicion by both colonisers and the colonised, derided in pejorative terms. Referring to a novel by Trinidadian-British Nobel laureate V.S. Naipaul, whose work explored postcolonial identity, historian Andreas Eckert for instance dubbed African office clerks "mimic men".[11] Indeed, one can argue that they constituted what in postcolonial studies has been termed "a 'blurred copy' of the colonizer that can be quite threatening", because the act of "mimicry", as reflected upon by Homi Bhabha, is "never far from mockery, since it can appear to parody whatever it mimics".[12]

This chapter focuses on office spaces and their users in late colonial Congo (1945-1960), during the era of "developmental colonialism". It examines the interplay between bureaucratic practices and the infrastructures that supported them, illuminating the intersection of architectural "hardware" and managerial "software" in colonial governance.[13] Given the deep entanglement of power between the state, commercial enterprises and the church – what has been termed the colonial trinity – we extend the discussion beyond offices directly associated with the colonial state.[14] Our analysis of the spatial dimension of bureaucracy examines various scales, from the micro-level of office furniture to the macro-level of segregated urban spaces. Images serve as the starting point for our reflection: by bringing together a variety of visual sources that depict phenomena across these scales – photographs, architectural drawings, illustrated press, books and art – we seek to establish new connections and insights into the workings of colonial power. Many of these images were explicitly conceived as instruments of propaganda, contributing to what Stuart Hall termed "regimes of representation", where authorities crafted visual dichotomies to reinforce hierarchical divisions.[15] Other visuals, while serving different functions – such as private keepsakes or internal documents – still operated within this broader regime, either reinforcing or challenging its ideologies.

Our analysis combines reading "against the grain" (as suggested by Christraud M. Geary), to deconstruct the propagandistic elements of these images, with reading "along the archival grain" (following Ann Laura Stoler) to understand their role within colonial bureaucracy.[16] In this regard, it is telling that Stoler's seminal work *Along the Archival Grain* (2009), which explores the centrality of archives in shaping colonial knowledge and power, opens with a 1910 photograph of a government office interior in Batavia, the capital of the Dutch East Indies.[17] Showing white administrators alongside "indigenous" lower-ranking clerks, this photo illustrates how "accumulations of paper and edifices of stone were both monuments to the asserted know-how of rule, artifacts of bureaucratic labor duly performed [and] artifices of a colonial state declared to be in efficient operation".[18] The image, like those below on the Congo, underscores that colonial office spaces were indeed crucial sites of power, which the nervous colonisers shared with mimic men – sometimes also mimic women – who were determined to carve out an in-between space for themselves within a segregated society.

BUILDING THE SCAFFOLDING OF THE NERVOUS STATE

In 1949, authorities launched the "Ten-Year Plan for the Social and Economic Development of the Belgian Congo". Mirroring long-term policy initiatives in British and French African colonies, and responding to mounting criticism from the African population and the United Nations, this plan aimed to establish a colonial version of the welfare state in the territories under Belgian control. It proposed ambitious projects in fields such as urban planning, housing, healthcare, education, agriculture and transport infrastructure.[19] The Ten-Year Plan represented a pivotal moment in the administration of the Belgian Congo, laying the foundation for what contemporary observers, both domestically and internationally, would soon hail as a "model colony" (*colonie modèle*). The legacy of buildings resulting from this plan is a key element by which the success of this *colonie modèle* was often measured in the decades after 1960, particularly by those who sought to counter criticism of colonial rule. After all, did the Belgians not build "an immense number of schools and hospitals"?[20]

The official publication *Investir c'est prospérer: Les réalisations du Plan décennal* (c. 1959-1960) provides a comprehensive quantitative survey of all new edifices constructed since 1949 (Fig. 9.2.). Of particular significance in the context of this chapter are the numbers listed in the section "administrative buildings": "For central and provincial administrations: 11; for district administrations: 8; for territorial administrations: 74; [...] for the police, security, customs, taxes, public markets: 79." The list continues with buildings for communication and the meteorological service (147), judicial administrations (17), penitentiary services (21), and a large number of residential units for administrative staff, totalling over 13,000.[21] This enumeration illustrates the vast workforce required by the

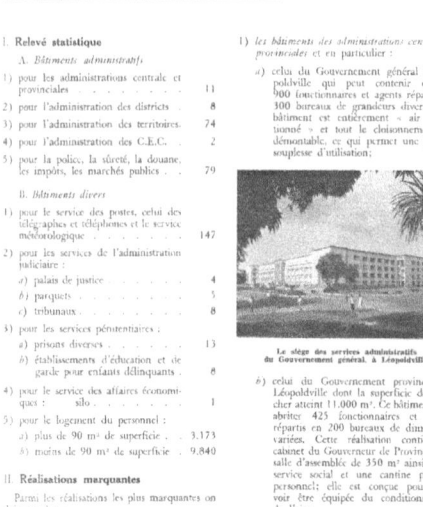

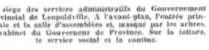

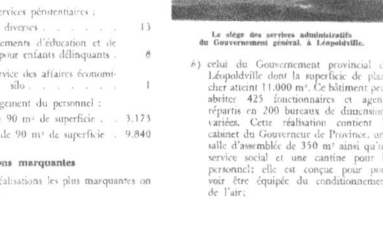

Fig. 9.2. List of achievements in the field of "public buildings, warehouses and urban planning". (Investir c'est prospérer: Les réalisation du Plan décennal [Brussels, s.d.], 38-39.)

colonial administration, highlighting that the Belgian Congo possessed "the densest administration in Africa".[22] A geographic mapping of the colonial state's office infrastructure – an exercise that can be undertaken using the detailed building programme data included in the annual reports presented by the Ministry of Colonies – reveals the extent to which this construction effort penetrated deep into the territory, in line with the hierarchical structure of the colonial administration, with its provinces, districts, sectors, *chefferies* and at one point even *sous-chefferies*.[23] Drawing on a concept proposed by architectural historian Peter Scriver, this built infrastructure (and the administrative workforce it accommodated) can be regarded as the "scaffolding" of the Belgian colonial "empire".[24] Among its components were office buildings in major urban centres and provincial capitals, designed to be representative of colonial authority. A striking example is the vast, five-storey provincial headquarters built in the mid-1950s in Mbandaka/Coquilhatville (Equator Province), where a landscaped park – depicted on the construction plans – was intended to reinforce the building's symbolic presence (Fig. 9.3.). Designed by architects employed by the colonial state but also, on occasion, outsourced to metropolitan architects, such monumental structures asserted power and prestige.

Fig. 9.3. Drawing (detail) of an office complex with a surrounding park for the provincial administration, Mbandaka (Equator Province), 1955, architect J. Petit. (Archives of the Ministry of Colonies, Brussels, AA 3DG[814]3.)

They were embedded within broader urban layouts that also included more utilitarian buildings conceived by technicians from the Public Works Department residing in Congo. Alongside offices, schools and hospitals, this infrastructure extended to prisons and what *Investir c'est prospérer* referred to as "educational and custodial institutions for delinquent children": facilities that were often characterised by inhumane conditions and decrepit infrastructure.[25] In this respect, Nancy Rose Hunt has noted that "by the time of Belgian Congo's famed postwar developmentalist schemes, a shining infertility clinic stood near a bleak penal colony", aptly encapsulating the "nervous state" that governed the territory.[26]

THE *PORTRAIT-ROBOT* OF EUROPEAN AND AFRICAN WHITE-COLLAR WORKERS

Colonial bureaucracy required not only a vast infrastructure of buildings, but also a corresponding workforce of clerks, both black and white. Historian Martin Klein has argued that the high salaries of European office workers, which consumed a significant portion of colonial budgets, prompted many colonial authorities to educate large numbers of African clerks to sustain the colonial enterprise.[27] The Belgian Congo was no exception. Although comprehensive data on the number of Congolese staff employed by the colonial state and large companies is lacking, several indicators are revealing. Historian Daniel Tödt has noted that "secretarial assistants were trained in French, bookkeeping and typewriting" at vocational and technical schools (*écoles moyennes*), whose numbers increased significantly under the Ten-Year Plan. Additionally, specialised institutions such as the *Colonie scolaire* in Boma, run by the *Frères des écoles chrétiennes*, trained typists to meet the state's growing administrative needs.[28] During World War II, the number of office workers grew by 70%, reaching 15,000; by 1946, this number had climbed to 18,000. However, the real boom was yet to come.[29] Statistics from a book published by the *Banque du Congo belge* in 1959 highlight this postwar expansion: in 1945, the bank employed 93 white and 489 black staff members; by 1959, these numbers had risen to 236 and 1,512 respectively.[30]

The post-war period coincided with the aforementioned Belgian "developmental" colonialism. As Tödt explained, during this time, there was a resurgence in the assimilation doctrine, which emphasised the responsibility of Congolese individuals to "learn the lessons of civilized life [...] by imitating Europeans".[31] Photographs from the 1950s, distributed by official press services such as Congopresse and Inforcongo, depict the archetypal European administrative worker in the Congo: dressed in a white shirt and tie, the clerk – almost always male – is shown diligently seated behind his desk, reading documents or composing correspondence, pen in hand.[32] Top-ranking officials were often portrayed through similar "*portraits-robots*": a 1950 photograph of Vice-Governor Ivan de Thibault, for instance, shows him in his ceremonial uniform, fully engaged in paperwork (Fig. 9.4.).[33] On another portrait, most likely from the same period, we see Dr. Georges Neujean, the inspector of the medical laboratories and director of the Institute for Tropical Medicine in Kinshasa, similarly engaged in administrative duties (Fig. 9.5.).[34]

The many services of the colonial state thus produced vast numbers of documents, which today form the extensive archival holdings of the former Ministry of Colonies and *Gouvernement Général*. Not coincidentally, in colonial parlance, Kinshasa was dubbed the "capital of paper". Indeed, in line with the hierarchical organisation of colonial bureaucracy, decision-making processes necessitated time-consuming communication across all levels of administration, with final approval required from top-ranking officials in both Kinshasa and Brussels. It is no wonder that, much like in the metropole, the cumbersome nature of bureaucratic

Figs. 9.4.–9.5. White men at work in the colony: Ivan de Thibault (left) and Georges Neujean (right). Photo by J. Mulders for Inforcongo, October 1950 (left), and C. Lamote for Inforcongo, 1950s (right). (RMCA, HP.1955.17.20 and HP.1955.96.234. © RMCA/Mulders [left]; © RMCA [right].)

activities was frequently criticised, both in acerbic texts and through humour and satire. The immense flow of paperwork arriving and leaving the colonial capital was already mocked during the interwar period in a short satirical story by Henri Stevelinck, first published in the newspaper *L'Avenir colonial belge*. Entitled *"La papyrusserie"*, it was reprinted in 1932 in the book *Chroniques de Stinkopolis*, which collected stories depicting daily life in the colonial capital.[35] Another example can be found in the final chapter of *Les bavardages du cancrelat* (The Chattering of the Cockroach), written by W. Vigneron and published in 1945.[36] Beginning with the sentence "Scribbling [in bureaucracy] leads to sluggishness, lethargy and morbidity", the chapter presents a satirical portrait of a European white-collar worker in Lubumbashi/Élisabethville. An accompanying cartoon portrays a white clerk seated at a rudimentary desk, insufficiently sized for his needs, draped with a worn tablecloth (Fig. 9.6.). As described in the text, his face shows "carefully crafted and perfected disguises", including "a forehead etched with symptomatic wrinkles that betray anxiety" and "eyebrow arches that convey the subtle nuances mirroring the contours of the problem".[37]

This ironic portrayal of lower- and medium-ranking white clerks undermined the developmentalist doctrine of "imitation" (as the behaviour of Europeans frequently fell short of the expectations set by the colonial administration), while also standing in stark contrast to

Fig. 9.6. Cartoon by W. Vigneron, published in his book *Les bavardages du cancrelat* (Élisabethville, 1945, 205).

the official propaganda photographs that were intended to convey the colony's efficiency. Reflecting the crude nature of much colonial humour, the satirical depictions of office workers are jarring from a present-day perspective, especially when rooted in racial stereotypes. A handwritten caption, found in an early 1930s album on the port city of Matadi, reading *"Un nègre-blanc: Percepteur à Matadi"* (A white negro: Tax collector in Matadi), next to a photograph of a European clerk sitting at a desk in front of a stacked filing cabinet, offers a telling example (Fig. 9.7.). This photograph foreshadows the *portrait-robot* of the Congolese clerk, as part of a photographic genre that proliferated after World War II and focused on categorising different types of workers. Tellingly, like manual labourers, clerical workers were almost always depicted as generic members of the "indigenous" population and rarely represented as individuals with a name. (In French, the term *nègre* also referred to anonymous copywriters or ghostwriters, adding a layer of irony to the caption of the 1930s photo that further underscores the clerk's perceived lack of individuality and status.) Likewise, in their detailed analysis of propaganda films, Francis Ramirez and Christian Rolot have highlighted an almost fetishist

Fig. 9.7. "*Un nègre-blanc*" shown in a photo album by Mainguin, post office clerk in Matadi between 1930 and 1933. (RMCA, HP.2005.58.1-24.)

emphasis on the "tool" (*outil*) in post-1945 portrayals of Congolese striving for social mobility: it was the tool, rather than the personality, that defined workers' identity. Just as the microscope became synonymous with the Congolese medical assistant and the handsaw with the Congolese carpenter, tools like the typewriter, calculator and telephone thus came to symbolise the idealised image of the Congolese office worker – despite the fact that this role remained reserved for a small minority of the black population.[38]

As with white clerks, the tools of the black clerk could also become objects of satire in the eyes of colonisers. In the 1952 film *À chacun son métier* (To Each His Own Trade), directed by the prominent Abbé Cornil, the typewriter was used to mock the "pretensions" of a black clerk: "Utterly incompetent, he racks up typing errors, tears paper from the roll, and ultimately resigns himself to a less prestigious job than that of secretary".[39] This satirisation was undoubtedly fuelled by a palpable fear among colonisers, emerging in the postwar period, when the emancipatory actions of an increasing number of black office workers began to challenge social norms, particularly the discriminatory regime of the "colour bar". These grievances found expression not only in private circles but also more frequently in public venues such as the periodical *La Voix du Congolais*.[40] As we will explore, Congolese office workers – emblematic of the "mimic men" – constituted a distinct group within the elite circles of so-called *évolués*.[41] Over time, they also made use of their newfound status to carve out space and agency for themselves in a rigidly segregated colonial society, thus challenging the stark divide between black and white (Figs. 9.8.–9.9.).

Figs. 9.8.–9.9. Anonymous office workers in the 1940s. The captions describe them as "an indigenous clerk at work in the offices of a large agricultural enterprise in Binga (Congo-Ubangi district)" (left), and as an example of the fact that "the indigenous people of the Congo are valuable assistants in telegraph services", with "the most skilled black operators transmitting or receiving telegrams in Morse code at a rate of 100 to 120 words per minute" (right). Photo by E. Lebied for Inforcongo, 1947 (left), and Gérard de Boe for Inforcongo, 1944 (right). (RMCA, HP.1956.15.13052 and HP.1956.15.3232. © RMCA/Lebied [left]; © Royal Film Archive of Belgium [right].)

SEGREGATED OFFICE SPACES FOR SEGREGATED CITIES

In 1947, the Brussels-based architect Georges Ricquier was commissioned to design a new headquarters building in Kinshasa for the Agence Maritime Internationale (AMI), a company involved in operating shipping routes between Matadi and Antwerp.[42] Constructed shortly thereafter, the new headquarters served a variety of functions (Fig. 9.10.). The ground floor included storage spaces, a garage, a dressing room and two shops. The *piano nobile* accommodated offices, a waiting room, and a large double-height public hall, directly accessible from the street via a centrally located staircase. This hall featured an elongated counter placed in front of an open office area. The first floor contained additional office rooms of varying sizes; the second floor was reserved as an apartment for visiting senior company officials. The building stood out in the streetscape, not only because of its height (surpassing the one-storey buildings of the 1910s and 1920s), but also because of its remarkable grid-like *claustra* and a series of galleries on the main façade. According to the description of the planned building, these architectural features were designed to counter the challenging orientation and the building's exposure to the intense late afternoon sun.

Fig. 9.10. Main façade of the AMI headquarters, 1949. Photo by L. Denis for Inforcongo. (RMCA, HP.1956.30.92. © RMCA/Denis)

Located on a corner plot, the AMI headquarters followed the principle of axial symmetry, which informed both the overall exterior appearance and the internal spatial organisation, including the circulation patterns. Intriguingly, this design element was employed to subtly reinforce the spatial separation embedded in the colonial context, in line with the pervasive colour bar that shaped life in colonial Congo.[43] While the public staircase leading to the main hall on the *bel étage* was open to all, the floor plans reveal the presence of two other staircases accessible via entrances on the opposing side façades. Neither the façade drawings nor photographs of the building indicate that these staff entrances were intended for different users. However, a closer examination of the *bel étage* floor plan reveals the segregationist logic underlying the design: in the top left corner, one sees a vertical circulation node featuring a lift and a spacious staircase labelled as the "European" one (*escalier des Européens*), with a separate toilet. In the bottom right corner, a more cramped "indigenous

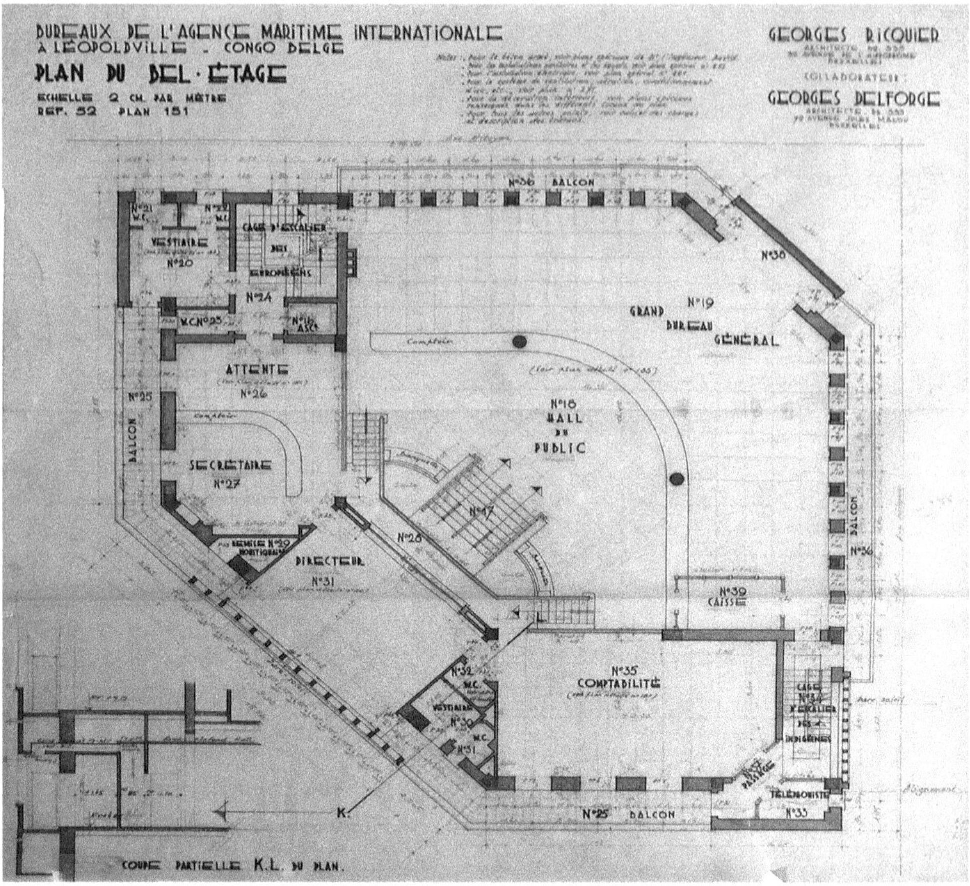

Fig. 9.11. Floor plan of the AMI headquarters in Kinshasa designed by Georges Ricquier, c. 1947. (CIVA/AAM, Brussels.)

workers' staircase" (*escalier des indigènes*) can be discerned (Fig. 9.11.). Ricquier was outspoken on this issue, stating in a brief text on the "complexity of architectural problems regarding administrative buildings in the Belgian Congo" that "the vastly different level of development between the two races demands particular provisions unknown in Europe, which also influences the plan".[44]

The ground floor plan further emphasised this segregation, with vertical circulation nodes connected to separate street entrances. However, no written signage was placed above these entrances, as would have been the case in apartheid South Africa. The racial divide was further reflected in the modes of transport used by black and white office workers. The plan

Fig. 9.12. Rear view of the *Gouvernement Général* headquarters in Kinshasa (c. 1952-1955), showing the covered parking spaces for the cars of European employees. Photo by C. Lamote for Inforcongo. (RMCA, HP.1955.17.223. © RMCA)

designates a "garage for cars" and a "garage for bicycles", leaving little doubt about which mode was assigned to whom. It is precisely by examining mundane spaces such as staircases and garages that one can better understand the racial segregation embedded in the office architecture of colonial Congo. The segregation principle was applied by architects and urban planners on various scales, from individual buildings to the broader urban form. Since the 1930s, colonial urban planning practices in the Belgian Congo, following trends across sub-Saharan Africa, had mandated the strict separation of the "European city" (*ville européenne*) from the "indigenous quarters" (*cités indigènes*), where most African office workers resided. In this context, it is worth noting that Ricquier was also the author of a 1949 urban master plan for Kinshasa (entitled *le Grand Léo*), which explicitly incorporated segregation through a continuous "neutral zone" of at least 400 metres running throughout the urban area.[45]

Fig. 9.13. Photo of cyclists riding along the Avenue Roi Baudouin (1951), which was widely published in colonial times. In the popularising account *Images du Congo: Léopoldville, Kwango-Bas-Congo* (Brussels, s.d.), it was accompanied by the caption: "Approximately three hundred thousand Congolese are taking part in the feverish life of the capital." Photo by C. Lamote for Inforcongo. (RMCA, HP.1977.43.14.40. © RMCA)

A segregationist logic also underpinned the impressive complex built in the early 1950s along Avenue Pierre Ryckmans (Kinshasa) to house large numbers of staff in various administrations of the *Gouvernement Général*. It was a building that, in terms of dimensions, most explicitly embodied the "density" of the colonial bureaucracy – even though, tellingly, the twin building that was supposed to be erected on the opposite side of the avenue was never constructed.[46] Through the monumental classicist style of its main entrance and the location on Kinshasa's primary urban axis of political power, the building symbolised the importance placed on office work. A view of the building's rear reveals a series of covered parking spaces, underscoring the effort to ensure the comfort of white workers (Fig. 9.12.). Although they only lived a few kilometres away, they

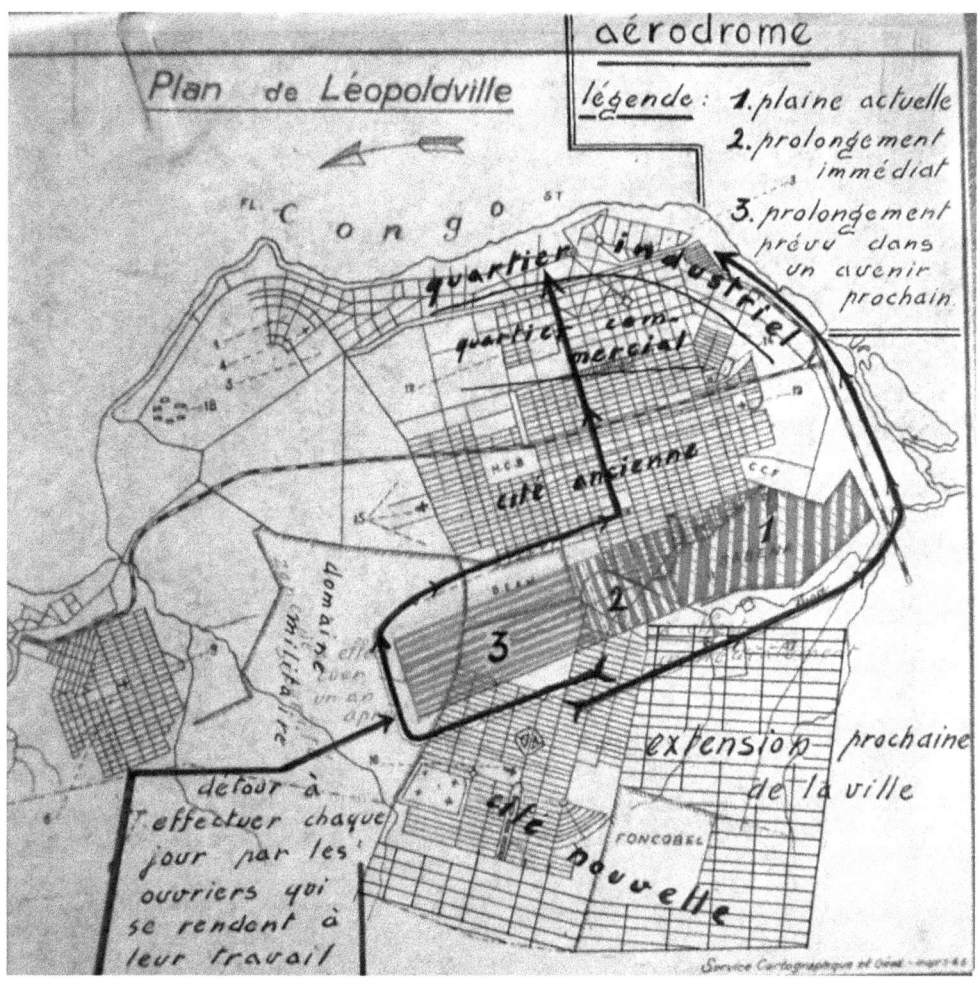

Fig. 9.14. Map indicating the impact of the planned extension of the runway at N'Dolo Airport on mobility between the new urban neighbourhoods and the commercial and industrial quarters of Kinshasa, c. 1947. (Archives of the Ministry of Colonies, Brussels, 3DG 1486.)

commuted by car, avoiding strenuous journeys on foot or by bicycle in the oppressive tropical heat. By contrast, Congolese workers commuted by bicycle, and it is no coincidence that photographs of Congolese cycling from the new *cités indigènes*, situated at a considerable distance from their place of work, became a recurring motif in the visual propaganda of post-war colonial Kinshasa (Fig. 9.13.). This massive daily flow of African workers along specific routes between the *cités* and the *ville européenne* – with Avenue Roi Baudouin undoubtedly the most important – formed a crucial part of daily life and shaped urban planning decisions. In 1947, for example, a debate arose over the need to preserve Avenue Roi Baudouin when a proposal to extend the runway of N'Dolo Airport threatened to block the route, which would have compelled Congolese from the *cités* to undertake a lengthy detour on their daily commute (Fig. 9.14.).[47] Ultimately, the project was cancelled, and the Avenue was maintained as the primary route for black workers – whether dockers or railwaymen employed at the port or railway yards, or clerks in the numerous buildings housing public and private administrations. When examining office spaces in colonial Congo, it is therefore essential to consider how these spaces were connected to the broader social and spatial fabric – from the desks where administrative tasks were performed to the *cités* where office workers lived. This approach indeed reveals how racial segregation shaped every level of colonial society, embedding inequality in both workplace design and urban planning.

OPEN OFFICES IN THE TROPICS

The AMI building discussed above exemplifies an early effort to construct in a manner that responded to the specific conditions of the tropics. It was not until the late 1940s that European architects began to develop a substantive understanding of how to achieve thermal comfort in an environment characterised by persistently high temperatures and extreme humidity. This period also saw the emergence of a more scientific approach to the orientation and design of buildings in relation to the sun's trajectory, which, in sites near the equator, differs significantly from conditions in Europe. Although the AMI building marked a preliminary step towards the adoption of open office concepts, other projects arguably offer a clearer perspective on the specificities of this typology within a tropical context. One pertinent example is the new headquarters of the Central Bank of the Belgian Congo (*Banque du Congo belge*), inaugurated in 1953 (Fig. 9.15.). Designed in 1949 by architect Maurice Houyoux as part of a larger complex that included multistorey residential buildings for the bank's staff, the edifice was frequently showcased in architectural publications of the 1950s and hailed as a hallmark of what has since been termed "tropical modernism": an architectural idiom that places particular emphasis on the tropical climate as a determinant of form and spatial organisation.[48]

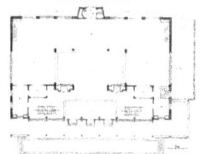

Fig. 9.15. The new headquarters of the *Banque du Congo belge* in Kinshasa, designed by architect Maurice Houyoux, as presented in the architectural magazine *Rythme* (March 1954, 18-19).

The project description highlighted the particular design of each façade to address the challenges posed by solar radiation. This approach is evident in the use of elongated, slender awnings above the windows, the covered portico with its elegant columns spanning the main street-facing façade, and the *claustras* on the smaller side façades. The sectional drawing of the building, included in the project's presentation in the architectural periodical *Rythme*, underscores Houyoux's prioritisation of cross-ventilation as a key principle of tropical modernist architecture. This approach necessitated façades conceived as "breathing walls" and roofs designed as ventilated umbrellas or parasols.[49] In a 1956 interview, Houyoux articulated the guiding principle of tropical modernism as "entirely forgetting the existence of air-conditioning" in favour of "alternative means of protection" against the hot and humid climate.[50] This strategy can be contrasted with the path taken in post-war Japan, whose sub-tropical climate similarly created architectural challenges – but

Fig. 9.16. Interior of the former premises of the *Banque du Congo belge* in Kinshasa, as photographed between 1943 and 1948, showing "a group of native typists (*dactylographes indigènes*) at work", as described in the original caption. Photo by J. Costa for Inforcongo. (RMCA, HP.1956.15.2731. © RMCA/Costa)

where active climatisation techniques did gain currency, as explained in Tatsuya Mitsuda's contribution to this volume.

The new headquarters of the *Banque du Congo belge* demonstrate that designing a climate-responsive building required an integrated approach to façades, roofs, sections and plans. A photograph taken by C. Lamote in 1949 of the office spaces previously occupied by the bank in Kinshasa illustrates the evolution of architectural philosophy (Fig. 9.16.). The image depicts a whitewashed room with heavy columns supporting reinforced concrete beams or arches, without visible windows. Congolese office workers sit at desks arranged in a rigid orthogonal layout, supervised by two European men in shirts and ties. The ceiling appears to be approximately 4 metres high, in accordance with the erstwhile building regulations of the Belgian Congo. Small openings near the ceiling may have served as

Les bureaux de la Banque à Léopoldville.

Mécanographe au travail.

Fig. 9.17. Office spaces inside the new Kinshasa headquarters of the *Banque du Congo belge*, c. 1956. (Banque du Congo belge, 1909-1959 [Brussels, 1959], 165.)

ventilation points to allow foul, warm air to escape. The 1949 photograph reflects a belief, prevailing from the late 19th century until the 1930s, that maximising air volume was crucial for maintaining comfort in tropical environments.[51] Evoking an almost stifling atmosphere, it could not contrast more sharply with the images of the new headquarters designed by Houyoux, which were included in the coffee table book *Banque du Congo belge 1909-1959*, published to mark the bank's 50th anniversary. Bird's-eye views reveal an open atrium around which U-shaped platforms with open offices were arranged, with a spacious ground-floor hall containing counters for client services. One photograph shows a bright, open office space filled with workers, embodying the post-war reorganisation – or, in the bank's own words, the "true transformation" – aimed at making the bank "a modern international credit institution" committed to maximising "efficiency, speed and the quality of all services" (Fig. 9.17.).[52] The mid-century modernist office architecture combined older Taylorist principles of spatial organisation – well-suited to banking's serial tasks like transaction processing – with newer priorities of spatial transparency and integrated design. For a public financial institution, this approach indeed conveyed progress, efficiency and trustworthiness.

AFRICANISING THE GENERIC OFFICE DESK?

The example of the Central Bank illustrates that the drive for efficiency extended not only to the architectural design of new office buildings, but also to the furnishings and equipment within them. Modular and standardised furniture, which had become a staple in many European office interiors from the interwar period onward, gradually made its way into the colonies after 1945. Archival records related to the construction of the main seat of the *Gouvernement Général* in Kinshasa – the most iconic symbol of colonial Congo's bureaucracy – include a 1951 folder containing the tender specifications of such items. With staggering detail, the document depicts and describes every piece in the future offices, including the number of drawers in filing cabinets, the materials to be used for desk surfaces and chair coverings, the number of hooks on coat hangers, and the size of waste-paper baskets (Figs. 9.18.–9.21.). Meticulously prescribed at the upper echelons of colonial governance, these banal objects reveal the deeply bureaucratic nature of colonial rule. While colonialism is rightly associated with exploitation and violence, there was also a counterpart to these overt forms of domination, evident in the minutiae of administrative control. The careful planning of even the most mundane items indeed demonstrates how colonialism was sustained not only through force, but also through a constant focus on bureaucratic routines and infrastructures.[53] The waste-paper basket, though completely neglected in scholarship, was one of many objects playing a role in this process:

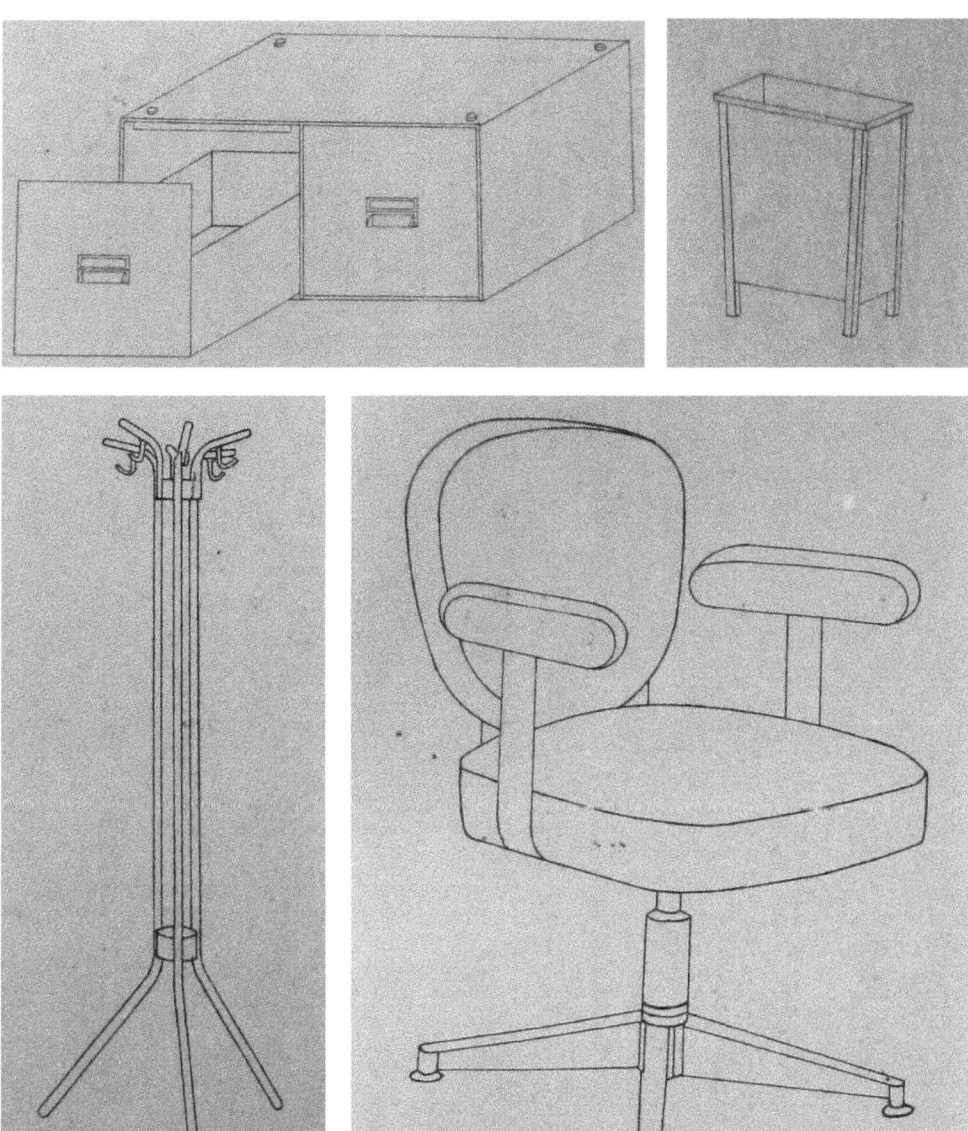

Figs. 9.18.–9.21. Examples of items depicted in the tender specifications for the construction of the *Gouvernement Général* headquarters in Kinshasa, 1951: filing cabinet (top left), wastepaper basket (top right), coat hanger (bottom left), and office chair (bottom right). (Archives of the Ministry of Colonies, Brussels, AA GG942.)

Fig. 9.22. A worker of the *Service de l'information du Gouvernement Général* in the 1950s. The original caption states: "Having long been excluded from progress because of traditional prejudices, Congolese women are beginning to take their place in the intellectual and social development of the country; increasingly, they are occupying roles as secretaries, saleswomen, typists and nurses, which were previously reserved for men." Photo by C. Lamote for Inforcongo. (RCMA, HP.1958.1.56. © RMCA)

as office technology historian Jos Legrand has pointed out, it served as a repository for all that went "wrong" and interrupted the "efficient" flow, such as discarded drafts and documents with typing errors.[54] Clearly, Belgian colonial planners were fully aware of this function, incorporating such practical considerations into their office designs. At the same time, the careful top-down planning of furniture and office equipment created a façade of order and rationality, obscuring the underlying contradictions and anxieties of colonial administration.

In the provision of standardised steel office furniture, efficiency – instead of ornamentation – was the guiding principle. However, given the density of colonial bureaucracy, the high demand for furniture meant that locally produced, non-standardised pieces continued to be used alongside

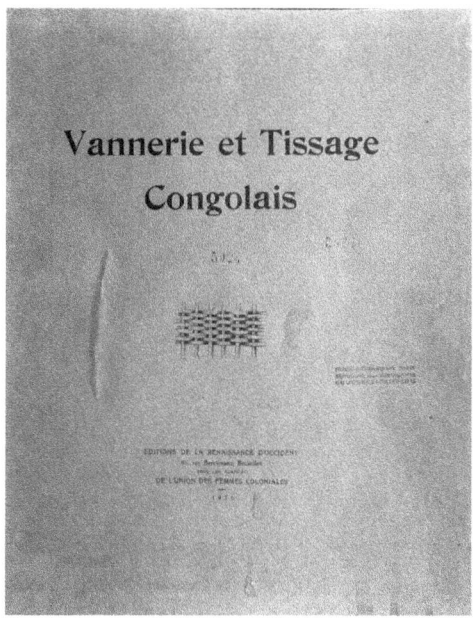

Figs. 9.23.–9.24. Cover of the book *Vannerie et tissage congolais* (Brussels, 1926), alongside an image of a textile (*natte*) included in the book, showing a motive close to the one on the wooden desk featured on the preceding photo.

Fig. 9.25. Cover of a 1952 volume by A. Bonnelange from the *Bibliothèque de l'Étoile* series on carpentry, translated into Lingala by Raphaël François Elema (Leverville, 1952).

imported items. A late 1950s propaganda photograph of a female telephone operator employed by the *Service de l'information du Gouvernement Général* in Kinshasa not only illustrates the rise of Congolese women in clerical roles, but also unintentionally documents the importance of locally produced furniture (Fig. 9.22.). The image shows a heavy wooden desk with intricate carvings, standing out amid more generic office equipment such as a telephone, folders and pens. The desk highlights the role of missionary-run carpentry workshops, which, since the early days of colonisation, had been producing furniture in the Congo as both an educational project and a means of generating economic revenue, supplying pieces to colonisers' homes and offices. An inquiry published by the *Bulletin de l'Union des femmes coloniales* in the late 1920s reveals that much of the furniture in colonial households originated from such workshops. While the magazine did promote furniture by Belgian and foreign firms between the 1930s and 1950s, local production of wooden pieces continued to flourish throughout this period.[55] For some Congolese, crafting such furniture was considered aspirational, with multiple volumes in the *Bibliothèque de l'Étoile* series of instructional books – some of which were translated into Lingala – explaining how to design and construct chairs, tables and cupboards.[56]

What distinguishes the desk in the photograph is not only its solid wooden construction but also its intricate decorative carvings. The geometric patterns on the front panel evoke motifs commonly found in traditional culture, including bodily scarification, artefacts and textiles associated with ethnic groups like the Kuba and Kongo peoples.[57] From the interwar period onwards, such motifs became an integral part of the decorative vocabulary in Congolese art and architecture, promoted by the colonial regime as part of broader efforts to preserve local arts and crafts. For example, in 1929, the *Union des femmes coloniales* published *Vannerie et tissage congolais*, a lavishly illustrated volume on Congolese textiles with geometric motifs, aimed at inspiring embroidery projects in missionary schools for girls (Figs. 9.23.–9.24.).[58] The motifs depicted in the book found their way into furniture production (including the office desk in the *Service de l'information*) as well as onto the covers of *Bibliothèque de l'Étoile* carpentry manuals (Fig. 9.25.).[59] Furniture adorned with such motifs may have appealed to European colonisers seeking to infuse their private interiors with a sense of *couleur locale*, but its presence in office spaces of the colonial bureaucracy was likely driven more by pragmatic considerations – such as the need for faster and more cost-effective production – than by any ideological aim to "Africanise" the "generic" office.

THE UNSETTLING "MIMIC MAN"

A photograph of a canvas, entitled *Le bureau du clerc* (The Clerk's Office), likely dating from the late 1940s and attributed to the Congolese artist Louis Koyongonda, provides a compelling basis for further analysing the *portrait-robot* of the Congolese office worker (Fig. 9.26.).[60] The clerk is placed in a modest office setting, seated behind a desk with files, against a backdrop of a brick wall and a large clock. His refined attire – a chequered suit jacket, a bowtie and glasses – suggests a high- or mid-ranking position, contrasting with most of the clerks depicted in the aforementioned photographs of the *Banque du Congo belge*, who were largely part of the anonymous lower-ranking workforce. To the left of the composition stands a woman, equally well-dressed, whose role remains ambiguous; she could represent either the clerk's spouse or a visitor seeking assistance. Their elegant clothing positions both figures as members of the emerging elite of *évolués*, a colonial term denoting Africans who had embraced European customs. Belgian authorities considered *évolués* to have attained the highest level of "civilisation" possible for Congolese, yet one still deemed inferior to that of Europeans. Koyongonda's clerk has indeed adopted the posture of a European white-collar worker, while the female figure embodies the ideal of the Congolese spouse, educated to become the compliant housewife envisioned by colonial authorities.[61]

Historians have argued that African office workers constituted a distinct social group within colonial societies. In French West Africa, for instance, local populations referred to these employees as "white-blacks", a term that encapsulated "their role as representatives of the white colonial state".[62] Although most African clerks held low-ranking positions that "bestowed little official authority", they could function as the "hidden linchpins of colonial rule", facilitating administration across vast territories with relatively few European officials.[63] Scholars have suggested that these roles provided African clerks with a "bargain of collaboration", which they could use to "accumulate wealth, power and prestige", enabling some to rise within the colonial hierarchy.[64] Daniel Tödt has indeed shown that clerks were among the most prominent Congolese to obtain a *carte du mérite civique* or a *carte d'immatriculation*: legal documents granting them privileges associated with crossing the colour bar.[65] This achievement, however, was viewed by some colonisers as an unacceptable encroachment on white privilege.[66] It is this perception that may also

Fig. 9.26. *Le bureau du clerc* by Louis Koyongonda. Photographed around 1948 by H. Goldstein for Inforcongo. (RMCA, HP.1949.34.1. © Sofam/Koyongonda)

have informed the photograph caption of a white clerk portrayed as *"un nègre-blanc"*, discussed earlier.

In this regard, Patrice Lumumba (1925-1961), the first prime minister of independent Congo and a national hero following his assassination, exemplifies the social mobility associated with the clerical profession.[67] Lumumba began his career as a low-ranking office worker in Kisangani/Stanleyville, later joining the city's postal service. He pursued a year-long postal training programme in Kinshasa to enhance his administrative and French language skills. Rising rapidly through Kisangani's local bureaucracy, Lumumba became politically active in the mid-1950s, notably as president of the city's *Association des évolués*. Convicted in 1956 for allegedly embezzling postal funds and sentenced to one year in prison, Lumumba was released early and subsequently appointed as sales director of the *Brasserie de Léopoldville et du Bas-Congo*, a brewery in Kinshasa. While there is an extensive iconography of Lumumba as a

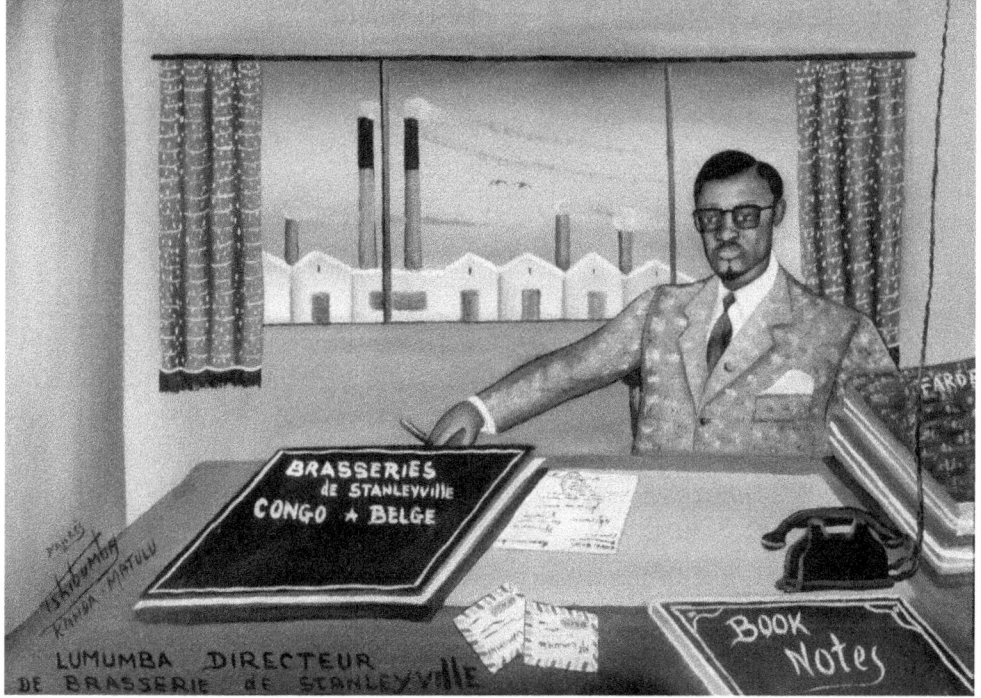

Fig. 9.27. *Lumumba, Director of the Stanleyville Brewery* by Tshibumba Kanda Matulu (1974). Kanda Matulu mislocated the brewery in Kisangani/Stanleyville instead of Kinshasa. (Wereldmuseum, Amsterdam/Leiden/Rotterdam, TM-5867-36. © Tshibumba Kanda Matulu)

statesman, no photographs exist of him as an office clerk.[68] However, in 1974, the Congolese artist Tshibumba Kanda Matulu did include a portrayal of Lumumba as brewery director in his *Histoire du Zaïre* painting series, showing a desk with files, a telephone and, notably, two airmail envelopes – symbols of the international correspondence crucial to the independence movement (Fig. 9.27.).[69] Lumumba's confident posture reflects his professional and political rise, and even though he appears less slender than in later photographs as prime minister, his resemblance to Koyongonda's 1940s clerk, with the chequered jacket, bow tie and glasses, is striking.

In colonial Congo, attire carried profound significance, and it would be a mistake to dismiss its importance. While, in the eye of colonisers, the well-dressed Congolese symbolised the success of the *mission civilisatrice*, clothing could also function as a tool of resistance. In 1950s Kinshasa, members of street gangs like the Hindubill, for instance, dressed as cowboys, defying colonial norms.[70] Scholars such as Didier Gondola and Manuel

Charpy have explored *sapologie*, the extreme elegance of the *Société des ambianceurs et des personnes élégantes* (Society of Tastemakers and Elegant People): originating in Congo-Brazzaville in the 1910s and spreading to Kinshasa, their mimicry of European fashion often served as a provocation, particularly when *sapeurs* pushed dandy-like elegance to its limits.[71] Charpy has pointed out an intriguing detail in various photographs of well-dressed Congolese: why, from the 1910s onwards, did individuals in European attire often check their ostentatiously broken watches with such apparent confidence?[72] Was this negligence, misunderstanding or defiance? Or was it "a sign of the 'laziness of the negroes', a stereotype propagated since the early 19th century?"[73] In any case, it is clear that such acts subtly challenged colonial authority, which placed great emphasis on time discipline. A 1947 propaganda film produced by the *Service de l'information du Gouvernement Général*, for instance, promoted the use of watches for "better time management". It ridiculed those who ignored the clock, such as a traveller missing a train, a schoolboy arriving late for class, or a worker losing a day's pay for failing to show up on time. These figures were contrasted with the *"indigènes modèles"* (model natives): a lorry driver, a postal worker, a pilot and a radio operator. The entire film thus revolved around the motto: "To avoid trouble in life, learn to read the time on watches."[74] Yet what colonial authorities failed to understand – or, if they did, could not admit – was that the practice of "broken watches" fundamentally subverted the colonial system itself. As such, Charpy's analysis invites a reconsideration of the clock in Koyongonda's 1940s painting: rather than taking such images at face value, we should view them as artefacts "to think with" (Elizabeth Edwards) when interrogating the bureaucracy of the colonial "nervous state".[75] And rather than viewing Congolese clerks as merely emulating the European white collar worker, we should understand them as "mimic (wo)men", acknowledging the ambivalence that, as Homi Bhabha argued already in the 1990s, is connoted by this term.

CONCLUDING REMARKS: AN ENDURING LEGACY

We would do well to take colonial office spaces seriously, as they provide insights into the paradoxes of both colonial governance and bureaucratic power in general. While the colonial "nervous state", reliant on bureaucratic control, was in many ways designed to suppress and exploit the population, its offices also offered the colonised a route to partake in the universalising drive towards "modernity". For the Congolese, engaging in office work was perhaps the most important strategy to acquire empowerment and agency, not only socially but also politically – as exemplified by Patrice Lumumba, whose bureaucratic experience undoubtedly contributed to the downfall of the colonial "nervous state". Yet following independence, certain aspects of bureaucratic nervousness never really vanished, as they were – and remain – embedded in the framework of *all* administrative systems. As sociologist Robert Merton observed, bureaucracies can produce what he termed the "neurocrat", an individual more concerned with maintaining institutional procedures than addressing real-world needs.[76] Max Weber's "iron cage" metaphor further illustrates this concept, describing how bureaucratic systems, over time, risk becoming dehumanising by swapping means and ends, trapping both bureaucrats and the subjects they govern in an impersonal, rules-driven environment.[77]

In post-independence Congo, the legacy of the colonial "paper regime" remains highly visible. While numerous new office buildings have been constructed since 1960 (especially since the turn of the 21st century), many administrations still operate within structures established during the colonial era. Indeed, all the buildings discussed in this chapter still stand and continue to function as office spaces. The recent work of photographers such as Guy Tillim and Carl De Keyzer shows how the interiors of these buildings continue to evoke the bureaucratic atmosphere of the past, with their generic desks and filing cabinets imported in the 1950s.[78] But the legacy is not only material. Much like in colonial times, receiving an official letter with a signature and a stamp remains essential for accessing services or even favours in Congo's daily life. Despite the country's frequent portrayal as being in perpetual crisis – marked by gruesome wars and sweeping epidemics, it is often referred to, albeit too simplistically, as "a failed state" –, paper and bureaucracy continue to play a central role in how people make do and reinvent order, particularly in Kinshasa. However, this often occurs in ways that have "nothing to do with Weberian political order, with its functioning bureaucracy, democratically elected representatives, tax collectors, law enforcement agents and impartial judicial system" (Theodore Trefon).[79] A common saying in present-day Congo captures this irony: "*Article 15: Débrouillez-vous*" (Article 15: Sort it out yourself). Ostensibly referring to a clause in some official code, the phrase has become "the country's most important law", symbolising how Congolese must rely on ingenuity, improvisation and resilience rather than government support – a popular commentary on both the ubiquity and limits of bureaucratic power.[80]

ACKNOWLEDGEMENT

We would like to thank Anne Welschen (Royal Museum for Central Africa, Tervuren) for her invaluable assistance in locating archival materials and organising their reproduction.

NOTES

1. For this overview, see Christopher Dandeker, Surveillance, Power and Modernity (Cambridge, 1990), 9-10.
2. On the new "responsibilities" associated with the 1908 takeover, see for instance Guy Vanthemsche, Belgium and the Congo, 1885-1960 (New York, 2012), 76; Isidore Ndaywel è Nziem, Théophile Obenga and Pierre Salmon, Histoire générale du Congo: De l'héritage ancien à la République Démocratique (Paris, 1998), 360-361; Jean Stengers, Congo, mythes et réalités: 100 ans d'histoire (Brussels, 1989), 168-178. For the developmentalist era, see Guy Vanthemsche, 'The Congo, a Colony Heading for "Development"?', in Idesbald Goddeeris, Amandine Lauro and Guy Vanthemsche (eds.), Colonial Congo: A History in Questions (Turnhout, 2020); Guy Vanthemsche, Genèse et portée du "Plan Décennal" du Congo belge (1949-1959) (Brussels, 1994).
3. For a presentation of the hierarchical structure of the Belgian colonial administration, see Julien L.L. Vanhove, Histoire du Ministère des Colonies (Brussels, 1968). Throughout this chapter, we will use the present-day geographical names, followed (at the first mention) by the colonial names.
4. Benoît Henriet, Colonial Impotence: Virtue and Violence in a Congolese Concession (1911-1940) (Berlin, 2021), 32.
5. Nancy Rose Hunt, A Nervous State: Violence, Remedies and Reverie in Colonial Congo (Durham, 2016).
6. On the notion of "paper regimes" in colonial contexts, see Uma Dhupelia-Mesthrie, 'Paper Regimes', in Kronos: Southern African Histories, 40 (2014). On the importance of paperwork, see also for instance Matthew S. Hull, Government of Paper: The Materiality of Bureaucracy in Urban Pakistan (Berkeley, 2012); Patrick Joyce, 'Filing the Raj: Political Technologies of the Imperial British State', in Tony Bennett and Patrick Joyce (eds.), Material Powers: Cultural Studies, History and the Material Turn (London, 2010), 104-105.
7. In colonial Congo, the most striking and ironic example of a government building that remained unfinished in 1960 was the residence for the Governor General in Kinshasa. See Johan Lagae, '"Le petit Belge a voulu faire grand": The Troublesome Construction of the Résidence du Gouverneur Général du Congo Belge in Leopoldville (1922-1960)', in METU: Journal of Architecture, 20/1-2 (2000).
8. For Port's observation, see M.H. Port, Imperial London: Civil Government Building in London, 1850-1915 (New Haven, 1995), 27-28.
9. Benjamin N. Lawrance, Emily Lynn Osborn and Richard L. Roberts, 'Introduction', in idem (eds.), Intermediaries, Interpreters and Clerks: African Employees in the Making of Colonial Africa (Madison, 2006), 5.
10. On the notion of cultural commuters, see Andreas Eckert, 'Cultural Commuters: African Employees in Late Colonial Tanzania', in Lawrance, Osborn and Roberts, Intermediaries.
11. *The Mimic Men* is the title of a 1967 novel by Naipaul. See ibid., 265.
12. Mimicry has become a central notion in postcolonial thinking; see Bill Ashcroft, Gareth Griffiths and Helen Tiffin (eds.), Post-Colonial Studies: The Key Concepts (London, 2000), 139. Homi Bhabha developed his reflections on this notion in an essay that explicitly drew on Naipaul's novel; see Homi Bhabha, The Location of Culture (London, 1994), 121-131.
13. See the introduction to this volume for an exploration of these notions, which have been derived from the work of Delphine Gardey. For our analysis of the office buildings of the

colonial administration in Brussels, see Jens van de Maele and Johan Lagae, '"The Congo must have a presence on Belgian soil": The Concept of Representation in Governmental Discourses on the Architecture of the Ministry of Colonies in Brussels, 1908-1960', in The Journal of Architecture, 22/7 (2017).

[14] Historian Jean Stengers has emphasised the joint actions of the state, the church and enterprises, arguing that the Belgian colonial undertaking was a "national project", a "civilizing mission", and geared towards exploitation. See Stengers, Congo, 179-280. On the collaboration between the colonial state and enterprises, see also Jean-Luc Vellut, Congo: Ambitions et désenchantements, 1880-1960 (Paris, 2021), 95-113. More recently, scholars have started to question the hegemony of the colonial trinity by paying attention to the differences in the agendas of the three actors, especially during the late colonial period.

[15] Stuart Hall, 'The Spectacle of the "Other"', in idem (ed.), Representation: Cultural Representations and Signifying Practices (London, 1997), 232 and 249. For another application of this concept in the context of colonial history, see for instance Katharina Jörder, Building a White Nation: Propaganda, Photography and the Apartheid Regime Between the Late 1940s and the Mid-1970s (Leuven, 2023), 272.

[16] Ann Laura Stoler, Along the Archival Grain: Epistemic Anxieties and Colonial Common Sense (Princeton, 2009); Christraud M. Geary, In and Out of Focus: Images from Central Africa, 1885-1960 (London, 2002), 39. On the analytical deconstruction of photos from colonial Congo, see also Sandrine Colard, 'African Writings and the Colonial Time's Pictures', in idem (ed.), Recaptioning Congo: African Stories and Colonial Pictures (Tielt, 2022); Johan Lagae, 'Unsettling the "Colonizing Camera": Curatorial Notes on the "Congo belge en images" Project', in Photography & Culture, 5/3 (2012).

[17] Stoler, Along the Archival Grain, ii. On Stoler's work being an exponent of the recent "archival turn", see Max Kemman, Trading Zones of Digital History (Berlin, 2021), 26-27.

[18] Stoler, Along the Archival Grain, 2.

[19] Vanthemsche, 'The Congo, a Colony Heading for "Development"?'; Frederick Cooper, Africa Since 1940: The Past of the Present (Cambridge, 2002).

[20] For a critical unpacking of this notion of the *colonie modèle*, see Simon De Nys-Ketels, 'Myths and Realities of the Belgian Medical Model Colony: A Genealogy', PhD thesis (Ghent University), 2021.

[21] Investir c'est prospérer: Les réalisations du Plan décennal (Brussels, s.d.), 38.

[22] On this density, see also Martin Klein, 'African Participation in Colonial Rule: The Role of Clerks, Interpreters and Other Intermediaries', in Lawrance, Osborn and Roberts, Intermediaries, 274.

[23] Simon De Nys-Ketels et al., 'Planning Belgian Congo's Network of Medical Infrastructure: Type-Plans as Tools to Construct a Medical Model Colony, 1949-1959', in Planning Perspectives, 34/5 (2019); Lissa Camerlinck, 'The Construction of the Colonial Welfare State: Tracing Design Strategies in the Belgian Congo's Ten Year Plan, 1949-1959', MA thesis (Ghent University, 2017).

[24] Peter Scriver (ed.), The Scaffolding of Empire: 4th International Symposium of the Centre for Asian and Middle Eastern Architecture (Adelaide, 2007); Peter Scriver, 'Empire-Building and Thinking in the Public Works Department of British India', in Peter Scriver and Vikramaditya Prakash (eds.), Colonial Modernities: Building, Dwelling and Architecture in British India and Ceylon (Abingdon, 2007).

[25] Investir, 38. On the penitentiary facilities, see Pieter De Coene, Margot Luyckfasseel and Gillian Mathys, 'Voices from Exile: The Mpadist "Mission des noirs" in Oshwe's Prison Camps in the Belgian Congo (1940-1960)', in International Journal of African Historical Studies, 55/1 (2022); Bérengère Piret, Florence Renucci and Xavier Rousseaux, Les cent mille briques: La prison et les détenus de Stanleyville (Lille, 2014).

[26] Hunt, The Nervous State, back cover.

[27] Martin Klein, African Participation, 274.

[28] Daniel Tödt, The Lumumba Generation: African Bourgeoisie and Colonial Distinction in the Belgian Congo (Berlin, 2021), 50 and 56; Daniel Tödt, 'The Colonial State and the African Elite: A History of Subjugation?' in Goddeeris, Lauro and Vanthemsche, Colonial Congo. See also Jean-Marie

Mutamba, Du Congo belge au Congo indépendant, 1940-1960: Emergence des "évolués" et genèse du nationalisme (Kinshasa, 1998).
29   Tödt, The Lumumba Generation, 73.
30   Banque du Congo belge 1909-1959 (Brussels, s.d. [1959]), 165 and 168.
31   Tödt, The Lumumba Generation, 81.
32   For a discussion of this official visual propaganda, see Anne Cornet and Florence Gillet, Congo Belgique 1955-1965: Entre propagande et réalité (Brussels, 2010).
33   We are borrowing the notion *portrait-robot* (idealised portrait) from Jean Pirotte, Périodiques missionnaires belges d'expression française: Reflets de cinquante années d'évolution d'une mentalité 1889-1940 (Leuven, 1973).
34   Likewise, Léon Pétillon, Governor-General from 1952 to 1958, was known as a technocrat who spent long hours at his desk, often working late into the night. For his self-representation, see Léon A.M. Pétillon, Congo 1929-1958 (Brussels, 1985); Léon A.M. Pétillon, Courts métrages africains pour servir à l'histoire (Brussels, 1979).
35   Henri Stevelinck, Chroniques de Stinkopolis (Léopoldville, 1932).
36   W. Vigneron, Les bavardages du cancrelat (Élisabethville, 1945). The author probably used a pseudonym.
37   Ibid., 204.
38   Francis Ramirez and Christian Rolot, 'Noirs modèles et modèles de noirs', in Patricia Van Schuylenbergh and Mathieu Zana Aziza Etambala (eds.), Patrimoine d'Afrique centrale – Archives films: Congo, Rwanda, Burundi, 1912-1960 (Tervuren, 2010), 110. See also Francis Ramirez and Christian Rolot, Histoire du cinema colonial au Zaïre, au Rwanda et au Burundi (Tervuren, 1985).
39   Ramirez and Rolot, Noirs modèles, 116.
40   Tödt, The Lumumba Generation, 84.
41   Tödt defines *évolués* as "Congolese people who had been trained as office clerks, teachers or priests", and sees an equivalence with what in French colonies were termed *lettrés*, and *assimilados* or *civilizados* in Portuguese Africa. See Tödt, The Colonial State, 219.
42   Georges Ricquier designed several buildings for AMI in Congo, the most significant of which was a landmark office building in Matadi. The Kinshasa building was designed in association with his colleague Georges Delforge. See Georges Ricquier, 'Complexité des problems architecturaux des bâtiments d'administration au Congo belge', in Rythme, 17 (1954). This section is based on the project descriptions mentioned in the *Rythme* article, as well as on the original construction drawings. For the latter, see CIVA, Brussels, Georges Ricquier collection. See also Johan Lagae, 'Georges Ricquier', in Anne Van Loo (ed.), Repertorium van de architectuur in België van 1830 tot heden (Antwerp, 2003). The building also features prominently with two photographs in Whyms, Léopoldville: Son histoire 1881-1956 (Brussels, 1957), 53 and 65.
43   On the colour bar in Belgian Congo, see part 3 in Goddeeris, Lauro and Vanthemsche, Colonial Congo.
44   Ricquier, Complexité, 9.
45   For this plan, see Maurice Heymans (ed.), Urbanisme au Congo belge (Brussels, s.d. [1950]), 32. For a discussion of segregationist urban planning in colonial Kinshasa, see Luce Beeckmans and Johan Lagae, 'Kinshasa's Syndrome-Planning in Historical Perspective: From Belgian Colonial Capital to Self-Constructed Megalopolis', in Carlos Nunes Silva (ed.), Urban Planning in Sub-Saharan Africa: Colonial and Post-Colonial Planning Cultures (Abingdon, 2015); Bruno De Meulder, Kuvuande mbote: Een eeuw koloniale architectuur en stedenbouw in Kongo (Antwerp, 2000), 159-170.
46   For a discussion of Avenue Pierre Ryckmans as an axis of power, see Johan Lagae and Bernard Toulier (eds.), Kinshasa (Brussels, 2013); De Meulder, Kuvuande mbote, 159-170. The twin building appears on Ricquier's master plan and reappears again in 1959 on a master plan drawn by the last chief urbanist of colonial Kinshasa, Léon Henrard.
47   On this debate, see Johan Lagae et al., 'Vers une radioscopie de la ville coloniale: Episodes dans la génèse de l'Avenue Kasa-Vubu, Kinshasa', in Mathieu Zana Etambala and Pamphile Mabiala Mantuba-Ngoma (eds.), La société congolaise face à la modernité, 1700-2010: Mélanges eurafricains offerts à Jean-Luc Vellut (Paris, 2016).

48 On the Central Bank project, see 'Coup d'œil sur l'histoire de la Banque du Congo belge', in Belgique d'outremer, 290 (1959), 274-281; 'Siège de la Banque du Congo belge à Léopoldville', in Rythme, 17 (1954), 18-19. On the tropical modernism concept, see Hannah le Roux, 'The Networks of Tropical Architecture', in The Journal of Architecture, 8/3 (2003). For the Congolese context, see Johan Lagae, '"Kongo zoals het is": Drie architectuurverhalen uit de Belgische kolonisatiegeschiedenis 1920-1960', PhD thesis (Ghent University, 2002), chapter II.2.
49 Daniel A. Barber, Modern Architecture and Climate: Design Before Air Conditioning (Princeton, 2020).
50 'Grandeurs et servitudes de l'architecture en pays tropicaux: Un interview avec M. Houyoux-Diongre, architecte de la section de l'Afrique belge', in Objectif, 58/9 (1955), 9.
51 On this belief, see E. Devroey and E. De Backer, La réglementation sur les constructions au Congo belge (Brussels, 1941), 107-108.
52 Banque du Congo belge, 165.
53 On the notion of "system" in office cultures, see for instance Markus Krajewski, Paper Machines: About Cards & Catalogs, 1548-1929 (Cambridge MA, 2011); Jon Agar, The Government Machine: A Revolutionary History of the Computer (Cambridge, 2003), 144, 163 and 410; Alexandra Lange, White Collar Corbusier: From the "Casier" to the "Cité d'affaires", in Grey Room, 9 (2002), 61-63; O. de Wit and H. Buiter, De opkomst van de moderne administratie, in J.W. Schot et al. (eds.), Techniek in Nederland in de twintigste eeuw (I) (Zutphen, 1998), 219-223; JoAnne Yates, Control Through Communication: The Rise of System in American Management (Baltimore, 1989).
54 Jos Legrand, The Paradox of the Waste Paper Basket: The Waste Paper Basket in the American Office Between 1870 and 1930 (Maastricht, 2015).
55 On the bulletin, see Johan Lagae, 'Educating the Colonial Spouse or Pushing the Agenda of Tropical Modernism in the Belgian Congo? Architecture and the Coloniser's House in the Pages of the Bulletin de l'Union des femmes coloniales', in Alice Santiago Faria, Anne Shelley and Sandra Ataíde Lobo (eds.), The Built Environment through the Prism of the Colonial Periodical Press (Abingdon, 2023).
56 Igor Bloch, 'House Construction and Social Engineering in the Beaux métiers and Formation sociale Manuals of the Bibliothèque de l'Étoile (1943-1966)', in ABE Journal, 23 (2024).
57 See for instance these catalogues of Congolese artefacts: Els De Palmenaer (ed.), 100 x Congo: Un siècle d'art congolais à Anvers (Antwerp, 2020), Gustaaf Verswijver et al. (eds.), Schatten uit het Afrika-Museum Tervuren (Tervuren, 1995). Ethnographic albums from the turn of the century display a notable focus on bodily scarifications with similar motifs. We are grateful to Els De Palmenaer for directing us to these cultural expressions featuring such motifs.
58 Émile Jean Baptiste Coart, Vannerie et tissage congolais (Brussels, 1926). For insights into how such patterns informed artisanal training in (missionary) schools, see Sarah Van Beurden, 'Missions et artisanats d'art au Congo', in De Palmenaer, 100 x Congo; Patricia Van Schuylenbergh and Françoise Morimont, Rencontres artistiques Belgique-Congo, 1920-1950 (Louvain-la-Neuve, 1995).
59 While the French editions featured cover images of Congolese workers in aprons, the translated Lingala editions prominently displayed geometric patterns.
60 The accompanying caption describes Koyongonda as specialising in "paintings on tablecloths and napkins" and possessing a talent for drawing "superior to most painters of his generation". Born in Kisangani/Stanleyville in 1918, Koyongonda was part of a group of Congolese artists working in Laurent Moonens' atelier in Kinshasa during the late 1940s. He later became one of the favourite artists of Maurice Alhadeff, a prominent patron of the arts. See Jean-Luc Vellut et al., Het ontstaan van de hedendaagse schilderkunst in Midden-Afrika, 1930-1970 (Tervuren, 1992), 23, 31 and 67. The attribution is somewhat surprising: the style of the painting, which is reminiscent of the so-called peinture populaire depicting scenes of everyday life, stands out in the oeuvre of Koyongonda, who is reputed for his expressive portraits, market scenes and landscapes.
61 On the role of the Congolese spouse, see Tödt, The Lumumba Generation.
62 Lawrance, Osborn and Roberts, Introduction, 3-4.
63 Ibid., 4.
64 The notion "bargain of collaboration" is borrowed from the work of historian Ronald Robinson; see ibid., 6.

65 The number of *évolués* remained limited throughout the colonial era, and those who received a *carte du mérite civique* or a *carte d'immatriculation*, which gave them access to facilities previously only open to Europeans, were even fewer: 2,325 in total on the eve of independence. See Tödt, The Colonial State, 221.
66 Tödt, The Lumumba Generation, 282. Interesting in this respect is a statement from 1956 by Paul Bolya, who was a medical assistant: "We experienced paradoxical situations a few years ago: receiving in the morning the confirmation card for the baptism of civilisation [i.e. the *carte d'immatriculation*]… and in the evening being turned away from the door of a cinema, a hotel or a shop on the grounds that ebony skin is not the colour of the usual customers of these places." Cited by Jacob Sabakinu Kivilu, 'Paul-Gabriel-Dieudonné Bolya: De l'assistant médical à l'homme politique', in Jean-Luc Vellut et al. (eds.), La mémoire du Congo: Le temps colonial (Ghent, 2005), 238. On this matter, see also a counter-text to the "official" visual depiction of the *évolué* family: Koli Jean Bofane, 'Évolué, What's That?', in Colard, Recaptioning Congo.
67 On Lumumba's early career, see Jean Omasombo Tshonda and Benoît Verhaegen, Patrice Lumumba: Jeunesse et apprentissage politique, 1925-1956 (Paris, 1998).
68 For this iconography, see Matthias De Groof (ed.), Lumumba in the Arts (Leuven, 2020); Pierre Petit, Patrice Lumumba: La fabrication d'un héros national et panafricain (Brussels, 2016).
69 Johannes Fabian, Remembering the Present: Painting and Popular History in Zaïre (Berkeley, 1996), 72-73 and 229. On the crucial importance of the postal service, the possibility of international communication, and distance learning in Lumumba's training, see Pedro Monaville, Students of the World: Global 1968 and Decolonization in the Congo (Durham, 2022), 23-41. Even though the artwork in question bears the inscription "after Tshibumba Kanda-Matulu", it is effectively made by him. Johannes Fabian has explained this "intriguing" signature – which occurs on many of the artist's paintings – as follows: "Did Tshibumba think of a given painting as the copy of a model? Such an interpretation might be construed for genre pictures, which almost by definition are copies; much more likely is that Tshibumba used the expression as a formula of oral discourse (as in *d'après moi*, 'as I see it') in order to emphasize his authorship not only of the painting but also of the historical narrative for which he takes responsibility." See Fabian, Remembering, 237 and 238 (citation).
70 Didier Gondola, Tropical Cowboys: Westerns, Violence, and Masculinity in Kinshasa (Bloomington, 2016).
71 Manuel Charpy, 'Une histoire de la sapologie africaine', podcast (11 Jan. 2017) (via www.ifmparis.fr); Didier Gondola, 'La sape des mikilistes: Théâtre de l'artifice et représentation onirique', in Cahiers d'études africaines, 153 (1999).
72 Manuel Charpy, 'La montre cassée', in Gil Bartholeyns and Manuel Charpy (eds.), L'étrange et folle aventure du grille-pain: De la machine à coudre et des gens qui s'en servent (Paris, 2021).
73 Ibid., 89.
74 Van Schuylenbergh and Etambala, Patrimoine, 240.
75 Elizabeth Edwards, 'Thinking Photography Beyond the Visual?', in J.J. Long, Andrea Noble and Edward Welch (eds.), Photography: Theoretical Snapshots (Abingdon, 2009).
76 Merton's notion is cited by Ceri Sullivan, Literature in the Public Service (Houndmills, 2013), 11.
77 Sullivan, Literature, 11.
78 Carl De Keyzer, Congo (Belge) (Tielt, 2009); Guy Tillim, Avenue Patrice Lumumba (Munich, 2008).
79 Theodore Trefon, 'Introduction: Reinventing Order', in idem (ed.), Reinventing Order in the Congo: How People Respond to State Failure in Kinshasa (London, 2004), 2.
80 On *article 15*, see for instance Sachka Vincent, 'Wit privilege in onafhankelijk Congo: Over "Terug naar Congo" (1987) van Lieve Joris', in Knack, 8 April 2021.

BIBLIOGRAPHY

Jon Agar, The Government Machine: A Revolutionary History of the Computer (Cambridge, 2003).
Bill Ashcroft, Gareth Griffiths and Helen Tiffin (eds.), Post-Colonial Studies: The Key Concepts (London, 2000), 139-142.
Daniel A. Barber, Modern Architecture and Climate: Design Before Air Conditioning (Princeton, 2020).
Luce Beeckmans and Johan Lagae, 'Kinshasa's Syndrome-Planning in Historical Perspective: From Belgian Colonial Capital to Self-Constructed Megalopolis', in Carlos Nunes Silva (ed.), Urban Planning in Sub-Saharan Africa: Colonial and Post-Colonial Planning Cultures (Abingdon, 2015), 201-224.
Homi Bhabha, The Location of Culture (London, 1994).
Igor Bloch, 'House Construction and Social Engineering in the *Beaux métiers* and *Formation sociale* Manuals of the Bibliothèque de l'Étoile (1943-1966)', in ABE Journal, 23 (2024).
Koli Jean Bofane, 'Évolué, What's That?', in Sandrine Collard (ed.), Recaptioning Congo: African Stories and Colonial Pictures (Tielt, 2022), 137-165.
A. Bonnelange and Raphaël François Elema, Ngai mo-kabinda mpenza I (Leverville, 1952).
Lissa Camerlinck, 'The Construction of the Colonial Welfare State: Tracing Design Strategies in the Belgian Congo's Ten Year Plan, 1949-1959', MA thesis (Ghent University), 2017.
Manuel Charpy, 'Une histoire de la sapologie africaine', podcast (11 Jan. 2017) (via www.ifmparis.fr).
Manuel Charpy, 'La montre cassée', in Gil Bartholeyns and Manuel Charpy (eds.), L'étrange et folle aventure du grille-pain: De la machine à coudre et des gens qui s'en servent (Paris, 2021), 75-89.
Émile Jean Baptiste Coart, Vannerie et tissage congolais (Brussels, 1926).
Sandrine Colard, 'African Writings and the Colonial Time's Pictures', in idem (ed.), Recaptioning Congo: African Stories and Colonial Pictures (Tielt, 2022), 14-21.
Frederick Cooper, Africa Since 1940: The Past of the Present (Cambridge, 2002).
Anne Cornet and Florence Gillet, Congo Belgique 1955-1965: Entre propagande et réalité (Brussels, 2010).
Christopher Dandeker, Surveillance, Power and Modernity (Cambridge, 1990).
Pieter De Coene, Margot Luyckfasseel and Gillian Mathys, 'Voices from Exile: The Mpadist "Mission des noirs" in Oshwe's Prison Camps in the Belgian Congo (1940-1960)', in International Journal of African Historical Studies, 55/1 (2022), 89-114.
Matthias De Groof (ed.), Lumumba in the Arts (Leuven, 2020).
Carl De Keyzer, Congo (Belge) (Tielt, 2009).
Bruno De Meulder, Kuvuande mbote: Een eeuw koloniale architectuur en stedenbouw in Kongo (Antwerp, 2000).
Simon De Nys-Ketels, 'Myths and Realities of the Belgian Medical Model Colony: A Genealogy', PhD thesis (Ghent University), 2021.
Simon De Nys-Ketels et al., 'Planning Belgian Congo's Network of Medical Infrastructure: Type-Plans as Tools to Construct a Medical Model Colony, 1949-1959', in Planning Perspectives, 34/5 (2019), 757-778.
Els De Palmenaer (ed.), 100 x Congo: Un siècle d'art congolais à Anvers (Antwerp, 2020).
E. Devroey and E. De Backer, La réglementation sur les constructions au Congo belge (Brussels, 1941).
Uma Dhupelia-Mesthrie, 'Paper Regimes', in Kronos: Southern African Histories, 40 (2014), 11-22.
Andreas Eckert, 'Cultural Commuters: African Employees in Late Colonial Tanzania', in Benjamin N. Lawrance, Emily Lynn Osborn and Richard L. Roberts (eds.), Intermediaries, Interpreters and Clerks: African Employees in the Making of Colonial Africa (Madison, 2006), 248-272.
Elizabeth Edwards, 'Thinking Photography Beyond the Visual?', in J.J. Long, Andrea Noble and Edward Welch (eds.), Photography: Theoretical Snapshots (Abingdon, 2009), 31-48.
Johannes Fabian, Remembering the Present: Painting and Popular History in Zaïre (Berkeley, 1996).
Christraud M. Geary, In and Out of Focus: Images from Central Africa, 1885-1960 (London, 2002).
Didier Gondola, 'La sape des mikilistes: Théâtre de l'artifice et représentation onirique', in Cahiers d'études africaines, 153 (1999), 13-47.
Didier Gondola, Tropical Cowboys: Westerns, Violence, and Masculinity in Kinshasa (Bloomington, 2016).
Stuart Hall, 'The Spectacle of the "Other"', in idem (ed.), Representation: Cultural Representations and Signifying Practices (London, 1997), 223-289.

Benoît Henriet, Colonial Impotence: Virtue and Violence in a Congolese Concession (1911-1940) (Berlin, 2021).

Maurice Heymans (ed.), Urbanisme au Congo belge (Brussels, s.d. [1950]).

Matthew S. Hull, Government of Paper: The Materiality of Bureaucracy in Urban Pakistan (Berkeley, 2012).

Nancy Rose Hunt, A Nervous State: Violence, Remedies and Reverie in Colonial Congo (Durham, 2016).

Patrick Joyce, 'Filing the Raj: Political Technologies of the Imperial British State', in Tony Bennett and Patrick Joyce (eds.), Material Powers: Cultural Studies, History and the Material Turn (London, 2010), 102-123.

Katharina Jörder, Building a White Nation: Propaganda, Photography and the Apartheid Regime Between the Late 1940s and the Mid-1970s (Leuven, 2023).

Max Kemman, Trading Zones of Digital History (Berlin, 2021).

Jacob Sabakinu Kivilu, 'Paul-Gabriel-Dieudonné Bolya: De l'assistant médical à l'homme politique', in Jean-Luc Vellut et al. (eds.), La mémoire du Congo: Le temps colonial (Ghent, 2005), 235-239.

Martin Klein, 'African Participation in Colonial Rule: The Role of Clerks, Interpreters and Other Intermediaries', in Benjamin N. Lawrance, Emily Lynn Osborn and Richard L. Roberts (eds.), Intermediaries, Interpreters and Clerks: African Employees in the Making of Colonial Africa (Madison, 2006), 273-288.

Markus Krajewski, Paper Machines: About Cards & Catalogs, 1548-1929 (Cambridge MA, 2011).

Johan Lagae, '"Le petit Belge a voulu faire grand": The Troublesome Construction of the Résidence du Gouverneur Général du Congo Belge in Leopoldville (1922-1960)', in METU: Journal of Architecture, 20/1-2 (2000), 6-27.

Johan Lagae, '"Kongo zoals het is": Drie architectuurverhalen uit de Belgische kolonisatiegeschiedenis 1920-1960', PhD thesis (Ghent University), 2002.

Johan Lagae, 'Georges Ricquier', in Anne Van Loo (ed.), Repertorium van de architectuur in België van 1830 tot heden (Antwerp, 2003), 475.

Johan Lagae, 'Unsettling the "Colonizing Camera": Curatorial Notes on the "Congo belge en images" Project', in Photography & Culture, 5/3 (2012), 327-342.

Johan Lagae, 'Educating the Colonial Spouse or Pushing the Agenda of Tropical Modernism in the Belgian Congo? Architecture and the Coloniser's House in the Pages of the Bulletin de l'Union des femmes coloniales', in Alice Santiago Faria, Anne Shelley and Sandra Ataíde Lobo (eds.), The Built Environment through the Prism of the Colonial Periodical Press (Abingdon, 2023), 130-157.

Johan Lagae and Bernard Toulier (eds.), Kinshasa (Brussels, 2013).

Johan Lagae et al., 'Vers une radioscopie de la ville coloniale: Episodes dans la génèse de l'Avenue Kasa-Vubu, Kinshasa', in Mathieu Zana Etambala and Pamphile Mabiala Mantuba-Ngoma (eds.), La société congolaise face à la modernité, 1700-2010: Mélanges eurafricains offerts à Jean-Luc Vellut (Paris, 2016), 309-343.

Alexandra Lange, White Collar Corbusier: From the "Casier" to the "Cité d'affaires", in Grey Room, 9 (2002), 58-79.

Benjamin N. Lawrance, Emily Lynn Osborn and Richard L. Roberts, 'Introduction', in idem (eds.), Intermediaries, Interpreters and Clerks: African Employees in the Making of Colonial Africa (Madison, 2006), 3-36.

Jos Legrand, The Paradox of the Waste Paper Basket: The Waste Paper Basket in the American Office Between 1870 and 1930 (Maastricht, 2015).

Jens van de Maele and Johan Lagae, '"The Congo must have a presence on Belgian soil": The Concept of Representation in Governmental Discourses on the Architecture of the Ministry of Colonies in Brussels, 1908-1960', in The Journal of Architecture, 22/7 (2017), 1178-1201.

Pedro Monaville, Students of the World: Global 1968 and Decolonization in the Congo (Durham, 2022).

Jean-Marie Mutamba, Du Congo belge au Congo indépendant, 1940-1960: Emergence des "évolués" et genèse du nationalisme (Kinshasa, 1998).

Isidore Ndaywel è Nziem, Théophile Obenga and Pierre Salmon, Histoire générale du Congo: De l'héritage ancien à la République Démocratique (Paris, 1998).

Léon A.M. Pétillon, Courts métrages africains pour servir à l'histoire (Brussels, 1979).

Léon A.M. Pétillon, Congo 1929-1958 (Brussels, 1985).
Pierre Petit, Patrice Lumumba: La fabrication d'un héros national et panafricain (Brussels, 2016).
Bérengère Piret, Florence Renucci and Xavier Rousseaux, Les cent mille briques: La prison et les détenus de Stanleyville (Lille, 2014).
Jean Pirotte, Périodiques missionnaires belges d'expression française: Reflets de cinquante années d'évolution d'une mentalité 1889-1940 (Leuven, 1973).
M.H. Port, Imperial London: Civil Government Building in London, 1850-1915 (New Haven, 1995).
Georges Ricquier, 'Complexité des problems architecturaux des bâtiments d'administration au Congo belge', in Rythme, 17 (1954), 9-16.
Hannah le Roux, 'The Networks of Tropical Architecture', in The Journal of Architecture, 8/3 (2003), 337-354.
Peter Scriver, 'Empire-Building and Thinking in the Public Works Department of British India', in Peter Scriver and Vikramaditya Prakash (eds.), Colonial Modernities: Building, Dwelling and Architecture in British India and Ceylon (Abingdon, 2007), 69-92.
Peter Scriver (ed.), The Scaffolding of Empire: 4th International Symposium of the Centre for Asian and Middle Eastern Architecture (Adelaide, 2007).
Jean Stengers, Congo, mythes et réalités: 100 ans d'histoire (Brussels, 1989).
Henri Stevelinck, Chroniques de Stinkopolis (Léopoldville, 1932).
Ann Laura Stoler, Along the Archival Grain: Epistemic Anxieties and Colonial Common Sense (Princeton, 2009).
Ceri Sullivan, Literature in the Public Service (Houndmills, 2013).
Guy Tillim, Avenue Patrice Lumumba (Munich, 2008).
Theodore Trefon, 'Introduction: Reinventing Order', in idem (ed.), Reinventing Order in the Congo: How People Respond to State Failure in Kinshasa (London, 2004), 1-19.
Daniel Tödt, 'The Colonial State and the African Elite: A History of Subjugation?' in Idesbald Goddeeris, Amandine Lauro and Guy Vanthemsche (eds.), Colonial Congo: A History in Questions (Turnhout, 2020), 215-224.
Daniel Tödt, The Lumumba Generation: African Bourgeoisie and Colonial Distinction In the Belgian Congo (Berlin, 2021).
Jean Omasombo Tshonda and Benoît Verhaegen, Patrice Lumumba: Jeunesse et apprentissage politique, 1925-1956 (Paris, 1998).
Sarah Van Beurden, 'Missions et artisanats d'art au Congo', in Els De Palmenaer (ed.), 100 x Congo: Un siècle d'art congolais à Anvers (Antwerp, 2020), 97-113.
Julien L.L. Vanhove, Histoire du Ministère des Colonies (Brussels, 1968).
Patricia Van Schuylenbergh and Françoise Morimont, Rencontres artistiques Belgique-Congo, 1920-1950 (Louvain-la-Neuve, 1995).
Guy Vanthemsche, 'The Congo, a Colony Heading for "Development"?', in Idesbald Goddeeris, Amandine Lauro and Guy Vanthemsche (eds.), Colonial Congo: A History in Questions (Turnhout, 2020), 160-168.
Guy Vanthemsche, Belgium and the Congo, 1885-1960 (New York, 2012).
Guy Vanthemsche, Genèse et portée du "Plan Décennal" du Congo belge (1949-1959) (Brussels, 1994).
Jean-Luc Vellut, Congo: Ambitions et désenchantements, 1880-1960 (Paris, 2021).
Jean-Luc Vellut et al., Het ontstaan van de hedendaagse schilderkunst in Midden-Afrika, 1930-1970 (Tervuren, 1992).
Gustaaf Verswijver et al. (eds.), Schatten uit het Afrika-Museum Tervuren (Tervuren, 1995).
W. Vigneron, Les bavardages du cancrelat (Élisabethville, 1945).
Sachka Vincent, 'Wit privilege in onafhankelijk Congo: Over "Terug naar Congo" (1987) van Lieve Joris', in Knack, 8 April 2021.
Whyms, Léopoldville: Son histoire 1881-1956 (Brussels, 1957).
O. de Wit and H. Buiter, De opkomst van de moderne administratie, in J.W. Schot et al. (eds.), Techniek in Nederland in de twintigste eeuw (I) (Zutphen, 1998), 219-235.
JoAnne Yates, Control Through Communication: The Rise of System in American Management (Baltimore, 1989).

Chapter 10
Between Hierarchy, Efficiency and Pragmatism: Picturing Portuguese Government Offices in Historic Buildings during the Estado Novo Dictatorship

Ana Mehnert Pascoal

In recent times, the *Terreiro do Paço* has taken on the value of a national symbol. The square, with the buildings that frame it, has acquired [...] significance of the highest importance in the life of the nation. The government's determination to promote the concentration of public services around the square reinforces this. Bearing in mind the respective proportions, different functions and various political nuances, we talk about the *Terreiro do Paço* like someone who mentions the Sublime Porte, the Kremlin, Downing Street, the White House, the Elysée [...]. But we must not lose sight of the fact that the buildings at *Terreiro do Paço* are a contested space, with public services vying for every metre.[1]

In 1949, architect Raul Lino highlighted the limited space available for ministerial departments on Lisbon's *Terreiro do Paço* (also known as *Praça do Comércio*). Constructed after the 1755 earthquake on the site of the former royal palace, this square had gradually come to house the government ministries and departments (Fig. 10.1.).[2] During the late 1940s, the government initiated a renovation plan for the square's buildings to improve the quality of the public services located there. These buildings served multiple purposes: besides being workplaces for cabinet members and civil servants, they were symbols of both governmental authority and institutional identity. Although the history of the civil service and the role of architects and planners in designing ministerial workplaces have been explored across various countries, the everyday use of these spaces remains significantly under-researched.[3] This visual essay examines the case of Portugal's Estado Novo dictatorship (in power from 1933 to 1974), drawing on photographs of various departments within the Ministry of

Fig. 10.1. *Terreiro do Paço*, with the north and east wings of the government complex, 1930s. Photo by Horácio Novais. (FCG – Biblioteca de Arte e Arquivos, CFT164.160145.)

Public Works – particularly from the 1950s and 1960s – to help mitigate the scarcity of written records on civil servant experiences from this era.[4]

While the Portuguese dictatorship did invest in constructing modern buildings to showcase its commitment to progress and innovation, it prioritised the restoration of monuments and historic structures to legitimise its nationalist ideology and reinforce a sense of continuity with the country's imperial past. This approach often required adapting the evolving managerial needs of ministerial departments to historic buildings, which posed significant challenges for office organisation and necessitated constant improvisation. Under the Estado Novo, the civil service was both strongly centralised and hierarchical.[5] Below the ministers and secretaries of state, secretariats-general and directorates-general oversaw subdepartments, subsections and external directorates.[6] This organisational structure aimed to rationalise work processes and reflected early-20th-century managerial principles of task division (as found in scientific management) alongside the authoritarian state's emphasis on centralised authority. However, complaints about insufficient or poorly distributed space within the 18th-century office buildings on *Terreiro do Paço* were frequent between the 1950s and the early 1970s, reflecting the persistent tension between modern administrative demands and the limitations of historic architecture.[7]

In the 1950s, plans to construct a new monumental building for the Ministry of Public Works were abandoned, resulting in the ministry's continued occupation of the east wing of the *Terreiro do Paço* complex, alongside other government departments, including the Under-Secretariat of Corporations and Social Welfare. By 1953, the Public Works Department employed approximately 800 civil servants, many of whom were technically trained, such as engineers and architects.⁸ Because of the deteriorating state of the buildings, several renovations were carried out in the 1950s, including the cleaning and painting of walls, as well as minor transformations of sanitary facilities and modifications to lighting. In some cases, wooden and glass partitions were introduced, while in others, non-load-bearing walls were removed. The overarching objective was to preserve the historic building in its original state, in contrast to the more transformative remodelling solution applied to the adjacent Ministry of Finance. Individual offices were allocated only to the minister, the directors-general and the heads of departments, with these offices strategically placed close to their respective teams. Yet, despite such efforts to improve efficiency and administrative "coordination" – concepts first articulated during Prime Minister António de Oliveira Salazar's financial reorganisation in the 1930s – spatial limitations continued to hinder effective connections and workflows.⁹ Furthermore, the need for multiple ministerial departments to share a single building exacerbated the challenges.

A photograph taken in 1959 shows the recently renovated personal office of the Minister of Public Works, a space designed to balance administrative work with ceremonial gravitas (Fig. 10.2.). As Adrian Forty noted, the interior design of government buildings typically seeks to convey not only efficiency but also the hierarchy of power within the state.¹⁰ Far from being a mere workspace, this Portuguese office indeed served as both a venue for professional meetings and a stage for symbolic display, reflecting the minister's position at the apex of the state apparatus. Located on the first floor of the ministerial building, the office was positioned within a spatial hierarchy: surrounding it were an antechamber, the office of the minister's personal secretary, the office of the Under-Secretary of State, a waiting room, and the office of the head of the ministerial cabinet. The "depth" of the minister's position reflected power dynamics: as Thomas Markus observed, in public buildings, spatial depth is often indicative of authority, with "the person [having] the greatest power [...] at the tip of a tree, reached through corridors, stairs, outer and inner offices and waiting rooms".¹¹ This design emphasised the minister's authority and physical distance from the more "accessible" areas of the building. Furnishings were carefully selected to project both professional dignity and prestige, further highlighting the minister's status.¹² While new items such as sofas, a carpet and a folding screen are visible in the photograph, much of the furniture appears to date from older times, including a Renaissance-style glass-topped desk, D. José chairs, and an opulent chandelier and table

Fig. 10.2. Personal office of the Minister of Public Works, September 1959. Photo by Analide Óscar. (Património Cultural, I.P., FOTO.00513941.)

clock, all of which conveyed an air of historical gravitas.[13] Tellingly, Portuguese ministers were actively involved in selecting furnishings for their offices, and they often expressed a preference for traditional, historicist pieces over contemporary styles.[14] This preference reflected not only personal taste but also financial pragmatism, as the restoration and reuse of existing furniture were often justified on economic grounds.

Let us turn our attention to the working spaces of civil servants, a first example of which is offered by a photograph – taken between 1930 and 1950 – of a shared office belonging to the Affordable Housing Department (Fig. 10.3.). An accounting calculator and a scale suggest that this room was used by the treasury section. The desks, with books, papers, inkstands, blotters and rubber stamps arranged on them, provide a glimpse of the administrative tasks performed. The absence of partitions between desks again reflects tenets of scientific management, prioritising efficiency and managerial oversight. The space is organised into three rows of adjoining desks, with a single perpendicular desk aligned with the door. This desk, likely for a senior official, is positioned to supervise the others and stands near the room's only telephone – a clear symbol of authority. The first row

Fig. 10.3. Undated photo (taken between 1930 and 1950) of civil servants working for the Affordable Housing department. Photo by Alvão. (Centro Português de Fotografia, PT/CPF/ALV/005074.)

of desks faces the other two and includes accounting equipment and desk calendars, indicating that the clerks seated here likely held higher ranks than their six colleagues. This position allowed them to set an example, reflecting the importance placed by the French managerial theorist Henri Fayol (1841-1925) on discipline and strong leadership. Fayol's principles of discipline, obedience and proper conduct are further reflected in the portrait of Salazar: hung above photographs of housing projects, it reinforced the expectation that civil servants served the regime above all else.[15] A 1951 government report captured this ethos: "In the public service, one must breathe and feel the authority and [...] discipline that is imposed on everyone."[16] Although Portugal's civil service was officially framed as neutral and apolitical, and the Estado Novo routinely presented governance as a "technical" endeavour, civil servants were expected to follow political commands without question.[17] The blending of scientific management's focus on efficiency with the regime's authoritarian ideals thus demonstrates how office design was used to reinforce dictatorial power.

The fact that the adaptation of government workspaces to historic buildings required constant pragmatism is also underscored by the

Figs. 10.4.–10.5. The Noble Hall in the 1960s. (Património Cultural, I.P., FOTO.00536301 and FOTO.00536305.)

following two photographs from the 1960s, which show the Noble Hall in the *Terreiro do Paço* complex being used by unidentified departments (Figs. 10.4.–10.5.). Originally conceived as a venue for important events and gatherings, this double-height hall was used by the Minister of Corporations until he was relocated to a new building around 1966. These

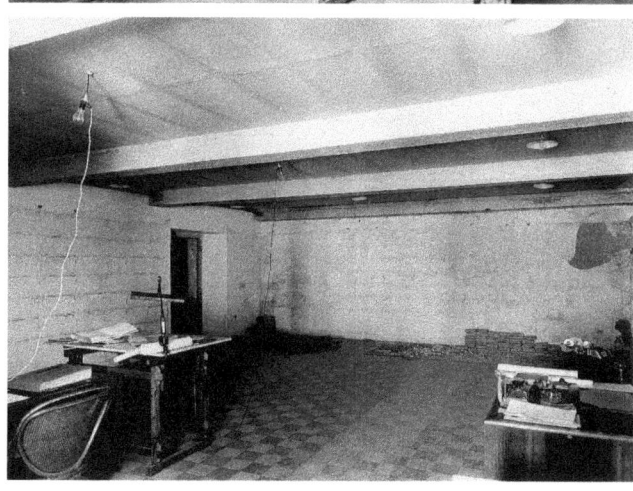

Figs. 10.6.–10.8.
First section of the Directorate-General of National Monuments and Buildings: secretariat (top), draughtsmen's office (middle), and technical agents' office (bottom), 1950. (Património Cultural, I.P., FOTO.00512489, FOTO.00513937 and FOTO.00512488.)

photographs, which appear less staged than the previous one, reveal a striking contrast between ornamentation – obvious in the ornate stucco ceiling and luxurious crystal chandelier – and "functional" office furniture in different styles. The large windows, the ventilation openings above the curtain-covered door and the fan on the top of a cabinet point to both active and passive strategies for climate control. A row of metal filing cabinets, positioned centrally within the space, served as a spatial divider: a typical example of "non-intentional design", adding another layer of user experience to the categories discussed in this volume by Craig Robertson.[18]

The last three images portray the secretariat and drawing section of the Department of Construction Services, part of the Directorate-General of National Monuments and Buildings (Figs. 10.6.–10.8.). In this setting, notions of scientific management are less apparent. Photographed outside working hours, the scenes may have been intended to draw attention to suboptimal working conditions – insufficient lighting, poor ventilation and inadequate thermal comfort – frequently criticised in reports by senior civil servants.[19] The varied assortment of wooden desks and chairs reflects a cost-effective approach, prioritising the reuse and repair of older furniture. Such practices were regarded as a model of moderation and frugality, values that epitomised Portuguese governance at the time. This emphasis on thrift overshadowed the idea that uniform furniture could project efficiency and productivity. The theme of frugality is particularly evident in photograph 10.8., which shows renovation work – either ongoing or stalled – on the floor. Regardless of the renovation's status, conventional standards of efficiency were overlooked: if the work was ongoing, desks were neither vacated nor protected from dust; if stalled, clerks were left to perform their duties in a visibly unfinished and unpolished environment.

In sum, the offices depicted in all the photographs reflect the Estado Novo regime's conceptualisation of the civil service. It was seen as the backbone of a centralising state, where the individuality of civil servants was subordinated to their collective role in serving the nation. This centralisation led to excessive bureaucratisation, further reinforced by the adoption of a highly hierarchical organisational structure in government offices located within historic buildings, with clear distinctions based on status. Intentions to implement scientific management theories coexisted with a degree of improvisation. The economic benefits of repurposing existing spaces and furniture were accentuated by the heritage value ascribed to historic buildings. However, as Raul Lino noted, the office spaces on *Terreiro do Paço* were contested by various administrative departments, leading to pragmatic adaptations.

A lack of investment in training for civil servants, identified as a key challenge in public administration reform during the 1960s, likely contributed to their continued subordination. By this time, the images of offices for lower-ranking clerks show that little attention was given to these non-representational spaces, where environmental comfort and room capacity were less than ideal. The issues were masked by the symbolic significance of the façades. Further research, especially through a comparative approach that includes international cases, could shed light on whether these office layouts and functions were an expression of authoritarian power or rather a pragmatic response to the socio-economic realities of Portugal at the time.

NOTES

1. Património Cultural, I.P., Arquivos e Coleções Documentais da Ex-DGEMN (Lisbon) [hereafter ACD Ex-DGEMN], PT/DGEMN/DSID-001/011-1351, Letter (13 April 1949).
2. Joana Estorninho de Almeida, 'A Cultura Burocrática Ministerial: Repartições, Empregados e Quotidiano nas Secretarias de Estado na Primeira Metade do Século XIX', PhD thesis (University of Lisbon), 2008.
3. On the history of ministerial buildings, see for example Jens van de Maele, Architectures of Bureaucracy: The Politics of Government Office Buildings in Interwar Belgium (Berlin, 2025); Emmanuel Pénicaut, 'Un ministère en quête d'identité? Une histoire du Ministère de la Défense par ses bâtiments, des années trente à nous jours', in In situ, 34 (2018); Adam Sharr and Stephen Thornton, Demolishing Whitehall: Leslie Martin, Harold Wilson and the Architecture of White Heat (London, 2013); Michael H. Port, Imperial London: Civil Government Building in London, 1850-1915 (New Haven, 1995).
4. A more elaborate analysis of the Estado Novo case can be found in Ana Mehnert Pascoal, 'Os "Palácios da Representação Nacional": Identidade e Poder nos Edifícios do Governo no Estado Novo', PhD thesis (University of Lisbon), 2023.
5. Diogo Freitas do Amaral, 'Administração Pública', in Joel Serrão (ed.), Dicionário de História de Portugal, vol. VII (Porto, 1999).
6. Decree-Law 26115, 23 Nov. 1953.
7. Correspondence from senior officials confirms the need for improvement. See for instance ACD Ex-DGEMN, PT/DGEMN/DNISP-001-0121/02/5 and PT/DGEMN/DNISP-001-0001/04, Correspondence, 1950 and 1957-1961. The responses to a survey conducted in 1973 by the recently established Secretariat for Public Administration, within the context of an ongoing administrative reform, also offer valuable insights on this subject: Arquivo Contemporâneo do Ministério das Finanças (Lisbon), Fundo Secretaria-Geral do Ministério das Finanças, 462-13.
8. For this number, see 25 Anos de Administração Pública: Ministério das Obras Públicas (Lisbon, 1953), 17.
9. In his capacity as Minister of Finance from 1928 onwards, Salazar pursued the objective of stabilising public finances. He argued against the duplication of services and the accumulation of positions, advocating instead for the concentration of services and the simplification of bureaucracy within the civil service. See António de Oliveira Salazar, A Reorganização Financeira: Dois Anos no Ministério das Finanças, 1928-1930 (Coimbra, 1930). Nevertheless, the debate surrounding

the ineffectiveness of public administration only gained prominence in the 1950s. See Ana Carina Azevedo, 'Reformar a Administração Pública ao Sabor das Prioridades do Estado Novo', in Portuguese Studies Review, 26/2 (2018).

[10] Adrian Forty, Objects of Desire: Design and Society since 1750 (London, 1995), 147-150. On the symbolism of government buildings, see also Lawrence J. Vale, Architecture, Power and National Identity (New Haven, 1992), 3.

[11] Thomas Markus, Buildings and Power: Freedom and Control in the Origin of Modern Building Types (London, 2004), 16.

[12] On the relationship between hierarchical position and levels of furnishing and decoration, see Christopher Baldry, 'The Social Construction of Office Space', in International Labour Review, 136/3 (1997), 368; Linda Stewart Gatter, 'The Office: An Analysis of the Evolution of a Workplace', PhD thesis (Massachusetts Institute of Technology), 1982, 8.

[13] The D. José style, named after King José I (1714-1777), dates back to the second half of the 18th century and was influenced by English rococo and French ornamentation.

[14] An example of this can be found in the active intervention of the Minister of Finance during the renovation of his office in the early 1950s, when he overruled the architect's plans and demanded the installation of specific historicist furniture, as well as the addition of a mural tapestry, without informing the committee in charge. See ACD Ex-DGEMN, PT/DGEMN/DSARH-005/125-2509/02 and PT/DGEMN/DNISP-001-0129/02/4, Correspondence (1952-1960) and report (April 1952).

[15] On these "Fayolist" principles, see Henri Fayol, Administration industrielle et générale (Paris, 1920).

[16] Cited by João Paulo Martins, 'Móveis Modernos: A Atividade da Comissão para Aquisição de Mobiliário no Âmbito da Direção-Geral dos Edifícios e Monumentos Nacionais', in idem (ed.), Móveis Modernos: Mobiliário para Edifícios Públicos em Portugal 1940-1980 (Lisbon, 2014), 14.

[17] On Salazar's technocratic self-image, see Fernando Rosas, Salazar e o Poder: A Arte de Saber Durar (Lisbon, 2013), 36. In accordance with the constitutional stipulation that civil servants were obliged to serve the community (rather than any political party or organisation with a private interest), the formation of syndicates, which were themselves subject to state control, was not permitted. See Maria Cristina Rodrigues, 'Portugal e a Organização Internacional do Trabalho (1933-1974)', PhD thesis (University of Coimbra), 2012, 270.

[18] On the notion of non-intentional design, see Uta Brandes and Michael Erlhoff, Non Intentional Design (Cologne, 2006).

[19] ACD Ex-DGEMN, PT/DGEMN/DNISP-001-0208/01/1, PT/DGEMN/DNISP-001-0001/04 and PT/DGEMN/DSARH-005/125-1199/06, Report (Feb. 1953), letter (17 March 1954) and letter (9 Oct. 1958).

BIBLIOGRAPHY

Joana Estorninho de Almeida, 'A Cultura Burocrática Ministerial: Repartições, Empregados e Quotidiano nas Secretarias de Estado na Primeira Metade do Século XIX', PhD thesis (University of Lisbon), 2008.

Diogo Freitas do Amaral, 'Administração Pública', in Joel Serrão (ed.), Dicionário de História de Portugal, vol. VII (Porto, 1999), 51-58.

Ana Carina Azevedo, 'Reformar a Administração Pública ao Sabor das Prioridades do Estado Novo', in Portuguese Studies Review, 26/2 (2018), 177-198.

Christopher Baldry, 'The Social Construction of Office Space', in International Labour Review, 136/3 (1997), 365-378.

Uta Brandes and Michael Erlhoff, Non Intentional Design (Cologne, 2006).

Henri Fayol, Administration industrielle et générale (Paris, 1920).

Adrian Forty, Objects of Desire: Design and Society since 1750 (London, 1995).

Linda Stewart Gatter, 'The Office: An Analysis of the Evolution of a Workplace', PhD thesis (Massachusetts Institute of Technology), 1982.

Thomas Markus, Buildings and Power: Freedom and Control in the Origin of Modern Building Types (London, 2004).

João Paulo Martins, 'Móveis Modernos: A Atividade da Comissão para Aquisição de Mobiliário no Âmbito da Direção-Geral dos Edifícios e Monumentos Nacionais', in idem (ed.), Móveis Modernos: Mobiliário para Edifícios Públicos em Portugal 1940-1980 (Lisbon, 2014), 10-21.

Jens van de Maele, Architectures of Bureaucracy: The Politics of Government Office Buildings in Interwar Belgium (Berlin, 2025).

Ana Mehnert Pascoal, 'Os "Palácios da Representação Nacional": Identidade e Poder nos Edifícios do Governo no Estado Novo', PhD thesis (University of Lisbon), 2023.

Emmanuel Pénicaut, 'Un ministère en quête d'identité? Une histoire du Ministère de la Défense par ses bâtiments, des années trente à nous jours', in In situ, 34 (2018).

Michael H. Port, Imperial London: Civil Government Building in London, 1850-1915 (New Haven, 1995).

Fernando Rosas, Salazar e o Poder: A Arte de Saber Durar (Lisbon, 2013).

Adam Sharr and Stephen Thornton, Demolishing Whitehall: Leslie Martin, Harold Wilson and the Architecture of White Heat (London, 2013).

Maria Cristina Rodrigues, 'Portugal e a Organização Internacional do Trabalho (1933-1974)', PhD thesis (University of Coimbra), 2012.

António de Oliveira Salazar, A Reorganização Financeira: Dois Anos no Ministério das Finanças, 1928-1930 (Coimbra, 1930).

Lawrence J. Vale, Architecture, Power and National Identity (New Haven, 1992).

Chapter 11
Office Life in Chandigarh

Ruth Baumeister (text), Shaun Fynn (photography)

Photography is a kind of preservation. In it, architecture is a lived event.
(Vikramāditya Prakāsh, 2017)[1]

Modernist architects regarded the office as a paradigmatic typology of the 20th century. For figures such as Frank Lloyd Wright, Ludwig Mies van der Rohe, Gio Ponti, Arne Jacobsen, Alvar Aalto and Le Corbusier, it served as a testing ground for the conceptual, technical and material innovations of their time. Flexibility, transparency and innovation were the new paradigms – and these architects knew how to meet such demands through open-plan layouts in curtain-walled buildings of glass, steel, concrete and drywall. Some of their office buildings became icons of modernism and contributed to an architectural canon that defined the basis for much historical scholarship. Le Corbusier's office buildings for the city of Chandigarh in India, which were built between 1950 and 1965 and are pictured in the following photographs by Shaun Fynn, form part of this canon. As noted in the introduction to the present volume, the canonical focus on the great ideas and ambitions of architects and their clients has shaped a narrative that has reinforced the legacy-building of individual (typically male) architects. However, when revisiting these canonical buildings in the context of today's global environmental crisis, this approach offers only limited insight.

For example, when considering aspects of sustainability – such as the thermal performance of buildings, the durability of their structures and materials, and the well-being of office workers – many of the shortcomings for which modernism is criticised today become apparent. Glass façades were conceived at a time when energy and resource supplies were assumed to be unlimited. As a result, these façades are a significant source of heat loss during colder seasons and necessitate extensive air conditioning during warmer periods. Replacing entire façades with better-performing glass presents yet another challenge, as the production of such glass is highly energy-intensive. The flexibility offered by the open-plan design has also driven the constant renewal of interior spaces, resulting in the disposal of fully functional building materials such as drywall, doors and carpets. The analysis by Nicholas Poot and Rem Koolhaas of data from the New York Department of Building's Information System on interior alterations to Mies van der Rohe's Seagram Building (1958) revealed that, between 1990 and 2013 alone, there were 467 interior refurbishment projects. This insatiable drive for innovation led to the disposal of vast quantities of drywall panels: the authors calculated that if all these panels were stacked, the resulting pile would exceed the height of the 156-metre building itself.[2] Another overlooked issue is the impact of modernist workplaces on their occupants. Office workers were often exposed to malfunctioning ventilation systems and toxic materials, including inks, adhesives and solvents. These conditions led to a range of health problems such as headaches, rashes and immune system disorders. By the early 1990s, Sick Building Syndrome had become one of the most common occupational illnesses among office workers in the United States.[3]

With few exceptions, high-profile clients and architects prioritised the representational value of their buildings' exteriors, as evidenced by the often-elaborate designs of façades, entrances, lobbies and overall building volumes. In contrast, workplaces were typically designed to be inexpensive and quick to construct; as long as they met basic working standards or labour laws, considerations such as aesthetics or the well-being of users were largely secondary. The design of specific workplace interiors was often left to consultancies or, at best, furniture companies. Their primary focus was on creating efficient spatial layouts to ensure the smooth functioning of work processes, while factors such as indoor air quality, ergonomics and user comfort were treated as secondary concerns. Within the design and architectural communities, working on office interiors was neither highly regarded as a profession nor considered a field of creative expression. Moreover, as the American architectural historian Henry-Russell Hitchcock argued, the architecture of workplaces was usually more a product of bureaucracy than a stroke of genius.[4]

The pandemic of the early 2020s radically transformed our work lives, prompting a shift in how we perceive offices. Covid-19 once again accelerated the adoption of remote working, blurring the boundaries between private and professional life. Out of necessity, and often in an improvised manner, people set up workspaces in kitchens, living rooms, on terraces, or wherever space allowed. This led both companies and employees to question whether physically working in an office is truly essential. Today, countless office buildings in urban centres around the world stand idle. In light of the current climate crisis and increasing resource scarcity, abandoning or demolishing urban centres is no longer justifiable; rather, their transformation into sustainable and adaptable spaces is essential. This compels architects and urban planners to grapple with what has long been regarded as the "banality" of the office. Furthermore, it raises significant questions for entrepreneurs, public institutions and architects about the future of office workspaces, including prevailing standards and labour laws. Where do we go from here? What lessons can be drawn from the 20th-century office building as a historical artefact, and how might these inform our approach to the office of the future?

We are familiar with office buildings primarily through representations in books, magazines and social media. These images often depict them in pristine condition, paradoxically devoid of the office workers for whom they were designed. Such representations convey an understanding of architecture as a finished, static object, failing to recognise its performative nature. By erasing the presence of users, these images also deny the social spaces created within these buildings. The workplaces provided by these offices, along with the everyday life once lived or still unfolding within them, largely remain hidden. As the French writer Georges Perec (1973) asked:

> What speaks to us, seemingly, is always the big event, the untoward, the extraordinary: the front-page splash, the banner headlines. [...] Behind the event there has to be a scandal, a fissure, a danger, as if life reveals itself only by way of the spectacular, as if what speaks, what is significant, is always abnormal: natural cataclysms or historical upheavals, social unrest, political scandals. [...] The daily papers talk of everything except the daily. [...] What's really going on, what we're experiencing, the rest, all the rest, where is it? How should we take account of, question, describe what happens every day and recurs every day: the banal, the quotidian, the obvious, the common, the ordinary, the infra-ordinary, the background noise, the habitual?[5]

The work of designer and photographer Shaun Fynn, capturing clerks at work in Le Corbusier's office buildings in Chandigarh, focuses precisely on this dynamic. The Swiss-French architect's project for the new capital of Punjab has been extensively criticised by postcolonial theorists for imposing Western ideals and values through architecture and urban planning, while disregarding local cultures, urban life and building practices. Although not necessarily intended as such, Fynn's photographs can be interpreted as visual evidence supporting this criticism.[6] However, the aim here is neither to engage directly with this discourse nor to romanticise working conditions that might be deemed precarious or intolerable by Western standards. Furthermore, this contribution does not seek to provide a legacy-focused analysis of Le Corbusier's office buildings. Such an approach would merely foreground the intentions of a single architect or client, amplifying the voices of those in power while simultaneously neglecting the labour of all others who contributed to the realisation of these buildings.

Instead, this visual essay shifts the focus from the creator and the static, representational office building to an exploration of everyday life within these spaces. Over several years of living and working in Chandigarh, Fynn independently explored the city in its many facets with his camera, publishing his reflections on Le Corbusier's project in a book.[7] His photographs offer a rare glimpse into the interior life, presenting perspectives typically absent from architectural monographs. Rather than freezing a single moment in time, Fynn's photographs – produced from 2012 to 2014 – illuminate the buildings' performance over time by revealing what takes place behind office doors and by consciously highlighting the traces left by everyday office use. In doing so, they open up a new layer of discourse. By distancing themselves from the canonical approach, these photographs uncover a reality concealed behind the representational façade, demonstrating how bodies interact with, move through and sit within "Corbusian" workspaces. Fynn's images embrace, rather than conceal, the messiness of the office. Indirectly, they capture moments in the buildings' life not just at the time of their inauguration – when spaces are typically "clean" and meticulously staged – but in a neo-realist manner, documenting users and traces of use accumulated over the years.

Particularly striking is the apparent disorder of these spaces and the apparent indifference of the clerks towards it when photographed. The images reveal files piled up in corners and makeshift workstations with electric cords hanging from ceilings. Furniture designed by Pierre Jeanneret, which could fetch high prices at auctions in Europe or North America, is carelessly stacked in storage spaces. In these offices, bespoke furniture pieces designed for the complexes coexist inconspicuously with generic, mass-produced items. The photographs capture bureaucracy in action: personalised workspaces, cheap suspended ceilings, and fans perched on tables, mounted on ceilings or placed in windows. Personal items, such as drawings, calendars pinned to walls, desktop telephones, and traces of food and drink, are scattered throughout. Together, after decades of administrative work, these elements form a palimpsest of working lives, as Fynn's images unfold before us. They invite reflection on the ways in which precarity fosters creative practices of social production and spatial reconfiguration. At the same time, the photographs attest to the resilience of the Corbusian spaces. They illuminate the habits and rituals of daily work life, showing how the architecture either succeeded or failed to meet the needs of individual office workers and how the latter adapted to these conditions.

It has been said that Prime Minister Jawaharlal Nehru was once asked whether he liked Chandigarh, to which he replied that it was not a matter of liking but rather a profound statement intended to "make you think".[8] This perspective becomes especially relevant when examining these photographs. What we see invites us to reconsider Western standards that govern the physical dimensions of office work, such as indoor air quality, comfort, noise and lighting: standards designed to ensure occupational health but ultimately aimed at enhancing worker efficiency. If, as Perec asserts, "what we need to question is bricks, concrete, glass, our table manners, our utensils, our tools, the way we spend our time, our rhythms",[9] then Fynn's photographs urge us to do precisely that.

Fig. 11.1. Secretariat, Capitol complex, 2013. (© Shaun Fynn – All rights reserved)

Fig. 11.2. Office, Chandigarh Bus Terminal, 2012. (© Shaun Fynn – All rights reserved)

Fig. 11.3. Government office, 2013. (© Shaun Fynn – All rights reserved)

Fig. 11.4. Government office, 2013. (© Shaun Fynn – All rights reserved)

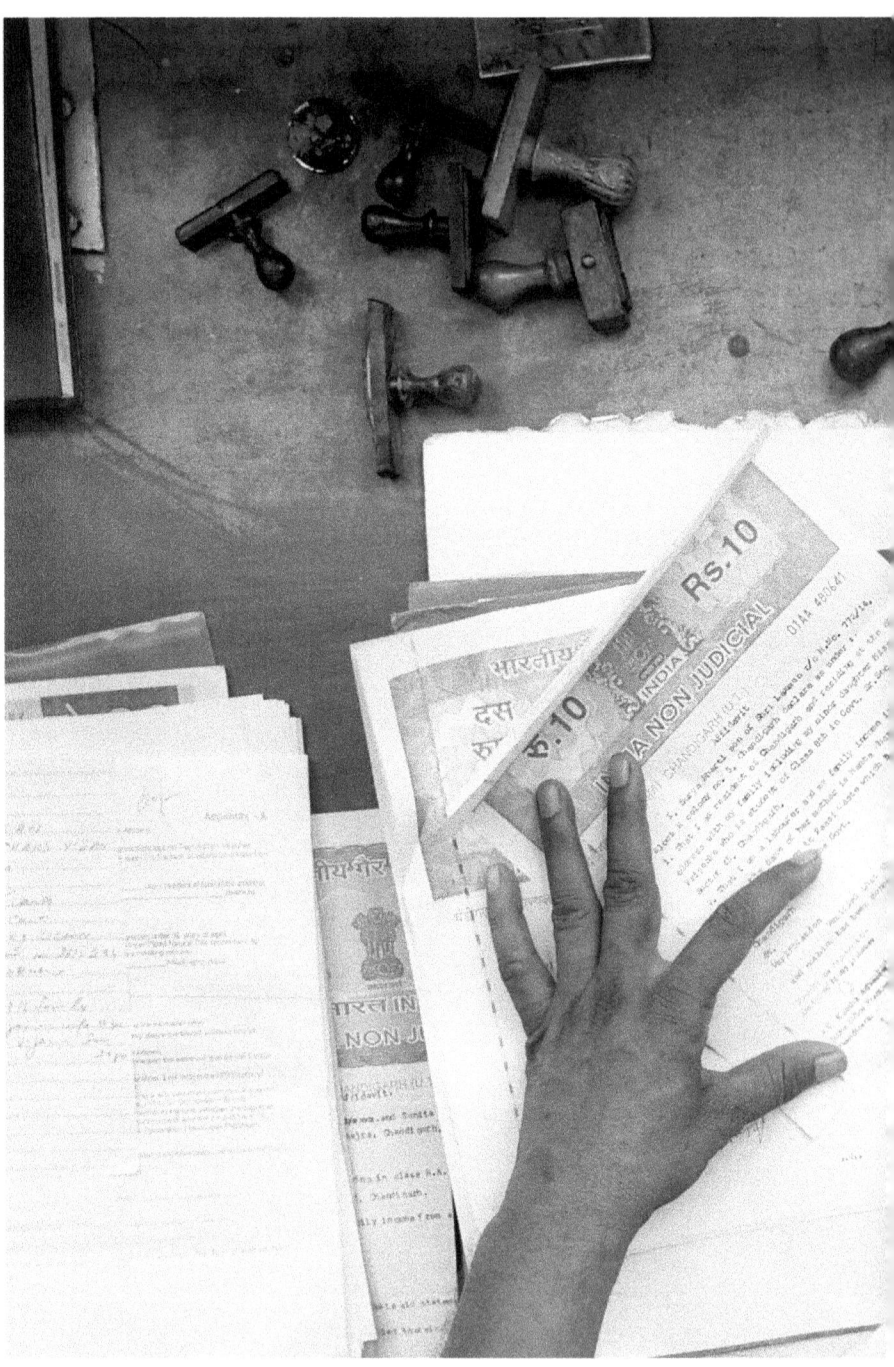

Fig. 11.5. Public notary desk, 2012. (© Shaun Fynn – All rights reserved)

Fig. 11.6. Government office, 2013. (© Shaun Fynn – All rights reserved)

Fig. 11.7. Government office, 2012. (© Shaun Fynn – All rights reserved)

Fig. 11.8. Furniture storage on the roof of the High Court, 2014.
(© Shaun Fynn – All rights reserved)

NOTES

1. Vikramāditya Prakäsh, '"L. Corbusier" and the State of the Nation-State', in Shaun Fynn, Chandigarh Revealed: Le Corbusier's City Today (New York, 2017), 231.
2. Rem Koolhaas and Nicholas Potts, 'Seagram Building', in Ruth Baumeister, Stephan Petermann and Marieke van den Heuvel, Back to the Office: 50 Revolutionary Office Buildings and How they Sustained (Rotterdam, 2022).
3. Michelle Murphy, Sick Building Syndrome and the Problem of Uncertainty: Environmental Politics, Technoscience and Women Workers (Durham, 2006).
4. On the latter two matters, see also the introduction to this volume.
5. Georges Perec, 'Approaches to What?' in idem, Species of Spaces and Other Pieces (ed. by John Sturrock) (London, 1999), 209-210.
6. Fynn confirmed in a conversation with the author on 2 October 2024 that this was not his intention.
7. Fynn, Chandigarh. See also Shaun Fynn, Departures: A Journey with India (s.l., 2022).
8. Prakäsh, L. Corbusier, 231.
9. Perec, Approaches, 210.

BIBLIOGRAPHY

Shaun Fynn, Chandigarh Revealed: Le Corbusier's City Today (New York, 2017).
Shaun Fynn, Departures: A Journey with India (s.l., 2022).
Rem Koolhaas and Nicholas Potts, 'Seagram Building', in Ruth Baumeister, Stephan Petermann and Marieke van den Heuvel, Back to the Office: 50 Revolutionary Office Buildings and How They Sustained (Rotterdam, 2022), 164-172.
Michelle Murphy, Sick Building Syndrome and the Problem of Uncertainty: Environmental Politics, Technoscience and Women Workers (Durham, 2006).
Georges Perec, 'Approaches to What?' in idem, Species of Spaces and Other Pieces (ed. by John Sturrock) (London, 1999), 209-211.
Vikramäditya Prakäsh, '"L. Corbusier" and the State of the Nation-State', in Shaun Fynn, Chandigarh Revealed: Le Corbusier's City Today (New York, 2017), 230-231.

Epilogue

Martin Kohlrausch and Andreas Fickers

The office is one of the more inconspicuous places of the 20th century, banal in its ubiquity and seemingly insignificant in its relative lack of scholarly visibility. A 2005 book on "Places of Modernity" (*Orte der Moderne*) interestingly included the apartment alongside more spectacular places like the submarine or the strip club, but there was no mention of the office.[1] This lack of attention probably says as much about researcher preferences as it does about the specific characteristics of the office that place it outside major research trends. These very characteristics, however, may well be what makes it so historically important. The introduction to this edited volume convincingly makes the case that the office should be seen as the prime locus of the redefinition of work in the 20th century. Just as we continue to live with 19th-century factories (even though they no longer function, smell or look as they once did, both on the inside and often also on the outside), the office is unlikely to disappear. After the Covid-19-induced success of working from home, offices – our presence in, access to and arrangement of them – have become a space in which postmodern society has literally and metaphorically tried to find its locus.[2]

This collection makes a concerted effort to address gaps – some that readily come to mind, others that become apparent only on closer examination – revealing their relevance in the process. In this way, the volume offers a state-of-the-art perspective on a dynamic and evolving field, introducing new categories for understanding the office in its broader social and cultural context and linking it to themes such as efficiency, control, emancipation and social change. This epilogue will sketch, with a very broad brush, two dimensions which feature prominently in the preceding contributions, while also showing the potential for further developing the theme of the office. We do so by zooming out, hinting at a perspective related to the political relevance of the office that could be further explored; and by zooming in, suggesting even more radical ways than those explored in this volume to scrutinize a user's perspective of the office by applying the findings of research on the material dimension of media.

When focusing on the office as a *political* space, a number of tensions spring to mind. Literary depictions of the office have effectively captured the tension between the elusive and the banal on the one hand, and the increasing force, coercion and sheer power associated with the office on the other. One may think here of Franz Kafka's *The Trial*, in which the office both loses its character as a secure space for protagonist Josef K., a bank clerk, and at the same time serves as a space in which unclear charges are prepared against him, further blurring the boundaries of private and public, coercion and freedom, safety and persecution. In Eugène Ionesco's *Rhinoceros* the office is the symbolic space in which order and (liberal) civilisation collapse after the intrusion of the eponymous animals, which symbolise the lure of totalitarianism.

One could argue that the office became a central space in 20th-century life, not only as the workplace of a growing number of employees but also as the site where anonymous bureaucratic processes enabled the defining political developments of the era. From war economies and planned economies to the bureaucratised execution of the Holocaust, the office merged administration with "rationalised" violence.[3] Already in the late 19th century, the Prussian General Staff – through its military role and considerable political and cultural influence – had established the office as a key site for planning complex social processes of force and violence, foreshadowing the two most extreme ideologies of the "Age of Extremes" (fascism and communism). In moving the locus of decision-making from the frontlines to an anonymous space behind the scenes, in which criteria other than personal example-setting and courage apply, background ideologies like efficiency, control and planning, all associated with the office, came to be acknowledged as decisive. This development encompassed liberal-democratic, authoritarian-fascist and state-socialist systems and found its most extreme and lethal expression in the systems of control and eventually extermination developed by totalitarian systems, particularly the Holocaust organised by Nazi Germany. The link between bureaucratic rationality and systematic extermination has been examined in Hannah Arendt's controversial notion of the "banality of evil" and, in a more systematic way, in Zygmunt Bauman's influential but contested study on modernity and the Holocaust.[4]

To illustrate the shifting "politics of the office" in the 20th century, it is useful to examine stratification and hierarchy in both vertical and horizontal dimensions. In his seminal 1925 text *Urbanisme* – and later, though with some modifications, in *La ville radieuse* (1930) – Le Corbusier envisioned a city centre dominated by skyscrapers that housed the political, administrative and economic elites. These towers functioned as power hubs and focal points of a technologically driven modernity. The supporting classes, by contrast, were relegated to lower-rise buildings in less central locations.[5] Less immediately apparent is the way power could transcend the static, enclosed nature of the office through horizontal mobility.[6] Robert Moses, the notorious driving force behind New York's postwar infrastructure transformation and a key figure in modern public administration, commanded a network of offices, each staffed and ready for his arrival. Moving between them in a limousine kitted out as a mobile office, his secretaries following in a separate car, he turned mobility itself into an extension of bureaucratic control.[7] Already around 1900, a more classic leader, German Emperor Wilhelm II, had escaped administrative routines in Berlin and Potsdam by moving his office to his yacht *Hohenzollern* and his royal train for large parts of the year.[8] Perhaps the most infamous example is Adolf Hitler's *Führerhauptquartier*, which followed the advancing and retreating German Wehrmacht, involving hundreds of bureaucratic staff keeping files and securing communications in makeshift bunker-cum-offices.[9] By comparison, Air Force One appears as a resolutely civil form of office mobility, yet it confirms the notion that political power even today is wielded by those who are able to render an office mobile and transcend its inherent static nature.

The political dimension of the office as a symbol and agent of power is thus closely linked to the ideologies of rationalisation and efficiency that are deeply rooted in the age of industrial capitalism and modernity. From a media-materialist perspective, the (pseudo-)scientific ideas of Taylorism and management were reflected in the many technological innovations that turned the office into a privileged place of renegotiation of social and economic relationships, especially when considering their impact on the division of labour between men and women. The most iconic object in this respect was the typewriter, which started its triumphant progress in the 1880s. Within a period of twenty to thirty years, the office turned from a nearly all-male preserve into a female-dominated domain. The emergence of this "new economy of writing", based on new technologies of classifying, archiving and transmitting information, placed female office workers at the forefront of a new bureaucratic era. After the First World War, the "typewriter girl" displaced men from their leading role in clerical employment, and female typists successfully embodied visions of mechanical speed, impersonality and professional habitus. As Martyn

Lyons explains in *The Typewriter Century*, "establishing a 'rational' work routine and a productive office layout in a new corporate culture turned typists into pieces of mechanical apparatus".[10]

As Taylorist principles of scientific management were transferred from the factory to the office, "speedometers" were attached to typewriters, measuring the number of words a typist was able to write per minute. As public and private administrations expanded, service industries proliferated and new machines and methods of bookkeeping, communication and data storage entered the office, which subsequently became populated by new filing systems, calculators, addressing machines, cash registers, telephone exchanges, dictating machines, photocopiers and finally computing technologies. As Craig Robertson and David Owen have shown with the examples of the filing cabinet and the photocopier, new technologies for information management, storage and reproduction have deeply affected the professional structures and social relationships of office work.[11] Each of these technologies has changed the "socio-technological regime of the office", which is characterised by a high degree of specialised labour and the complex integration of different office technologies and infrastructures.[12]

While most historical studies of offices highlight the organisational and structural changes of office work as a result of new economic, administrative and technological realities, a focus on "office objects" and their uses may enrich the current scholarship by pointing historians to the intricate relationship between "things" (and the sociotechnical imaginaries they embody)[13] and their power as "actants" in the tissue of bureaucratic/administrative procedures and human-workplace interactions. Telephones and Dictaphones, typewriters and personal computers have deeply affected human communication and interaction and gradually "regendered" office work throughout the 20th century. In addition, the infrastructural affordances of modern communication and information technologies have shaped new architectural plans and office designs, reflecting the procedural logic of collecting, storing and disseminating information based on paper, cable or wireless technologies. It is this interplay of infrastructural "hardware" and system-based "software" that characterises modern administrative systems and bureaucratic practices – practices that require careful historical consideration when trying to "look behind the door" to understand the seminal role and function of offices as a "crime scene" of 20th-century history.

NOTES

1. Alexa Geisthövel and Habbo Knoch (eds.), Orte der Moderne: Erfahrungswelten des 19. und 20. Jahrhunderts (Frankfurt/M., 2005).
2. On the emergence of the home office, see Elizabeth A. Patton, Easy Living: The Rise of the Home Office (New Brunswick, 2020).
3. Edwin Black, IBM and the Holocaust (New York, 2001).
4. Hannah Arendt, Eichmann in Jerusalem: A Report on the Banality of Evil (New York, 1963); Zygmunt Bauman, Modernity and the Holocaust (Cambridge, 1989).
5. Le Corbusier, Urbanisme (Paris, 2025 [first ed. 1925]).
6. On the problem of horizontal mobility, see Yves Cohen, Le siècle des chefs: Une histoire transnationale du commandement et de l'autorité (1890-1940) (Paris, 2013), 620-623.
7. Robert Caro, The Power Broker: Robert Moses and the Fall of New York (New York, 1974), 266-267.
8. Birgit Marschall, Reisen und Regieren: Die Nordlandfahrten Kaiser Wilhelms II (Hamburg, 1991).
9. Felix Hartlaub (ed. by Gabriele Lieslotte Ewenz), Aufzeichnungen aus dem Führerhauptquartier (Frankfurt/M., 2022).
10. Martyn Lyons, The Typewriter Century: A Cultural History of Writing Practices (Toronto, 2021), 59.
11. Craig Robertson, The Filing Cabinet: A Vertical History of Information (Minneapolis, 2021); David Owen, Copies in Seconds: Chester Carlson and the Birth of the Xerox Machine (New York, 2004).
12. J. van den Ende, 'Kantoortechnologie in de twintigste eeuw', in J.W. Schot et al. (eds.), Techniek in Nederland in de twintigste eeuw (Vol. 1) (Zutphen, 1998).
13. Sheila Jasanoff and Sang-Hyon Kim (eds.), Dreamscapes of Modernity: Sociotechnical Imagination and the Fabrication of Power (Chicago, 2015).

BIBLIOGRAPHY

Hannah Arendt, Eichmann in Jerusalem: A Report on the Banality of Evil (New York, 1963).
Zygmunt Bauman, Modernity and the Holocaust (Cambridge, 1989).
Edwin Black, IBM and the Holocaust (New York, 2001).
Robert Caro, The Power Broker: Robert Moses and the Fall of New York (New York, 1974).
Yves Cohen, Le siècle des chefs: Une histoire transnationale du commandement et de l'autorité (1890-1940) (Paris, 2013).
J. van den Ende, 'Kantoortechnologie in de twintigste eeuw', in J.W. Schot et al. (eds.), Techniek in Nederland in de twintigste eeuw (Vol. 1) (Zutphen, 1998), 328-339.
Alexa Geisthövel and Habbo Knoch (eds.), Orte der Moderne: Erfahrungswelten des 19. und 20. Jahrhunderts (Frankfurt/M., 2005).
Felix Hartlaub (ed. by Gabriele Lieslotte Ewenz), Aufzeichnungen aus dem Führerhauptquartier (Frankfurt/M., 2022).
Sheila Jasanoff and Sang-Hyon Kim (eds.), Dreamscapes of Modernity: Sociotechnical Imagination and the Fabrication of Power (Chicago, 2015).
Le Corbusier, Urbanisme (Paris, 2025).
Martyn Lyons, The Typewriter Century: A Cultural History of Writing Practices (Toronto, 2021).
Birgit Marschall, Reisen und Regieren: Die Nordlandfahrten Kaiser Wilhelms II (Hamburg, 1991).
David Owen, Copies in Seconds: Chester Carlson and the Birth of the Xerox Machine (New York, 2004).
Elizabeth A. Patton, Easy Living: The Rise of the Home Office (New Brunswick, 2020).
Craig Robertson, The Filing Cabinet: A Vertical History of Information (Minneapolis, 2021).

Contributors

Ruth Baumeister is associate professor at Aarhus School of Architecture. She received a PhD from TU Delft with a thesis on Asger Jorn's concept of architecture. Her architectural research spans the effects of globalisation, the role of gender, the history of the post-war European avant-gardes, and cultures of maintenance and repair. She is co-author of *Back to the Office: 50 Revolutionary Office Buildings and How They Sustained* (2022).

Nicola Bishop is academic enhancement lead at De Montfort University (Leicester), and researches and writes widely about popular culture, representations of class and educational practice. Her first monograph (*Lower-Middle-Class Nation*, 2021), focused on the representations of white-collar workers in novels, film and television, looking at examples from 1850 to the present day. She has recently published pieces on contemporary crime fiction, suburban comedy, and office-based sitcoms and film.

Joeri Bruyninckx is assistant professor in science and technology studies at Maastricht University's Faculty of Arts and Social Sciences. He is author of *Listening in the Field: Recording and the Science of Birdsong* (2018). His current project investigates the interplay of ergonomic science, design and use in shaping 20th-century office environments.

Andreas Fickers is professor for contemporary and digital history and founding director of the Luxembourg Centre for Contemporary and Digital History (C²DH). His research focuses on European history of technology, transnational and intermedial media history, experimental media archaeology, digital history and hermeneutics, and transmedia storytelling in history. He is editor-in-chief of the *Journal of Digital History*.

Shaun Fynn is the founder of StudioFYNN, a New York-based design, research and communication agency. His photographic work explores the human condition, architecture, consumption, materiality and impermanence in the context of our increasingly urban world. He is the author and photographer of *Chandigarh Revealed*: *Le Corbusier's City Today* and *Departures: A Journey* *with India*. He is currently an adjunct professor at Parsons School of Design in New York City. www.studiofynn.com / www.shaunfynn.com

Bernd Holtwick holds a PhD in Modern German history. From 2000 to 2005, he worked at the *Haus der Geschichte Baden-Württemberg*. He later oversaw cultural affairs in Biberach, including the Kürnbach open-air museum. Since 2011, he has led exhibitions at DASA Working World Exhibition, a museum in Dortmund that explores how work shapes people's lives. His research focuses on modern labour issues and how exhibitions foster public dialogue.

Martin Kohlrausch is professor of European political history and member of the research group Modernity and Society 1800-2000 at KU Leuven. He examines the interplay between mass media and politics, and the role of experts – particularly architects – in shaping European history. His key publications include *Building Europe on Expertise: Innovators, Organisers, Networkers* (with Helmuth Trischler, 2014) and *Brokers of Modernity: East Central Europe and the Rise of Modernist Architects* (2019).

Johan Lagae is professor at Ghent University, where he teaches 20th-century architectural history with a global focus. His research focuses on architecture and urbanisation in (post)colonial Central Africa, including the Congolese cities Kinshasa, Lubumbashi and Matadi. He is co-editor-in-chief of *ABE Journal*, and contributed to many Congo/Africa-related exhibitions. He was the recipient of various grants and fellow at the Paris Institute for Advanced Study.

Jens van de Maele is a postdoctoral member of the research group Modernity and Society 1800-2000 at KU Leuven. He focuses on architectural history and urban environmental history. He has co-curated several award-winning history exhibitions. Recent publications include the monograph *Architectures of Bureaucracy: The Politics of Government Office Buildings in Interwar Belgium* and the edited volume *Mediating the Decline of Industrial Cities* (co-editor).

Ana Mehnert Pascoal holds a PhD in art history. She is a researcher at University Institute of Lisbon, collaborating in the project *Understanding Everyday Modern Architecture and Urban Design in the Iberian Peninsula (1939-1985)*. Her main research interests encompass architecture and bureaucracy, collective memory and the built environment, and the built and artistic heritage of 20th-century dictatorships.

Tatsuya Mitsuda is associate professor at Keio University's Faculty of Economics. His research spans the social and cultural histories of food, animals and climate. He is currently finishing a book on the history of sweets in Japan and preparing a monograph on the history of animal health in 19th-century Germany.

Marco Ninno is a predoctoral member of the research group Modernity and Society 1800-2000 at KU Leuven. His research examines the relationship between the materiality of European Commission office spaces and the institution's practices and identities. With a background in international and global history, and a strong interest in memory cultures, his work explores the intersection of architecture, political history and material culture.

Craig Robertson is professor of communication studies at Northeastern University (Boston, MA). His research focuses on the relationship between paper and information, specifically how the recording, classification and storage of information on paper affects not only who gets to handle and access information, but also how information is conceptualised as something people can use. His most recent book is the award-winning *The Filing Cabinet: A Vertical History of Information* (2021).

Petra Seitz is a PhD candidate at the Bartlett School of Architecture (UCL) and principal investigator on the Chandigarh Chairs project. Her research interests lie within the field of mid-century interiors and furniture, as well as the relationship between politics, particularly political economy, and design. She has lectured in architectural history and theory at the University of Greenwich.

Amy Thomas is associate professor at TU Delft, researching the intersections of architecture, social life and urban change. She authored *The City in the City* (2023) and co-edited *Teaching Design for Values* (2022). A recipient of the NWO VENI grant, she focuses on gender and workplace design. She teaches and supervises on topics including architectural history, urbanism, gender and representation, blending theory with creative practice.

Index

Aalto, Alvar, 327
Ábalos, Iñaki, 33
Abe, Makoto, 130
Abramson, Daniel, 47
Ackermann, Marsha, 123
Action Office, see Herman Miller
Adams, J.S., 258
Adams, Nicholas, 18
Adams, Richard, 103
Adler, David, 250
Ahmed, Sara, 73
Alborn, Timothy, 102, 103
Albrecht, Donald, 21
Albrow, Martin, 26
Anderson, Gregory, 97, 110
Anderson, Perry, 25
Ann Arbor (MI), 227
Antwerp, 286
Arendt, Hannah, 348
Arsenault, Raymond, 122
Baldry, Christopher, 21
Ban, Carolyn, 250
Banville, Scott, 94, 100
Barnes, Julian, 94
Batavia, 278
Battersea, 179
Bauman, Zygmunt, 348
Becker, Dana, 190
Bell Labs Building (Holmdel, NJ), 223
Bell Telephone Laboratories, 158
Benjamin, Walter, 13, 19, 39
Bennett, Arnold, 94, 98, 99, 102, 109
Bentham, Jeremy, 20, 23, 25, 27, 30
Beranek, Leo, 155, 156, 157
Berebitsky, Julie, 27, 97
Berlaymont Building (Brussels), 254, 256, 263
Berlin, 11, 129, 203, 349
Bernasconi, Gianenrico, 14, 124
Besant, Walter, 99
Bhabha, Homi, 278, 304
Biebl, Sabine, 11
Bishop, Nicola, 24
Bjelopera, Jerome, 102
Blake, Peter, 33
Blamires, Cyprian, 26
Bodson, Victor, 252, 258
Böhme, Hartmut, 20

Böhrs, Hermann, 258
Bolt Beranek and Newman, 155, 156, 157, 159, 160, 163
Bolt, Richard, 155
Boma (Congo), 282
Boven, Erica van, 99
Brandt, Willy, 206
Braverman, Harry, 172, 233, 239
Brett Young, Francis, 110
Brighton, 184
British Illumination Engineering Society, 152
British Society for Social Responsibility in Science, 172, 178, 179
Broikos, Chrysanthe, 21
Brussels, 249, 276, 282
Building Research Station (U.K.), 149, 150, 153, 154
Bullock, Shan, 94, 98, 104, 107
Bunshaft, Gordon, 18, 223
Bürolandschaft, 15, 33, 34, 35, 37, 159, 265
Butera, Federico Maria, 31, 32
Calnan, Michael, 182
Canning, Victor, 107, 110
Caplan, Ralph, 237
Carey, John, 98
Çelik Alexander, Zeynep, 16
Centraal Beheer Building (Apeldoorn), 15, 16, 17, 191
Certeau, Michel de, 37
Chadwick, Don, 227
Chang, Jiat-Hwee, 138
Charlemagne Building (Brussels), 256
Charpy, Manuel, 304
Chicago, 83, 121, 127, 129
Christie, Agatha, 106
Clarke, Joseph L., 33, 35
Collins, J.B., 150
Collins, Norman, 108, 109
consociational democracy, 34
Coppé, Albert, 252, 258
Covid-19, 47, 100, 112, 191, 328, 347
Craig, Barbara L., 46
Craig, Marianne, 171, 172, 173, 176
Crisell, Andrew, 101
Croft, David, 107
Crosland, T.W.H., 95
Crossick, Geoffrey, 97

Crozier, Michel, 97
cubicle, 104, 224
Cuisinier, Jacques, 256
Cupers, Kenny, 31
cybernetics, 33
Daiichi Insurance Building (Tokyo), 125
Daniels, Greg, 93
De Keyzer, Karl, 305
Delderfield, R.F., 107, 109
Delgado, Alan, 21
Denver (CO), 227
De Pree, D.J., 226, 237
De Pree, Hugh, 227, 231, 232, 234
Deutsches Institut für Normung, 210, 211
Dewey, Melville, 75
Dickens, Charles, 94, 96, 101, 103, 104, 111
Dircks, Rudolf, 99
Dorson, James, 14, 15, 33
Dortmund, 200, 206, 208
Dreyfuss, Henry, 42
Duffy, Francis, 14, 18, 21, 31, 32, 100, 189, 259
Dumoulin, Michel, 263
Eames, Charles, 226
Eames, Ray, 226
Eckert, Andreas, 278
Eckert-Mauchly Computer Corporation, 131, 132
Edwards, Elizabeth, 45, 304
Ehime (Japan), 137
Eley, Joanna, 189
Elias, Norbert, 22, 29
Eliot, T.S., 94, 107
Élisabethville, see Lubumbashi
Elton, Ben, 107
Emerson Jennings, Eugene, 29
environmental psychology, 146
ergonomics, 15, 146, 150, 160, 200, 201, 205, 207, 209, 211, 212, 213, 224, 328
Ergonomics Research Society (U.K.), 205
Euratom, 251, 252, 253
European Coal and Steel Community, 251
European Commission, 249
European Economic Community, 211, 251
European Productivity Society, 205
Evans, Dan, 97
Farrell, Ranger, 160, 162
Farrell, William R., 157
Faut, Roger, 259
Fayol, Henri, 28, 29, 34, 36, 319
Fechner, Gustav, 149
Felski, Rita, 97, 102, 112
Fickers, Andreas, 78
Fiji, 179
Fischer, Gustave-Nicolas, 21

Ford (car manufacturer), 131, 226
Forster, E.M., 95
Forty, Adrian, 30, 34, 43, 185, 317
Foucault, Michel, 20, 21, 22, 23, 24, 25, 27, 29, 30, 37, 123
Friedmann, Georges, 13
Fritz, Hans-Joachim, 21, 22, 29, 30, 43
Frost, Carl, 234, 238
Gardey, Delphine, 21, 30, 39, 46
Garnisonen Building (Stockholm), 18
Gavron, Hannah, 181
Gay, Peter, 35
Geary, Christraud M., 278
German Democratic Republic, 11
Gervais, Ricky, 93
Gilbreth, Frank B., 203
Gissing, George, 99, 109
Glasgow, 176
Glew, Helen, 97
GM Technical Center (Warren, MI), 223
Gondola, Didier, 303
Grandjean, Etienne, 205
Grand Rapids (MI), 234
Gropius, Walter, 223
Grossmith, Charles, 99, 100, 107
Grossmith, George, 95
Grossmith, Weedon, 95, 99, 100, 107
Haan, Francisca de, 27
Haggett, Ali, 103
Haigh, Gideon, 14
Hallstein, Walter, 253, 254, 266
Hall, Stuart, 278
Hamme, Richard, 160
Hammerton, James, 99
Hannay, Patrick, 18
Harrisburg (PA), 80
Harvard University, 156, 158
Hatoyama, Ichirō, 125
Healy, Stephen, 122
Heidegger, Martin, 13
Heller, Michael, 97
Henriet, Benoît, 276
Herman Miller, 15, 37, 159, 160, 162, 223
Hermans, Willem Frederik, 9
Herreros, Juan, 33
Hertzberger, Herman, 15, 17, 191
Herzberg, Frederick, 204
Higgins, Richard, 99
Hitchcock, Henry-Russell, 17, 328
Hitler, Adolf, 349
Hohenschönhausen (Berlin prison), 11
Honeyman, Gail, 104
Hopkinson, Ralph G., 149, 150, 151, 152, 153, 154

Houyoux, Maurice, 292, 293, 295
Howard, Elizabeth Jane, 105
Hughes, Thomas, 110
human relations (management school), 15, 34, 35, 146
Huntington, Ellsworth, 129
Hunt, Nancy Rose, 276, 281
IBM, 131, 226
Idenburg, Florian, 38
industrial hygiene, 204, 205, 211
International Energy Agency, 122
Ionesco, Eugène, 348
Ishiguro, Kazuo, 112
Iwasa, Hisashi, 135
Jacobsen, Arne, 327
James, P.D., 105
Jeacle, Ingrid, 93
Jeanneret, Pierre, 330
Jerome, Jerome K., 110
Johansen, Michelle, 96, 102
John Deere Headquarters (Moline, IL), 223
Johnson, B.S., 105, 106
Johnson Wax Building (Racine, WI), 15
Jordan, Paul, 102
Joyce, Patrick, 28
Kafka, Franz, 103, 111, 348
Kanda Matulu, Tshibumba, 303
Kasumigaseki Building (Tokyo), 135, 136, 139
Katsuki, Shinji, 130
Kaufmann Buhler, Jennifer, 30, 31, 33, 159
Kinshasa, 276, 282, 289, 290, 294, 296, 300, 302, 303
Klein, Martin, 281
Klein, Viola, 181
Klingender, F.D., 97
Klockenberg, Erich Alexander, 203
Knobel, Lance, 36
Kobayashi, Yōtaro, 133
Koolhaas, Rem, 19, 328
Koyongonda, Louis, 301, 303, 304
Kracauer, Siegfried, 35
Laak, Dirk van, 23
Lacroix, Max, 252, 253, 255, 257, 258, 259, 260
Lamb, Charles, 94
Lamote, C., 294
Lanchester, John, 106
Larkin Building (Buffalo, NY), 15, 16, 17
Lawrence, D.H., 109
Le Corbusier, 127, 327, 329, 330, 348
Lefebvre, Henri, 37, 263
Leffingwell, William Henry, 34
Legrand, Jos, 298
Leigh Star, Susan, 12

Leonard, Hugh, 105
Leopold II, 275
Léopoldville, see Kinshasa
Lever House (NYC), 18, 223
Levinson, Harry, 29
Lewis, Jeremy, 103
Library Bureau (company), 75, 79, 81, 82, 86, 89
Lino, Raul, 315, 322
Lisbon, 315
Liverpool, 110, 145
Lloyd Wright, Frank, 15, 16, 17, 125, 327
Lockwood, David, 97
London, 102, 105, 129, 179, 276
Long, Vicky, 178
Los Angeles, 81
Lowe, Graham, 97
Lubumbashi, 283
Lukács, Georg, 109
Lumumba, Patrice, 302, 305
Luxembourg, 251
Lyons, Martin, 350
MacArthur, Douglas, 125
MacNeil, Heather, 46
Manning, Peter, 145, 146
Markus, Thomas, 317
Marmot, Alexi, 189
Marmot, Michael, 187
Martin, Reinhold, 12
Marunouchi Building (Tokyo), 130
Marxism, 14, 97, 233, 239
Marx, Karl, 97, 240
Massachusetts Institute of Technology, 156, 157
Matadi, 284, 286
Mayer, Arno, 14
McKibbin, Ross, 97
McKinlay, Alan, 26, 27
Merton, Robert, 305
Mexico, 122
Michelmann, Hans, 251
Mihm, Stephen, 97
Milam Building (San Antonio), 121
Miura, Toyohiko, 130, 133
Moses, Robert, 349
Munich, 207
Murphy, Michelle, 21, 27, 30, 37, 42, 130, 139, 174, 181
Mutō, Kiyoshi, 135
Myrdal, Alva, 181
Naipaul, V.S., 278
Nakabayashi, Yoshikatsu, 130
Naunhof, 9, 10
Nazi Germany, 126, 348
Nehru, Jawaharlal, 331

Nellen, Stefan, 14, 124
Nelson, George, 224, 227, 228, 229
Netherlands, 27
Neufert, Ernst, 41
Neujean, Georges, 282
Newman, Bob, 155
New York, 83, 87, 121, 127, 129
New Zealand, 108, 179
Nobbs, David, 105
Noël, Émile, 266
Noguchi, Isamu, 227
Noiriel, Gérard, 37
Norway, 189
Oever, Annie van den, 78
office landscape, see Bürolandschaft
Ōhira, Masayoshi, 137
Oliveira, Andreia Alves de, 10
Olsen, Christopher, 93
Olwell, Victoria, 89
omniopticism, 28, 33, 38
Orwell, George, 94, 110, 112
Osaka, 126
Owen, David, 350
Ōya, Hitomi, 134
PanAm Building (NYC), 223
Panayiotou, Alexia, 100
panopticism, 20, 23, 25, 26, 27
Paris, 129
Paris, Rainer, 24
Parker, Lee, 93
Pasco, Allan, 101
Patrão, André, 25
Pélegrin-Genel, Élisabeth, 10, 14, 16
Perec, Georges, 329, 331
Perry, Jimmy, 107
Pevsner, Nikolaus, 17
Pile, John, 26, 33, 34, 35
Pilkington Research Unit (Liverpool), 145, 146, 153
Ponti, Gio, 327
Poot, Nicholas, 328
Port, Michael Harry, 276
Potsdam, 349
Prakäsh, Vikramāditya, 327
Price, Leah, 99
Priestley, J.B., 108, 110
Propst, Robert, 160, 162, 227, 228, 229, 231, 238, 239, 240, 241
psychophysics, 149, 158
psychotechnics, 203, 204, 205
Pugh, Edwin, 98, 99, 102, 105
Quantrill, Alexandra, 164

Quickborner Team, 15, 33, 34, 35, 36, 159
Ramirez, Francis, 284
Raw, Gary, 189
Reinhard, CarrieLynn, 93
Remington Rand, 79, 132
Rhodes, Carl, 100
Ricquier, Georges, 286, 288
Ripnen, Kenneth H., 252, 257
Robertson, Craig, 124, 350
Robertson, Nicole, 97
Rohde, Gilbert, 226
Rohe, Ludwig Mies van der, 15, 17, 223, 327, 328
Rolot, Christian, 284
Rose, Jonathan, 98, 111, 112
Royale Belge Building (Brussels), 263
Rumpfhuber, Andreas, 33, 34
Saarinen, Eero, 223
Salazar, António de Oliveira, 317, 319
Salmon, Geoffrey, 154
San Antonio, 121
Scanlon, Joseph, 232, 233, 235, 236
Schmidt, Sigurd O., 101
Schnaithmann, Christine, 16
Schoneboom, Abigail, 112
Schonfield, Katherine, 185
Schulze, John William, 149
Schwenger, Hannes, 9
Scientific Management, see Taylorism
Scriver, Peter, 280
Seagram Building (NYC), 15, 17, 223, 328
Sick Building Syndrome, 30, 37, 42, 174, 186, 187, 188, 189, 191, 263, 328
Sigge, Erik, 18
Silicon Valley, 223
Singapore, 123, 138
Siry, Joseph, 122
Skidmore, Owings and Merrill, 18
South Africa, 288
Spain, Daphne, 29, 188
Stevelinck, Henri, 283
Stoler, Ann Laura, 278
Strasser, Daniel, 255
Stumpf, Bill, 227
Sue, Natalie, 112
Suen, LeeAnn, 38
Sweden, 19, 189
Swinnerton, Frank, 98, 99, 105
Taut, Bruno, 126
Taylor, Frederick Winslow, 36, 107, 122, 203
Taylorism, 13, 14, 15, 21, 22, 28, 32, 33, 34, 73, 97, 108, 122, 146, 204, 211, 296, 316, 318, 322, 349, 350

Terry, George R., 129
Thatcher, Margaret, 183, 190
Thibault, Ivan de, 282
Thomas, Amy, 17, 18
Thompson, Emily, 155
Thompson, Graham, 24, 26
Three Mile Island, 178
Thurshwell, Pamela, 99
Tilburg, 9, 10
Tillim, Guy, 305
Tödt, Daniel, 282, 301
Tokyo, 124, 126, 127, 128, 130, 131, 132, 135, 136
Trefon, Theodore, 305
Tremaine, Herbert, 99
United Nations, 279
Vemer Andrzejewski, Anna, 28
Verlinden, Jasper, 14, 15, 33
Vigneron, W., 283
Wainwright, David, 182
Wånggren, Lena, 99
Waterhouse, Keith, 109
Watters, B.G., 157

Weber, Max, 22, 103, 275, 305
Wells, H.G., 99, 107, 110
Westwood, Robert, 100
Wild, Jonathan, 98, 99
Wilhelm II, 349
Williams, Nigel, 106
Willis, Carol, 121, 127
Wilson, Robbie Guerriero, 26, 27
Winter, Tim, 138
Wit, Onno de, 32
Wodehouse, P.G., 94, 109
Wodka, Michael, 162
Women and Work Hazards Group (U.K.), 171, 173, 174, 175, 176, 178, 179, 181, 183, 184, 185, 186, 187, 188, 191
Wood, John C., 29
Wood, Michael C., 29
Worthington, John, 189
Zakim, Michael, 110
Zeeland (MI), 226, 227
Zimmeck, Meta, 97

www.ingramcontent.com/pod-product-compliance
Lightning Source LLC
Chambersburg PA
CBHW041438300426
44114CB00026B/2928